LIFESTYLE IN SIBERIA AND THE RUSSIAN NORTH

Lifestyle in Siberia and the Russian North

Edited by Joachim Otto Habeck

OpenBook
Publishers

ISBN Paperback: 978-1-78374-717-7
ISBN Hardback: 978-1-78374-718-4
ISBN Digital (PDF): 978-1-78374-719-1
ISBN Digital ebook (epub): 978-1-78374-720-7
ISBN Digital ebook (mobi): 978-1-78374-721-4
ISBN XML: 978-1-78374-722-1
DOI: 10.11647/OBP.0171

Cover image: Ulan-Ude, 2009. Participants of a brass band open-air festival are returning to their hostel from the main square where they've just performed. Photo: Luděk Brož, CC-BY.

Cover design: Martina Tóthová and Anna Gatti.

Contents

Note on transliteration

In the main text of this volume, certain geographic and other terms widely known to an English-speaking readership are given in their conventional forms (e.g. Buryatia, intelligentsia, Moscow, Yakutia). All other words and phrases transliterated from Cyrillic script are rendered in accordance with the ALA-LC (American Library Association and Library of Congress) romanisation table, available at https://www.loc.gov/catdir/cpso/romanization/russian.pdf, with the exception of the Cyrillic letters е, ю, я — rendered in this volume as ye, yu, ya when at the *beginning* of a word. Words and phrases from Sakha language may also include ө, ү and h, rendered in this volume as ö, ü and h.

Cyrillic	Latin	Cyrillic	Latin
А а	A a	Р р	R r
Б б	B b	С с	S s
В в	V v	Т т	T t
Г г	G g	У у	U u
Д д	D d	Ф ф	F f
Е е	e Ye* ye*	Х х	Kh kh
Ё ё	Ё ё	Ц ц	Ts ts
Ж ж	Zh zh	Ч ч	Ch ch
З з	Z z	Ш ш	Sh sh
И и	I i	Щ щ	Shch shch
Й й	I i	ъ	"
К к	K k	Ы ы	Y y
Л л	L l	ь	'
М м	M m	Э э	E e
Н н	N n	Ю ю	iu Yu* yu*
О о	O o	Я я	ia Ya* ya*
П п	P p		

*at the beginning of a word

Publications in Russian and Sakha are referenced in accordance with the above transliteration; publications in English of authors from Russian-speaking countries are referenced in accordance with the respective publication itself. For this reason, the rendering of names may differ.

Note on translations

Unless marked otherwise, all the research project's interviews quoted in this volume were conducted in Russian, and translated by the respective author(s). Likewise, translations of material quoted from Russian publications (books, articles, online sources, etc.) have been made by the author(s) of the respective chapter, unless indicated otherwise.

Notes on Contributors

Tatiana Barchunova is Associate Professor at the Institute of Philosophy and Law of Novosibirsk State University. She worked as a Research Affiliate at the Siberian Studies Centre of the Max Planck Institute for Social Anthropology from 2008 to 2013. She has published widely on gender, religion, and live-action role-playing in Russian and English. She recently translated Raewyn Connell's *Gender and Power* into Russian, (*Gender i vlast'*, 2015).

Luděk Brož is the Head of the Department of Ecological Anthropology at the Institute of Ethnology, The Czech Academy of Sciences, Czech Republic. After receiving his doctorate from the University of Cambridge (2008) he was Research Associate at the Siberian Studies Centre of the Max Planck Institute for Social Anthropology, from 2008 to 2011. With Joachim Otto Habeck, he co-edited a theme section on mobility in the Far North in the journal *Mobilities*, vol. 10 (4), published in 2015. With Daniel Münster, he co-edited *Suicide and Agency: anthropological perspectives on self-destruction, personhood and power* (2015).

Joachim Otto Habeck teaches Anthropology at the University of Hamburg, Germany. From 2003 to 2013 he was Coordinator of the Siberian Studies Centre of the Max Planck Institute for Social Anthropology. He received his doctorate from the University of Cambridge in 2004. He is author of *What It Means to Be a Herdsman: the practice and image of reindeer husbandry among the Komi of Northern Russia* (2005) and *Das Kulturhaus in Russland* (2014). With Brian Donahoe, he co-edited *Reconstructing the House of Culture* (2011). His sphere of interest comprises popular culture, practices of distinction, and the concept of lifestyle in postsocialist countries.

Joseph J. Long is Research Manager for Scottish Autism. He is also Honorary Research Fellow in Anthropology at the University of Aberdeen and an associate of the Edinburgh Centre for Medical Anthropology. From 2010 to 2013, he was Research Fellow in the Siberian Studies Centre at the Max Planck Institute for Social Anthropology. He has undertaken long-term fieldwork in Buryat communities in the Baikal region of Siberia where his research interests include ritual and performance practices, kinship, civic cultural institutions, and the politics of indigeneity. He received his doctorate from the University of Aberdeen in 2010.

Jaroslava Panáková is a research fellow at the Institute of Ethnology and Social Anthropology, Slovak Academy of Sciences; and teacher at the Comenius University in Bratislava, Slovakia. She received her doctorate from the Saint Petersburg State University and was Research Associate at the Siberian Studies Centre of the Max Planck Institute for Social Anthropology from 2008 to 2011. Jaroslava has conducted her field research on northern peoples in Saint Petersburg and in Chukotka, looking comparatively at mobility, identity, and visual representations. Since her research stay at the CNRS in Paris from 2014 to 2015, she has attempted to link the themes of death and visuality of commemoration.

Eleanor Peers is the Arctic Information Specialist at the library of the Scott Polar Research Institute at Cambridge. She holds a doctorate in sociology from the University of Cambridge (2010), was Research Associate at the Siberian Studies Centre of the Max Planck Institute for Social Anthropology (2010-2013), and undertook a postdoctoral fellowship at the University of Aberdeen (2015-2017). Eleanor has conducted fieldwork in Buryatia and the Republic of Sakha (Yakutia) and has published on post-Soviet popular culture, ethnic revival in Siberia, and post-Soviet shamanism.

Artem Rabogoshvili is a Senior Lecturer at the Department of International Relations, History and Oriental Studies (MOIV) at the Ufa State Petroleum Technological University. He was member of the Siberian Studies Centre of the Max Planck Institute for Social Anthropology, from 2010 to 2013. His publications in Russian, English, and Chinese cover the topics of migration, ethnicity, nationality politics, and social and religious movements.

Ina Schröder is associate researcher at the Max Planck Institute for Social Anthropology. She has conducted field research in western Siberia for her doctorate on indigeneity, gender, and the importance of youth camps for ethnic revivalism. Her dissertation is entitled "Shaping Youth: quest for moral education in an indigenous community in western Siberia" and was defended at Martin-Luther-Universität Halle-Wittenberg in 2017.

Masha Shaw (née Maria Nakhshina) is a Researcher Development Adviser at the Postgraduate Research School, University of Aberdeen. She holds a doctorate in anthropology from the University of Aberdeen (2011), was a Research Associate in the Siberian Studies Centre at the Max Planck Institute for Social Anthropology (2010-2013) and undertook a postdoctoral fellowship at the University of Aberdeen (2013-2016). She has conducted long-term research in rural areas along the White Sea coast in the northwest of Russia. Her research interests include small-scale fisheries, fishing collective farms, perception of space and place, Pomory identity, the politics of ethnicity, and resource governance in post-Soviet Russia.

Dennis Zuev is Research Fellow in the Centre for Research and Studies in Sociology (CIES-ISCTE) and Associate Researcher at the Institute of Oriental Studies, University of Lisbon, Portugal. He was associate researcher at the Max Planck Institute for Social Anthropology (2010-2013), and lecturer in Sustainable Mobilities at Nuertingen-Geislingen University, Germany (2017-2019). He was involved in the project "Low-Carbon Innovation in China" at Lancaster University, UK (2013-2016). In 2018 he published *Urban Mobility in Modern China: the growth of the E-bike* with Palgrave Macmillan. His research interests comprise sustainable tourism, circumpolar societies, Chinese Studies and visual sociology. He conducted fieldwork in Siberia, China, Portugal and Argentina.

Preface

This book, a collection of essays written by ten anthropologists, is dedicated to our friends far and near. Far, inasmuch as the region portrayed here — Siberia and the Russian North — exerts its own specific challenges when it comes to spatial distance. But for us it is simultaneously close, for our ties with many of the individuals we introduce in this volume have been maintained over many years, and increasingly so via new means of telecommunication. The latter were not yet available in the years when each of us began to conduct ethnographic fieldwork, but we were more than willing to spend months or years in an unfamiliar setting away from home, and to explore ways of living that differed markedly from our own. Anthropology is based on a sustained sense of curiosity and surprise. We deem ourselves lucky to have taken curiosity as motivation for the research project that brought us together, and to have been granted help and open-mindedness by so many people all across the region.

The initiative was first conceived at the Max Planck Institute for Social Anthropology in Halle, Germany. In the first place, I would like to thank Bettina Mann who, in a serendipitous moment in 2007, encouraged me to focus on the concept of *lifestyle*, to fathom the depth of the sociological debates around it, and to lay out a research design for a study of lifestyle in Siberia. Since then, she has contributed in manifold ways to the success of the project.

Why lifestyle in Siberia? Because it embraces more than the conventional notions of "tradition" and "crisis", often associated with this part of the world. Crisis cannot be wiped away: it is part of so many of the biographies of our interviewees; and yet crisis engenders a stronger awareness of one's circumstances and sparks a desire for change. Lifestyle as a concept reaches out towards a deeper level of personal commitment, sense of life, hope, and belonging. Our acquaintances and friends in different parts of Siberia and the Russian North had the courage to talk about these aspects in a very candid manner.

In this volume, we combine the idea of lifestyle — as an expressive, routinised and stylised mode of identification — with the changes that this part of the world has seen in terms of technology, telecommunication, visual self-presentation, connectedness, transport, and mobility. Intrinsically, the chapters of the book all engage with the Soviet and post-Soviet notion of *modernity*, which exerts a sublime and yet pervasive influence on how people in the region picture themselves and the society in which they live. The concept of lifestyle connects very strongly with debates on vernacular views and meanings of "being modern" — but then, Siberia and the Russian North have been widely neglected in that debate, notwithstanding far-reaching anthropological debates on socialism, post-socialism, and shifting dynamics of identification.

We are grateful to Chris Hann and Günther Schlee, the two founding directors of the Max Planck Institute, for their continual and enthused support of the project, paired with constructive criticism. The project itself was a collaborative one, with research questions, methods, research instruments, and data analysis defined before the actual field research. I believe that this was one of the strongest aspects of the collective endeavour (the Appendix to this volume offers more details on research design and methodology). It all developed within the organisational framework of the Siberian Studies Centre, a research unit of the Max Planck Institute from 2002 to 2014. The predominant share of financial support for this project was granted by the Max Planck Society; and Kathrin Niehuus and her team always took good care of the project's finances. The project took its intellectual roots from the scientific agenda that the Max Planck Institute for Social Anthropology has fervently and successfully pursued since its beginnings in 1999.

This volume can also be read as one chapter in the history of the Siberian Studies Centre. Clearly, anthropological research on Siberia has moved from Halle to other academic centres, such as Aberdeen,

Rovaniemi, and Vienna; and of course, it is being pursued in St Petersburg, Moscow, and Siberia itself. But so have we, the contributors to this volume: we have moved to other responsibilities and personal commitments. And so have the people that we talk about in this book: many of them have moved to other places, experiencing their own existence in different ways from those captured here. Still, we believe it is worthwhile rendering their takes and views as expressed in the time around 2010, and we are positive that this volume provides for a close reading of everyday life in Russia's regions in the first decade of the new century. The last chapter of the volume sketches out the most important social trends that have occurred in Russia between 2010 and 2019, connecting them back to the topic of lifestyle.

We had many an opportunity to discuss our thoughts with other colleagues at the Max Planck Institute, working in different regions across the world, and since their number is truly large, we cannot do justice by listing all of them. In the initial phase of the project, Stephan Dudeck, Kirill Istomin, Elena Liarskaya, and Vladislava Vladimirova took part in discussions on the concept of lifestyle in 2008. Subsequently, there were more meetings of this kind, for example the one in Novosibirsk and Berdsk in 2012, and we would like to express our sincere thanks to Yuliia Druzhinina, Irina Oktiabr'skaia, Yurii Popkov, Tamara Popkova, and Iraida Udalova, who all took a vivid interest in the project presentation and endorsed it, even if they disagreed with some of our ideas. Likewise, our thanks go to Igor' Nabok, Nikolai Vakhtin, and their colleagues in St Petersburg for highly helpful consultation and support.

We would like to express our sincere gratitude not only to those we lived and spoke with in the different communities across Russia that feature in this volume, but also to those who worked as research assistants, translators, and language instructors: Nikolai Aipin, Natal'ia Beletskaia, Anna Gossmann, Roza Khaltueva, Stepan Kolodeznikov, Liubov' Kolodeznikova, Alexander Kymyechkin, Anna Larionova, Ariuna Matveeva, Dora Matveeva, Anna Ptitsyna, Anna Sysoeva, Fiodor Uiaganskii, Alexander Vamingu, and Rodion Vamingu. Anyone who has conducted ethnographic field research is aware of the difficulty of distinguishing between the roles of research assistant, informant/ interlocutor, and close acquaintance with whom interaction never really stops; in that sense, ethnographic fieldwork is never complete.

Notwithstanding, each project of this kind also necessarily involves moments when the flow of life should be cast into some mould: notably when it comes to compiling data, writing reports, connecting the immediacy of the fieldwork experience with a wider array of ideas, notably those debated in social-scientific scholarship. We are indebted and highly grateful to those who accompanied and helped us on this way, notably the student assistants and interns at the Siberian Studies Centre: Georgi Dietzsch, Friedemann Ebelt, Katja Mahler, Nadia Manitz *née* Mukhina, Stella Penkova, Mariya Petrova, Ricarda Scheffer, Alexander Seidel, and Andreas Zimmermann. All of them invested considerable time and energy in transcribing audio files of interviews. Claudia Ulbrich took care of administrative issues, along with Viktoria Giehler-Zeng and Berit Eckert. As a student apprentice to the Siberian Studies Centre, Christian Buchner designed a common framework for data management that proved to be helpful throughout and beyond the project's lifetime; he also assisted in transcribing interviews.

Closer towards the completion of the manuscript of this volume, admittedly and for personal reasons with a delay of more than five years, new colleagues and friends have accompanied our work and ambitions to finish the project. The anonymous reviews of the draft manuscripts were extremely helpful; in extension, we should like to express our sincere thanks to Frances Pine and Peter Schweitzer for their comments and support. All contributors would like to express their gratitude to the team at Open Book Publishers, notably to Alessandra Tosi, Luca Baffa, Lucy Barnes, Anna Gatti, Laura Rodriguez, Molly Byrne, and Corin Throsby. Jens Bussewitz took a special effort in the graphic design of the book cover and other illustrations, and so did Luděk Brož, Jaroslava Panáková, Martina Tóthová, and Jonas Büchel. We are happy and grateful for the support in the quantitative analysis of data, conducted by Andrej Mentel.

The Max Planck Institute has always been a personally and intellectually inspiring environment, as has the city of Halle. We would like to express our empathy and solidarity with our friends and colleagues in Halle after the recent anti-Semitic and xenophobic assault on the city. This atrocious attack reminds us of our aim as anthropologists: namely, to work towards a society that derives hope from diversity, that tries to understand human grief, and that attempts to create and maintain affective bonds between people across the globe. Hope is the theme that, after ten years of research and reflection, lies at the very core of the chapters presented in this book. We share this prospect with our friends far and near, whom we got to know at different moments and in different situations, from the inception to the completion of this research project.

Joachim Otto Habeck, on behalf of
all the members of the research team

October 2019

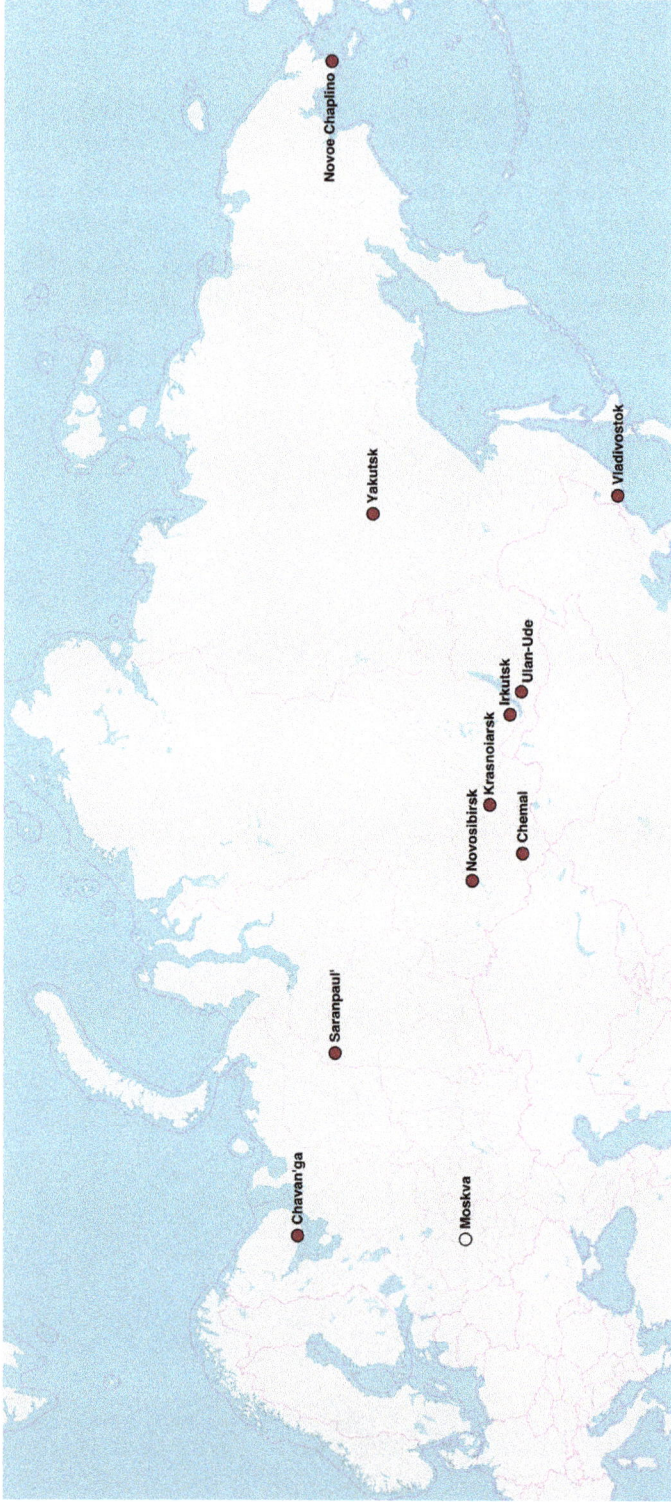

Map of the project's field research sites. Compiled from OpenStreetMaps (https://www.openstreetmap.org/copyright/en) by Jens Bussewitz, CC BY-SA

1. Introduction

Studying Lifestyle in Russia

Joachim Otto Habeck

This book is about lifestyle. More exactly, it is about the dynamics behind people's choices and needs, according to which they seek to live their lives practically and to furnish them with meaning. The authors of this volume — a research team of anthropologists and sociologists — have investigated this subject in Russia, predominantly in Siberia, where it has not been given scholarly attention until now. There are reasons for that, notably Siberia's reputation as a region in crisis, an area of environmental decay and rapid economic change that has detrimentally affected indigenous groups. In addition, anthropological research in the region was, until recently, generally limited to indigenous groups' traditional culture. In this book, however, we argue that these categories hardly suffice to explore the current realities of everyday life in this part of Russia. In order to explain how political, economic and technological changes create new possibilities for, and/or constraints on people's existence and self-perception, we found it most expedient to focus on lifestyle, a concept that has been widely applied and debated in sociology but not yet in anthropology, for the reasons sketched out below.

This brings us to the title of the research project, "Conditions and Limitations of Lifestyle Plurality in Siberia" (CLLP) (2008–2013), the main phase of which entailed ethnographic field work during the period 2010–2012 in ten different locations across Siberia and the Far

 https://doi.org/10.11647/OBP.0171.01

North of Russia. Our hypothesis was that the range of options given to an individual or group to pursue different ways of life has been changing over the recent past, and we want to understand the factors that influence that range. We do not claim that these options are always consciously *reflected* by the individual, nor that they are necessarily "good" for him or her. Nor do we assume that the range of possible ways of life was by necessity more limited in the Soviet period than in post-Soviet or present times. These assumptions, which are often made by social-scientific studies of modernity, need to be carefully examined; by presenting our research findings here we aim to contribute to such empirical examination.

The study of "modernity" (the constitution of modern society) or rather "modernities" (competing views of what defines modern life) is a key topic to which we seek to contribute, but it is not the only one. We also intend to explore (im)mobility, visuality, aesthetics, expression and displays of ethnic belonging, play, creativity, and self-presentation as aspects of sociability in this part of the world. The particular combination of topics is based to some extent on previous research undertaken by individual team members in Siberia; more importantly, however, it stems from certain subtle yet wide-ranging shifts in how people in Siberia frame their existence — shifts that researchers observed collectively and which came to occupy the centre of our intensive discussions.[1]

Outline of the book

The structure of the book reflects this attempt to demonstrate how the notion of lifestyle plays out in the context of, and in combination with, other concepts. Mobility and immobility are the main keywords of Chapters 2 to 5. Chapter 2, by Dennis Zuev and Joachim Otto Habeck, paints a portrait of the technological and infrastructural changes that have taken place in our field research sites over the past forty years,

---

[1]   As part of the discussion process, team members decided to look at the relationship between (1) changes in lifestyles, on the one hand, and (2) changes in the availability and actual use of technical devices and networks of communication, on the other, as revealed by two sets of practices: (a) habits of travel and (b) visual forms of self-presentation. In other words, (im)mobility and photography are the two lenses through which we study how the appearance of new technologies articulates with changes in lifestyles. See the Appendix for a more detailed description of the research design and instruments.

and we highlight how these changes have had a bearing on individual perceptions of, and strategies for, travelling, communication, and photographic displays. In Chapter 3, Masha Shaw takes readers to a remote village on the Kola Peninsula in northwest Russia. Inhabitants there have developed specific skills and strategies for overcoming the lack of predictable transport into and out of the village. The resulting isolation fosters creativity and enables individuals to pursue certain life projects that divert from or complement urban ones. Arguably more so than in urban areas, lifestyles in remote villages closely reflect collective practices of place-making. Chapter 4, by Luděk Brož and Habeck, compares late-Soviet versus present-day expectations of holiday-making and the use of tourism infrastructure, with the aim of assessing the shifting norms of what is desired when one is away from home. Partly, these shifts involve new interpretations of ethnic difference as a resource in tourism, as the display of ethnic symbols gradually underwent a process of commodification. Additionally, tourism and travel are now motivated by ideas of self-fulfilment that markedly differ from those in earlier decades. Joseph Long continues this line of inquiry in Chapter 5 on the basis of travel biography interviews conducted by himself and other research team members, examining the ways in which "home", travel destinations, and collectively-held spatial imaginaries come to be woven together in personal topographies. Photo albums and travelogues highlight the value of personal topographies and trajectories in the expression of a specific identity and style.

In Chapter 6, Jaroslava Panáková discusses how aesthetic conventions and their visual expression are subject to sudden change inasmuch as notions of the self and the collective have undergone modification in the post-socialist period. In addition, she explicates the methodological benefits and challenges of photo elicitation, a method employed by all the contributors in their field researches. Chapter 7 continues the investigation of aesthetics: Eleanor Peers focuses on performance in a particular group of events, notably public celebrations, aesthetic expressions, and artwork. She analyses the development of lifestyles in late Soviet times with reference to Yurchak's concept of *svoi* (communities of "ours") and provides a careful description of ethnicity and *kultur'nost'* (which we translate as "culturedness" or cultivated behaviour) in Soviet and post-Soviet times. While Chapter 7 discusses the practice and meaning of aesthetic displays of ethnic identities, Chapter 8, by Artem Rabogoshvili, elucidates to what extent attendance at such events, either as a performer on the stage or "just" as a member of the audience, is itself an indicator of a lifestyle that draws explicitly on ethnic affiliation and ethnic symbols. Rabogoshvili investigates the workings of national-cultural organisations in the Baikal region, contrasting old and new diaspora groups, and analyses the different degrees of involvement of individual actors.

In Chapters 9 and 10, we look at the significance of play for many people in their desire to create a sense of life that transcends their everyday existence, which they often associate with a lack of control and coherence. In Chapter 9, Ina Schröder investigates the importance of youth camps in the foothills of the Urals for the enactment and transmission of indigenous culture; these camps aim to enable young people in remote villages to embrace traditional indigenous lifestyles in a positive way and to gain a higher level of self-confidence. The protagonists of Chapter 10 (by Tatiana Barchunova and Habeck) are people who participate in live-action role-playing (LARP). Stylisation here is of great importance, in that attire and comportment are highly reflexive and intended to be taken as signifiers. Interestingly, the shift between the two modes of life — play versus ordinary life — usually requires some movement in space, and switching between these two modes is a form of mobility in its own right. The volume closes with an update on current social trends in Russia and a summary of research findings (Chapter 11) along with a description of the research design and methods (Appendix).

Having sketched out the content of this volume in general terms, the remainder of this introduction contains a literature review of how lifestyle has developed as a concept in European and US sociology and anthropology.[2] On this basis, the next section asks how lifestyle as a concept can and should be applied to non-western settings. A brief introduction to Siberia as a setting for social science research[3] and a comment on the Soviet modernisation project constitute the middle part of the introduction. Further, I will discuss the remarkable (albeit

---

2   The section comparing the positions of Bourdieu and Giddens is a revised version of the pertinent section in Habeck (2008).

3   The section on Siberia's image is a revised version of the pertinent section in Habeck (2008).

not well-known) strand of scholarship on lifestyle in late Soviet and post-Soviet social sciences; this focus on lifestyle (*stil' zhizni*) has occurred in parallel with — and sometimes complemented — research on everyday life (*byt*) and way of life (*obraz zhizni*). The final section of this introductory chapter offers some general insights gained in the course of the research, which will be elaborated in more detail in the conclusions given in Chapter 11.

The concept of lifestyle in sociological and anthropological literature

This section gives an overview of the (ramified) genealogy of the concept of lifestyle, from early and implicit usages such as those by Thorstein Veblen, Georg Simmel and Max Weber, to American contributions from the 1970s and 1980s by Benjamin D. Zablocki, Rosabeth Moss Kanter, and Michael Sobel. Many of the current conceptualisations of lifestyle build on the works of French and British authors, notably Pierre Bourdieu, Anthony Giddens, and David Chaney, with whose ideas I will complete this section. The selection of authors portrayed here captures only part of the range of relevant studies, but nonetheless it highlights key aspects of how the concept has been framed and reframed over time.

Early treatises on conspicuous consumption and lifestyle

The term lifestyle entered scientific usage around the beginning of the twentieth century. American economist Thorstein Veblen wrote what can be seen as a prelude to research into lifestyle in his book, *Theory of the Leisure Class* (1899). Already in this work, consumption is characterised as a major mechanism in capitalist societies by which boundaries between classes are created and maintained. It is through conspicuous consumption of expensive goods and services that members of the leisure class reassure themselves of their social status and present themselves to others as a distinct, privileged group. Moreover, Veblen argues that individuals of each class or group aspire to increase their status by emulating the tastes and preferences of those who are one step further up the social ladder, and their main motivation is to be recognised by others: "members of each stratum accept as their ideal of decency the scheme of life in vogue in the next higher stratum, and bend their energies to live up to that ideal" (1899: 84; cf. Brown 1998). This idea bears a striking resemblance to later expositions of social distinction, such as that by Bourdieu (see below).

German sociologist Georg Simmel employed the term lifestyle in his book *The Philosophy of Money* ([1900] 2004) in a twofold sense: he used the singular "style of life" (2004: 433ff.) to indicate a modern, contemporary form of existence in contrast to earlier periods, the modern form being increasingly impersonal, civic and mediated (notably, by money), and emotionally less colourful. This loss of character in modern times "may be designated as the objectivity of life-style" (ibid: 439). However, in the same context, Simmel applies the term in the plural form to point out the multitude of styles whereby "we are confronted with a world of expressive possibilities each developed according to their own norms, with a host of forms within which to express life as a whole" (ibid: 468). "The Problem of Style" is further discussed in a later essay ([1908] 1991), and Simmel's essay "On Fashion" (1904) offers relevant insights into the complex interaction of fashion and lifestyle: here he reveals the seemingly contradictory relationship between the effect of proudly emphasising individuality on the one hand, and the effect of opportunistically subjugating oneself to the latest fad, on the other.

An early occurrence of the notion of lifestyle can also be found in the work of Max Weber, notably in his treatise on class, status and political interest groups. Weber juxtaposes the expression of social order by status groups (e.g. the aristocracy) with that of the class system, arguing that the latter operates quite visibly through money, whereas the former hinges on the ascription of honour, the importance of conventions, and a tendency of stylisation that comes with these: "The decisive role of a 'style of life' in status 'honor' means that status groups are the specific bearers of all 'conventions.' In whatever way it may be manifest, all 'stylization' of life either originates in status groups or is at least conserved by them" (Weber [1922] 1946: 191). H. H. Gerth and C. Wright Mills, who translated this passage,[4] have been

---

4   The German original runs: "Denn die maßgebende Rolle der 'Lebensführung' für
       die ständische 'Ehre' bringt es mit sich, daß die Stände die spezifischen Träger aller
       'Konventionen' sind: alle 'Stilisierung des Lebens', in welchen Aeußerungen es auch
       sei, ist entweder ständischen Ursprungs oder wird doch ständisch konserviert"
       (Weber [1922] 1980: 537).

criticised for their imprecise rendering — indeed, mistranslation — of *Lebensführung* as "style of life" rather than "conduct of life" here and on many other occasions in Weber's text (Abel & Cockerham 1993; cf. Hartmann 1999: 15–20; Voß 1991). While this has led to considerable confusion, it is clear that Weber characterises the "stylisation of life" as an older, more traditional mechanism of expressing hierarchy. This is remarkable inasmuch as it contradicts many later authors who connect lifestyle with modernity, individualisation, and multiple processes of detraditionalisation, as will become clear from what follows.

Lifestyle as a topic of US sociology in the 1970s and 1980s

Drawing on Veblen and Weber, several US sociologists and psychologists employed the notion of lifestyle in their writings, and in very divergent ways. Zablocki and Kanter (1976) provided an early systematic overview of the concept, and their synthesis is still frequently quoted. Their central concern in that article was to complement the analysis of "classic forms of life-style differentiation" according to the categories of socio-economic status (1976: 272) with a conceptual framework to explain the proliferation of alternative lifestyles, which they claim to be independent of socio-economic status (ibid: 280 ff.). The classic forms are arranged into three categories: property-dominated lifestyles, comprising the landed rich as well as petty farmers; occupation-dominated lifestyles, with some occupations absorbing more time and individual loyalty than others; and poverty-dominated lifestyles, where the range of possible choices is severely limited (which calls into question the voluntary nature of lifestyle). Zablocki and Kanter argue that the emergence of alternative lifestyles is due to the loss of value coherence, as observed in US society in the late 1960s and early 1970s. They indicate a large number of alternative lifestyles — esoteric, green, revolutionary, isolationist, hedonistic, ascetic, tradition-oriented, ethnically defined communities and communes — and sketch out possibilities for grouping these. Mere description of lifestyles is not the ultimate goal: "not specific life-styles themselves but their range and diversity constitute the most interesting sociological problem for investigation" (1976: 293). Moreover, lifestyle research can help illuminate more general social phenomena, namely "the transmission of tastes and values, the nature of the collective experience [...], the correlates of commitment and social cohesion [...], or the transformation of social institutions as consumers shift their preferences" (ibid.).

As sociologists, working in a period when numerous counter-culture and liberation movements were emerging, Zablocki and Kanter (1976) pursued the express aim of disconnecting alternative lifestyles from widespread connotations of deviance and delinquency, and preparing the ground for social-scientific analysis. Michael Sobel, to whose work I will now turn, discarded this and similar attempts as one-sided: "Despite a great deal of undue attention, the relative frequency of these 'alternative' lifestyles is not great [...]. In other words, sociologists have written a great deal about an imperceptible fraction of the population, thereby failing to discuss lifestyle differentiation within the majority population" (Sobel 1981: 56).

Sobel described lifestyle as "set of observable behavioral choices that individuals make" (1981: 3 and 1983: 521) and defined it — with reference to conceptualisations of style in Art History — as "any distinctive, and therefore recognizable, mode of living" (1981: 28). He added that "To this definition the condition of expressiveness (alternative choice) is attached" (ibid.). In his as well as most other works on lifestyle, what comes to the fore is the idea of preference, or choice, within a limited range of options along with the obligation to choose: "it is through this creative participation in the normative order that individuals may generate status, meaning and self-esteem" (1983: 521). Sobel's emphasis on style and lifestyle as something "observable or deducible from observation" (1981: 28) led him to exclude values, attitudes and norms from the concept. Further, he argued that consumption (rather than work, and methodologically better than leisure) is the domain where lifestyles can be discerned; particularly so in American society, where, in the course of the twentieth century, consumption has become the prime sphere within which to build self-esteem and social recognition (1981: 31–48). Sobel thus initially built his empirical study around the criterion of household disposable income, and asked how it is spent for purchasing a range of goods. In a further step, he took specific categories of items as representative of four "factors", namely: visible status, maintenance, high life, and home life (1981: 157–64). They differ in level of expenditure (from necessary items to luxuries) and direction (with "visible status" and "high life" or party life being directed socially outward rather than home-bound).

Sobel's emphasis on consumption has two ramifications, one in terms of the region under study in this volume — Russia — and the other in terms of continuity and change. As to the first, he contrasted America's post-1945 consumer society with that in the Soviet Union, where, according to him, material conditions led to fewer options being available in the sphere of consumption; moreover, consumption "is not an officially recognized goal. Consumption is secondary to many other things, and at the individual level, consumption is not expressive, but severely constrained" (Sobel 1981: 41).[5]

As to the second, Sobel drew a clear conceptual line between lifestyle and stylistic unity (ibid: 118–20). The latter expresses the observation that certain items frequently co-occur with others, whereas other combinations are highly unlikely, to the degree of looking odd or "inconsistent". Patterns of consistency are subject to change, but also establish the condition of continuity and the recognizability of lifestyles: "The items that index a lifestyle are culturally arbitrary; however, the manner in which a sample of items hangs together, as revealed by the factor pattern, may not be so arbitrary. [...] there is a good deal of historical evidence that lifestyle forms have displayed considerable continuity over time" (Sobel 1983: 526). Implicitly, his argument suggests that patterns may be perpetuated through generations, with individuals displaying preferences they acquired in the household in which they grew up. Explicitly, Sobel contends that the household's income level and the occupational status belonging to the head of that household (i.e. the prestige conferred by the occupation) are more decisive in terms of lifestyle than is the level of an individual's formal education, the influence of which is more subtle (1981: 167–68).

Sobel's emphasis on consumption as key indicator of lifestyle may be too limited and biased; it comes over as rather conservative if compared

---

5   This leads us to ask if lifestyle in the Soviet Union may be retrospectively discerned more suitably in the sphere of work rather than consumption, or perhaps in people's positions in networks of allocation of goods, access to resources, and informal redistribution (see Chapter 7 in this volume; see Chapter 2A in Nielsen 1986 for a lively illustration of such networks in late socialist Leningrad). For a discussion of the concept of consumption and its relevance to the current constitution of a Russian middle class, see Gurova (2012).

to Zablocki and Kanter's (1976) attempt to make alternative lifestyles (including ascetic ones) accessible for sociological analysis, as discussed above. Nonetheless, Sobel has set some standards for further empirical research. By interpreting lifestyle as a link between social position (and, notably, class) and patterns in the symbolic use of material goods, his approach roughly corresponds with that of Bourdieu, the next scholar whose work I shall explore.

French, British, and German scholarship on the concept of lifestyle (1979–early 2000s)

Of central importance for research on lifestyle is the legacy of French sociologist and anthropologist Pierre Bourdieu, notably his comprehensive empirical study on social stratification in France in the 1960s, published under the title *Distinction* ([1979] 1984). He exposes lifestyles as concomitant — in fact, homologous — to different positions in social space. Both the social space (in the French original: *espace social*) and the space of lifestyles (*espace des styles de vie*) are defined by the criteria of economic capital and cultural capital. He thus promotes the idea that any analysis of social differentiation requires more than just the criterion of economic capital. Under the influence of Bourdieu, scientific models of social differentiation ultimately attained multidimensional shape. Bourdieu interprets the particular symbolic meanings of a wide range of goods, leisure activities, personal predilections and value judgements and the ways in which they express the individual's belonging to a certain class and milieu. Such localisation of social status can be illustrated by two brief examples: individual preference for high-carbohydrate and high-fat foods, rugby, and film star Brigitte Bardot indicate an individual's affiliation to the less affluent milieu of farm workers and employees in rural communities; whereas a person who shows sustained interest in Bach's musical oeuvre and bicycle tourism may be identified, with some probability, as a secondary-school teacher (Bourdieu 1984: 128–29).

Bourdieu argues that the elites seek to distinguish themselves from the middle class by means of taste. The members of the latter continually and breathlessly try to emulate elite taste. Here Bourdieu's argument strongly resembles that of Veblen, but it differs when it comes to the poorest strata of society: according to Bourdieu, the groups with lowest incomes do not participate in the hunt to develop ever more refined tastes; instead, by necessity they come to value the "practical" advantage — and hence, neatness — of those things affordable to them (ibid: 372ff.).

Taste, seemingly a domain of individual decision-making, follows socially established patterns. The individual does not usually reflect on his or her disposition, which conditions such choices. "Distinction" of social groups is perpetuated by the enactment of taste. The principle that, according to Bourdieu, creates the conditions for the existence of lifestyles is rooted in the *habitus*. Habitus is the mechanism that generates certain patterns of valorisation through taste, along with certain practices and works, which are liable to classification and simultaneously serve the purpose of classifying. These practices, productions and taste judgements engender a specific lifestyle (Bourdieu 1984: 173).[6] The habitus in turn results from the individual's position within the framework of "objectively inscribed" conditions of existence (ibid: 170). Individual dispositions are habitualised, routinised, embodied and usually not questioned; and yet, they can be transmitted from one actor to another.

The analysis provided by Bourdieu points to the high levels of congruence between aesthetic judgements and affiliation with a social stratum or milieu; it also explains how taste is continually reproduced. However, Bourdieu has little to say about the potential of certain actors to disengage wilfully from the struggle for symbolic recognition and "legitimate culture". Likewise, the possibility of creative, ironic, and subversive utilisation of symbols is not sufficiently captured in Bourdieu's analysis (cf. Chaney 1996: 66). If we follow Bourdieu, whatever it is that an actor perceives as an option just *seems* to be a matter of choice — in fact, however, a socially preconditioned, usually unconscious process stands behind the decision-making. In that sense, Bourdieu's take differs from that of Giddens, whose view shall be briefly sketched out in what follows.

---

6   "Taste, the propensity and capacity to appropriate (materially or symbolically) a given class of classified, classifying objects and practices, is the generative formula of life-style, a unitary set of distinctive preferences which express the same expressive intention in the specific logic of each of the symbolic sub-spaces, furniture, clothing, language or body hexis" (Bourdieu 1984: 173).

British sociologist Anthony Giddens discussed the term lifestyle as a key phenomenon of the late modern and post-modern era. In *Modernity and Self-Identity* (1991), Giddens defines lifestyle as "a more or less integrated set of practices which an individual embraces, not only because such practices fulfil utilitarian needs, but because they give material form to a particular narrative of self-identity" (1991: 83). Particularly incisive is the statement that precedes the above definition: "we all not only follow lifestyles, but in an important sense are forced to do so — we have no choice but to choose" (ibid.).

In contrast to Bourdieu, Giddens puts strong emphasis on the individuals' need to select consciously from many existing options: he conceptualises the self as a reflexive project. Taking this into account, our investigation of lifestyles should explicitly address the norms, predilections, orientations, and convictions according to which a person takes decisions about how to get on in life, whom to bond with, and how to present him- or herself in public. His notion of lifestyle carries generally positive connotations in the sense that people are satisfied with (or at least, have arranged themselves according to) the goals and activities that shape their everyday lives. This aspect of assenting emotions is complementary to the aspect of negative emotions, represented by such terms as "crisis" and "survival", which thus far appear to be the dominant rationale for anthropological and ethnographic research in Siberia. Not only suffering but also affirmative emotions and expressions are needed to sustain a sense of collective identity.

In view of the theoretical frame of our research project in Siberia, it is necessary to address the crucial difference between Giddens's notion of lifestyle as expression of individual self-reflection, and Bourdieu's emphasis on the mostly unreflective character of consumption practices and social distinction. Respondents' occasional assertions that important changes and turning points in the course of their lives "just happened" (*prosto poluchilos' tak*) cast doubt upon Giddens's idea of the self as a reflexive project. On the other hand, the rapid economic and symbolic shifts in post-Soviet society prevented most people from simply "carrying on" and induced them to compare the present with the past, to "rethink" their situation and aspirations. Giddens may well over-emphasise the individual's capacity to induce change, whereas

Bourdieu tends to underestimate this potential. His work depicts individuals as unavoidably inserted in a social hierarchy, leading a lifestyle they have not chosen but instead appropriated and learned to like. What emerges from Bourdieu's writings is the idea that lifestyles reproduce themselves through the people that enact and re-enact them. Changes in lifestyle are tied to class affiliation and hence they are a question of the individual or family ascending or descending on the social ladder. For Bourdieu it is not a question of choice by necessity, as Giddens would have it, or of choice as eclectic combination, as is claimed by postmodern sociologists. The aspect of (non-)choice and (non-)reflexivity will come up again in the remainder of this overview of theoretical works on lifestyle.

In the late 1980s and early 1990s, the different national traditions (US, French and British) in the debate on lifestyle gradually converged again, also incorporating contributions from West German sociologists,[7] whose engagement with the concept had been comparatively active throughout the 1980s (for example, Beck, Giddens & Lash 1994). Similar to Giddens, the German sociologists Ulrich Beck and Elisabeth Beck-Gernsheim treated the increasing diversity of lifestyles (*Lebensstil*) and life conduct (*Lebensführung*) as part of a more general social process: individualisation (cf. Zablocki & Kanter's "loss of value coherence" described above). "Standard biography transmutes [...] into a chosen biography, reflexive biography, bricolage biography. This does not have to be intended, nor does it have to be successful" (Beck & Beck-Gernsheim 1994: 13, my translation). Written some 25 years ago, this appraisal, as much as Giddens's position, referred to so-called western societies, that is, societies in western Europe and North America. In subsequent years, Beck and Beck-Gernsheim (2010: xv) stated that "we cannot simply assume that the process of individualization exhibits the same basic pattern in all regions of the world [...] On the contrary, it must be shown at the theoretical level that the specificity of the European path towards individualization becomes visible only when it is juxtaposed with extra-European paths [...]". The research pursued

---

7   Useful overviews of German-language publications on lifestyle have been given
     by Hradil (1992); Otte & Rössel (2011); and Spellerberg (1996). These publications
     themselves are in German. I am not aware of any comprehensive synthesis of this
     strand of scholarship in English.

by the authors of this book is rooted in a similar line of inquiry and asks about the specificities of self-expression in the context of Russia in late Soviet and post-Soviet decades. Along with Beck-Gernsheim and Beck, we may ask: To what extent has individualisation in Russia (and in Russia's remote regions) taken a *specific* trajectory? Is it specific at all? What may be specific about it?

David Chaney's treatise on lifestyle

Comprehensive and particularly informative, from our point of view, is British sociologist David Chaney's monograph with the straightforward title *Lifestyles* (1996). Chaney's position is quite close to that of Giddens, notably in his emphasis on reflexivity and a certain room for manoeuvre, or ambit of choice. Chaney offers more than one — in fact many different — definitions of lifestyle, and here I present one that may not be the most elegant, but is the most productive from our research team's point of view, because it combines practice with intentionality, display, and resources at hand: "Lifestyles are reflexive projects: we (and relevant others) can see (however dimly) who we want to be seen to be through how we use the resources of who we are" (Chaney 1996: 37). The concatenation of verbs summarises well, in our opinion, the various processes at work at the intersection of normative and unconscious practice paired with reflexivity, willful display, and a desire for self-expression: "Lifestyles are reflexive projects: we (and relevant others) can see [*perception*] who we want [*intention*] to be seen [*recognisability*] to be [*aspired status*] through how we use [*practice*] the resources [*capital*] of who we are [*status quo*]".

Elsewhere in his book (ibid: 114) Chaney (again, in agreement with Giddens) states that lifestyle offers the symbolic means to express a narration of *self*. He argues *against* limiting the lifestyle concept to patterns of consumption and material aspects only. To be sure, the latter do have strong significance inasmuch as they make up a vast part of the inventory for self-stylisation; yet in many cases, consumer practices and decisions do not automatically follow the conventions and intentions that come with an item. Rather, we can often detect that individuals pursue their *mise-en-scène* in a consciously weird, sometimes ironic manner. By taking things out of their original context and intended meaning, people occasionally manage to create new symbols of lasting currency (1996: 99; see also Miller 1995; Moore 2011).

Apart from *self*, two more keywords in Chaney's book deserve to be explained here: *surfaces* and *sensibilities*. *Surfaces* is a shorthand for the phenomenon, already observed by Simmel, that attire, accessories and other attributes worn by a person make that person "recognisable" or legible for others immediately on first sight. It is this phenomenon that enables a rapid, albeit preliminary, appraisal of passers-by in an increasingly urban and thus anonymous social environment (Chaney 1996: 94, 99–111). The notion and relevance of *surfaces* is further discussed in Chapters 8 and 10 of this volume.

The third term, *sensibilities*, serves as a metaphor for collective concerns, moral judgements, "big issues", and perhaps one might also add the term *social imaginaries*. Chaney speaks of "a way of responding to certain events […] that has a certain pattern" and is imbued "with ethical and aesthetic significance" (ibid: 8). One example provided by Chaney are collective concerns and debates about animal rights, hunting and meat consumption, which have undergone diverse modifications over several centuries; another is the emergence of the cultural practice of attending public concerts and the emergence of "distinct taste publics" (ibid: 10). To give another illustration, the purposes and practices of holiday-making (in the mountains, at the sea) are based, to a large extent, on health-related sensibilities that emerged during a specific period in history. Sensibilities also comprise individual and collective reflections about morality, as is exemplified by the raising importance of religion in the everyday lives of many of Russia's inhabitants (see first section of Chapter 11). Sensibilities have a clear temporal dimension, and they reflect what some people find tolerable, but others think of as less acceptable or unacceptable. Individuals with shared sensibilities tend to cluster in some way; they constitute milieus, that is, groups of individuals that may assume each other to have similar opinions on moral and political issues. *Sensibilities* as a key concept is further elaborated in more detail in Chapter 7, it is also discussed in Chapters 2, 4, 8, 9, and 10 of this volume.

Towards a definition of lifestyle to be used in a post-Soviet context

For the team of contributors to this book, Chaney's analysis has provided inspiration in manifold ways. We connected it with the endeavour of formulating a general theoretical framework for the study of identity and identification at the Max Planck Institute for Social Anthropology, the outcome of which is captured in Donahoe et al. (2009). Further, Chaney's work helped us to revise and sharpen our working definition of lifestyle.[8] I argue that lifestyle can be seen as a particular *mode* of identification. Lifestyle is an expressive, routinised, and stylised mode of identification: (i) it is expressive, insofar as individuals connect choices and practices with statements about themselves to be recognised by others; they invest them with some sense of *importance* that they also seek to convey to others. (ii) It is routinised (and habitualised) insofar as such practices and choices are performed repeatedly, and predilections can be predicted with some probability. (iii) It is stylised insofar as this mode of identification combines a seemingly contradictory mixture of subjecting the self to social conventions and yet emphasising one's own difference and distinction. This mixture is one of the basic properties of fashion, as Simmel has pointed out.

All three elements of our definition — lifestyle as an expressive, habitualised and stylised mode of identification — will be of significance in this book. Is the concept of lifestyle applicable to non-western societies? As mentioned, there is a certain challenge in the way lifestyle is embedded in a particular discourse on modernisation, urbanisation and individualisation, all part of a grand scheme called Modernisation Theory. Take the following statement by Giddens as an example: "Lifestyle is not a term which has much applicability to traditional cultures, because it implies choice within a plurality of possible options, and is 'adopted' rather than 'handed down'" (Giddens 1991: 83).

In a similar manner, Stefan Hradil, a German sociologist, states: "The analytical power of the lifestyle concept has narrow limits when

---

8   In 2008, research team members formulated a working definition: *Lifestyle is what one does in order to be what one thinks one should be.* We soon came to realise that this definition of ours had some resemblance with that provided by Chaney (1996: 37), presented in the main text (p. 14). On the process of formulating the working definition and on other aspects of research design, see the Appendix.

applied in societal settings with low freedom of choice, such as prisons, among primitive peoples (*Naturvölker*) or at the level of the livelihood of a single parent with three children who depends on social support payments. Empirical evidence indicates that a relatively large plurality of lifestyles for many people exists in modern societies only, and within these, it is larger in higher social strata than in lower ones" (Hradil 2001: 275, my translation).[9]

However, very few sociological or anthropological studies have thus far seriously approached the question of the analytical power of the lifestyle concept in non-urban settings outside Europe and North America. Hence the question: what can we say about lifestyle plurality in Siberia, notably among erstwhile *Naturvölker*, and how traditional is Siberia today? A first approximation of an answer to this question is pursued in the next section, on Siberia and the Soviet quest for modernity.

Towards research on lifestyle in Siberia: some remarks on the regional context

The Soviet modernisation project

Let us take a brief look at how a peculiar Soviet modernisation project sought to propel social change among the indigenous peoples of Siberia (and more generally, not only in that part of the Soviet Union, but throughout the country — and ultimately regardless of ethnic particularities). As a reminder, the Soviet Union aspired to pursue a path of economic and social development in marked contrast to that of the capitalist world. In a way, the intention was to become even more modern than the rest of the world. This alternative path of development was connected with an emancipatory project from above, enacted in a more explicit and forceful way than what we know from many other historical settings.

---

9   Many authors seem to share the understanding that "style of life" (or "lifestyles") is *not* an attribute of traditional society, even though Weber quite explicitly spoke about it as a traditional phenomenon (see footnote 4), and Ulrich Beck followed Weber's interpretation to some extent. Weber remarked that style of life is often "corporatively conserved" (*"ständisch konserviert"*, Weber [1922] 1980: 537); Beck extended this point when portraying lifestyles as "a relic of pre-capitalist, pre-industrial traditions" (Beck 1983: 49, my translation).

Siberia is inhabited by many different indigenous peoples, and according to Marxist-Leninist logic, these were supposed to be on different stages of the evolutionary ladder.[10] The task was to have these peoples "leap forward", to integrate them into socialist society. Generally speaking, we can characterise the Soviet modernisation project as one of the many attempts of social engineering in the twentieth century. Particular to the Soviet version, however, was the speed and geographic scope with which social change was induced, plus the accompanying promise of a bright future, narrated as a unilinear evolutionist process. The main components of modernisation within the entire country — collectivisation, industrialisation, forceful replacement of political and functional élites, literacy and education — had their correlates in the far-flung areas of the country, including large swathes of Siberia: there, the Soviet government sought to make nomadic groups sedentary, invested in large-scale extraction of mineral resources, introduced "industrial methods" and mechanical equipment in all branches of agriculture, persecuted *kulaki* (wealthy people) and shamans as the most influential representatives of traditional social order, created new indigenous élites, established alphabets and textbooks in indigenous languages, obliged indigenous parents to send their children to Soviet schools, etc. The more or less orchestrated implementation of these strategies and their ambivalent effects have been discussed in detail elsewhere (e.g. Slezkine 1994; Ssorin-Chaikov 2003; Ulturgasheva 2012; Vitebsky 2005).

Some of the many ramifications of the modernisation project should be emphasised here: as part of this strategy, different groups within the indigenous population of Siberia were co-opted more directly than others, with women being seen as potentially the most reliable allies of the Soviet modernisation project (Povoroznyuk et al. 2010). New professions came into existence, notably in the sphere of administration, education, infrastructure, transportation, and trade. Through media and school education the inhabitants of even the remotest areas of the country came to embrace new items of

---

10   For a recent treatment of pre-Soviet and Soviet traditions of evolutionary thought in ethnography, see Sokolovskiy (2017). A volume published by Open Book Publishers and edited by Anderson, Arzyutov & Alymov (2019) traces the long history of *etnos*, a concept that gained popularity in Soviet ethnography in the 1960s, partly in response to earlier orthodox views on evolution.

consumption and "cultivated" life — either in the form of desire or in actual appropriation (see Volkov 2000). Moreover, the Soviet ideal of "cultivated" life also implied new genres of self-improvement, self-expression, and aesthetic self-formation (cf. Foucault 2000; Rabinow & Dreyfus 2000) that were generally in line with the idea of the development of a socialist personality (Habeck 2011). To use Chaney's terminology, the Soviet period established new sensibilities; it also obliged individuals "to surface", show their commitment to the overall social project, and to express themselves in public (cf. Kharkhordin 1999). Finally, in the sphere of identity-building, ethnicity was made a legitimate register of personal identity, to be expressed through certain genres of display — whereas other, politically incorrect and "backward" aspects of ethnic difference were separated, relegated to museums and banned from everyday life (Vitebsky 1995).

While the Soviet period is often linked with the loss of traditional culture, the post-Soviet period *also* saw serious impoverishment: the promise of development, of a bright future, was abandoned. And simultaneously, that which was supposed to replace the Soviet world order after 1991, namely a transition towards a free-market economy and democracy, seems to have got "stuck"; or at least, it has generally lost its appeal. For many of our Siberian interlocutors, progress, modernity, conservatism, tradition, and neo-tradition appeared to be jumbled, they did not make sense anymore even though they were still widely in use; and there was no clear trajectory of "development" anymore. However, over the last two decades, a new state ideology has been emerging; it becomes visible in the emphasis on good citizenship, law and order, and patriotism, as portrayed in Chapter 11.

Having claimed that lifestyle is usually discussed within the framework of Modernisation Theory, and having claimed that Soviet modernisation was strong, but *is no more*, what can we say about the explanatory power of lifestyle in a non-western setting such as present-day Russia? Are notions of modernity and progress relevant in the contemporary context of Siberia (and in extension, provincial Russia)? If yes, for what vision of progress do people strive?

The image of Siberia

Siberia is commonly perceived and described by outsiders as a desolate, cheerless and uncultured part of the world. As one fellow social scientist aptly formulated: "Russia in particular continues to evoke overwhelmingly negative reporting and imagery in much of the mass media which informs popular understanding in the west. [...] There is, it seems, no good news to come out of Russia and less still to come out of Siberia" (Kay 2006: 213). Notwithstanding occasional accounts that are more complex in their judgement, connotations of icy confines, unpopulated expanses, forced labour camps, unsustainable resource extraction, and environmental degradation dominate the discourse about Siberia among the publics of western Europe and North America. To be sure, climatic conditions in Siberia are difficult, the technical infrastructure is insufficient in many regions, and for this and other reasons one may conclude that the conditions of everyday life are harder here than elsewhere. This does not necessarily mean, however, that people in Siberia suffer more privation and misery than in other parts of the world.

Many inhabitants of the Russian Federation do live under precarious circumstances, and the description and analysis of their life conditions are among the most relevant tasks that fall to social science research. However, this commitment can easily distort the realities of everyday life in Siberia in all their manifestations. Since the early 2000s, Russia has witnessed considerable economic growth, for the most part on the basis of oil and gas exports (although the economic crisis of 2008 caused a temporary decrease in incomes and security). It is unclear (and deserves to be studied) whether and to what extent rural inhabitants and urban lower-income groups have benefited from the oil and gas revenues. One may assume that overall economic growth has generally led to higher and more stable monetary income, but the effect is probably experienced very differentially by the various population segments. Thus, on the one hand, spending power and possibilities for consumption have increased noticeably in some Siberian communities; for many people the economic situation is no longer as grave as it was some twenty years ago. On the other hand, new patterns of social inequality are manifest in the non-participation and exclusion of less affluent groups from public spaces and facilities. On these grounds, research on consumer practices, lifestyles, and forms of representation of individual and collective identity is of growing topicality and deserves more attention in social science scholarship on Siberia.

Most inhabitants of Siberia (and of Russia, in general) usually associate the 1990s with chaos and wildness, whereas the subsequent two decades can be generally characterised as a period of economic, cultural, and societal consolidation, with a marked tendency towards conservatism and a resurgence of religious organisations, notably the Orthodox Church. We are witnessing, on the one hand, many signs of growing diversity of lifestyles in this region; on the other hand, the state's current emphasis on patriotism, family values, and proper moral education indicates a normative, mainstreaming tendency, with the possible result that spaces for alternative lifestyles and projects will be limited (see Chapter 11).

The concept of lifestyle in Russian social science literature

The question arises if and how the concept of lifestyle has weight and currency in Russian social sciences, and, with a view to past decades, if and how it was used in Soviet social science. In search of an answer, we first need to turn to concepts that complement, compete with or precede the concept of lifestyle: for the socialist and post-socialist period, these are *byt* (roughly corresponding to the notion of "everyday life") and *obraz zhizni* (roughly equivalent to "way of life"). These terms were and continue to be espoused by some scientific disciplines more than by others.

Byt (everyday life), *obraz zhizni* (way of life) and *stil' zhizni* (lifestyle)

With regard to the first of these three terms, Natal'ia Pushkareva (2005) offers a complex history of the scientific usage of *byt*, which gained currency in pre-revolutionary Russian historiography and ethnography, but underwent a conceptual redefinition in early Soviet times. It came to stand for material culture and livelihood, for household reproduction and leisure (i.e. for the things people habitually do when they are not engaged in production). However, she notes that even "the most meticulous description of *byt* [...] was unable to represent any man or a woman of the past [as a being] endowed with plans that came true, or dreams that failed to be realised" (Pushkareva 2005: 25). Further, she argues that, thanks to paradigmatic shifts in (western) historiography and social sciences in general, the study of *byt* regained explanatory power in the late twentieth century, but this time under the label "history of everyday life" (*istoriia povsednevnosti*). She holds that such an approach — unlike the conventional ethnography of *byt* — can account for the ways in which individuals and groups do not just follow rules and habits, but also how they divert from them (ibid: 30–31). From my point of view, it would be unfair to claim that ethnography in the post-Soviet decades has been entirely ignorant of people's aspirations and ambitions, and yet it seems that the notion of *byt* is still much more strongly geared to the material aspects of *habitus*, and in that sense is reminiscent of Bourdieu's understanding of lifestyle as a largely unreflective pattern of behaviour; at any rate, it lacks the sense of *self*, sensibility and reflexivity that we find in Chaney's characterisation of lifestyle.

Ralf Rytlewski (1990: 16, 22) draws interesting parallels between the Soviet concept *obraz zhizni* and the German equivalent *Lebensweise*, which in the 1970s became a central category in social science research on citizens' everyday lives in the German Democratic Republic. *Lebensweise* in turn stands in a complex juxtaposition with *Lebensstil*, which was more widely employed by West German sociologists during the same period. Against the backdrop of Pushkareva's argument (see above), it would be apposite to explore how strongly GDR scholarship on *Lebensweise* interacted with Soviet academic conceptualisations not just of *obraz zhizni*, but also of *byt*, since in both the Soviet Union and the GDR the study of "everyday life", peasant and workers' culture attained popularity among historians during the late socialist period.

Stil' zhizni, by contrast, emerged within the discipline of sociology. When perusing the relevant literature, it appears that by the early 1980s the concept of lifestyle (*stil' zhizni*) became methodologically established by a group of sociologists in Kiev, Ukrainian SSR, under the aegis of Lidiia Vasil'evna Sokhan'[11] (Sokhan' & Tikhonovich 1982). In order to carry out this task, the authors first had to delineate *stil' zhizni* (lifestyle) from the much more common term *obraz zhizni*, usually translated as "way of life". The latter term will be explored in more detail here. It recurred frequently in late Soviet and then post-Soviet social science research to describe the combination of material, technological, and cultural aspects of how people live their lives. To point out the difference between the two concepts, Sokhan', Tikhonovich and colleagues argued, "Lifestyle, from such an approach, emerges as the reflection of the individual in the social, [whereas] way of life is the reflection of the social in the individual" (ibid: 9). Repeatedly, the authors emphasised the importance of the "agentive, creative role of the human being as designer of his/her life conditions and him/herself" (*deiatel'naia, sozidatel'naia rol' cheloveka kak tvortsa uslovii svoei zhizni i samogo sebia*) (ibid: 9–10).

Remarkably, sociological scholarship on lifestyle continued in Kiev after the dissolution of the Soviet Union, with Liubov' Dmitrievna Bevzenko being among the senior scholars (Bevzenko 2007, 2008) and Anna Domaranskaia (2014) among the younger generation of colleagues working in this field. These authors also explicitly draw a line between lifestyle (*stil' zhizni*) and way of life (*obraz zhizni*), the latter being related to the "physical parameters" of existence, such as rural versus urban residence or healthy versus unhealthy ways of life; whereas the former is attributed to the culturally and socially defined necessities, such as maintenance of social status (Bevzenko 2007: 148). A definition of lifestyle offered by Bevzenko is thus: "Lifestyle is [a] system of practices which are closely linked with and continually repeat themselves in the everyday expressions of the individual. It [comprises] practices that correspond with different social fields: leisure and consumption, work, politics, religion, health, education and so forth. All this in its totality is signified as practices of lifestyle" (ibid: 134). All of the authors quoted offer ways to use the concept in empirical research. For example, Domaranskaia (2014: 470) investigates

---

11   Lidiia Vasil'evna Sokhan' was born and grew up in a remote village of Novosibirsk Oblast, thus she has an immediate understanding of everyday life in rural Siberia. Later she moved to Kiev and worked as a senior scientist in the Department of Social Psychology, Institute of Sociology, Ukrainian Academy of Sciences, until 1994 (source: ru.wikipedia.org).

the correlation of leisure activities and social position as defined by income, type of work, and prestige of profession; the resulting graphs resemble those presented by Bourdieu (see above). One of the results concerning contemporary Ukrainian society (and I would argue, post-Soviet societies more generally) is the finding that the "classic" élite pursuits of theatre and fine arts are not so much in demand from the most affluent and influential social layers, but rather by middle-class intellectuals (ibid: 477).

In Russia too, several social scientists have been employing lifestyle as a conceptual basis for their theoretical and empirical writings (Burtonova 2017; Gurova 2012, 2014; Ionin 1996; Omel'chenko 2003; Osadchaia 2002; Ostroukh 2006; Roshchina 2007; Viktorova 2017; Voz'mitel' 2002).[12] It is difficult, though, to identify a particular academic centre or school with long-term, sustained interest in this line of research. While some authors — among them Ionin — drew their conceptual inspiration from Weber, Simmel, and Bourdieu, others have developed definitions that are very pronouncedly based on classic Marxist readings, e.g. Voz'mitel' & Osadchaia (2009: 62). Of theoretical relevance is their differentiation between way of life (*obraz zhizni*), lifestyle (*stil' zhizni*) and mode of life (*sposob zhizni*). "Mode of life" is defined as indicator of the individual's approach to turning social potentialities (opportunities, options) into reality. "Lifestyles" are characterised as manifold and more strongly related to personality, perhaps also more volatile. Lifestyles blend into "way of life" to create a more encompassing reality, namely that of larger collectives or parts of society, and, according to the authors, they denote the objective situation within society, or even society at large. The authors conclude with a rather categorical reassertion of binaries: "And exactly in this sense we have talked, and [continue to] talk, about

---

12   A recent application of the concept of lifestyle to a Siberian urban setting (Ulan-Ude) has been presented by Burtonova (2017). To a considerable extent, research on the conditions and limitations of lifestyle plurality can draw conceptually on the seminal work of the erstwhile Centre for Contemporary Cultural Studies (CCCS) at the University of Birmingham, with its focus on the development of youth cultures and "subcultures". Urban lifestyles, youth cultures and "subcultures" in Russia have been explored in the 1990s and 2000s by sociologists (notably, Omel'chenko 2003; Pilkington et al. 2002); these studies are usually confined to the European part of Russia; for one of the rare examples of a study on subculture in the Far North, see Pilkington (2014). Studies on youth cultures were occasionally interpreted as closely related and partly compatible with research on lifestyle (Dittrich & Hölscher 2001: 153, 164).

socialist and bourgeois, Christian and Muslim, American and Soviet ways of life" (Voz'mitel' & Osadchaia 2009: 62).[13]

To summarise, the term *obraz zhizni* is favoured by a larger number of social scientists in Russia over *stil' zhizni*. Furthermore, it has also found wide application in studies on public health, recently endorsed by the nationwide, policy-driven quest for a healthy way of life (*zdorovyi obraz zhizni*) (e.g. Silin & Koval'zhina 2017, based on research in West Siberia). However, the concept of *obraz zhizni* is somewhat problematic for our purposes because of its implicit focus on macro processes (long-term social change, large-scale phenomena, e.g. transition from a nomadic to a settled way of life), with the result that micro processes, i.e. personal choices and behaviour in small groups, remain out of sight. In other words, research on *obraz zhizni* does not yield a satisfactory answer as to why somebody might want to live a certain kind of life or want to pursue certain activities. *Obraz zhizni* may continue to be a fruitful concept, yet it can benefit from a closer analysis of how people come to accept and assert certain way(s) of life or reject and substitute them with others.

Transferring the concept of lifestyle to Russia: an early attempt

In closing this section, it should be noted that, to many experts and lay people alike, *stil' zhizni* may have the ring of a term imported to Russia from "the west". We cannot quite discard such apprehensions. In fact,

---

13 In 1990, Krisztina Mänicke-Gyöngyösi (1990) provided a study of early-Soviet changes in urban lifestyles, based on secondary sources from the 1920s onwards. Her methodologically interesting attempt starts with an explanation of why lifestyle is chosen over way of life (*obraz zhizni*). She questioned if a consistent "normative status" of the term *obraz zhizni* has ever been found. She argued it is used ambivalently, to denote on the one hand the connection between material conditions and the activities of certain social groups and classes, which can be empirically investigated; and to describe on the other hand a general principle of everyday conduct. In this latter sense, the term is often used to characterise the socialist mode of production in everyday life. The term therefore serves to "idealise the real conditions of life and asserts the standardisation of these in the sense of a *socialist way of life*" (Mänicke-Gyöngyösi 1990: 161, her emphasis, my translation). Further she held that for a study of social processes in the 1920s (as hers is) the term *obraz zhizni* is not applicable, since sociological scholarship was based, back then, on "different traditions, and it its development was interrupted at the beginning of the thirties" (1990: 162).

there has been a sociological study that analysed exactly if and how the concept of lifestyle could be transferred to studying post-Soviet Russian society. The authors, Dittrich & Hölscher (2001) were motivated by the rapid transformation of post-socialist societies in the east of Europe and in Russia, and they chose Russia for an assessment of how lifestyle can be employed theoretically and methodologically. However, they found this to be a challenge because some of the tenets usually associated with high-modern or post-modern societies — most importantly, the tenet of growing individualisation — seemed to be inappropriate for, or not applicable to, Russian society. Likewise, some of the indicators utilised in lifestyle research seemed not to work, possibly because of a fundamentally different approach to consumption (Dittrich & Hölscher 2001: 88; see Gurova 2012 for an overview of research on consumption in late Soviet and post-Soviet Russia).

Influenced by the developments of the comparatively chaotic and boisterous 1990s, and taking an approach that was admittedly very general, Dittrich and Hölscher listed key characteristics of Russia's historical otherness as compared to societies in the west of Europe (2001: 82–83). Their diagnosis includes: historically strongly hierarchical relations between those ruling and those ruled, and thence a particular, apprehensive relationship between state and individual; a preference for collectivity over individuality — not the least because of the necessity to obtain access to vitally important resources — and the persistence of rather traditional gender roles despite changes in women's status and roles in Soviet times. To be sure, these generalised tenets have been explored repeatedly (among many others, by Kharkhordin 1999; Ledeneva 1998 and Nielsen 1986; Zdravomyslova & Temkina 2004) and deserve further exploration in detail (Chapters 3–11 of this book contribute to these long-standing debates).

Nonetheless, from our point of view and for our purpose here, we concur with Dittrich and Hölscher on at least two methodological points: firstly, that data collection has thus far been focused only on the largest cities and it has been insufficiently pursued in the smaller cities and the rural (and more remote) regions of Russia; and secondly, that the collection of quantitative data on consumer behaviour etc. needs to be corroborated by exploratory approaches that shed light on the ways interview partners perceive and reflect their own situation (2001: 40, 134).

When designing our research project on the conditions and limitations of lifestyle plurality in Russia, we had very similar goals in mind.

First insights obtained in the course of the research project

Against the backdrop of theoretical writings and earlier research on lifestyle in Russia, and on the basis of a collectively developed research design (see Appendix), research-team members made themselves acquainted with a range of different communities. Here I present some general insights from the collective research.

Firstly, the theoretical tenet that lifestyles are best studied through patterns of consumption (maintained by Sobel, see above) does not fully suffice to identify and explain the breadth and complexity of existing lifestyles. Many of the lifestyles portrayed in this volume do not necessarily hinge upon such patterns of consumption. It is true that attitudes to consumption (e.g. the valorisation of self-made objects or home-grown food, and ironic play with the meaning of objects) differ in relation to specific lifestyles, and these differences have a distinctive quality. In that sense, Chaney's notion of *sensibilities* comes to include the sphere of consumption.

Second, it is this very notion of *sensibilities* that lies at the core of lifestyles, for lifestyles — from our empirical observation — constitute practical responses to certain sensibilities, questions of morality, and reflections on one's opportunities and ambitions to follow a certain path, or style, in one's life.

Third, the stronger the degree of involvement and the intensity of commitment to a certain activity (be it in the domains of leisure or work or both), the more likely an individual is to develop a certain style, along with the skills and knowledge connected to that activity.

Fourth, and resulting from the previous point, with regard to the question of reflexivity, we side with Chaney and other authors who treat lifestyles as self-formative (and in many cases, creative) projects that have a self-reflexive quality, and again the degree seems to vary with different degrees of involvement. Having said that, we consider Bourdieu's point of habitualised forms of taste and practice as highly relevant, because our study does reveal a strong dependence of habits and choices on social background (including the criterion of class). It also supports the idea that *sensibilities*, inasmuch as they emerge and are promoted at a social rather than an individual level, may often be taken for granted, with individuals practically responding to them but not necessarily opting for divergent or alternative sensibilities.

Fifth, the current trend towards conservative and traditional values in Russian politics and also in everyday life (portrayed in Chapter 11) is an example of changing sensibilities, promoting new or renewed practical responses and lifestyles in some fields while simultaneously potentially sidelining other modes of living, and part of this mechanism is the devaluation and ridiculing of certain sensibilities.[14]

Sixth, and with reference to the first point, the allegedly close connection of lifestyle with consumption, in tandem with an ambivalent attitude in Russian society towards consumerism, may explain why the concept of lifestyle has limited theoretical clout in Russian-language sociological and other scientific literature; admittedly, this is not so much a research finding as a hypothesis that derives from the insights summarised above.

Finally, we argue against the idea that lifestyle is intrinsic only to high-modern or post-modern settings and also against the tenet that lifestyle is characteristic of urban parts of society. Instead, we argue that the Soviet modernisation project, and also current social trends (broadly conservative, but geared towards technological and infrastructural modernisation) offer rich opportunities for empirical research on how certain sensibilities emerge and come to eclipse others; how self-formation is connected with collective goals; and how individual predilections and tastes develop around, and feed back into, social imaginaries and public debates on morality.

Beyond the theoretical approach that guided the design and content of this collaborative research project, we hope that the subsequent chapters of this volume will illustratively and respectfully account for our interlocutors' own understandings of everyday life and life projects in Russia — in large cities as well as remote places of Siberia and the Far North.

---

14   To give but one example: the devaluation of feminism and gender-related emancipation projects, the latter being sidelined by concerns about reproduction, upbringing, and a healthy nation (see Chapter 11).

References

Abel, Thomas & William C. Cockerham. 1993. "Lifestyle or Lebensführung? Critical remarks on the mistranslation of Weber's 'Class, Status, Party'". *The Sociological Quarterly*, 34 (3): 551–56, https://doi.org/10.1111/j.1533-8525.1993.tb00126.x

Anderson, David G., Dmitry V. Arzyutov & Sergei S. Alymov (eds). 2019. *Life Histories of Etnos Theory in Russia and Beyond*. Cambridge: Open Book Publishers, https://doi.org/10.11647/OBP.0150

Beck, Ulrich. 1983. "Jenseits von Klasse und Stand? Soziale Ungleichheit, gesellschaftliche Individualisierungsprozesse und die Entstehung neuer sozialer Formationen und Identitäten" [Beyond class and status? Social inequality, social processes of individualisation, and the emergence of new social formations and identities]. In: *Soziale Ungleichheiten*, ed. Reinhard Kreckel, pp. 35–74. Göttingen: Otto Schwartz.

— & Elisabeth Beck-Gernsheim. 1994. "Individualisierung in modernen Gesellschaften: Perspektiven und Kontroversen in einer subjektorientierten Soziologie" [Individualisation in modern societies: perspectives and controversies in a subject-oriented sociology]. In: *Riskante Freiheiten: Individualisierung in modernen Gesellschaften*, ed. Ulrich Beck & Elisabeth Beck-Gernsheim, pp. 10–39. Frankfurt am Main: Suhrkamp.

— & Elisabeth Beck-Gernsheim. 2010. "Foreword: varieties of individualization". In: *iChina: the rise of the individual in modern Chinese society*, ed. Mette Halskov Hansen & Rune Svarverud, pp. xiii–xx. Copenhagen: NIAS [Nordic Institute of Asian Studies] Press.

—, Anthony Giddens & Scott Lash. 1994. *Reflexive Modernization: politics, tradition and aesthetics in the modern social order*. Cambridge: Polity Press.

Bevzenko, Liubov' Dmitrievna. 2007. "Zhiznennyi uspekh, tsennosti, stili zhizni" [Success in life, values, lifestyle]. *Sotsiologiia: teoriia, metody, marketing*, 4: 132–51, http://ecsocman.hse.ru/data/2010/12/25/1214866400/09_Bevzenko.pdf

—. 2008. *Stili zhizni perekhodnogo obshchestva* [Lifestyles of transitional society]. Kiev: Institut sotsiologii Natsional'noi Akademii Nauk Ukrainy, https://www.twirpx.com/file/348065

Bourdieu, Pierre. 1984 [1979]. *Distinction: a social critique of the judgement of taste*, trans. Richard Nice. London: Routledge & Kegan Paul.

Brown, Doug. 1998. "Be all you can be: invidious self-development and its social imperative". In: *Thorstein Veblen in the Twenty-First Century: a commemoration of the Theory of the Leisure Class (1899–1999)*, ed. Doug Brown, pp. 49–69. Cheltenham: Edward Elgar.

Burtonova, Vera Nikolaevna. 2017. "Stil' zhizni gorozhanina kak sotsial'nyi mekhanizm konstruirovaniia gorodskikh granits" [Lifestyle of city dwellers as social mechanism of constructing city limits]. *Vlast'*, 12: 38–42, http://www.jour.isras.ru/index.php/vlast/article/view/5546

Chaney, David. 1996. *Lifestyles*. London: Routledge, https://doi.org/10.4324/9780203137468

Dittrich, Rita & Barbara Hölscher. 2001. *Transfer von Lebensstilkonzepten: zu den Voraussetzungen interkultureller Vergleichsforschungen* [Transfer of Lifestyle Concepts: on the preconditions of intercultural comparative researches]. Münster: Waxmann.

Domaranskaia, Anna Aleksandrovna. 2014. "Stil' zhizni: strukturnye i lichnostnye determinanty" [Lifestyle: structural and personal determinants]. In: *Sotsiologicheskii Almanakh*, vol. 5, ed. Ivan V. Kotliarov et al. Minsk: Belaruskaia navuka, pp. 464–78, https://cyberleninka.ru/article/n/stil-zhizni-strukturnye-i-lichnostnye-determinanty

Donahoe, Brian, John Eidson, Dereje Feyissa, Veronika Fuest, Markus V. Hoehne, Boris Nieswand, Günther Schlee & Olaf Zenker. 2009. "The formation and mobilization of collective identities in situations of conflict and integration". Halle (Saale): Max Planck Institute for Social Anthropology. *Max Planck Institute for Social Anthropology Working Paper Series*, 116, http://www.eth.mpg.de/pubs/wps/pdf/mpi-eth-working-paper-0116

Foucault, Michel. 2000. "Technologies of the self". In: Michel Foucault, *Ethics: subjectivity and truth*, ed. Paul Rabinow, pp. 223–51. London: Penguin.

Giddens, Anthony. 1991. *Modernity and Self-Identity: self and society in the late modern age*. Stanford, CA: Stanford University Press.

Gurova, Olga. 2012. "'We are not rich enough to buy cheap things': clothing consumption of the St. Petersburg middle class". In: *The social class in Russia*, ed. Suvi Salmenniemi, pp. 149–66. Farnham: Ashgate.

—. 2014. "'U vas tak yarko odevaetsia narod!': sotsial'nye razlichiia v potreblenii odezhdy v Sankt-Peterburge i Novosibirske" ["People dress so brightly here!": social distinctions through clothing in St Petersburg and Novosibirsk]. *Etnograficheskoe obozrenie*, 3: 52–70.

Habeck, Joachim Otto. 2008. "Conditions and limitations of lifestyle plurality in Siberia: a research programme". *Max Planck Institute for Social Anthropology Working Paper Series*, 104, https://www.eth.mpg.de/pubs/wps/pdf/mpi-eth-working-paper-0104

—. 2011. "Introduction: cultivation, collective, and the self". In: *Reconstructing the House of Culture: community, self, and the makings of culture in Russia and beyond*, ed. Brian Donahoe & Joachim Otto Habeck, pp. 1–25. New York: Berghahn.

Hartmann, Peter H. 1999. *Lebensstilforschung: Darstellung, Kritik und Weiterentwicklung* [Research on Lifestyle: presentation, critique, and further development]. Opladen: Leske & Budrich.

Hradil, Stefan. 1992. "Alte Begriffe und neue Strukturen: die Milieu-, Subkultur- und Lebensstilforschung der 80er Jahre" [Old terms and new structures: milieu-, subculture-, and lifestyle-related research in the 1980s]. In: *Zwischen Bewusstsein und Sein: die Vermittlung "objektiver" Lebensbedingungen und "subjektiver" Lebensweisen*, ed. Stefan Hradil, pp. 15–55. Opladen: Westdeutscher Verlag, https://doi.org/10.1007/978-3-322-99582-7

—. 2001. "Eine Alternative? Einige Anmerkungen zu Thomas Meyers Aufsatz 'Das Konzept der Lebensstile in der Sozialstrukturforschung'" [An alternative? Some remarks on Thomas Meyer's article on "The concept of lifestyles in the study of social structure"]. *Soziale Welt*, 52 (3): 273–82.

Ionin, Leonid Grigor'evich. 1996. "Kul'tura i sotsial'naia struktura" [Culture and social structure]. *Sotsiologicheskie issledovaniia*, 3: 31–42, http://ecsocman. hse.ru/data/878/896/1217/005Ionin.pdf

Kay, Rebecca. 2006. *Men in Contemporary Russia: the fallen heroes of post-soviet change?* Aldershot: Ashgate.

Kharkhordin, Oleg. 1999. *The Collective and the Individual in Russia: a study of practices*. Berkeley, CA: University of California Press.

Ledeneva, Alena V. 1998. *Russia's Economy of Favours: blat, networking and informal exchange*. Cambridge: Cambridge University Press.

Mänicke-Gyöngyösi, Krisztina. 1990. "Zum Wandel städtischer Lebensstile in der Sowjetunion" [On change of urban lifestyles in the Soviet Union]. In: *Lebensstile und Kulturmuster in sozialistischen Gesellschaften*, ed. Krisztina Mänicke-Gyöngyösi & Ralf Rytlewski, pp. 160–90. Cologne: Wissenschaft und Politik.

Miller, Daniel. 1995. "Consumption and commodities". *Annual Review of Anthropology*, 24: 141–61, https://doi.org/10.1146/annurev.an.24.100195.001041

Moore, Henrietta. 2011. *Still Life: hopes, desires and satisfactions*. Cambridge: Polity Press.

Nielsen, Finn Sivert. 1986. *The Eye of the Whirlwind: Russian identity and Soviet nation building — quests for meaning in a Soviet metropolis*. Oslo: [no publisher], http://www.anthrobase.com/Txt/N/Nielsen_F_S_03.htm

Omel'chenko, Yelena Leonidovna. 2003. "Kul'turnye praktiki i stili zhizni rossiiskoi molodezhi v kontse XX veka" [Cultural practices and lifestyles of Russian youth at the end of the twentieth century]. *Rubezh: al'manakh sotsial'nykh issledovanii*, 18: 145–66, http://www.ecsocman.edu.ru/rubezh/msg/141484.html

Osadchaia, Galina Ivanovna. 2002. "Stil' zhizni molodykh gorozhan: transformatsiia i regional'naia differentsiatsiia" [Lifestyle of young city dwellers: transformation and regional differentiation]. *Sotsiologicheskie issledovaniia*, 10: 88–94, http://www.ecsocman.edu.ru/socis/msg/214464.html

Ostroukh, Irina Germanovna. 2006. "Metroseksual — stil' zhizni, forma samorealizatsii i samosoznanie muzhchiny v postindustrial'nom prostranstve" [Metrosexual: lifestyle, shape of self-realisation and self-consciousness in postindustrial space]. *Etnograficheskoe obozrenie*, 4: 14–22.

Otte, Gunnar & Jörg Rössel. 2011 (publ. 2012). "Lebensstile in der Soziologie" [Lifestyles in sociology]. In: *Lebensstilforschung*, ed. Jörg Rössel & Gunnar Otte, pp. 7–34. Wiesbaden: Springer. (*Kölner Zeitschrift für Soziologie und Sozialpsychologie*, special issue, 51/2011).

Pilkington, Hilary. 2014. "Sounds of a 'rotting city': Punk in Russia's Arctic hinterland". In: *Sounds and the City: popular music, place and globalization*, ed. Brett Lashua, Karl Spracklen & Stephen Wagg, pp. 162–82. Basingstoke: Palgrave Macmillan, https://doi.org/10.1057/9781137283115

—, Elena Omel'chenko, Moya Flynn, Uliana Bliudina & Elena Starkova. 2002. *Looking West?: Cultural globalization and Russian youth cultures*. University Park, PA: Pennsylvania State University Press.

Povoroznyuk, Olga, Joachim Otto Habeck & Virginie Vaté. 2010. "Introduction: On the definition, theory, and practice of gender shift in the North of Russia". *Anthropology of East Europe Review*, 28 (2): 1–37, http://scholarworks.iu.edu/journals/index.php/aeer/article/view/929/1037

Pushkareva, Natal'ia L. 2005. "'Istoriia povsednevnosti' i etnograficheskoe issledovanie byta: raskhozhdeniia i peresecheniia" ["History of everyday life" and ethnographic inquiries into the quotidian: divergences and intersections]. *Glasnik Etnografcheskog Instituta SANU*, 53 (1): 21-34, https://www.ceeol.com/search/viewpdf?id=578849

Rabinow, Paul & Hubert Dreyfus. 2000. "On the genealogy of ethics: an overview of work in progress" [interviews with Michel Foucault]. In: Michel Foucault, *Ethics: subjectivity and truth*, ed. Paul Rabinow, pp. 253–80. London: Penguin.

Roshchina, Yana Mikhailovna. 2007. "Differentsiatsiia stilei zhizni Rossiian v pole dosuga" [Lifestyle differentiation among Russians in the leisure sphere]. *Ekonomicheskaia sotsiologiia*, 8 (4): 23–42, https://cyberleninka.ru/article/n/differentsiatsiya-stiley-zhizni-rossiyan-v-pole-dosuga

Rytlewski, Ralf. 1990. "Lebensstandard, Lebensweise, Lebensstil: einige problem- und methodenkritische Anmerkungen zum Vergleich moderner Gesellschaften in Ost und West" [Life standard, way of life, lifestyle: some comments on the problems and methods of comparison of modern societies in the east and the west]. In: *Lebensstile und Kulturmuster in sozialistischen Gesellschaften*, ed. Krisztina Mänicke-Gyöngyösi & Ralf Rytlewski, pp. 15–24. Cologne: Wissenschaft und Politik.

Silin, Anatolii Nikolaevich & Larisa Sergeevna Koval'zhina. 2017. "Zdorovyi obraz zhizni v Tiumenskom regione" [Healthy way of life in the region of Tiumen']. *Vestnik Instituta Sotsiologii*, 8 (2): 96–107, https://elibrary.ru/item.asp?id=29407319

Simmel, Georg. 2004 [1900]. *The Philosophy of Money*, ed. David Frisby, trans. Tom Bottomore, David Frisby & Kaethe Mengelberg. London: Routledge. Originally published as *Philosophie des Geldes*, Leipzig: Duncker & Humblot.

—. 1957 [1904]. "Fashion". *American Journal of Sociology*, 62 (6): 541–58. Originally published as "Fashion". *The International Quarterly*, 10: 130–55, https://doi.org/10.1086/222102

—. 1991 [1908]. "The Problem of Style". *Theory, Culture & Society*, 8: 63–71, https://doi.org/10.1177/026327691008003004

Slezkine, Yuri. 1994. *Arctic Mirrors: Russia and the small peoples of the North*. Ithaca, NY: Cornell University Press.

Sobel, Michael E. 1981. *Lifestyle and Social Structure: concepts, definitions, analyses*. New York: Academic Press.

—. 1983. "Lifestyle expenditures in contemporary America: relations between stratification and culture". *American Behavioral Scientist*, 26 (4): 521–33.

Soeffner, Hans-Georg. 2005. *Zeitbilder: Versuche über Glück, Lebensstil, Gewalt und Schuld* [Time Images: essays on happiness, lifestyle, violence, and guilt]. Frankfurt am Main: Campus.

Sokhan', Lidiia Vasil'evna & Vsevolod Aleksandrovich Tikhonovich (eds). 1982. *Stil' Zhizni Lichnosti: teoreticheskie i metodologicheskie problemy* [Lifestyle of Personality: theoretical and methodological problems]. Kiev: Naukova Dumka.

Sokolovskiy, Sergey. 2017. "Anthropology in Russia: tradition vs. paradigm shift". In: *European Anthropologies*, ed. Andrés Barrera-González, Monica Heintz & Anna Horolets, pp. 85–108. New York: Berghahn.

Spellerberg, Annette. 1996. *Soziale Differenzierung durch Lebensstile* [Social Differentiation through Lifestyles]. Berlin: Edition Sigma.

Ssorin-Chaikov, Nikolai. 2003. *The Social Life of the State in Subarctic Siberia*. Stanford, CA: Stanford University Press.

Ulturgasheva, Olga. 2012. *Narrating the Future in Siberia: childhood, adolescence and autobiography among the Eveny*. Oxford: Berghahn.

Veblen, Thorstein. 1899. *The Theory of the Leisure Class: an economic study in the evolution of institutions*. London: Macmillan, https://doi.org/10.4324/9781315135373

Viktorova, Ol'ga Viktorovna. 2017. "Tipologizatsiia sotsial'nykh grupp na osnove stilia zhizni" [Typology of social groups on the basis of lifestyle]. *Istoricheskie, filosofskie, politicheskie i yuridicheskie nauki, kul'turologiia i iskusstvovedenie: voprosy teorii i praktiki*, 10: 36–39, https://cyberleninka.ru/article/n/tipologizatsiya-sotsialnyh-grupp-na-osnove-stilya-zhizni

Vitebsky, Piers. 1995. "From cosmology to environmentalism: shamanism as local knowledge in a global setting". In: *Counterworks: managing the diversity of knowledge*, ed. Richard Fardon, pp. 182–203. London: Routledge, https://doi.org/10.4324/9780203450994

—. 2005. *Reindeer People: living with animals and spirits in Siberia*. London: Harper Collins.

Volkov, Vadim. 2000. "The concept of *kul'turnost'*: notes on the Stalinist civilization process". In: *Stalinism: new directions*, ed. Sheila Fitzpatrick, pp. 210–30. London: Routledge.

Voß, Gerd Günter. 1991. *Lebensführung als Arbeit: über die Autonomie der Person im Alltag der Gesellschaft* [Life Conduct as Work: on the autonomy of the person in everyday life of society]. Stuttgart: Enke.

Voz'mitel', Andrei Andreevich. 2002. Diversifikatsiia obraza zhizni (sposoby i stili zhizni v postsovetskom sotsial'nom prostranstve) [Diversification of way of life (modes and styles of life in post-Soviet social space)]. *Mir Rossii*, 11 (1): 97–113, https://cyberleninka.ru/article/v/diversifikatsiya-obraza-zhizni-sposoby-i-stili-zhizni-v-postsovetskom-sotsialnom-prostranstve

— & Galina Ivanovna Osadchaia. 2009. "Obraz zhizni: teoretiko-metodologicheskie osnovy analiza" [Way of life: theoretical-methodological foundations of analysis]. *Sotsiologicheskie issledovaniia*, 8: 58–65, http://ecsocman.hse.ru/data/961/411/1224/Vozmitel.pdf

Weber, Max. 1946 [1922]. "Class, status, party". In: *From Max Weber: essays in sociology*, trans. & ed. Hans H. Gerth & C. Wright Mills, pp. 180–95. New York: Oxford University Press, https://doi.org/10.4324/9780203759240

—. 1980 [1922]. *Wirtschaft und Gesellschaft: Grundriss der Verstehenden Soziologie* [Economy and Society: an outline of interpretive sociology]. 5th ed., ed. Johannes Winckelmann. Tübingen: J. C. B. Mohr (Paul Siebeck).

Zablocki, Benjamin D. & Rosabeth Moss Kanter. 1976. "The differentiation of life-styles". *Annual Review of Sociology*, 2: 269–98, https://doi.org/10.1146/annurev.so.02.080176.001413

Zdravomyslova, Elena & Anna Temkina. 2004. "Gosudarstvennoe konstruirovanie gendera v sovetskom obshchestve" [The state's construction of gender in Soviet society]. *Zhurnal issledovanii sotsial'noi politiki*, 1 (3–4): 299–321, https://cyberleninka.ru/article/n/gosudarstvennoe-konstruirovanie-gendera-v-sovetskom-obschestve

2. Implications of Infrastructure and Technological Change for Lifestyles in Siberia

Dennis Zuev and Joachim Otto Habeck

This chapter will explore how the changing habits in mobility and use of media technology have contributed to the pluralisation of lifestyles in Siberia, and how these new technologies are being used to express new social disparities.[1] We aim to show how technological changes have directly influenced people's lives in Siberia.

The chapter has seven sections. After a brief overview of the last three decades' infrastructural and related social changes, we will provide our own biographical experiences about the role of technical devices in everyday life. In doing so, we use an experiential approach that is usually absent in descriptions of infrastructure[2] and technology in the Soviet Union and the Russian Federation. Next, we portray the linkages between peripherality and lifestyle choices through the prism of infrastructure, mobility, and telecommunication. After that,

---

[1] We would like to express our gratitude to all our colleagues in the research team who helped compile data on infrastructure in the respective communities where they conducted field work.

[2] Vakhtin (2017: 9–10) expresses some concern about the loose use of the term infrastructure in social sciences, including Anthropology. Our use is limited to "hard" infrastructure (transport routes, lines of communication and supplies) and technical arrangements that provide for telecommunication, including online.

  https://doi.org/10.11647/OBP.0171.02

we will briefly characterise the different field sites of the comparative research project, sketching out the infrastructural development of the respective community on the basis of a variety of published material (books, articles, information on the internet), our own memories and those of our interlocutors. These portraits of cities and villages will be followed by an extended overview of changes in transportation, as well as changes in telecommunication, TV and radio, computers and the internet, audio and video equipment, and photography. The chapter will conclude with a general assessment of how people in rural and urban Siberia perceive the symbolic and practical significance of mobility, telecommunication, and "modernity" when thinking about their own biographies and ambitions.

Major infrastructural and related social changes during the last three decades

The most salient trends in post-Soviet infrastructural change are: a shift towards individual means of transportation, notably cars; rapid decrease of aviation to remote settlements, and simultaneously a decrease in railway passenger numbers as airborne transport has become more affordable between major cities; and finally the introduction and rapid expansion of mobile telephony into nearly all parts of Siberia. However, internet access is highly unequal across the region. Along with these trends, the last two decades have seen a rejuvenation of certain infrastructural networks (such as the Baikal-Amur Mainline), increasing cargo transport along the Northern Sea Route, and renewed northward expansion of extractive industries after a period of out-migration from the north in the 1990s.

Owing to state subsidies, traveling from one place to another was comparatively cheap in Soviet times, or at least this is how it is remembered.[3] However, the number of taxis, tickets, seats, fuel, etc. was limited. The scarcity of certain goods and services created peculiar forms of sociability: the 'community' of the queue with its mixture of apprehensiveness and hope, and the complicity of semi-public

---

3   For an extensive online discussion on the cost of different modes of travelling, see "Tseny na proezd: SSSR vs. RF [Transportation expenses: USSR vs Russian Federation]", http://germanych.livejournal.com/71959.html

arrangements. In contrast to Soviet times, availability is now less of a problem, but affordability is an issue. In the light of the international economic sanctions imposed on Russia in 2014 and the gradual inflation of the rouble, prices for goods and services have risen, altering the conditions of travel in Russia and in Siberia in particular. This has had a significant impact on social cohesion that is based on visits, communication and travelling.

Social cohesion was felt more intensely in Soviet times because it was largely based on favours and personal ties. Today, money enables access to goods and services that were previously limited, but the perception that money can buy anything (which seems to be the case in Moscow) is not necessarily true for Siberia: kinship ties are of crucial importance, not only in rural settlements but also in cities.[4]

Many of the criteria that regulate inclusion and exclusion have changed. Privileges that came with belonging to influential political and professional networks have less immediate value now. Positions of informal power (*khlebnoe mesto*) have shifted: typical gatekeeper functions of previous decades have been replaced by a range of new ones. The mafia-like provision of security by criminal organisations, which was typical in the 1990s, has given way to open and formalised market-economy procedures, though corruption and arbitrary allocation of investments are still widely perceived as a problem.

Along with the monetisation of transportation resources, patterns of communication among passengers have changed, too: now, one observes fewer and/or shorter verbal exchanges between fellow travellers in the immediate physical environment (train carriage, railway ticket counters, shops, etc.). Simultaneously, mobile phone and internet use allow communication with friends, relatives, and colleagues, so that physical distance seems less of a problem than it used to be. In other words, while there is less sociability among strangers travelling together, one can have more conversations on the phone with people one knows. Internet services have become affordable for almost everyone except in very remote communities, so online and mobile phone applications

---

4   This is particularly important in the capitals of the ethnically defined republics, notably the Republic of Sakha (Yakutia) and Buryatia (Argounova-Low 2007; Humphrey 2007). On the social importance of informal ties in the socialist planned economy, see Ledeneva (1998) and Verdery (1996).

(Skype, WhatsApp, etc.) now facilitate interpersonal and familial ties. In the following section, we provide vignettes illustrating the changes in infrastructure and related social processes in Siberia since the late Soviet days.

Entering the post-Soviet 1990s: personal experiences

Car, TV, and phone: the material triad of a happy life (Dennis Zuev)

When I started to think about the changes in infrastructure in Siberia over the last thirty years, I could not forget the stories I had heard from my family members and from older people in my home city of Krasnoiarsk, as well as my own experiences of growing up in that city. Here I shall offer a few examples of how various technologies entered our lives before the 1990s. My parents were engineers, one working in civil engineering and the other at the SibTiazhMash factory.[5] They stood in line and queued for several things: a car, TV set, and landline telephone connection.

It took more than sixteen years from registering their wish to have a phone number at home to actually having it. We also had a problem obtaining the telephone itself — they were not so easy to find in the 1990s. Eventually, we had our phone installed, but after five years it was taken away and we had to share the line with another number. So sometimes, when my parents wanted to make a call, they could not because someone (in the same building) was using the phone. In the early 2000s the internet operated through a modem connection, which meant that whenever somebody wanted to use the internet, nobody else could use the phone. Although nowadays everyone has a mobile phone in our family, the landline phone is still used for "long" talks, while the mobile is essentially used among family members for calls to and from the *dacha*.

A *dacha* is a summer house with a vegetable garden outside the city. In the 1980s and 1990s, due to the lack of construction materials and access roads, owners had to build these houses from any

---

5   SibTiazMash is the acronym of Sibirskii Zavod Tiazhelogo Mashinostroeniia (Siberian Plant of Heavy Machinery Construction).

materials they could get hold of, often using scrap or other discarded items (planks, pipes, sheets of metal, etc.). Nearly every factory worker had a *dacha*, yielding some vegetables and crops which then had to be stored — preferably in a *podval* (cellar). For the purpose of storing vegetables, as well as children's sledges and skis, construction materials for the *dacha* etc., one would build a garage with such a cellar. Across the Soviet Union, this type of building has become a characteristic feature of the urban landscape (Tuvikene 2010) with multiple functions beyond storage, for example acting as a social venue for car owners who shared the same garage space. I remember that our balcony was full of things, and we needed an extra storage area. Having a garage with an inspection pit and a cellar underneath seemed to be the best option for the family's needs. But it was not so simple to build a proper garage[6] — in order to be entitled to do so, one had to own a vehicle. And it was not so easy to obtain a vehicle.[7] My parents bought an old motorcycle *IZH Yupiter 3* from our friends in Igarka (1,700 kilometres down the Yenisei) and had it transported by ship, so that we would finally be entitled to build a garage. My father never had a driver's licence and never drove the motorcycle; in the 1980s he would have preferred to have a car — but by the time he was able to acquire a car he was no longer interested. He was already a pensioner and preferred to walk rather than take public transportation, let alone go by car. He explained his lack of enthusiasm for a motor vehicle with two reasons: a desire to save money and a passion for walking.

The television set that we obtained in 1987, the Lithuanian *Silelis* with the innovative remote-control wire, was a real hit and despite its small size it was a high-status possession. There were only two of this kind in the entire yard (which consisted of four large apartment blocks with approximately 700 inhabitants). We were no ordinary family with this TV set! It still stands on one of the refrigerators in the kitchen as an artefact; my parents have no desire to throw it out. It is a reminder of the battle we won and also of the things we never got.

---

6   Compare the film *Garazh* [Garage] directed by Eldar Ryzanov, 1979.
7   See Siegelbaum (2008a, 2008b). Cf. *Krupnyi Vyigrysh*, a film produced by Khoshor Shahum in 1980.

Fig. 2.1. New apartment blocks are rising all over Krasnoiarsk, displacing single-storey timber houses, especially in the central districts. The large Soviet-era garage complexes for private cars occupy considerable parts of the urban space. Garages continue to be used for private storage, often including cellars to store produce grown on the *dacha*; sometimes they are used for car-repair businesses or workshops. Photograph by Dennis Zuev, 31 March 2018, CC-BY.

Hello, Tura! (Joachim Otto Habeck)

My desire to explore the remoter parts of Eurasia developed in my early years; my first travels to the Soviet Union and Siberia took place in 1990–1995. Parallel to my studies in geography and anthropology, I took up a job as telephone operator for long-distance calls within the reunified Germany, and between Germany and other countries. (I will have to write a separate book on this.) It should be noted that in Germany, there were still a small number of places that could be reached only via operator; this situation only came to an end in November 1993, which is not so long ago. In comparison with Poland, Romania and some other countries in eastern central Europe, the telephone network of the Soviet Union and its successor states was quite well developed. But it seemed that nobody in the west had tried to find out about the area codes that were introduced with the automatisation of telephony in the Soviet Union in the 1980s. With a colleague of mine, I embarked on nightly conversations with operators throughout what had just ceased to be the Soviet Union, harvesting area codes hitherto unknown to western operators. This helped considerably to accelerate the process of making phone calls between Berlin and the whole of Russia, a development that did not go unnoticed in telecom offices in other parts of Germany. Placing a phone call from Germany to far-flung district centres (*raionnye tsentry*) in Siberia remained a real challenge, however; very few customers (actually, they were not called "customers" but "subscribers" back then) would venture to call places below the level of a district centre.

I remember my first phone call from the Berlin office to Tura, the capital of Evenkia, with its 5,000 inhabitants. I mention this place because it soon became important for me in a different context. There was no phone line to Tura in 1992; there was a very scratchy and noisy radio connection from Krasnoiarsk to Tura that I was put onto, and it required a lot of shouting.

In summer 1993, I travelled to Tura for the first time. That journey was comparatively easy. Having obtained a Russian visa and a train ticket to Krasnoiarsk, the most logical and convenient way to reach Tura was by airplane. Air transportation to district centres (such as Tura) was possible, but onward airborne connections to subordinate villages like Yessei, Chirinda and Ekonda,[8] some seven hundred kilometres further in what really is the Far North, had been abandoned because state subsidies for kerosene were no longer sufficient to cover the expenses. Trying to visit *taiga* settlements, I was lucky to be offered a ride in a small steamer up the Nizhniaia Tunguska with youngsters belonging to a folklore ensemble that was travelling to perform songs and dances for the small communities upstream. Not unlike airplane timetables, boat trips and in fact everything organised by the state had become unreliable and erratic, with the exception of the railway services, which kept functioning.

To be sure, transportation in the remote parts of Siberia, the Far North and the Far East was also irregular throughout Soviet times, owing to sudden changes in the weather — the imponderables of rain, fog, snow, and ice. One had, and still has, to be patient. All of the researchers on this project can tell numerous stories about waiting: they have been waiting for many hours of their lives (though not necessarily wasting those hours, see below). Sometimes, one would have to wait for days or weeks. The

---

8   On Ekonda and the sudden immobility, see Campbell (2003).

appearance of helicopters, airplanes, boats, etc. were rare opportunities that one would not want to let go. The difference, then, between earlier and later forms of unpredictable transportation lay in the degree of state control over mobility, of mechanisation and individual dependence, and of being able to resort to alternative modes of travelling (Habeck 2013; cf. Urry 2007: 53–54, 139–40). The things one was waiting for also changed. Earlier — up until the 1960s, before helicopters came into use — one waited for the ice to become stable or, alternatively, to melt, so that one could cross it by sledge or use a boat, whereas later, one would wait for the hovering fog to disperse and for the sound of a helicopter.[9] The image of Siberia as a vast territory becomes more palpable when one tries to imagine the countless hours of waiting for a lift, for a chance to carry on. Waiting can turn into a habit, a well-developed social convention (cf. Ries 1997: 135). More often than not, people wait together. The *communitas* of expectation and longing brings them together.[10] They sit in airport lounges, *taiga* camps, at the embankment of a road or railway line platform. (The same mode of waiting for the expected thing to happen unexpectedly was also characteristic of the phone call to Siberia, when the telephone operator might call in the middle of the night to say that the other party is now on the line.) What has also changed are the modes of waiting, as new technological devices permit one to keep oneself busy, reading and sending text messages, making phone calls, playing games, or listening to music.

Movement, telecommunication, and lifestyle in peripheral settings

Consumption alone does not suffice to describe lifestyles; rather, lifestyles evolve around specific sensibilities, they constitute a particular

---

9   Particularly cumbersome are situations when the traveller is dependent on different means of transportation that all require certain weather conditions. For example, in Chukotka, during the winter one has to wait for the ice to become stable to get to the airport, where one would then pray for a clear sky to take off. In this season one can use both road transport (sledge, jeep, military vehicles) and air transport (helicopter). Summer is the season of *podushka* (hovercraft, used between Anadyr' and its airport on the other side of the bay, at Ugol'nye Kopi).

10   We are reminded by our colleagues that this *communitas* could occasionally turn into nasty competition, depending on the product or service to be acquired.

mode of identification inasmuch as they are *expressive, routinised* and *stylised* (as argued in Chapters 1 and 11). On the basis of these three attributes, lifestyles do influence patterns of consumption. They also entail specific attitudes towards consumption, as does past biographical experience of the availability of goods and services. In the region under study — Siberia and the North of Russia — consumer choices were limited in Soviet times, and at present they continue to be limited by infrastructural constraints, in particular with regard to telecommunication, and patterns of mobility. There are thus manifold ways in which the development and availability of technology and infrastructure both constitute and limit the range of lifestyles.

Peripherality can be understood as the experience of a lack of infrastructure: transportation of goods is more expensive and services are limited (see below). If we accept that the availability of a broad range of consumer goods and services is a precondition for diverse self-stylisation and individual distinction, then we arrive at the conclusion that peripheral places offer fewer lifestyle choices. In some cases, however, limitation itself is a source of pride ("we can do without", "we are not dependent on such gadgets", "we are inventive") and provides the basis for a particular form of distinction. Self-stylisation in peripheral places often employs references to personal inventiveness (for example, see Shaw in Chapter 3 discussing Chavan'ga), vigour and vitality, purity, authentic life, and straightforwardness. These values also play an essential role in urbanites' ideas about the countryside, and inform and affect tourism. However, it is reasonable to assume that many — if not most — inhabitants of peripheral places would want to move to a more central place, or to be able to travel to the nearest city more easily, or, alternatively, to see improvement in the range of goods and services offered at their place of residence. Mobility is therefore crucial, and so are imagined ideas about distant places (see Long, Chapter 5) and thoughts about a better life elsewhere.

As we have discussed, movement and travel can be unpredictable. In many parts of Siberia, mobility planning is largely dependent on transportation timetables, weather conditions, and the ready availability of money. Here we postulate that the predictability of travel is one factor (among others) that determines the feasibility of life projects. The less a person is able to plan their departures and arrivals, the more difficult it is to steadily pursue long-term goals. Unpredictability does not necessarily impinge on one's quality of life or an individual's feeling of happiness (in some situations, people seek adventures), but it does mean that things are more likely to happen by coincidence or providence rather than intention.

In Siberia in particular, regimes of mobility have changed drastically. Freedom of movement and mobility have become essential resources for self-formation: compared with the Soviet period, the majority of people now have more freedom to plan their movements within the country and abroad, for leisure, for work or for educational purposes. In Soviet society, different forms of mobility were associated with certain professional occupations and privileged positions (for example, party officials, high-rank military, scientists and journalists), whereas in post-Soviet Russia, money has become the most decisive criterion in determining people's ability to travel: money has an equalising effect in terms of entitlement to services, yet simultaneously the disparity of monetary income creates social inequalities and lifestyle limitations (Lipchinskaia 2012; Zubarevich 2013). It should be noted that incomes are generally higher in urban and suburban than in rural areas, with the result that rural inhabitants are disadvantaged when it comes to long-distance mobility.

Collectivist ideology and Soviet practices of holiday-making (Brož & Habeck, Chapter 4) have not become extinct, but a new generation of young people have appropriated more individualised leisure activities. This goes hand in hand with the adoption of the computer by the urban upper and middle classes. For many elderly rural inhabitants, personal computers are still novel and unusual, and the advent of the internet in rural communities is a very recent phenomenon (see the penultimate section of this chapter).

Mobility in its various forms has particular relevance for young people in Siberia. Mobility itself, or the expressed desire to be able to travel, can be an important ingredient of self-stylisation (as exemplified by the practice of free-travelling, Zuev 2008). Young people are relatively mobile because educational and career opportunities are often connected with relocating to a larger city, but by the same token, they are relatively immobile owing to financial constraints, and these constraints are particularly prominent in rural regions. In autonomous regions such as Chukotka or Sakha (Yakutia), the administration offers stipends for outstanding students to go elsewhere for higher education. At the same time, the internet and social media enable young people to connect to the world outside Siberia, and virtual mobility is on the list of attainable goals. Here one can see a particular and new aspect of distinction: access to the internet.

Money has to some extent replaced social capital as the main currency — in the big cities more so than in rural areas, where personal ties continue to play a comparatively decisive role. Older (Soviet) constraints on getting things done, and habitual ways of doing so, have thus been partially dislodged by forms of exchange in which money is the only currency. Simultaneously, we can observe that money has partially diminished the value of social ties, of informal networks, of mutual support, and also of public recognition that an individual receives from others. Obviously, the unequal availability of economic capital goes hand in hand with social stratification and it is the main factor that limits individuals' options for choice and action. Even for those whose lifestyle and self-stylisation do not depend on consumerism (by which we mean consumption as a purpose in itself), money is the factor that enables and restricts all sorts of activities. It also essentially enables and restricts physical movement, and this is now more strongly felt than in Soviet times.

Technically, the means of transportation (railway, airplanes, cars etc.) have not changed fundamentally over the last three decades; it is their availability and the conditions of their use that have changed, particularly with regard to cars.[11] Telecommunication and visual technologies are very different cases. These have changed drastically in technical terms: devices and systems that are commonly used by nearly everybody these days — mobile phones in particular — were simply not available thirty years ago. Photography and television have acquired fundamentally new qualities through their combination with computers, smartphones, and the emergence of the internet, and they have laid the ground for modes and strategies of self-presentation

---

11   The increasing number of cars has also resulted in new priorities in urban planning and new ways of socialising, which will be discussed below (see also Broz & Habeck 2015; Popov 2012).

that were downright unthinkable a few decades ago. There is a general trend away from centralised control over media and a top-down distribution of media content, to networked, rhizomatic forms of media organisation and user-generated content. Visual self-presentation nowadays happens in a digital commons. Photographs and other forms of content can be shared so widely and generally that ownership becomes a questionable category. Obviously, similar trends can be observed all over the world, but what is particular about Russia is the rupture of state control over people's movements and media content that occurred in the late 1980s and 1990s (Burrell & Hörschelmann 2014); today, however, the state is regaining, to some extent, influence on many types of media (as observed already in the 2000s by Hutchings & Rulyova 2009).

Social distinction is expressed not simply in the purchase of this or that brand of smartphone, tablet, and so forth, but also by the consumption of particular web-based products and services, participation in, and communicative behaviour on, social networking sites and online games, and — generally speaking — individual management of one's online existence (Athique 2013: 103–05; Boellstorff 2008). All this is relatively new, and in fact pertains only to a part of Siberia's population. It is clear, however, that in the communities under study, the use of these technologies and the flow of ideas and images give rise to new sensibilities, in Chaney's sense (1996: 8). In other words, personal judgements and public debates unfold along with new moral issues and aesthetic options, created by the diffusion of new technologies. In subsequent chapters of the book, the authors will pursue these developments in more detail and explore some of the pertinent aesthetic conventions.

Ways of engaging with social norms have changed, and the ethical and aesthetic significance of these methods has changed, too. One of the contradictions in Siberia has been the gap between new sensibilities and material limits — the fact that different technologies usually come to Siberia from Moscow and are initially available to people only in the big urban centres. People in the small towns and rural areas had to order such items through relatives or friends in the big cities. This is still partly the case today, even if the internet now provides improved possibilities for the purchase of goods and services.

Table 2.1. Field sites of the CLLP Project, sorted by number of inhabitants. Abbreviations in the last column: CN for China; FIN for Finland; KZ for Kazakhstan; MN for Mongolia; USA for the United States of America. Population data compiled from Wikipedia, based on the Federal State Statistics Service. Data on distance to the nearest tarmac or federal road/railway station/border-crossing point compiled from http://maps.google.de and http://km-km.ru

Name of settlement	Administrative status	Population as of 1 Oct 2010	Population as of 1 Jan 2018	Nearest tarmac or federal road (overland distance, km)	Nearest railway station (overland distance, km)	Nearest border crossing (overland distance, km)
Novosibirsk	Centre of Federal Subject	1,473,754	1,612,833	0	0	c. 440km, Karasuk (KZ)
Krasnoiarsk	Centre of Federal Subject	973,826	1,090,811	0	0	c. 1,050 km, Erzyn (MN)
Vladivostok	Centre of Federal Subject	592,034	604,901	0	0	c. 180 km, Suifenhe (CN)
Irkutsk	Centre of Federal Subject	587,891	623,869	0	0	c. 310 km, Mondy (MN)
Ulan-Ude	Centre of Federal Subject	404,426	434,869	0	0	c. 230 km, Kiakhta (MN)
Yakutsk	Centre of Federal Subject	269,691	311,760	0	35 km, Nizhnii Bestiakh	1,790 km (CN), Blagoveshchensk
Chemal	District Centre	3,973	4,670	0	180 km, Biisk	c. 480 km, Tashanta (MN)
Saranpaul'	Village	2,575	2,921	c. 400 km, Priob'e	c. 400 km, Priob'e	c. 1,200 km, Kazakhstan
Novoe Chaplino	Part of a larger municipality	419	Data not available	c.1,550 km, Omsukchan	c. 3,400 km, Nizhnii Bestiakh	120 km (sea), St Lawrence Island (USA)
Chavan'ga	Village	officially: 87 seasonal: 170	Data not available	187 km, Umba	335 km, Apatity-1	610 km, Kuolaiarvi (FIN)

Overview of field sites

In what follows we will give a brief overview of the sites where researchers carried out fieldwork for the CLLP Project. These are: Novosibirsk, Krasnoiarsk, Irkutsk, Ulan-Ude, Vladivostok, Yakutsk; Chemal (in the Altai Republic), Saranpaul' (in the Khanty-Mansi Autonomous Region — Yugra), Chavan'ga (Murmansk Oblast), and Novoe Chaplino (Chukchi Autonomous Region). Each of these sites will be briefly introduced below (see Table 2.1; information on the number of interviews conducted in specific places is given in the Appendix to this volume). We will discuss their remoteness or accessibility as a function of their administrative status and several other variables. Predictability of travel as a criterion is seldom found in geographic analyses of mobility and access, yet in some of our field sites it is the most important factor because it overrides and shapes people's plans and hopes.

Administrative status and dendritic infrastructure

The different field sites can be categorised according to their administrative function. Six of our field sites are capitals of large administrative units (Republic, Oblast, or Okrug); each city has a population of several hundreds of thousands of people. Of these, five are cities in the southern part of Siberia, located along the main transport artery, the Trans-Siberian railway; the sixth, Yakutsk, used to be much less privileged in terms of connectedness. Further down on the administrative hierarchy, we find district (*raion*) centres that nowadays usually also constitute municipal entities, and on the lowest level there are villages and hamlets. Our study includes four villages of different sizes. Two of them (Chavan'ga and Novoe Chaplino) are very remote settlements on the northern coasts; one (Saranpaul') is a very remote *taiga* village, and one (Chemal) is a mountain village that can be easily accessed by car.

The administrative status of a settlement is a prime factor when decisions are made about infrastructure development and accessibility. In a centrally planned economy like that of the Soviet Union, the flows of goods, people, and information were structured more hierarchically than in the market-economy countries of western Europe and the USA (cf. Humphrey 2014). We use the term "dendritic infrastructure" as a

Fig. 2.2. Krasnoiarsk is one of the large urban centres in Siberia with a significant number of timber-made houses (*chastnyi sektor*, in the foreground). The city has gradually expanded on both banks of the river. Many of its *dacha* communities occupy the surrounding hills, as can be seen in the background. Photograph by Dennis Zuev, 31 March 2018, CC-BY.

shorthand for this territorially arranged hierarchy of transportation and telecommunication. Dendritic infrastructure was also characteristic of other socialist countries,[12] although its effects were more pronounced in Russia because of the country's low population density and environmental conditions. The socialist state had to invest significantly in the development of infrastructure, and Siberia is an exemplary case. In many respects and for many individuals, it was the Soviet state that facilitated movement and exchange in the first place; however, owing to the enormous costs of transportation development — and also because of the bureaucratic nature of the system — these movements and exchanges occurred up and down the chain of command i.e. the administrative hierarchy, from village to district centre to the regional capital (and further to Moscow). In the Far North and central Siberia, regional borders were drawn in 1926–1930; they were often delineated with respect to ethnic criteria and existing patterns of indigenous economic activity, yet they later came to cement those very patterns. Within a centrally planned

---

12   In many countries of western Europe and North America, transportation networks were (and still are) also organised dendritically, but since there were more cross-country connections in these cases, the effect was less drastic.

economy, it became easier to travel to the regional capital — because of the needs of the administrative hierarchy — but more difficult, in many cases, to travel laterally, to a nearby village on the other side of the regional border (Habeck 2013; Kuklina & Holland 2018). The effect of dendritic infrastructure is also felt today; it affects nearly all parts of Siberia, the Far North and the Far East.

Predictability of travel

The position of a settlement in the administrative hierarchy is an important factor, but it is not the only thing that shapes the remoteness or accessibility of a place. The conditions of the natural environment (hydrographic location, landscape and relief, permafrost, etc.) are obviously very decisive. Moreover, many of the Soviet infrastructure development schemes in the Far North and Far East were guided by the needs of geological exploration and extraction; this was the case, for example, in the Autonomous Republic of Sakha (Yakutia), where road planning initially followed the necessities of the diamond-mining industry, with the effect that the western part of Sakha (Yakutia) stands out from other parts of the republic in terms of availability of paved roads. Another example is the north-western part of Siberia, where the transportation network is comparatively dense and dynamic in its development, serving the needs of the gas and oil industries. A further factor is geopolitical strategic relevance. Both Novoe Chaplino and Chavan'ga are located near the outer boundary of the Russian Federation, in proximity with Norway and the United States of America (member states of NATO). Chavan'ga has experienced infrastructural changes due to militarisation and demilitarisation processes. Novoe Chaplino is, like many other settlements along the northern coast, subject to the border-zone entry regulations, which require travellers to obtain a permit before going there.

Much has been written about this multitude of factors in geography, economics, and area-studies publications on Russia (Göler 2007; Hill and Gaddy 2003; Lazhentsev 2015; Pallot 1990; Rodgers 1990). Our point here is not to repeat these in detail, but rather to show how these conditions bear out in the everyday lives of people in different settlements. Comparative studies on this topic from different parts of the Russian Far North are rare, the exemplary article by Bolotova, Karaseva & Vasilyeva (2017) being a welcome exception. The issue of transportation is in some places the most decisive factor in people's daily existence, shaping all other plans and considerations, and thus it is also a factor that limits lifestyle choices. This is most apparent in the cases of Chavan'ga (see Chapter 3) and Novoe Chaplino (see Chapter 6) but it also emerges in the case of Saranpaul', where people say: "We live like on an island: you can't get here, but once you are in Saranpaul', you can't leave again" (see Chapter 9).

These and other examples induce us to discuss remoteness and accessibility in connection with plans and life projects: what becomes crucial, then, is not distance as such, but the *predictability* of transport and communication. "Average travel time" cannot serve as suitable indicator of remoteness in a situation where each journey depends on many imponderables, as is illustrated by a recent study on roads and remoteness in the Sayan Mountains (Kuklina & Holland 2018). In cities like Novosibirsk and Vladivostok, one can rely on the train and aviation timetables and one can count on the bus service. On the contrary, in remote villages such as Saranpaul' or Novoe Chaplino, transportation is hard to predict; and all decisions are subordinate to the one question: how and when is travel going to happen? Hence the importance of waiting and of taking chances when they appear on the horizon.

Urban field sites as transportation hubs

Krasnoiarsk, Irkutsk, and Ulan-Ude were established in the seventeenth and eighteenth centuries, as garrison towns by the Cossacks on their mission to conquer Siberia for the Russian empire. In the nineteenth century, the fortress of Vladivostok was built on the site of an old Chinese fishing village; since then it has been the strategic base for the Russian Pacific Fleet. The early twentieth century saw the completion of the Trans-Siberian railway that connected these places and provided the backbone of transportation throughout the whole of Asiatic Russia. The railway triggered a spectacular demographic and economic growth. It is the trunk from which the dendritic infrastructure fans out to the Far North, and thus the cities along the trunk line represent the industrial, cultural and educational urban nodes of Siberia and the Far East.

Later than the aforementioned cities, some 120 years ago the settlement that is now called Novosibirsk came into existence when the first railway bridge across the River Ob' was constructed. Novosibirsk is Siberia's largest city, with numerous industrial enterprises; it is an important node of transportation in every respect. It has seen several periods of rapid in-migration, and most of the current migrants arrive from nearby Kazakhstan and other Central Asian countries. Tourists from North America and European countries pass by in large numbers but usually do not stop for a longer period. The brisk growth of the city has not produced many architectural landmarks. Despite the construction of a subway (*metro*), there are several factors, natural and man-made, that lead to frequent congestion on the city's main thoroughfares.

Krasnoiarsk is one of the oldest cities in Siberia (founded in 1628) and this makes it quite attractive for tourists. It is the third largest city in Siberia and the administrative centre of Krasnoiarsk Region, which, in terms of its size, occupies second place in Russia after the Republic of Sakha (Yakutia). As is the case with Novosibirsk, Krasnoiarsk has become an attractive destination for migrants from Central Asia (Kyrgyzstan and Uzbekistan). Krasnoiarsk is known for its industrial base, with the Krasnoiarsk Aluminium factory (KRAZ) currently the biggest enterprise, while the creation of Siberia's Federal University in 2006 made it one of the educational centres of Siberia. Due to its defence- and space-related industries, in Soviet times it was closed to foreigners (unlike Irkutsk or Novosibirsk, the city centres of which were always open).

Irkutsk was the administrative centre of the whole of East Siberia from 1803 to 1917, and as such it also served as an important hub for trade and exchange, notably with Mongolia and China. However, its position in the administrative hierarchy and its economic importance are no longer as singular as they used to be, for other cities grew in importance and attained similar functions. Nonetheless, of all cities in Siberia, it is still Irkutsk that attracts the largest numbers of visitors from abroad. The influx of both domestic and foreign tourists, which is mostly due to the proximity of Lake Baikal, has exerted a noticeable influence on the city's infrastructure (more so than in Novosibirsk and Krasnoiarsk). To give just one example, it fostered the relatively early emergence of free wi-fi hotspots and internet cafés (Zuev 2013a) in this city.

Probably most distinct among the cities mentioned is Vladivostok. It is the terminus of the Trans-Siberian railway and an important contact zone for Russia in the east. From 1958 to 1991, it was a closed city, due to being the Russian Pacific Fleet's naval base. Now it serves as a symbolic stronghold, and a showcase of Russia's presence on the Pacific coast. Vladivostok's proximity to China, the Koreas and Japan has conditioned the growth of trade and cross-border material exchanges, as well as diplomatic representation, which facilitates human cross-border movement. Few cities in Russia can compete with Vladivostok when it comes to the scenery of the surrounding landscape. However, in terms of settlement structure and urban planning, Vladivostok shares many features with most other Siberian cities: a fairly underdeveloped tourism infrastructure and an expanding urban sprawl.

Two of our fieldwork sites, Ulan-Ude and Yakutsk, are capitals of ethnically defined territories, notably the Republic of Buryatia and the Republic of Sakha (Yakutia). Ulan-Ude shares many characteristics of the "Trans-Sib" cities, yet it is distinct in view of its proximity to Mongolia and its function as cultural capital and administrative centre of a region with a Mongol-speaking population. Yakutsk, while of the same status in the administrative hierarchy as Ulan-Ude, has a very different significance. Yakutsk is an example of a transportation hub for an expansive region, remote from the big Siberian cities of the Trans-Siberian belt. The city serves as the base from which to fly to to all the districts of the Republic of Sakha (Yakutia), which is the largest territory of all of Siberia and Russia. Several scholars (Argounova-Low 2012; Ventsel 2011; Vitebsky 2000, 2005: 351–65) have explored different aspects of mobility in Sakha — the driving experience of the truckers, the mobility of the traders, and the groups that venture into the most remote places — the hunters and reindeer herders. Two significant features of Sakha transportation are the river Lena, which is navigable from Ust'-Kut via Yakutsk to the Arctic Ocean port of Tiksi, and the Kolyma Highway, which connects Yakutsk with Magadan on the Okhotsk seacoast. Yakutsk has been awaiting the "arrival" of a railway connection since late Soviet times. By 1985, a railway from the Trans-Siberian and Baikal-Amur Mainline (BAM) to the southernmost part of Yakutia had been completed (Mote 1990). Construction of the remaining section of 800 kilometers took 25 years, and a passenger station in Nizhnii Bestiakh started fully operating as late as summer 2019, not far from Yakutsk but on the opposite bank of the River Lena. A bridge across that stream is yet to be built (cf. Schweitzer, Povoroznyuk & Schiesser 2017).

Rural field sites: peripherality and the experience of infrastructural shortcomings

In Siberia, more than elsewhere, there is a very steep gradient between centrality and peripherality, and the rural-urban divide has been a continual concern in Soviet and post-Soviet infrastructural planning (Jähnig 1983; Pallot 1990). In very stark contrast to the cities described above, which possess comparatively developed technical infrastructure, the rural field sites of our research project are characterised by infrastructural shortcomings. We suggest that these places represent the remotest branches and twigs of the dendritic infrastructure (see above). What is more, the different components of infrastructure are developed very unevenly — and in some cases they are completely absent — so that each place experiences telecommunication and transportation problems in its own particular way. People develop work-around or "coping" strategies, which become part of the local knowledge. Clearly, such technological shortcomings create limitations in the range of possibilities for the life projects and self-stylisation of individual people, though in some cases it is the very dearth or absence of technology that is seen as a spark for creativity, inventiveness, and pride: namely, the skill to live independently of complicated gadgets and to overcome technical difficulties (cf. Davydov 2017; Mankova 2018). In what follows, we briefly introduce three highly peripheral rural communities — Saranpaul', Chavan'ga, and Chaplino — and then contrast them with one community — Chemal — which has seen rapid development fuelled by tourism, and thus experiences a seasonal mass influx of people, rather than year-round peripherality.

Saranpaul', discussed in Chapter 9, is the administrative centre of a municipal unit that includes ten villages with a total population of 4,480 people, about half of them belonging to one of the several indigenous ethnic groups (Mansi, Khanty and Komi). Saranpaul' itself has 2,575 inhabitants. As in many other isolated places in the Far North, public-sector jobs and pensions provide a modest monetary income that is distributed among family members; some people have a plot or a greenhouse for growing vegetables; and hunting and fishing are important forms of subsistence. Reindeer husbandry also adds to the local economy. However, the popularity of such work has gradually undergone a decline and appears to be an unattractive occupation for young people because of low salaries and the complex challenges of transportation between the reindeer herders' camps and the central village. At the same time, reindeer meat is highly valued among local people. In Saranpaul', money does not have the universal power it has elsewhere: the value of social networks remains more pronounced than in big cities. If there are not enough places in the helicopter, informal ties with the local administration, or with staff of the regional airline UTAir, are instrumental. Social networks are important for travelling and accommodation, for example in order to get a place in a truck on a winter road (i.e., a road seasonally arranged across ice and snow). It is good to have friends in a big city, for example Tiumen', who can enhance your mobility by hosting you, sending you things, or booking vouchers for you to go on holidays abroad (the same voucher in the nearby, smaller city of Berezovo is more expensive than in Tiumen').

As in other places, the changes in transportation and telecommunication technology have been accompanied by the gradual development of new skills and the degradation of others. Navigation and orientation skills are still useful for finding one's way without relying on public transport, while the skills of driving a reindeer sledge or making one's own boat from the right type of wood are becoming rare. Instead, knowledge regarding the strength of coverage of different mobile phone companies is important when it comes to deciding which operator to choose. In terms of spatial information, there has been a shift in the last fifteen years from maps[13] to GPS, while the use of the internet as source of information is still limited to public institutions (school, administrative bodies), since it is rarely accessible from private households in Saranpaul'. The system of registering for goods has been

---

13   Detailed (large-scale) maps were classified as secret in Soviet times. Plans of cities were available, but they were based on schematic representations without topographical accuracy. Today, a large number of navigation and cartographic apps are accessed by smartphone users for trail-finding (cf. Popov 2012: 164–65).

replaced by the habit of buying things on credit. In terms of private transportation, snowmobiles and motorboats continue to be essential.

Chavan'ga, the focus of Chapter 3, is a village on the Terskii coast of the White Sea in the region of Murmansk; officially it has 87 permanent inhabitants. The main occupation is fishing for salmon, which has also been one of the local currencies (bartered for all-terrain vehicles, offered as a payment for favours to helicopter pilots, etc.). As in Saranpaul', one has to rely significantly on personal ties to get a place on a helicopter. There are no proper road connections to other settlements; with an off-road vehicle it is possible to get through to the nearest tarmac road within a few hours. There is also a winter road. People have owned private cars since Soviet times, and they are used for subsistence activities such as fishing or berry picking. Spatial knowledge is not dependent on maps, but rather on word-of-mouth advice and personal experience. Computers appeared only in 2008 and GSM coverage in 2015. In a situation in which infrastructure is incomplete, people use technical devices in vernacular ways: they apply their own makeshift practices (Istomin 2013). People with digital cameras who do not own a computer have to rely on someone else's device to transfer images. In terms of private transportation, the motorbike is the most widespread, but quadrocycles are becoming popular.

Novoe Chaplino (mentioned in Chapter 6) is located in the extreme east of the Chukchi Autonomous Okrug, which in turn is the north-easternmost part of the Russian Federation. Situated at the shore of the Bering Sea, this settlement, with 419 inhabitants, is the only place in Russia with a majority of Yupik (Eskimo) inhabitants. They used to maintain close connections with their relatives, the Yupik communities on the Alaskan shore of the Bering Sea and on St Lawrence Island, but these connections were cut during the Cold War, when the Chukchi Peninsula became a sensitive border zone. The settlement of Novoe Chaplino itself came into existence in 1958 as the result of the amalgamation (*ukrupnenie*)[14] of several small collective farms and pertinent settlements.

---

14   The process of *ukrupnenie* took place in waves in nearly all of the regions of the Soviet Union. It aimed to reduce the number of collective farms and small rural settlements, which were deemed to be "without prospect" for further development, and to concentrate the population in larger rural settlements, thereby providing better access to infrastructure and facilities (Pallot 1990; Allemann 2013: 79–89 for Murmansk Oblast; Habeck 2013 for Evenkia; Vitebsky 1990 for an example from the Yakut ASSR).

The 1990s saw renewed connections across the Bering Sea: people could travel to St Lawrence Island by boat. However, as a result of some tragic accidents and the newly invigorated border surveillance, boat journeys to the United States are no longer permitted by the Russian border guards. Flights from the nearby airport of Provideniia to Alaska occur rarely, usually once every summer. Novoe Chaplino is connected with Provideniia by a gravel road about 25 kilometres long. All transport now goes through Provideniia, which is the district centre with a port and military base.

The main source of livelihood is whaling and seal-hunting, activities that became especially crucial between 1996–1998, a time of food deprivation that was caused by particularly poor regional governance, aggravated by the country's overall economic crisis. When Roman Abramovich, a renowned entrepreneur and politician, became governor of the Chukchi Autonomous Okrug in 2002, Novoe Chaplino (along with other settlements) saw a complete overhaul: all of the inhabitants moved into newly built "prefab" houses and a school and local bakery were erected. Under Abramovich, plastic cards were introduced as means of payment for local services (possibly with the side-effect of limiting cash flows and combatting alcohol abuse). Notwithstanding the brand-new buildings and infrastructure, internet use and mobile telecommunication remain difficult. Even though a few individuals owned mobile phones as early as 2005 (and started using smartphones to take photographs), GSM connection arrived in Novoe Chaplino as late as 2012. Landlines are available and a few individuals have used the internet via modem since 2011. The sharing of technological devices — while characteristic of all northern communities — seems to be of particular value in Novoe Chaplino. Devices such as cameras or mobile phones can serve as status markers only if the owner shares them with others.

The community of Chemal is very different from the preceding rural field sites; it features in the chapter on tourism (Chapter 4). It is unusual in several respects. It is located in a relatively peripheral region, south of Siberia's spinal cord, the Trans-Siberian railway. Previously a rural settlement in one of the valleys of the Altai mountains, Chemal saw the erection of a hydropower station, the construction of a road, and later the emergence of tourism. Thus, in contrast to the remote and hard-to-access places in the Far North, Chemal attracts thousands of people every summer. Many of them come from Novosibirsk and other Siberian cities for a long weekend. Local inhabitants can predict the advent of the tourists every summer, and benefit economically; the tourists in turn can expect to find places to stay, to eat, or to enjoy the mountain landscape.

The technical infrastructure and availability of public services in all the above-mentioned rural and urban field sites are defined, to a great extent, by severe climatic conditions and the geographic particularities that affected the implementation of modernisation and industrialisation in Soviet times. In the next section, we will discuss the changes that affected mobility and infrastructure in Siberia, the Russian Far East and the Far North.

Means of transportation

This section will focus on different means of transportation, with a focus on our respondents' and our own experiences. A complete overview of infrastructural changes would have to include: a comprehensive history of industrial development and resource use; general changes in urban and rural planning; the advent of new media facilitating information exchange and mobility; the availability of leisure and sport facilities; communal services; cultural institutions; religious services; restaurants, cafés, and bars; and public spaces in a general sense. Some of these aspects have been researched elsewhere in more detail — see Humphrey (2007) on the effects of privatisation on the infrastructural development of Siberian cities; Hurelbaatar (2007) on changes in religious sites in the case of the Buryatia; and Habeck & Belolyubskaya (2016) on the diverse typology of buildings and problems of urban planning in the city of Yakutsk.[15] What we intend to account for in this chapter is the domain of the physical movement (transportation) of passengers, telecommunication, and media technology.

---

15   There is still a large number of timber-made houses in Siberian cities. Such areas are scattered throughout the cities, which makes them "splintered" in terms of access to basic utilities. Timber houses usually have no central heating, sewage, waste disposal or water supply. In the winter, the heating of houses with coal and wood adds to higher levels of air-pollution, which is aggravated by the growing use of motor vehicles.

Rail

It is hard to overestimate the influence that the construction and operation of the Trans-Siberian railway line, in combination with later additions to the network, have had on the economic development of Siberia (Lamin 2005; Marks 1991). It is easy, however, to forget that the current network of railways covers only the southern and western part of Siberia, with many villages and cities in the other parts being hundreds or thousands of kilometres away from the nearest railway station. Obviously, railways connect places and people. Yet in many cases, it is the railway itself that has created places and defined their *raison d'être*, providing employment and income for hundreds of families (cf. Povoroznyuk 2018; Schweitzer, Povoroznyuk & Schiesser 2017).

The cities along the railway expanded rapidly,[16] and as an extension of the urban sprawl, *dacha* settlements appeared in Soviet times along the railway corridors, sometimes a hundred kilometres away from the city centre. Since the *dacha* is such an important ingredient of leisure and perceived by many as a symbol of the good life (Caldwell 2012; Zavisca 2003), one may conceive of short-distance trains as shuttle services between different spheres of individual experience or even domains of reality.

In the following interview (conducted by Joachim Otto Habeck), Vasilii, a pensioner from Novosibirsk, talks about the *dacha* as a necessity, and about the journey to the *dacha* on the train being one of the most gruelling experiences of the *dacha* lifestyle for those without private transportation:

> JOH: Am I right to suggest that the *dacha* plays an important role in your life, in your biography?
>
> Vasilii: Well, it is not important; it is simply a necessity. Necessity to help. I helped Zhenia [his partner] to work on the *dacha*. I liked to be there during the summer. The only thing I did not like was the journey to the *dacha*. [You have to take] the suburban train, especially in the summer, it is hot, it takes a lot of your energy, one can't breathe — there are so many *dacha* owners [...] One and a half hours [by train] one way. And then you have to walk for

---

16 This rapid development along the main railway line occurred to the detriment of other, historically important cities, such as Tomsk and Yeniseisk.

> twenty minutes from the station [...] But when Zhenia got ill, we
> abandoned the *dacha*, there were other [more important] things...

While such journeys to the *dacha* usually take a few hours and occur on a regular basis, long-distance train journeys may extend over several days and bring about memorable, quite intensive experiences of transitory spaces. They are subject to particular rules and practices to such a degree that we can speak of trains as constituting a social sphere in their own right, complete with "institutionalised" inmates who perceive time, space, and each other in very special ways (Simonova 2007). For some, long-distance train journeys occur on a regular basis, notably for shift workers commuting between the oil and gas fields of the Far North and the more central regions of Russia (Saxinger 2015, 2016: 121–28). For many others, long-distance train trips are exceptional. Comings and goings, arrivals and departures seem to create more anxiety and stress and require more intensive social support than anywhere in Europe or North America. Tourists from abroad visiting Siberia do not simply use the railway to get from one place to another; rather, for the majority, the experience of the Trans-Siberian railway is itself the purpose of their journey (Zuev 2013a).

Fig. 2.3. Long-distance train passengers using a longer stop at Irkutsk railway station for a smoking break or communication by mobile phone (during the train ride, network coverage is often weak or non-existent). Photograph by Joachim Otto Habeck, 17 July 2017, CC-BY.

Certain railway-related professions, such as long-distance conductor (*provodnik*), are accompanied by such specific everyday conditions that they create particular subcultures. Between the big cities, along the line, smaller villages and their inhabitants live according to the rhythm of the trains that call by. Village dwellers could increase their meagre income by selling food on the platform to train passengers (until about 2009, when this was forbidden, officially because of incidents of food poisoning). In a few cases, railway stations became known for the produce traded there (notably, whitefish locally known as *omul'* at Sliudianka,[17] cedar nuts at the station of Taiga, potato pies at Vikhorevka).

Considering the ups and downs in other means of transportation in the "wild" post-Soviet years, the railway fared remarkably well. To be sure, the number of passenger trains were reduced, and ticket prices went up in the 1990s and ever since (about which more below). However, services ran on time throughout that difficult period, almost no lines were abandoned, and employees in transportation enterprises were less severely affected by payment arrears than employees of other branches of the public sector (Lehmann, Wadsworth & Acquisti 1999). At present, the different territorial branches of the Russian railways are among the biggest employers in the country.

If in terms of overland transportation, the twentieth century in Siberia was the century of the railway and of aviation, the twenty-first century is likely to become the era of the automobile. In Soviet times, the number of people owning cars was rather small, but now the car competes with the train as the most popular means of transportation in many parts of Siberia. This signals an important change in mobility patterns (Popov 2012), habits of travel, and probably also in perceptions of space. When one travels by train (or airplane or helicopter), one confides oneself to a vast machinery; one has no influence on its workings. Among other imponderables, one does not know with whom one will share the cabin or carriage for hours or days. Travelling by car, by contrast, is often associated with a high degree of personal freedom — admittedly for men more than women in rural settings — with the drivers and passengers being able to determine themselves with whom to travel, where to stop,

---

17 When in 2013 the sale of *omul'* was prohibited in Sliudianka, the local population organised a protest, declaring this business to be a crucial source of income.

and which shortcut to take (Broz & Habeck 2015). In present-day Siberia, we can discern a shift from a nexus system of transportation, in which "The whole is only able to function if every component works", towards a serial system of transportation, "in which each component is roughly like every other component", to use John Urry's distinction (2007: 94).

Long-distance railway journeys in Siberia (and more generally throughout the former Soviet Union) resemble trips by airplane in many respects. Since its beginnings, the railway has been an institution that overrides and shapes individual predilections, and it continues to do so: this is not only the case during the journey itself, but even while preparing the trip, individuals have to accept what the system offers and choose from a limited set of options.

In Soviet and early post-Soviet years, there were significant problems with the lack of availability of tickets. In part, this deficit was artificially created: thus, even if a train was half-empty, it was impossible to buy tickets. Sometimes one had to buy return tickets several months in advance. Travellers were advised at the ticket counter to travel a day earlier or three days later, to travel by third-class sleeper (*platskartnyi*) rather than second-class (*kupe*) or first-class (*SV*). Long queues for tickets were a very widespread phenomenon in the 1990s, whereas nowadays they have become rare, with more customers buying tickets online.[18] The physical and emotional tension connected with the purchase of long-distance railway tickets has disappeared. Train fares have been going up steadily since the early 1990s, not only as a long-term response to monetary inflation but also owing to the reduction of state subsidies. Travelling by train, even third class, is now usually more expensive than travelling by bus on the same route. Still, for some small towns and numerous villages, the railway continues to be the only way out and the only way back.

There are several ethnographic studies that trace the changes in the most elementary aspects of life once the railway "reaches" a place (Povoroznyuk 2011: 94, 136). There are many parallels between the inauguration of a railway track and that of a road, when a village or town becomes connected to the country-wide network. From our own observations we can say that, typically, some members of the

---

18 In the early 1990s, some individuals bought tickets in large quantities to resell them informally at a higher price. In 1994, a new regulation was introduced in order to prevent such abuses: to purchase a train ticket, one had to show a passport.

community complain about the uncontrolled influx of strangers and an increase in criminal acts (though we cannot judge if such statements are empirically grounded). On the other hand, becoming connected to the road or railway network usually results in the arrival of cheaper and more diverse food products, consumer goods and technical equipment. This has significance in the light of the discussion of consumption as one of the mechanisms of social distinction and the diversification of lifestyles. Connectedness also enhances the possibility of mobility: leaving the place simply becomes easier, but only for those who can afford the trip. By the same token, the innovation of a new means of transportation (for example, the helicopter) usually also has a detrimental effect on other, older means (such as the reindeer sledge); this in turn transforms skills and spatial perception, as mentioned above.[19] The ways in which the existence or absence of infrastructure in a place is perceived by the individuals who live there depends to no small degree on their personal plans for staying in that place or leaving it (Gavrilova 2017).

Returning to the symbolic significance of the railway in contemporary Russia, this section closes with the observation that large-scale plans and projects are still underway. Among these are the extension of the railway line beyond Yakutsk to the shores of the Pacific Ocean, and partial reconstruction of the so-called Transpolar railway line[20] to connect the Northern Urals with River Yenisei. The railway network of Siberia is still due to expand, for example, into the Republic of Altai, Tyva, to Sakhalin and towards Magadan (Strategiia 2030). Railway construction is heavily loaded with the symbolic power of the grand modernisation project, which has survived the end of the Soviet Union.

---

19   See Campbell 2003 and n.d.; Habeck 2013; see also Aporta (2013) and Aporta & Higgs (2005) for a discussion of how older and newer technological artefacts are integrated into Inuit practices of travelling and wayfinding. Istomin (2013) and Stammler (2013) give similar accounts with regard to Nenets reindeer herders and fishermen.

20   Activities to build this railway peaked in the 1940s and 1950s, when a large contingent of labour camp inmates were forced to build the line across the swamps and forest of north-western Siberia (Haywood 2010: 100–03; Mote 2003). Immediately after Stalin's death, the line was partially disbanded. Construction was partially resumed in later decades. Forced labour along the Transpolar railway was one of the gloomiest examples of how the Soviet modernisation project held sway over individual bodies, turning civil life into "bare life" (Agamben 1998).

The construction of new railways is still tantamount to hope for a better future (Povoroznyuk 2018).

The tariff policies of the Russian Railway Company (RZhD, *Rossiiskie Zheleznye Dorogi*) result in the adjustment of ticket prices at particular periods. The lowest prices are usually available around important public holidays, while the summer period has the highest prices. This pricing policy offers advantages for less affluent groups of people who are able to be flexible about when they travel, such as, notably, pensioners, who prefer to choose the low-tariff season for their trips. Moreover, in response to the under-use of *kupe* (second-class) carriages, for several years the Russian Railway Company has promoted low pricing for upper berth *kupe* places. During peak seasons and on popular routes (Krasnoiarsk-Moscow, or to anywhere along the BAM in summer) it is difficult to buy *platskart* (third-class) tickets from the railway station's counter. An artificial deficit of tickets was at times created locally so that the cashier could receive a small service fee and a share of tickets that were sold informally. With the introduction of the internet, tickets can be bought online by people who have a computer and know how to do it — in many cases children buy the tickets online for their parents. In general, the ticket situation has much improved, although the traditional ticket shortage remains for the summer vacation trains to the Black Sea resorts and the spas in the foothills of the Caucasus.

One of the trends since the 2000s has been the reduction of suburban train services in the outskirts of the large Siberian cities, probably partly in response to the growing number of individually owned automobiles (see below). This trend of scaling-down has also affected local (mid-range) passenger train services,[21] and it is related to the state railway company's policy of making operations commercially more efficient. The most recent trend, however, has been the growth of affordable air travel, which has significantly reduced railway passenger numbers between Siberian cities.

---

21   For instance, in the Krasnoiarsk Region over the last two years, out of three local trains from Khakassia on the route to Saianskaia and Taishet, two have been cancelled. Some routes have simply been shut down, for example, between Krasnoiarsk and Lesosibirsk (Dennis Zuev, interview with a railway officer in Krasnoiarsk, March 2018). At the same time, many big towns and settlements on the Baikal-Amur Mainline depend on this railway much more than those cities on the Trans-Siberian railway depend on that famous line.

Fig. 2.4. Many airplane journeys within the Russian Far East are subsidised through a federal programme, which makes trips from Vladivostok to smaller towns in the region more comfortable and faster than those by coach, for residents and non-residents. Photograph by Dennis Zuev, August 2011, CC-BY.

Air

Since 2015, there has been renewed interest in studying the social dynamics related to infrastructure changes and new mobilities in Siberia and the Russian North;[22] some authors discuss this under the label of "recolonisation" of the Russian North (e.g. Kinossian 2016). However, since the seminal report by Vitebsky (2000) on aviation in Sakha, very little research has been done on transformations in, and indeed reduction of, small-scale aviation (*malaia aviatsiia*) and its effects on the livelihoods and lifestyles of the inhabitants of the North.

At the same time, one of the typical features of Siberian (im)mobility in the last three decades has been that people who moved to the north for work found themselves unable to return to the so-called mainland, or to afford frequent visits to their hometowns in the south. This is related to the fact that airplane tickets to northern destinations became more expensive in comparison to Soviet times. According to the Rosgosstat

---

22 Among these, Bolotova, Karaseva & Vasilyeva (2017); Gavrilova, Vakhtin & Vasilyeva (2017); Kuklina, Povoroznyuk & Saxinger (2019); Laruelle (2017); Schweitzer, Povoroznyuk & Schiesser (2017).

statistics, the number of people in Russia transported by air in 2008 was almost half of that in 1990 (Federal'naia sluzhba gosudarstvennoi statistiki 2009). In fact, the number of air passengers has always been very small in proportion to that of railway passengers. However, the figures show that railway passenger traffic since 1995 has decreased even more in comparison to previous years, while air passenger turnover increased, although not steadily, from 1995 to 2016.[23] Travel by airplane to the far-flung northern towns and settlements is controlled by a few providers, and is thus expensive. Informal arrangements can help passengers to save money, in particular when travelling within the Far North. Air travel to villages and many district centres in the Far North remains dependent on helicopters; it has to be booked in advance or else it must be "organised" through informal social ties.

Fig. 2.5. Helicopter landing for a brief stop near a Komi reindeer-herders' camp on the territory of the Nenets Autonomous Okrug. Photograph by Joachim Otto Habeck, 23 October 1998, CC-BY.

---

23   The number of railway passengers steadily decreased from 1,833 million in 1995 to 1,419 million in 2000 and 1,296 million passengers in 2008; since 2014 it has been relatively stable, amounting to 1,040 million passengers in 2016. The number of air passengers was 32 million in 1995; it decreased to 23 million by 2000, and increased almost twofold by 2008 to 51 million, reaching 91 million in 2016 (Federal'naia sluzhba gosudarstvennoi statistiki 2009, 2017). Apparently, the number of railway passengers comprises travellers on all categories of trains, and the number of air passengers all travellers on airplanes (using domestic and international connections) as well as helicopters. Compare data for the period 1980–2008 on passenger kilometres, specified for different means of transport (Popov 2012: 154).

At the same time, in some locations the air transport market has diversified: when the regional airline monopolists went bankrupt (as Krasnoiarsk-based KrasAir did in 2008), several new airlines appeared, resulting in the availability of cheaper tickets. With the decrease in price, the trajectories of the passengers have changed. During the KrasAir monopoly, Krasnoiarsk residents occasionally went to Novosibirsk by train in order to catch a cheaper flight (operated by S7 Airlines) to Moscow. In some cases, it is not possible to travel by plane from one Siberian city to another without flying through Moscow. Since the mid-2010s, flights between Siberian cities (e.g. from Novosibirsk to Krasnoiarsk or Irkutsk) are regularly on offer. Additionally, in contrast to earlier decades, there is now a greater range of international connections from the airports of Novosibirsk, Irkutsk, and Vladivostok to popular holiday destinations such as Thailand, so that people can now go abroad without necessarily travelling via Moscow. The opening of the borders and visa-free regimes for Russian citizens with an increasing number of countries has facilitated this change in travel trajectories (see below).

One of the current features of air transport is the federal programme that subsidises air travel from and within the Far Eastern regions, as well as travel for residents of the Far East to the central parts of the country during the summer period. This programme has been in effect for almost a decade and corresponds with the strategic and political goals of bringing the Far East closer to Russian citizens (Chemodanova 2018). For instance, in 2011 the airplane ticket from Vladivostok to Plastun, a coastal settlement of approximately 5,000 inhabitants in the north-eastern part of Primor'e, was 1,000 roubles (approx. 35 US dollars at that time), an amount equal to the fare of the coach for the route overland, which takes many hours on dusty and potholed roads. Understandably, travellers preferred the plane, as it took only one hour to get to the destination. The existence of this federal funding scheme was reported by one of our informants in Vladivostok, who used the plane to get to the wild and secluded beaches of the Sea of Japan near Plastun and to the Sikhote-Alin nature reserve. The absence of transport from the airport, with the only cars belonging to locals picking up their relatives, the wooden building of the airport, without any waiting room, and the sandy airstrip all remind travellers that in peripheral areas like this one, little has changed since Soviet times.[24]

Fig. 2.6. New airport terminal at Yemel'ianovo (Krasnoiarsk) under construction for the Universiade 2019. Photograph by Dennis Zuev, 21 September 2017, CC-BY.

At the time of field research, there were discussions in Russian society whether air travel was more affordable in Soviet times, in relation to average salaries.[25] With the emergence of low-budget airlines operating flights between major Siberian cities, airfares have become competitive with train fares. Regardless of the costs, people in many cases preferred to travel by plane rather than train, as the comment below demonstrates. Nastia, a Buriat woman aged forty-nine at the time of interview (conducted by Joseph Long) reflects on how she travelled in 1991 to visit her relatives in Moscow. Having a relative in Moscow was thought to be an asset, as the quotation indicates:

JL: So how [did you travel] to Moscow [from Irkutsk]? By train?

24   However, the residents of Plastun can be proud of such connectivity and may ignore the appearance of their airport. At the same time (in 2010) the airport terminal in Krasnoiarsk (with a million inhabitants, after all) did not even have the name of the city on it, the waiting halls until 2016 were equipped only with worn plastic chairs, and after check-in people had to wait in a narrow buffer zone. Only in 2017 was a new airport terminal opened, as Krasnoiarsk was preparing to host the Universiade in 2019 (Fig. 2.6).

25   In late Soviet times, the airfare from Krasnoiarsk to Moscow and back was equal to one third of an engineer's salary. It is about the same now.

Nastia: No! Only by plane. I could not stand going by train. [...] Because it would be three days with strangers. Here you get on the plane, then after seven hours you arrive. [...] My relative picked me up [at the airport] on the first visit, but all the other times I went to their place on my own. I remember I used to put aside some money. Yes, when I was a student at the university, I worked and my mom gave me some money too, I just packed up and went, I arrived at my sister's. All my coursemates envied me going so far away to visit my sister. And most importantly, it was fun.

We can see from this that people made their choices about means of travelling not only on the basis of their financial standing, but also the social networks they possessed. This example also shows that mobility could, and did, lead to heightened social status.

Water

The big rivers of Siberia — Ob', Yenisei, and Lena — generally flow in a northerly direction, and with the opening of the Trans-Siberian railway, transportation of freight and passengers on those rivers became livelier in Soviet times. However, the navigation period on these rivers and their tributaries lasts for only a few months per year. In several of the locations of our study, the waterways play a crucial role in transportation — both during the summer navigation period and during the winter, when frozen rivers serve as winter roads (see the next section).

The river fleet includes cargo boats, large passenger boats and smaller hydrofoil boats. In late Soviet times, passenger boat services were regular, though not cheap, despite the fact that many communities depended heavily on them. Since then, centralised transportation on some of the rivers, such as the Lena, has crumbled. Regular passenger services are now less coordinated or have been completely abandoned. Consequently, many villages along the river are now more difficult to reach. The same is true for coastal traffic (as we know from Chavan'ga and other villages along the shore of the White Sea). As an alternative to passenger boat trips on the big rivers, it is also possible as in the old days to rely on informal arrangements, such as getting a ride with an oil tanker or a barge that carries goods northward or southward.

While public services are in decline, in Vladivostok one can observe an increase in private motorboats and yachts, many of which have been obtained second-hand from Japan. This boat ownership has made previously inaccessible islands open for manifold leisure activities, from *shashlyk* (grilled meat from the skewer) excursions and summer camps to rave discos and live-action role-plays.[26]

For the rural communities along the coasts and on the shores of the countless rivers and lakes, fishing is a very important source of income, and nearly every household owns a boat and an outboard engine. In the salmon villages of Kola Peninsula, the sturgeon villages of the Yenisei and Ob', and the *omul'* (whitefish) villages of Lake Baikal, fish has become hard currency and can be exchanged for fuel, off-road vehicles or a seat in the helicopter. Similarly, in the Far East, seafood — sea urchins, trepang and other molluscs — were exchanged in the 1990s in Japanese ports for cars and electronic appliances.

One of key re-emerging routes for waterborne transport is the Northern Sea Route (Gavrilova, Vakhtin & Vasilyeva 2017). The construction of ports and vessels from the 1930s onwards was promoted as a major achievement of Soviet modernisation in the Far North. From 1932 to 1938, the administrators of the Northern Sea Route "managed the human resources, including indigenous population and arriving forced labour working in cooperation with GULAG" (Schweitzer, Povoroznyuk & Schiesser 2017: 76). For communities along the coasts of the Laptev and Bering Sea, supplies by ship were of the utmost importance. Closed for international traffic until the 1990s, the Northern Sea Route has received renewed attention in the 1990s; it is likely to see more traffic as a consequence of climate change in the Arctic Ocean (Khon et al. 2010; Lindstad, Bright & Strømman 2016). However, the enthusiasm about the further development of the Northern Sea Route may be exaggerated to some extent, in view of many technical and jurisdictional challenges (Farre et al. 2014), and the smaller communities along the coast might see few if any benefits from the transportation of crude natural resources between the Far East and Europe.

---

26   Similarly, one can see more yachts on the large rivers and reservoirs in the vicinities of Novosibirsk, Barnaul, and Krasnoiarsk.

Roads and automobiles

In the eastern half of Russia's territory, the few existing tarmac roads do not form a network as of yet. The long-awaited final section of the road between Moscow and the Far East of Russia was ultimately completed in 2010 — many decades after the completion of the Trans-Siberian railway. Regional road building continues to be strongly oriented towards the needs of resource-extraction enterprises, as is the case with the diamond-extracting cities of Mirnyi and Udachnyi in the western part of the Republic of Sakha (Yakutia). However, when contemplating a map of Siberia, non-Russian observers often forget that there is a network of winter roads (*zimnik*) that complements the few tarmac roads. It is in the winter that many cut-off places in the Far North actually become accessible. Winter roads are established on the ice of big rivers or across frozen swamps or mountain ranges, with heavy machinery preparing the way for subsequent, lighter lorries and cars. As drivers have to travel in caravans and rely on themselves in emergency situations, winter road journeys are considered very adventurous; they are therefore accompanied by many stories and legends (Argounova-Low 2012), and drivers derive a sense of pride, both personal and professional, from this.

Fig. 2.7. Bridge-building for a new road in the Saian Mountains (Kuraginskii Raion). Photograph by Dennis Zuev, 6 May 2009, CC-BY.

One element that obviously very strongly influences people's everyday existence in many parts of Siberia is the continental climate. A number of places are more easily accessible in the winter than in the summer, but that is precisely when unpredictable weather conditions present serious hurdles to travel, including by car. When temperatures drop to fifty degrees centigrade below zero, or when the winds are intolerably chilly, life slows down and one becomes confined to one's own home. However, it is not in winter but spring and autumn when mobility is most challenging: the weather is unstable, rivers are swelling, and many of the provincial roads become impassable.

Further in the south, particularly in the cities and in rural West Siberia, road networks do exist, and they are now overwhelmingly used by private cars. The massive increase in individual car ownership is arguably one of the most fundamental changes in the history of transportation in Siberia. Remembering that a private car was a prized commodity in Soviet times (and remembering the difficulties that came along with obtaining and maintaining it — see Zuev's account at the beginning of this chapter), the rapid increase in private cars brought about tremendous modifications in the spheres of work, leisure, and also settlement patterns.

In the 2000s, many young people who possessed a car also became interested in acquiring a second home in the countryside. People gradually started to realise that, with a car, urban lifestyles could be complemented by a temporary life outside the city. Dying villages suddenly saw a revival, as people from the city started buying cheap houses for summer holidays or weekends. As mentioned above, many of the *dacha* settlements initially developed along the railways with suburban train services; but many more are now growing along roads and by-ways. Building materials can be more easily acquired and transported than in the past. City dwellers have started to buy land outside the city, close to the roads, in order to spend more time in the forest and fresh air, rather than in anonymous apartment blocks in the polluted inner parts of the city. This "suburbia" tendency is particularly evident in Krasnoiarsk, Irkutsk, Ulan-Ude, and Vladivostok. Also, in smaller cities and towns such as Yakutsk or Novyi Urengoi, a sizeable number of *dacha* plots are now used for year-round residence (Stammler & Sidorova 2015: 584–86) and attain a more pronounced suburban character, facilitated by individual car ownership.

Fig. 2.8. Urban visitors using the bonnet of their car for a picnic on the occasion of the Day of the Reindeer Herder in Russkinskaia, Khanty-Mansi Autonomous Okrug — Yugra. Photograph by Stephan Dudeck, 30 March 2009. Courtesy of the photographer, CC-BY.

The second-hand car market in particular has provided opportunities for private entrepreneurs, especially in the 1990s. Siberia has seen second-hand car imports from two directions — western Europe and Japan. Vladivostok served as a major entry port for Japanese cars.[27] Adventurous car-dealers (*peregonshchiki*) drove thousands of kilometres to deliver a car to their customer elsewhere in Siberia. As one driver from Krasnoiarsk reported, the journey to Vladivostok to buy a car for later resale was an exciting trip to the Sea of Japan, conveniently combined with business. So far this part of mobility culture in Russia has received scant attention among researchers.

Notwithstanding the government's decision to increase the customs duty in January 2009, cars from Japan were still imported in subsequent years, in disassembled mode, with the frame cut into parts, later to be re-welded and furnished with a coat of paint. Needless to say, this was illegal — but it was hard for the police to keep track of such practices. As the second-hand car business used to be an important source of income

---

27 Vladivostok's proximity was instrumental in the development of outward tourism to Japan, China and Korea. The presence of several diplomatic missions (not including any country from the European Union) indicates that the city partakes of significant flows of goods and people from and to East Asian countries.

for a section of the male population in Vladivostok, there was great disappointment about the tax increase, which resulted in mass protests and activism. Car drivers participated in civil protest, especially in the wake of the government's decision to limit the import of cars from abroad (including Japan), and they organised themselves in drivers' associations, which had both practical and political goals (Lonkila 2011: 292, fn. 3).

In recent years, there seems to be a tendency towards buying new rather than second-hand cars. The increasing number of car sales resulted in more showrooms. Often the owners of a specific make of car would participate in joint activities, for example Subaru-club picnics in the outskirts of a big city or Mercedes-club cocktail events where one can have a free test drive. The owners of the cars also become engaged in "off-road" entertainment, facilitated by the availability of quads, cross-country motorcycles and snow-scooters, all of which now ply long-forgotten logging roads and off-road tracks around big cities.

With the increasing number of cars, there also come new roads, such as the new highway from the Far East westward, mentioned above. Urban sprawl and road construction unavoidably entail negative environmental impacts. These are perceived particularly strongly in cases of large-scale, prestigious construction projects.[28] Notwithstanding the trend towards sub-urbanisation and large-scale infrastructural investments, most rural districts rely on very modest infrastructure, and local residents often complain about the deplorable state of roads and services.

In the small villages of Tyva, Buryatia, Sakha (Yakutia), and others, the motorcycle is still among the most practical vehicles, occasionally with a side-car which can be used for transporting bulky loads, tent poles, etc. In many rural areas of southern and central Siberia, horses continue to be essential for transportation; in Altai, Tyva, and Buryatia

---

28 A good example is the bridge from Vladivostok to the nearby island Ostrov Russkii, completed shortly before the 2012 ASEAN summit. The bridge is part of the programme for making Vladivostok a Russian Pacific showcase city. Its cost amounted to 33 billion roubles, which is a steep sum considering that the bridge was primarily to serve a population of 5,000 inhabitants of the island plus the students and staff of the Far-Eastern Federal University. In addition to concerns about cost, there were fears that the island, previously a rather untouched spot, would turn into a place of mass picnics, and consequently suffer pollution by litter and waste.

they are used by shepherds and hunters. The availability of horses has spawned horse-trekking tourism in the Sayan and Altai mountains. In many parts of the tundra and forest tundra belt, reindeer or sledge dogs were widely used for transportation, though the role of these animals in overland transportation of goods, people, and postal deliveries has been declining since the 1960s, with few people still having the skills required.

Fig. 2.9. *Karakatitsa* (a light but robust vehicle for transport in roadless areas). Villagers of Chavan'ga (Kola Peninsula) assist in kick-starting the vehicle. Photograph by Masha Shaw, 25 July 2011, with the permission of the individuals depicted, CC-BY.

In many locations in the Far North one can see light off-road vehicles called *karakat* or *karakatitsa*, suitable for swampy roadless terrains. Home constructors assemble such vehicles from spare parts (cf. Usenyuk, Hyysalo & Whalen 2016); alternatively, they modify cars like *Lada Niva* or *UAZ*, furnishing them with oversized tyres. As the data from Chavan'ga demonstrate, in the 1990s the barter schemes included exchange of food for mechanical parts (in one reported case a barrel of salmon for a former military tracked vehicle). Thus, a surplus of food could be converted into mobility extensions. Such practices are known also from other regions, e.g. among reindeer herders who exchange reindeer meat for fuel.

Additional modes of public transport

Private means of transportation are not always available, hence the importance of public transport. The role of the railway has already been discussed; this section deals mainly with bus services, both within the cities and outside. Long-distance services between cities, towns, and larger villages are usually cheaper and sometimes faster than the railway on the equivalent connection. They are operated by public and private companies. The public companies run buses on the basis of timetables, the private ones use smaller vehicles — equipped with twelve to sixteen seats — that operate on the basis of actual demand. When the driver decides that a sensible number of passengers has accumulated, he starts going.[29] This system (*marshrutnoe taksi, marshrutka*) is in practice all over the former Soviet Union, and has been for more than 25 years.

Marshrutka lines have come to compete with bus lines not only between, but also within cities and towns. In the Soviet era, going by bus was more cumbersome: one often had to wait a long time and perhaps in vain because the bus would be full, with few routes servicing the city districts. Tramways, trolleybuses, and Hungary-imported Ikarus buses can be seen in the streets of the largest Siberian cities, but *marshrutka* vehicles are now much greater in number. With the arrival of private companies, the number of routes increased, and going from one point to another is now much easier and faster — generally, though not always (depending on traffic jams and accidents). A *marshrutka* ride costs fifty to 150 roubles,[30] roughly double the price of a single ticket for the tram or trolleybus. In cities like Irkutsk and Vladivostok, public transport, including *marshrutka*, ends at approximately 9:30pm, in Novosibirsk and Krasnoiarsk at about 11pm; after that, one has to take a taxi or a shared taxi. Even though the latter two cities count more than a million inhabitants each, there is no night service on public lines. This is also

---

29 Drivers and conductors of municipal buses and trolleybuses are either male or female, whereas drivers of commercial buses and *marshrutka* vehicles are always male. If there is a conductor on board, then this person is most likely a woman. This is an example of the division of labour between sexes in some vocational domains. For other examples in the Far North of Russia, see Povoroznyuk, Habeck & Vaté (2010).

30 The exchange rate between euro and rouble was one to forty in the summer of 2011. As of summer 2019, seventy roubles were roughly equivalent to one euro.

true for the two underground lines of Novosibirsk.[31] Whether one wants to return home from the club in the late evening or to catch an early-morning flight: one has to rely on friends for a ride or take a taxi.

Going abroad and crossing the borders

International mobility of Siberian residents is still a relatively new phenomenon. While for residents of remote locations like Chukotka or Sakha (Yakutia) it is still rather unusual, it is particularly relevant for the border areas in southern Siberia and the Far East and the big urban centres. The infrastructure for international mobility in Siberia is related to the availability of cultural centres, foreign consulates, and flights. In this respect, the major cities on the Trans-Siberian railway differ from each other.

Visa centres are a relatively new development: they serve as an intermediary between the individual applicant and the consulate. In the past, visa applications were received directly at the consulates. However, since 2008 many consulates terminated this service and established visa centres — which means an extra cost for the applicant (visa fee plus service fee). However, visa centres make it possible for people to avoid a trip to Moscow. One of the frequent student practices of "Work and Travel" requires that applicants come for an interview to Yekaterinburg or Moscow. In some cases, applicants had to make a trip from Krasnoiarsk or Irkutsk to Moscow — just to learn that they were refused their visa (see Zuev's interviews with these students in Chapter 5 in this volume).

The situation of cultural centres, such as the Goethe Institute or the British Council has changed over the years. British Council centres were opened in several Siberian cities. The council provided language materials and computer facilities for free use. The opening of such centres was seen as a positive change by young people in particular. Language learning became more available, which in turn made it easier for young people to go abroad independently. Having said that, the closure of regional offices of the British Council in 2007 and the complete cessation of its operation in March 2018 exemplify the consequences

---

31 Novosibirsk has had a metro since 1986; the construction of a metro in Krasnoiarsk started in 1995 but has been abandoned in 2012 and not yet resumed.

of international political tensions (cf. Kinnock 2018). As a side effect, such state policies are conducive to curbing international ("western") cultural influence.

Despite the presence of the consulates and visa centres, many visas still have to be processed in Moscow and most of the international traffic is routed via Moscow. To fly to Japan from Krasnoiarsk is still more convenient through the Russian capital, but routes via China and Korea are not impossible. Perhaps, travelling habits have been so strongly associated with Moscow that even now it is hard to imagine other routes. This is, however, not the case of the Russian Far East, which is more oriented eastward, so that tourism and especially student mobility are developing towards Asian destinations.

We estimate that thousands of young people go to work in Thailand and China. Moreover, Thailand has emerged as a highly popular tourist destination since approximately 2005 (King 2018: 8–9) and we know of a sizeable number of young citizens from Novosibirsk and other cities who prefer to work and relax in the tropical resorts of Thailand than endure the Siberian winter at home. Others spend extended periods in Goa or Bali, participating in music festivals and/or searching for spiritual enrichment (Buchner, forthcoming). In other words, for urban youth from Siberia, it is no longer unusual to spend weeks or months abroad. This new development seems to eclipse the attractiveness of Moscow or St Petersburg (Leningrad), which used to be the most coveted destinations of youth in the Soviet era. It also means that individual work biographies, practices of holiday-making, life projects, and aesthetic predilections are now more frequently connected with places outside Russia, and urban Siberians' connoisseurship of tastes, cultural expressions, and modes of living has come to embrace a more global ambit.

At the same time, strong tendencies of state-induced isolation can be discerned in Russia's politics over the last decade. Partly as a result of geopolitical conflicts (for example, sanctions in certain spheres of consumption), partly promoted by a self-centred turn towards patriotism (discussed in Chapter 11), a strong emphasis on all things Russian — for example, in the fields of cultural legacy, consumer goods, holiday destinations, and demeanour — goes hand in hand with growing apprehension of cultural imports, fashions, and styles from "the west". While the latter continues to be attractive in many regards, its importance as a source of inspiration or fascination is increasingly put into question.

In addition, one can observe that proximity to the border does not necessarily mean an openness to travel and trade. While during the Soviet time Russian cars imported to Finland were re-imported to Russia (Karelia and the Russian north), and the border trade with China and Mongolia has been booming since the 1980s, sensitive areas such as Chukotka remain closed to international border crossing. There is no regular connection across the Bering Strait and the practice of boat crossings introduced in the 1990s was prohibited after a few accidents, enhancing the unwillingness of the border guards to let people pass. By contrast, in the geopolitically sensitive South Sakhalin and Kuril Islands area, Japanese boats are allowed to make trips to the islands and there is a regular sea connection between Sakhalin and Japan. Vladivostok remains the centre of international sea connections to Korea and Japan, at the same time as ships from Vladivostok to the Kuril Islands and Sakhalin no longer operate.

With the growing presence of privately owned cars, short-distance and long-distance trips abroad have become more frequent. Until 2015, China did not allow the entrance of Russian cars; at present there are more than a dozen border-crossing points for passengers travelling by car.[32] The border areas that cater for Russian tourists provide a wide range of low-cost services. It has become common practice for residents of Vladivostok to go to China for a few days in order to enjoy a foot massage, eat Chinese food, change their whole set of tyres, and install a new set of teeth implants, as well as stock up on some new clothing and household appliances. In the beginning of the 2000s, the practice of *pomogai* (helper) was based on individual tours to China: each participant could enjoy a free bus ride with a two nights' stay in a hotel in return for twenty kilograms of duty-free goods transportation.

Finally, international sports events and conferences have made tourist numbers larger and international encounters more frequent — not only

---

32 *Pogranichnye punkty propuska* [Border-crossing points]. ISSA Tamozhenno-logisticheskii servis. http://issa.ru/forms/kpp/?curPos=70 — this page and subsequent pages 9–11 list all border-crossing points between Russia and China (accessed 28 July 2019).

in the European part of Russia. In the Russian Far East, for example, the University Forum of ASEAN (Association of Southeast Asian Nations) in September 2016 and the International Sports Games "Children of Asia", repeatedly held in Yakutsk, have contributed to cross-border contacts.

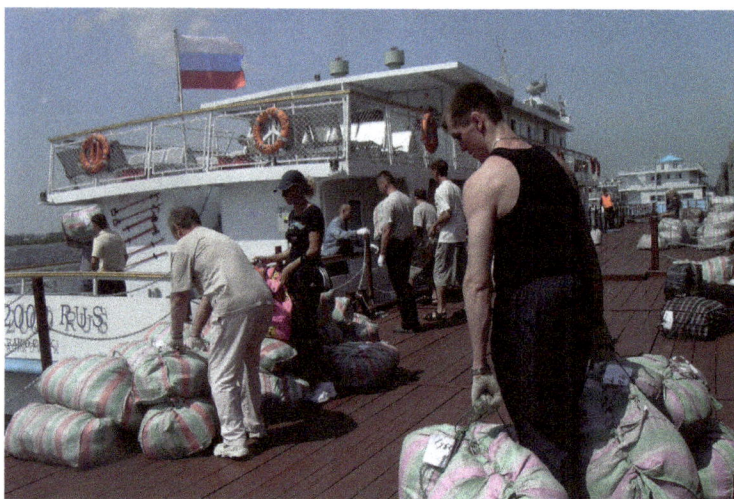

Fig. 2.10. Russian shuffle-traders (*chelnoki*) with typical striped bags (*risovki*) boarding the ferry from Heihe (China) to Blagoveshchensk (Russia) across the Amur. Photograph by Dennis Zuev, July 2007, CC-BY.

Telecommunication, media, social networks, and photography

One of the characteristics of Siberia is a spatially disproportionate availability of different technologies that mirrors the wide disparity in transportation options across the region. These disparities not only affect the daily running of people's lives, but also strongly influence the ways in which communities and individuals frame their past, their current existence, and their aspirations. The generation and circulation of images and imaginaries, of codes of conduct and commonalities of taste, are necessarily conditioned by the ways in which people can participate in telecommunication networks, or at least receive images and messages. This will be discussed in more detail in several subsequent chapters of the volume. Centrality and peripherality play out in this context as they do in the case of physical mobility — and yet in a very different way, as shall be demonstrated in this section.

Telecommunication (telegraph, telephones, mobiles)

Even before the railway, the telegraph came to Siberia, connecting European Russia and European countries with East Asia since 1871 (Weiss 2007: 158–61). For much of the world, the telegraph was overtaken by the newer technology of the telephone by the mid-twentieth century; in the Soviet Union, however, the period from the 1920s all the way through to the 1980s was the age of telegrams. Highly official orders and instructions, letters of congratulation, as well as requests for being picked up at the railway station were all transmitted by this technology. The railway became important as the backbone of transportation of goods and passengers, while the telegraph became the backbone of telecommunication across the whole country. In the mid-1990s, sending and receiving telegrams was still common practice. Each city had a telegraph office, usually in combination with the *mezhgorod* ("inter-city") telephone office, and queues were not unusual. The emergence of the telephone did not replace telegraphy, at least not in the official sphere, because printed messages had (and still have) a more binding force, as they can be archived and retrieved whenever necessary. By the same token, a telephone call is more expedient whenever the necessity for personal negotiations and arrangements arises.[33]

It was only when telefax and email (*elektronnaia pochta*) appeared in the larger and smaller cities that telegraphy was gradually abandoned. Telefax quickly spread over Siberian cities and villages in the first half of the 1990s, while email became widespread only after the year 2000.

Telecommunication was a sign of prestige and occupational status in the first post-Soviet years. The first mobile device acquired by businessmen (*biznesmeny*) in the big cities of Siberia was a pager (beeper), a one-way device for receiving messages. The pager served as a status symbol in the second half of the 1990s, then to be gradually substituted by the mobile phone, the possession of which was conspicuously demonstrated and shown off even during concerts or theatre performances. Since the 1990s, in Russia the number of mobile phone subscribers has grown immensely; it increased tenfold between 2003 and 2009 (Popov 2012: 163). Network coverage of different providers varies greatly, so that local residents sometimes combine a nation-wide

---

33　Rohozinski (1999: 7) stated that the larger number of phones on a desk, the more influential the boss.

provider (such as MTS, Megafon, or Beeline) with a regional one (for instance, YeniseiTelekom for Krasnoiarsk Region or BaikalVestKom for Irkutsk region). Not all villages are covered by GSM, not to mention the vast stretches of land in between permanent settlements. Florian Stammler (2013) has noted that, for the Nenets reindeer nomads in the Yamal Peninsula — in particular for the younger generation — the question of whether a certain area does or does not have mobile phone coverage influences where they decide to pitch their camp. Sometimes it helps to travel to a nearby hill to catch a network signal.

Smartphones combine many functions: audio player, radio, camera, TV, gaming device, navigation system, and communication device. In Russia as elsewhere, many people spend considerable time on their smartphone. This leads to the question of whether habits of communication have changed as such (see Popov 2012 on the emergence of "networked individualism" in Russia). One may assume that people visit each other less now that they can just phone each other. However, from our observations, mobile phone calls, text messages, emails, etc. do not reduce the number of personal encounters, they rather make it easier to arrange meetings at short notice.

Radio and television

From the late 1950s onwards, radio, and about two decades later, television became rapidly and widely available to households in the Soviet Union (Durham 1965: 15–16). Inexpensive radio receivers were placed in almost every apartment and every office; these were complemented by more sophisticated receivers that would also catch shortwave and other bands.[34] The content of the "First Programme" (*Pervaia programma Vsesoiuznogo radio*) as well as that of all other programmes was planned and produced centrally.[35] Alternative media

---

34 Some reindeer-herding brigades also possessed Latvian *Spidola* radios which provided news and entertainment.

35 According to Lapin (1975), five radio programmes were broadcast in 1975: the first programme with official news and a variety of themed broadcasts, including intermittent periods of music; the second (named *Maiak*) with a higher proportion of music, including music from abroad; the third with a pronouncedly high-culture profile and broadcasts for students; the fourth with Soviet and international music, broadcast on FM only; and the fifth with news and information "addressed to

content nonetheless found its way into Soviet society through inventive and partially subversive methods, such as *muzyka na rëbrakh*, i.e. LP-like audio records on disks made from discarded x-ray pictures (Yurchak 2006: 181–84). After 1990, more radio channels appeared, most of which were broadcast on FM bands.

In the 1980s, the typical Soviet household owned a television set by which to receive two channels via the communal antenna on the top of the residential building. Radio and television content came to beset knowledge, emotions, and collectively held imaginaries throughout the country. The magic of television fundamentally altered Soviet citizens' free-time habits: watching television became an all-important activity, to the detriment of social life in the street and artistic activities in public places (cf. Dubin & Zorkaia 2011: 28).

In the late 1980s, with the dispersion of video clubs and video recorders, *kooperativnyi* cable TV came into existence in some Siberian cities, providing an alternative to official (state-directed) television. There was a short-lived boom of public video rooms (*videosalon*) that showed mainly western commercial productions to an audience that was highly eager to watch films that had been shunned by Soviet TV stations. The practice of viewing films in small groups in video rooms was followed by more individual ways of watching pirated copies of films on VCR tapes, CDs, and DVDs. Some foreign channels, such as MTV, were slowly adapted for the Russian-language audience; the same happened with western talk-shows and entertainment shows. Individual aerials and satellite dishes gradually mushroomed in the cities and small towns. Currently, in each of the large cities there are several channels that provide regional news, entertainment shows, and films free of charge. In his study on media use in modern Russia, Pietiläinen (2008) observed that television remains the most important source of any sort of information for Russia's citizens. Similarly, Hutchings and Tolz argue that "television's role [in Russia] has been reinforced, rather than diminished, by the rise of new media technologies" (2015: i).

Soviet citizens outside the country (seamen, fishermen, polar staff and other)" (1975: 354–55). The first programme was broadcast in four identical but time-shifted versions, to cater for radio listeners in the different time zones of the Soviet Union.

Audio and video recorders

The development of devices for music storage for private use went from vinyl disks to audio tapes (music cassettes) and later to CDs and DVDs. In the 1980s it was possible to buy audio tapes in special kiosks or shops or even leave a blank tape at the shop for the desired recording to be made. In the vicinity of Krasnoiarsk, industries in the closed cities were engaged in "conversion" from military to civic production, and the Krasnoiarsk Electro Chemical Plant began to produce its own tapes using *BASF* technology, while the Soviet *MK-60* tapes became obsolete. Dennis Zuev recalls his personal experiences of using tape and video recorders in the 1990s:

> When I turned 14, I dreamt of a stereo. In 1992, I bought a *Vega* tape-recorder. These were produced in Berdsk and while being technically quite simple, nobody questioned their quality or functionality. In the 1990s, locally produced stereos were available and affordable to a wide public. Double-cassette recorders were still hard to come by and dubbing tapes was a widespread practice. Two single-cassette recorders would be linked by cable for dubbing and it took several hours to dub one tape. I made copies for myself, for my friends, and even sold some of the copies. This practice helped to socialise with friends and schoolmates with whom we exchanged music recordings; we dubbed them for each other and discussed which new ones to buy and who would buy them so we could listen to more. But things in the 1990s were changing very fast: in winter 1994 our family could not even think about buying a small good-quality Hi-Fi stereo in Krasnoiarsk, so I brought one home from my school exchange trip to the United States — only to discover that by summer 1995 the shops had a full stock of different foreign brands of audio-visual equipment stereos with television sets, video recorders, CD players, and CDs. These were slowly displacing the business of tape selling kiosks and tape-dubbing studios. The street markets were at the same time still supplied mostly by the cheap China-made products of counterfeit brands such as *Panasoanix, Sonic, Sonyo*, etc.

The practice of renting a videotape and later DVDs was still existent in most of the big cities until 2012. However, with the development of the internet these forms of video rental and music recording have petered out to online video streaming (including YouTube), torrent downloads, and MP3 file downloads. These, however, require high-speed internet, which is a privilege of urban centres and is not widely available in small district towns and villages. The prices for technical devices and other consumer goods used to be much higher in Siberia than in Moscow until approximately 2010, and it was common for Siberians to travel to Moscow to find a wider variety of goods at better prices. The increasing availability of new consumer goods in Siberian cities has often gone hand in hand with higher levels of small consumer loans and living "beyond one's means". Recent statistics demonstrate that inhabitants of Siberia now take fewer consumer loans but of larger amounts (Galaguz 2018). With the increasing practice of online shopping via Ebay, Amazon and the like, it has become possible to buy diverse items at comparatively low cost online, including books, music, sports equipment, and gadgets.

Computers and internet

Inexpensive computers such as the ZX Spectrum appeared in the households of urban residents by the 1980s. They were primarily used for computer games. The computer classes in city schools became part of the normal curriculum in the 1990s. A peculiarity of internet development in Siberia — and Russia in general — was Fidonet, a data transfer protocol that preceded the internet, based on modem-to-modem exchange of data badges (usually messages) during night hours, when phone calls could be made at a reduced charge. This was a non-commercial, grass-roots initiative of individual users. The first node of Fidonet in Russia was established in Novosibirsk in early 1991. There was a Fidonet community of up to 100,000 users in 1998 (Rohozinski 1999: 11). A few years later, however, the internet prevailed. Free access first appeared in Siberian universities in 1996 when the Soros Foundation jointly with the government of the Russian Federation launched a programme entitled "University Centres of Russia". Each student had two to four hours of free internet use (the use of somebody else's account was strictly prohibited). Computer salons and internet cafés in the cities were quite rare until the 2000s. From the first internet café in 1998 in Krasnoiarsk, internet provision developed to dozens of cafés with free wi-fi hotspots (see Table 2.2). State financed institutions caught up with this more slowly, for instance, in the Siberian Federal University wireless internet appeared in 2008.

In numerous district centres and occasionally in villages, libraries offer free — if slow — access to the internet. Using email and the internet on a regular basis was, for many inhabitants of Russia, the point when they started to learn some words of English, and to use the Latin (English) keyboard of the computer.

Table 2.2. Number of wi-fi hotspots registered at wifi4free.ru in selected cities of Russia (accessed 10 May 2013). The data given here provide a snapshot of the spread of wi-fi in the public sphere; since 2013, the number of registered hotspots has grown further (the website continues to be active). Population data compiled from the Russian version of Wikipedia, based on data of the Federal State Statistics Service (data of the Census on 1 October 2010).

City	Total number of wi-fi hotspots as of May 2013	Free of charge	Not free of charge	Population as of 1 October 2010
Moscow	1,397	1,163	234	11,503,501
St Petersburg	943	747	196	4,879,566
Kazan'	220	135	85	1,143,535
Krasnoiarsk	211	201	10	973,826
Yekaterinburg	190	180	10	1,349,772
Vladivostok	159	144	15	592,034
Novosibirsk	122	109	13	1,473,754
Omsk	112	96	16	1,154,116
Tomsk	55	53	2	524,669
Barnaul	49	36	13	612,401
Khabarovsk	41	41	0	577,441
Angarsk	27	25	2	233,567
Ulan-Ude	22	7	15	404,426
Surgut	20	19	1	306,675
Yakutsk	7	5	2	269,691
Magadan	1	1	0	95,982

The spread of internet usage in Russia has been recorded by the Yandex Institute in its annual reports (Analiticheskaia gruppa 2012).[36] They indicate that the Far Eastern Federal Okrug was the fastest growing region. The level of penetration of the internet (defined as the percentage of monthly internet users among the overall regional population) is particularly high in the Far East, whereas the Siberian Federal Okrug slightly lags behind the average level (ibid.). However, each location or region has its own specific properties and — generally

---

36   Yandex is known to be the largest Russian language search engine.

speaking — the internet is thus far more widely and easily accessible in urban areas, despite the fact that growth rates are currently higher in the villages than in the cities (cf. Gelvanovska, Rossotto & Gunzburger 2016; Rykov, Nagornyy & Koltsova 2017). According to the last Yandex report published in 2014, the share of the rural population connected to the internet increased significantly along with an increase of the share of senior users in urban areas. Visible decrease of the cost of mobile internet also clearly facilitated access to the internet in urban and economically developed areas (Analiticheskaia gruppa 2014).

There can be no doubt that the internet has contributed to the pluralisation of lifestyles: it is now the number-one platform of visual and verbal exchange for nearly all subcultures, minorities, and hobby groups — from death metal lovers to *estrada* (Russian language pop music) fans, from extremely conservative nationalist youth groups to queer activists, and from self-declared gardening experts to devoted live-action role players.

With regard to one of these groups — the live-action role players — we give an example from an interview conducted by Tatiana Barchunova with the key organiser of annual games in Novosibirsk, Vadim Zevlever (nickname: Makar, see Chapter 10 in this volume):

> TB: How do you think the preparation for the games has changed [with the development of the internet]?
>
> VZ: Immensely. Now the internet substitutes just everything. You don't need anything else. [...] Not just the internet but social media: first of all VKontakte. Because I sometimes even think that next year we won't even make a special website for Makarena [the annual event], I'll just upload everything in VKontakte. It is enough. This year we have a group in VKontakte and a website, but [...] I have all reason to believe that there are only few people who look at it. So I am thinking about closing down [the website] [...]
>
> TB: So as to not waste time on it?
>
> VZ: And money!

The internet has fundamentally changed the ways in which individuals can access information, plan their activities, make appointments with each other, etc. We have already mentioned its role in the purchase of tickets, music, media, and consumer goods. Moreover, the internet has also come to function as a specific element of tourist infrastructure, as is demonstrated by the case of the online couchsurfing hospitality communities along the Trans-Siberian railway (Zuev 2013a, 2013b). Travel arrangements no longer depend on official providers of local knowledge, such as municipal information desks (*gorspravka*) or tourist information offices. Foreign travellers can directly establish contact with locals and stay in their homes, enjoying the infrastructure that comes with hospitality.

As with the mobile phone, for urban residents the use of internet resources and social networking sites is now becoming habitual or, in fact, obligatory. Even those who express a sceptical attitude towards technological innovations and unnecessary "gadgets" are usually compelled to use online forums and resources. Not only does the internet serve as a backbone of communication and information exchange, it also redefines conventions of communication. Online forums and resources cater to an enormous variety of visual and textual impulses, yet they also shape the perceptions and channel the desires of individual users. They provide a format in which individuals see others and consequently come to see themselves and present themselves. In the following subsection, we briefly portray how the technical development of visual media have affected aesthetic conventions (a strand that will be explored more deeply in Chapter 6).

Photography

Photography's technical limitations and gradual improvements have led to new understandings of what pictures can (and should) tell and how they can (and should) be displayed. Photography in the Soviet Union of the post-war period was a serious business, a quite complex procedure, and a solemn moment for those in front of the camera. Professional photographers took pictures of assemblies, collectives, school classes, weddings, anniversaries, and similar events. People appeared in festive dress and tried to take on a proper posture. The number of snapshots was comparatively small. Up to the 1970s, holiday trips and excursions were equally documented by professional rather than amateur photographers. Many families kept a photo album as a collective biographical record and also as an important means to present themselves to visitors. The photographs themselves could serve as mnemonic devices to remember relatives, to talk about their achievements and adventures, and to recollect genealogies. Typically, these albums contained black-and-white pictures on grey cardboard, with colour photographs appearing in the 1970s and 1980s.[37]

Black-and-white photography gradually expanded from a merely professional business to an activity of some passionate amateurs, whereas colour photography remained largely the sphere of professionals. Since around the 1970s, residents of some cities could buy the tools and chemicals needed for the processing of black-and-white photographs, though our research reveals that availability of chemicals was very unequal across different geographical areas.[38] Roughly at the same time, Houses of Culture, youth centres, and schools started offering hobby groups (*foto-kruzhok*), which probably increased the popularity of amateur photography. By the early 1990s, numerous households had a camera, usually a *Smena, Liubitel'*, or *FED* — comparatively cheap and straightforward makes — and less frequently a *Zenit* or *Kiev* — more sophisticated and expensive types which had a changeable lens. From our colleagues' and our own interviews, we conclude that taking photographs and processing films was mainly a hobby of men rather than women, which reflects the close connotation of photography with technology, conventionally thought to be a male domain of activity.

With the arrival of Polaroid photography and then point-and-shoot cameras, photography expanded massively. The home-based processing of films became almost obsolete with the arrival of Kodak studios. The first Kodak shop in Krasnoiarsk appeared in 1995 and by the 2000s it was equipped with monitors where one could see the images and select the pictures individually. Masses of people acquired Kodak cameras, while more advanced users kept using their *SLR Zenit* or *Kiev* cameras. The mass photo studios like Kodak later gave way to digital photographs. These are no longer printed out at the previous scale, but instead they are shared and distributed by email, USB sticks, and social networking

---

37 Colour photography appeared very early in Russia, namely in the 1910s (Allshouse 1980), but then did not result in a widely available technology, which means that it became available for the masses only from the 1970s onwards.

38 Interviewees in Novosibirsk (with Habeck) stated that these items were cheap and always available, whereas in Krasnoiarsk interviewees (with Zuev) said that films and chemicals were hard to buy. In some remote villages — as we know from Panáková's interviews in Novoe Chaplino — there were one or several amateur photographers who took pictures on request, acting as substitutes for professional photo studios.

sites like VKontakte, Odnoklassniki, Instagram, Facebook or Moi Mir. To quote M., a woman aged 35 at the time of the interview (with Eleanor Peers), from Yakutsk:

> M: At first, I didn't like any digital pictures, because I preferred printed, because you can touch them and just have a look at them […]. But now I like digital. I am rather conservative […] maybe I need some time to get used [to new things], yes.

> EP: I mean, so do you sometimes print out your digital pictures?

> M: No. No, never.

> EP: And I mean, are you on VKontakte and Facebook?

> M: VKontakte and Facebook, yes, it was rather a new thing for me too, I just registered only in autumn, last autumn, in October or September [2010], I don't remember. Because everybody asked me: "Are you on VKontakte?" And I knew nothing about that and then I thought: "Am I old-fashioned, or what?" I should be on VKontakte and I registered there, yes. And I didn't even know how to write VKontakte, I thought that it was just "kontakt" and I typed it, I was surprised, then I had to use the Yandex search [engine] and I found VKontakte.[39]

The cardboard photo albums are kept as part of people's personal or familial belongings, but few people make the effort to update them; instead, they are substituted by folders of digital pictures on CDs and hard-drives. Contrary to the general trend towards digitalisation, the number of small one-photographer photo studios (*tochka*) providing *foto na dokumenty* has increased in bigger cities to satisfy the growing needs for passport photographs in line with biometric standards.[40]

Cameras built into mobile phones provide a wide sector of the population with an easy, at-hand medium of visual recording. Mobile phones and later smartphones have replaced photo cameras almost entirely. In fact, up to very recently, some residents of northern villages used their mobile phones primarily for taking pictures because the

---

39   The interview was conducted through English.
40   A search for "foto na dokumenty" (in Cyrillic) gives 124 addresses in Krasnoiarsk and 154 in Novosibirsk. mxkr.ru/ru/foto_na_dokumenty/ (accessed 28 July 2019). In future years, this service is likely to be partially replaced by automatic photo booths.

absence of any GSM signal did not permit them to make phone calls (cf. Chapter 6).

As a rule, information and communication technologies burgeoned in Siberia considerably later than in the European part of Russia. The Russian Far East differs in this respect, not the least because of its proximity to Japan. The booming border trade with China has also

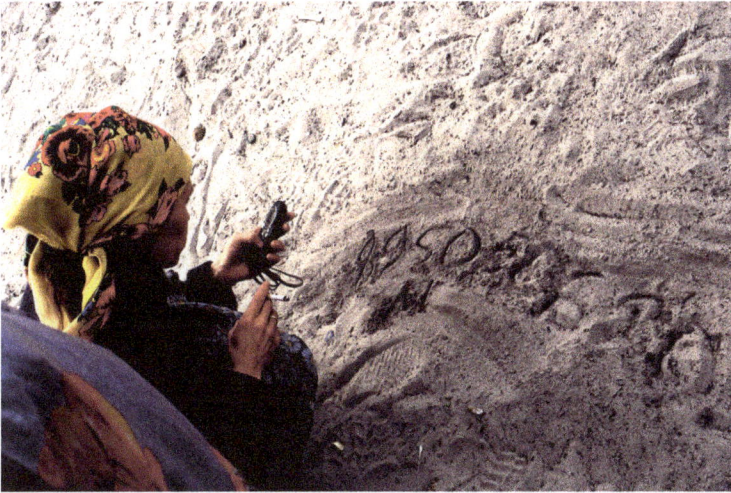

Fig. 2.11. Scribbling a phone number into the sand at the embankment of River Vakh, Khanty-Mansi Autonomous Okrug — Yugra. Photograph by Stephan Dudeck, August 2006. Courtesy of the photographer, CC-BY.

come to provide cheap alternatives for telecommunication gadgets, computers, and visual technologies. The use of mobile technology is no longer considered something extraordinary and prestigious or a conspicuous nuisance (as in the 1990s), although the material value of the object itself can still be used for status display. The ubiquity and ease of taking images has in some ways come to debase the professional and also artistic character of earlier photographic production. This popularisation of photography has allowed it to become a prominent feature of social networking sites, which also serve as archives for sharing images, social connection, and storage. Simultaneously, art photography or video production have turned into popular hobbies and taking pictures on the streets is no longer seen as a sign of journalism, but a mundane action.

Conclusion

Technology and infrastructure connect in multifarious ways with mobility and practices of distinction and lifestyles. As Vladimir Popov argues, "social preferences of a particular means of transportation are connected with various ways in the organization of daily life, with overall lifestyle" (2012: 154), and the same may be said of information technology. In Siberia, the most obvious aspect of this interconnection is the highly disparate availability of goods and services: in small places, this limits the number of domains in which distinction can be played out. Similar to other countries, it is mobility itself that serves as a marker of distinction; but in a much more elementary sense than in other countries, mobility can be crucially missing. Mobility is usually considered to enable people to pursue their goals: it is the precondition for creating and utilising social networks, for making plans come true. Where spatial mobility is limited, inventiveness and flexibility may serve as substitutes. Immobility can attain valorisations of stability, rootedness in a region, and stewardship of a place (for an example, see Chapter 3).

Muscovites may make condescending comments about the provinciality of Siberian cities; the residents of the latter may make malicious jokes about the district centres; and everybody may feel united in their negative attitude towards life in *glubinka* (very remote areas). However, there is a threshold where remoteness turns into an asset again. *Glubinka* can be likened with sincerity (in the sense of directness and intimacy), authenticity of human interaction, a certain purity of existence, and a special magic power, as is manifest in the sustained admiration and, sometimes, romanticism that many urban residents feel for traditional livelihoods, shamanism, and life in harmony with the natural environment. Sincerity and trust, we believe, are very persistent concerns in Russian society (cf. Boym 1994: 100–02; Ries 1997: 131, 158–60) and they are still relevant today. We can see this concern about purity of existence as a sensibility in its own right, along with other sensibilities, aesthetic choices, political issues, and moral convictions.

Lifestyles can be understood as communities of taste (Chaney 1996: 126), and their diversity seems to be determined by the range of domains available for the display of distinction and personal predilection. The domains themselves are subject to change inasmuch as sensibilities, aesthetic choices, political issues, and moral convictions grow or wane in public importance. The promotion of idols and imaginaries holds strong sway over the formulation of collective aspirations and personal desires. They play out in opinions and decisions about familial life and social ties, about emotions and responsibilities, about work and leisure, and also about material assets and residence. In the preceding paragraph, we have spoken about the attractiveness that a life close to nature holds for some. In this respect, certain areas of Siberia are particularly attractive. There has been an increasing willingness to relocate into a private *zagorodnyi dom* (a house outside the city) and even a revival of some long-abandoned *dacha* communities. This lifestyle choice has become largely possible with increased automobile ownership, as well as the internet and other technological amenities. Now it is possible to experience an autonomous mode of living, away from the city and yet in a "civilised" way. By the same token, the rapid increase in automobility constitutes a new challenge to Siberian cities, leading to traffic jams and contributing greatly to air pollution (Kirsheva 2016).

However, there is the opposite attractiveness of modernity, which for many decades used to be the dominant collective aspiration. In fact, modernisation constituted the core of Soviet ideology (see Chapters 1, 6, 7, and 11). Modernity continues to be one of the key sensibilities in Russia around which individuals and communities build their life projects. What we find is not simply that several generations of Siberians arrived to "open up" and "civilise" the Far North, and it is not simply that several generations of indigenous peoples underwent socialist education to embark on self-modernisation. What we also find is a profound feeling of "lagging behind", a zeal for catching up with the rest of Russia that characterises many people's self-perception in Siberian cities and villages. In this light, technology and infrastructure attain a tremendous symbolic importance.

In this chapter, we have discussed changes in transport, telecommunication, and use of media. These shifts have created entirely new modes of presenting oneself and relating to others. The flux of visual communication, of icons and inspirations has multiplied and diversified; we may thus assume that visual modes of communication have generally gained in significance. Authorship of media content — once the exclusive claim of a small number of state-paid professionals — is now diffusely distributed among substantial parts of society. The proliferation of digital cameras and mobile phones brings videos and self-produced images into a greater number of households. And yet, people's appropriation of new technologies occurs very unevenly across space. Access to the internet is a matter of not only the strength of the signal, but also the individual's or household's budget. The latter is even more decisive when it comes to buying technical devices. While nearly everybody can now afford to buy a mobile phone and personal computers are no longer a rare item in rural settlements, comparatively few people in rural settlements own a tablet or laptop.

We have also discussed changes in the availability and affordability of transportation. A general shift can be observed from collective towards individual means of transport. In addition, there is now a broader choice of tourist destinations. The combination of these two developments creates a new domain of distinction in which age and income, educational level, and place of residence inform choices on where to go and how to travel. Travel for recreation within Siberia remains a popular option — exactly because of remoteness (i.e. "purity") and the lack of infrastructure. Some parts of Siberia and the Far East — the Altai mountains, Lake Baikal, and the Pacific shore — experience a growing influx of tourists (which is subject to seasonal variation). The internet and open borders have greatly influenced the life of students in big cities and there are more opportunities for cultural exchange and "cosmopolitan learning" for young and middle-aged people (Zuev 2013a, 2013b). Young Siberians can get to know other people's languages and worldviews by going abroad, but also by communicating with visitors from abroad via computer-mediated social networks, which — despite a recent decrease in the popularity of couchsurfing — continue to form an important component in the tourist infrastructure in the cities along the Trans-Siberian railway.

Notwithstanding the pervasiveness of money as the primary currency for the exchange of commodities and services, some transactions and some travels are still more easily facilitated through social connections.

Social relations are still crucial for travelling as they reduce the financial costs and often compensate for the poor quality or the complete absence of commercial services (guesthouses and cafés, hotels and restaurants). Simultaneously, new apps such as *Bla Bla Car* make trips more predictable and cheaper, especially for the segment of travellers that is more accustomed to the secluded comfort of automobility rather than public transport.

We hope to have demonstrated that the Soviet-type dendritic infrastructure, which is based on administrative boundaries and the centrality of the Trans-Siberian railway, has largely remained in effect and continues to shape people's mobilities and travel biographies. At the same time the internet age has brought new developments and new types of affordances, such as social media, that allow for more convenient ways of planning individual physical movement. However, the limited availability of goods and scarcity of monetary resources remain a feature in the remoter parts of Siberia: despite the improvements of certain urban hubs, the transition to socially sustainable and inclusive mobility remains problematic and economically disadvantaged groups have only very limited access to places beyond their residence.

As a final remark, with the economic sanctions of western countries against Russia, the prospect of rising incomes and standard of living in Siberia is now less certain. This may limit the range of travel destinations and reduce the material means for individual expressions of taste and lifestyle. The necessity to support one's family and the aspiration of improving one's quality of life push many talented young Siberians to bigger cities and abroad. This does not always result in a permanent relocation, however: the familial, social and spiritual bonds with Siberia as a place of birth remain strong.

References

Agamben, Giorgio. 1998. *Homo Sacer: sovereign power and bare life*. Stanford, CA: Stanford University Press.

Allemann, Lukas. 2013. "The Sami of Kola Peninsula: about the life of an ethnic minority in the Soviet Union". *Senter for Samiske studier, skriftserie*, 19. Tromsø: University of Tromsø, Center for Sami Studies, http://septentrio.uit.no/index.php/samskrift/article/view/2546/2362; https://doi.org/10.7557/10.2546

Allshouse, R. H. (ed.). 1980. *Photographs for the Tsar: the pioneering color photography of Sergei Mikhailovich Prokudin-Gorskii*. London: Dial Press.

Analiticheskaia gruppa Departamenta marketinga kompanii "Yandeks". 2012. *Razvitie interneta v regionakh Rossii: vesna 2012* [Development of the internet in the regions of Russia: spring 2012], http://download.yandex.ru/company/ya_regions_report_spring_2012.pdf

—. 2014. *Razvitie interneta v regionakh Rossii: vesna 2014* [Development of the internet in the regions of Russia: spring 2014], https://download.yandex.ru/company/ya_internet_regions_2014.pdf

Argounova-Low, Tatiana. 2007. "Close relatives and outsiders: village people in the city of Yakutsk, Siberia". *Arctic Anthropology*, 44 (1): 51–61, https://doi.org/10.1353/arc.2011.0072

—. 2012. "Narrating the Road". *Landscape Research*, 37 (2): 191–206, https://doi.org/10.1080/01426397.2011.651113

—. 2012. "Roads and Roadlessness: driving trucks in Siberia". *Journal of Ethnology and Folkloristics* 6 (1): 71–88.

Aporta, Claudio. 2013. "From Inuit wayfinding to the Google world: living within an ecology of technologies". In: *Nomadic and Indigenous Spaces: productions and cognitions*, ed. Judith Miggelbrink, Joachim Otto Habeck, Peter Koch & Nuccio Mazzullo, pp. 246–58. Farnham: Ashgate, https://doi.org/10.4324/9781315598437

— & Eric Higgs. 2005. "Satellite Culture: global positioning systems, Inuit wayfinding, and the need for a new account of technology". *Current Anthropology*, 46 (5): 729–53, https://doi.org/10.1086/432651

Athique, Adrian. 2013. *Digital Media and Society: an introduction*. Cambridge: Polity Press.

Barchunova, Tatiana. 2010. "Shift-F2: female-to-female intimacy offline and online (Krasnoiarsk and Novosibirsk cases)". *Anthropology of East Europe Review*, 28 (2): 242–70, http://scholarworks.iu.edu/journals/index.php/aeer/article/view/940

Boellstorff, Tom. 2008. *Coming of Age in Second Life: an anthropologist explores the virtually human*. Princeton, NJ: Princeton University Press, https://doi.org/10.1515/9781400874101

Bolotova, Alla, Anastasia Karaseva & Valeria Vasilyeva. 2017. "Mobility and sense of place among youth in the Russian Arctic". *Sibirica: Interdisciplinary Journal of Siberian Studies*, 16 (3): 77–123, https://doi.org/10.3167/sib.2017.160305

Boym, Svetlana. 1994. *Common Places: mythologies of everyday life in Russia*. Cambridge, MA: Harvard University Press.

Broz, Ludek & Joachim Otto Habeck. 2015. "Siberian automobility boom: from the joy of destination to the joy of driving there". *Mobilities*, 10 (4): 552–70, https://doi.org/10.1080/17450101.2015.1059029

Buchner, Christian. Forthcoming. "Tropes of transgression in Siberia" [working title]. Doctoral thesis, Faculty of Humanities, Universität Hamburg.

Burrell, Kathy & Kathrin Hörschelmann. 2014. "Introduction: understanding mobility in Soviet and East European socialist and post-socialist states". In: *Mobilities in Socialist and Post-Socialist States*, ed. Kathy Burrell & Kathrin Hörschelmann. London: Palgrave Macmillan, pp. 1–22, https://doi.org/10.1057/9781137267290_1

Caldwell, Melissa L. 2011. *Dacha Idylls: living organically in the Russian countryside.* Berkeley, CA: University of California Press, https://doi.org/10.1525/california/9780520262843.001.0001

Campbell, Craig. 2003. "Contrails of globalization and the view from the ground: an essay on isolation in East-Central Siberia". *Polar Geography*, 27 (2): 97–120, https://doi.org/10.1080/789610230

—. [n.d.]. "Mobilization and isolation as outcomes of a dysfunctional Soviet landscape". Paper presented at the Havighurst Center for Soviet and Post-Soviet Studies Annual Young Researchers Conference "Russia in Global Context: Peoples, Environments, Policies", Oxford, OH, 7–9 November 2003, http://miamioh.edu/cas/_files/documents/havighurst/2003/campbell.pdf

Chaney, David. 1996. *Lifestyles.* London: Routledge, https://doi.org/DOI: 10.4324/9780203137468

Chemodanova, Kseniia. 2018. "Priblizit' Dal'nii Vostok: na l'gotnye polety po Rossii vydeliat 700 mln rublei" [To bring the Far East closer: 700 million roubles to be spent on subsidized flights in Russia]. *360° TV*, 25 June, https://360tv.ru/news/tekst/priblizit-dalnij-vostok/

Davydov, Vladimir. 2017. "Temporality of movements in the North: pragmatic use of infrastructure and reflexive mobility of Evenki and Dolgan hunters, reindeer herders, and fishers". *Sibirica: Interdisciplinary Journal of Siberian Studies*, 16 (3): 14–34, https://doi.org/10.3167/sib.2017.160302

Dubin, B. V. & N. A. Zorkaia. 2011. "Reading and society in Russia in the first years of the twenty-first century". *Russian Social Science Review*, 52 (4): 24–59, https://doi.org/10.2753/RES1060-9393520702

Durham, F. Gale. 1965. "Radio and television in the Soviet Union". Report of the Research Program on Problems of International Communication and Security. Cambridge, MA: Massachusetts Institute of Technology, http://www.dtic.mil/dtic/tr/fulltext/u2/651556.pdf; DOI: 10.21236/ad0651556

Farre, Albert Buixadé, Scott R. Stephenson, Linling Chen, Michael Czub, Ying Dai, Denis Demchev, et al. 2014. "Commercial Arctic shipping through the Northeast Passage: routes, resources, governance, technology, and infrastructure". *Polar Geography*, 37 (4): 298–324, https://doi.org/10.1080/1088937x.2014.965769

Federal'naia sluzhba gosudarstvennoi statistiki. 2009. *Rossiiskii statisticheskii ezhegodnik 2009* [Russian Statistical Yearbook 2009], http://www.gks.ru/bgd/regl/b09_13/IssWWW.exe/Stg/html4/17-01.htm

—. 2017. *Rossiiskii statisticheskii ezhegodnik 2017* [Russian Statistical Yearbook 2017], http://www.gks.ru/wps/wcm/connect/rosstat_main/rosstat/ru/statistics/publications/catalog/doc_1135087342078

Forsyth, James. 1992. *A History of the Peoples of Siberia: Russia's north Asian colony, 1581–1990*. Cambridge: Cambridge University Press.

Galaguz, Il'ia. 2018. "Sibiriaki stali chashche brat' krupnye potrebitel'skie kredity" [Siberians now use large consumer credits more frequently]. *Kommersant*, 21 July, https://www.kommersant.ru/doc/3694076

Gavrilova, Ksenia. 2017. "Temporal dimension of attitudes toward infrastructure and opportunities for relocation from the Northern town: the case of Kamchatka Krai". *Sibirica: Interdisciplinary Journal of Siberian Studies*, 16 (3): 35–56, https://doi.org/10.3167/sib.2017.160303

—, Nikolai Vakhtin & Valeria Vasilyeva. 2017. "Anthropology of the Northern Sea Route: introducing the topic". *The Polar Journal*, 7 (1): 46–57, https://doi.org/10.1080/2154896X.2017.1324691

Gelvanovska, Natalija, Carlo Maria Rossotto & Michael Lee Gunzburger. 2016. "Russia's Ambitious Broadband Goal: is the progress sustainable?". *Connections*, 4. World Bank, Washington, DC, https://openknowledge.worldbank.org/handle/10986/25012

Göler, Daniel. 2007. "Russia's northern periphery in transition: regional fragmentation of the Far North?" In: *Politics in the Russian Regions*, ed. Graeme Gill, pp. 188–203. Basingstoke: Palgrave Macmillan, https://doi.org/10.1057/9780230597280_8

Habeck, Joachim Otto. 2013. "Learning to be seated: sedentarization in the Soviet Far North as a spatial and cognitive enclosure". In: *Nomadic and Indigenous Spaces: productions and cognitions*, ed. Judith Miggelbrink, Joachim Otto Habeck, Peter Koch & Nuccio Mazzullo, pp. 155–79. Farnham: Ashgate, https://doi.org/10.4324/9781315598437

— & Galina Belolyubskaya. 2016. "Fences, private and public spaces, and traversability in a Siberian city". *Cities*, 56: 119–29, https://doi.org/10.1016/j.cities.2016.04.001

Haywood, A. J. 2010. *Siberia: a cultural history*. Oxford: Oxford University Press.

Hill, Fiona & Clifford Gaddy. 2003. *The Siberian Curse: how communist planners left Russia out in the cold*. Washington, DC: Brookings Institution Press.

Humphrey, Caroline. 2007. "New subjects and situated interdependence: after privatisation in Ulan-Ude". In: *Urban Life in Post-Soviet Asia*, ed. Catherine Alexander, Victor Buchli & Caroline Humphrey, pp. 175–207. London: University College London Press, https://doi.org/10.4324/9780203944875

—. [Kerolain Khamfri]. 2014. "Izmenenie znachimosti udalennosti v sovremennoi Rossii" [The changing significance of remoteness in contemporary Russia]. *Etnograficheskoe obozrenie*, 2014 (3): 8–24.

Hurelbaatar, Altanhuu. 2007. "The creation and revitalisation of ethnic sacred sites in Ulan-Ude since the 1990s". In: *Urban Life in Post-Soviet Asia*, ed. Catherine Alexander, Victor Buchli and Caroline Humphrey, pp. 136–56. London: University College London Press, https://doi.org/10.4324/9780203944875

Hutchings, Stephen & Natalia Rulyova. 2009. *Television and Culture in Putin's Russia: remote control.* London: Routledge, https://doi.org/10.4324/9780203091630

Hutchings, Stephen & Vera Tolz. 2015. *Nation, Ethnicity and Race on Russian Television: mediating post-Soviet difference.* London: Routledge, https://doi.org/10.4324/9781315722863

Istomin, Kirill. 2013. "From invisible float to the eye for a snowstorm: the introduction of GPS by Nenets reindeer herders of western Siberia and its impact on their spatial cognition and navigation methods". In: *Nomadic and Indigenous Spaces: productions and cognitions*, ed. Judith Miggelbrink, Joachim Otto Habeck, Peter Koch & Nuccio Mazzullo, pp. 203–20. Farnham: Ashgate, https://doi.org/10.4324/9781315598437

Jähnig, Wolfgang. 1983. "Die Siedlungsplanung im ländlichen Raum der Sowjetunion mit besonderer Berücksichtigung des Konzepts der 'Agrostadt'" [Settlement planning in the rural areas of the Soviet Union, with particular focus on the concept of "agro-town"]. *Osteuropa-Studien des Landes Hessen. Reihe I: Giessener Abhandlungen zur Agrar- und Wirtschaftsforschung des europäischen Ostens.* 123. Berlin: Duncker & Humblot.

Khon, Vyacheslav C., I. I. Mokhov, M. Latif, V. A. Semenov & W. Park. 2010. "Perspectives of Northern Sea Route and Northwest Passage in the twenty-first century". *Climatic Change*, 100 (3–4): 757–68, https://doi.org/10.1007/s10584-009-9683-2

King, Victor T. 2018. "Tourism and leisure in Thailand: Erik Cohen and beyond". *Universiti Brunei Darussalam Institute for Asian Studies Working Paper*, 40. Gadong: Universiti Brunei Darussalam Institute of Asian Studies, http://ias.ubd.edu.bn/wp-content/uploads/2018/09/working_paper_series_40.pdf

Kinnock, Stephen. 2018. "Russia is using the British Council as a political tool (op-ed)". *The Moscow Times*, 22 March, https://themoscowtimes.com/articles/russia-is-using-the-british-council-as-a-political-tool-op-ed-60913

Kinossian, Nadir. 2016. "Re-colonising the Arctic: the preparation of spatial planning policy in Murmansk Oblast, Russia". *Environment and Planning C: Politics and Space*, 35 (2): 221–38, https://doi.org/10.1177/0263774X16648331

Kirsheva, Irina. 2016. "Krasnoiartsy uezzhaiut iz-za gustogo smoga" [Citizens of Krasnaiarsk are leaving because of thick smog]. *Komsomolskaia Pravda*, Krasnoiarsk, Online Edition, 23 July, https://www.krsk.kp.ru/daily/26559.7/3575175

Konstantinov, Yulian. 2009. "Roadlessness and the person: mode of travel in the reindeer herding part of the Kola Peninsula". *Acta Borealia*, 26 (1): 27–49, https://doi.org/10.1080/08003830902951524

Kuhr-Korolev, Corinna. 2011. "Women and cars in Soviet and Russian Society". In: *The Socialist Car: automobility in the Eastern Bloc*, ed. Lewis H. Siegelbaum, pp. 186–203. Ithaca, NY: Cornell University Press, https://doi.org/10.7591/cornell/9780801449918.003.0012

Kuklina, Vera & Edward C. Holland. 2018. "The roads of the Sayan Mountains: theorizing remoteness in eastern Siberia". *Geoforum*, 88: 36–44, https://doi.org/10.1016/j.geoforum.2017.10.008

Kuklina, Vera, Olga Povoroznyuk & Gertrude Saxinger. 2019. "Power of rhythms: trains and work along the Baikal-Amur Mainline (BAM) in Siberia". *Polar Geography*, 42 (1): 18–33, https://doi.org/10.1080/1088937X.2018.1564395

Lamin, Vladimir. 2005. "The 'moving frontier': the Trans-Siberian Railroad". In: *The Siberian Saga: a history of Russia's Wild East*, ed. Eva-Maria Stolberg, pp. 109–18. Frankfurt am Main: Peter Lang.

Lapin, S. G. 1975. "Radioveshchanie" [Radio broadcast]. In: *Bol'shaia Sovetskaia Entsiklopediia*, 3rd ed., vol. 21, pp. 353–56.

Laruelle, Marlène (ed.). 2017. *New Mobilities and Social Changes in Russia's Arctic Regions*. New York: Routledge.

Lazhentsev, Vitalii N. 2015. "Theoretical results of research on spatial and territorial development (with examples on the European North of Russia)". *R-Economy*, 1 (4): 525–32, https://journals.urfu.ru/index.php/r-economy/article/view/2894; https://doi.org/10.15826/recon.2015.4.016

Ledeneva, Alena V. 1998. *Russia's Economy of Favours: blat, networking and informal exchange*. Cambridge: Cambridge University Press.

Lehmann, Hartmut, Jonathan Wadsworth & Alessandro Acquisti. 1999. "Grime and punishment: job insecurity and wage arrears in the Russian Federation". *Journal of Comparative Economics*, 27 (4): 595–617, https://doi.org/10.1006/jcec.1999.1616

Lindstad, Haakon, Ryan M. Bright & Anders H. Strømman. 2016. "Economic savings linked to future Arctic shipping trade are at odds with climate change mitigation". *Transport Policy*, 45: 24–30, https://doi.org/10.1016/j.tranpol.2015.09.002

Lipchinskaia, Ol'ga. 2012. "Gde v Vostochnoi Sibiri zhit' horosho" [Where to live well in eastern Siberia]. *Komsomolskaia Pravda*, Irkutsk, Online Edition, 27 March, https://www.irk.kp.ru/daily/25857/2825041/

Lonkila, Markku. 2011. "Driving at democracy in Russia: protest activities of St. Petersburg car drivers' associations". *Europe-Asia Studies*, 63 (2): 291–309, https://doi.org/10.1080/09668136.2011.547699

Mankova, Petia. 2018. "Homewarding remoteness: representations, agency and everyday life in a tundra village (NW Russia)". Doctoral thesis, UiT, The Arctic University of Norway, Tromsø, https://munin.uit.no/bitstream/handle/10037/12107/thesis.pdf

Marks, Steven Gary. 1991. *Road to Power: the Trans-Siberian Railroad and the colonization of Asian Russia, 1850–1917*. Ithaca, NY: Cornell University Press.

Mote, Victor. 1990. "The South Yakutian territorial production complex". In: *The Soviet Far East: geographical perspectives on development*, ed. Allan Rodgers, pp. 163–84. London: Routledge.

—. 2003. "Stalin's railway to nowhere: the 'Dead Road' (1947–1953)". *Sibirica: Interdisciplinary Journal of Siberian Studies*, 3 (1): 48–63, https://doi.org/10.1080/136173603200016802

Pallot, Judith. 1990. "Rural depopulation and the restoration of the Russian village under Gorbachev". *Soviet Studies*, 42 (4): 655–74, https://doi.org/10.1080/09668139008411895

Pietiläinen, Jukka. 2008. "Media use in Putin's Russia". *Journal of Communist Studies and Transition Politics*, 24 (3): 365–85, https://doi.org/10.1080/13523270802267906

Popov, Vladimir. 2012. "The culture of new mobility in Russia: networks and flows formation". *Mobilities*, 7 (1): 151–69, https://doi.org/10.1080/17450101.2012.631816

Povoroznyuk, Olga. 2011. *Zabaikal'skie evenki: sotsial'no-ekonomicheskie i kul'turnye transformatsii v XX–XXI vekakh* [Trans-Baikal Evenkis: social-economic and cultural transformations in the 20 and 21th centuries]. Moscow: Institut etnologii i antropologii im. N. N. Miklukho-Maklaia Rossiiskoi Akademii Nauk.

—. 2018. "The Baikal-Amur Mainline: memories and emotions of a socialist construction project". *Sibirica: Interdisciplinary Journal of Siberian Studies*, 18 (1): 22–52, https://doi.org/10.3167/sib.2019.180103

—, Joachim Otto Habeck & Virginie Vaté. 2010. "Introduction: On the definition, theory, and practice of gender shift in the North of Russia". *Anthropology of East Europe Review*, 28 (2): 1–37, http://scholarworks.iu.edu/journals/index.php/aeer/article/view/929/1037; https://doi.org/10.3167/sib.2019.180103

Ries, Nancy. 1997. *Russian Talk: culture and conversation during Perestroika*. Ithaca, NY: Cornell University Press.

Rodgers, Allan (ed.). 1990. *The Soviet Far East: geographical perspectives on development*. London: Routledge.

Rohozinski, Rafal. 1999. "Mapping Russian Cyberspace: perspectives on democracy and the Net". *United Nations Research Institute for Social Development Discussions Papers*, 115, http://unpan1.un.org/intradoc/groups/public/documents/untc/unpan015092.pdf

Rykov, Yuri, Oleg Nagornyy, & Olga Koltsova. 2017. "Digital inequality in Russia through the use of a social network site: a cross-regional comparison". In: *International Conference on Digital Transformation and Global Society*, ed. Daniel A. Alexandrov, Alexander V. Boukhanovsky, Andrey V. Chugunov, Yury Kabanov & Olessia Koltsova, pp. 70–83. Cham: Springer, https://doi.org/10.1007/978-3-319-69784-0_6

Saxinger, Gertrude. 2015. "Lured by oil and gas: labour mobility, multi-locality and negotiating normality & extreme in the Russian Far North". *The Extractive Industries and Society*, 3 (1): 50–59, https://doi.org/10.1016/j.exis.2015.12.002

—. 2016. *Unterwegs: Mobiles Leben in der Erdgas- und Erdölindustrie in Russlands Arktis* [On the road: mobile life in the gas and oil industry of Russia's Arctic]. Wien: Böhlau, https://doi.org/10.7767/9783205201861

Schweitzer, Peter, Olga Povoroznyuk & Sigrid Schiesser. 2017. "Beyond wilderness: towards an anthropology of infrastructure and the built environment in the Russian North". *The Polar Journal*, 7 (1): 58–85, https://doi.org/10.1080/2154896X.2017.1334427

Siegelbaum, Lewis H. 2008a. "Roadlessness and the 'Path to Communism': Building Roads and Highways in Stalinist Russia". *Journal of Transport History*, 29 (2): 277–94, https://doi.org/10.7227/tjth.29.2.8

—. 2008b. *Cars for Comrades: the life of the Soviet automobile*. Ithaca, NY: Cornell University Press.

Simonova, Veronika V. 2007. "TransSib: put' v zhizni, zhizn' v puti" [TransSib: route in life, life en route]. *Sotsiologicheskie issledovaniia*, 2007 (5): 103–13.

—. 2012. "Living taiga memories: how landscape creates remembering among Evenkis in the North Baikal, Siberia". Doctoral thesis, University of Aberdeen.

Stammler, Florian. 2013. "Narratives of adaptation and innovation: ways of being mobile and mobile technologies among reindeer nomads in the Russian Arctic". In: *Nomadic and Indigenous Spaces: productions and cognitions*, ed. Judith Miggelbrink, Joachim Otto Habeck, Peter Koch, & Nuccio Mazzullo, pp. 221–45. Farnham: Ashgate.

— & Lena Sidorova. 2015. "Dachas on permafrost: the creation of nature among Arctic Russian city-dwellers". *Polar Record*, 51 (6): 576–89, https://doi.org/10.1017/s0032247414000710

Strategiia 2030. No author. "Strategiia 2030" [Strategy 2030]. *Kommersant*, prilozhenie [supplement] 84: Business Guide (zheleznodorozhnyi transport) [railway transport], 25 May 2008, https://www.kommersant.ru/doc/891281

Tuvikene, Tauri. 2010. "From Soviet to post-Soviet with transformation of the fragmented urban landscape: the case of garage areas in Estonia". *Landscape Research*, 35 (5): 509–28, https://doi.org/10.1080/01426397.2010.504914

Urry, John. 2007. *Mobilities*. Cambridge: Polity Press, https://doi.org/10.4324/9781315595733

Usenyuk, Svetlana, Sampsa Hyysalo & Jack Whalen. 2016. "Proximal design: users as designers of mobility in the Russian North". *Technology and Culture*, 57 (4): 866–908, https://doi.org/10.1353/tech.2016.0110

Vakhtin, Nikolai. 2017. "Mobility and infrastructure in the Russian Arctic: das Sein bestimmt das Bewusstsein?". *Sibirica: Interdisciplinary Journal of Siberian Studies*, 16 (3): 1–13, https://doi.org/10.3167/sib.2017.160301

Ventsel, Aimar. 2011. "Siberian movements: how money and goods travel in and out Northwestern Sakha". *Folklore: Electronic Journal of Folklore*, 49: 113–30, https://doi.org/10.7592/FEJF2011.49.ventsel

Verdery, Katherine. 1996. *What Was Socialism, and What Comes Next?* Princeton, NJ: Princeton University Press.

Vitebsky, Piers. 1990. "Centralized decentralization: the ethnography of remote reindeer herders under Perestroika". *Cahiers du Monde Russe et Soviétique*, 31 (2–3): 345–55, https://doi.org/10.3406/cmr.1990.2234

—. 2000. "Coping with distance: Social, economic and environmental change in the Sakha Republic (Yakutia), northeast Siberia". Unpublished report. Scott Polar Research Institute, University of Cambridge.

—. 2005. *Reindeer People: living with animals and spirits in Siberia*. London: Harper Collins.

Weiss, Claudia. 2007. *Wie Sibirien unser wurde: die Russische Geographische Gesellschaft und ihr Einfluss auf die Bilder und Vorstellungen von Sibirien im 19. Jahrhundert* [How Siberia became ours: the Russian Geographic Society and its influence on the images and conceptions about Siberia in the 19th century]. Göttingen: V&R Unipress.

Yurchak, Alexei. 2006. *Everything Was Forever, Until it Was No More: the last Soviet generation*. Princeton, NJ: Princeton University Press, https://doi.org/10.1515/9781400849109

Zavisca, Jane. 2003. "Contesting capitalism at the Post-Soviet dacha: the meaning of food cultivation for urban Russians". *Slavic Review*, 62 (4): 786–810, https://doi.org/10.2307/3185655

Zubarevich, Natalia. 2013. "Four Russias: human potential and social differentiation of Russian regions and cities". In: *Russia 2025*, ed. Maria Lipman & Nikolay Petrov, pp. 67–85. London: Palgrave Macmillan, https://doi.org/10.1057/9781137336910

Zuev, Dennis. 2008. "The practice of free-traveling: young people coping with access in Post-Soviet Russia". *Young: Nordic Journal of Youth Research*, 16 (1): 5–26, https://doi.org/10.1177/110330880701600102

—. 2013a. "Couchsurfing along the Trans-Siberian Railway and beyond: cosmopolitan learning through hospitality in Siberia". *Sibirica: Interdisciplinary Journal of Siberian Studies*, 12 (1): 56–82, https://doi.org/10.3167/sib.2013.120103

—. 2013b. "Hosting Marco in Siberia: couchsurfing hospitality in an 'out of the way' place". In: *Couchsurfing Cosmopolitanisms: can tourism make a better world?*, ed. David Picard & Sonja Buchberger, pp. 65–82. Bielefeld: Transcript, https://doi.org/10.14361/transcript.9783839422557.65

3. Lifestyle and Creative Engagement with Rural Space in Northwest Russia

Masha Shaw (née Maria Nakhshina)

When colleagues in town asked me upon my return from yet another fieldwork trip to the village: *"Nu, i kak tam liudi zhivut?"* (So, how do people live there?), they usually met my enthusiastic reply that life in Chavan'ga was generally very good with a sceptical distrust. While acknowledging that deterioration of the social and economic provision has occurred in many if not most rural parts of post-Soviet Russia, I offer an account of situations when people in Russia today make a deliberate choice to live in the village in order to achieve what they think is best for them. I look at people's engagement with rural space as a lifestyle choice and a way of creative fulfilment of their desires and hopes.[1]

Academic, media, and everyday discourse often associate lifestyle with diversity and distinction, as well as the availability of spare time and money. This implies that rural dwellers in Russia and elsewhere

1   This study would not have been possible without the incredible support and hospitality of Chavan'ga's residents. In particular, Anna Yakovlevna, Vera Yegorovna, Ol'ga Pavlovna, and Nikolai Aleksandrovich hosted me on a number of occasions and have become my true mentors. The deputy chairman of Chavan'ga *kolkhoz*, Pavel Alekseevich, helped a lot with fieldwork logistics and administration. Finally, I would like to thank the young people of Chavan'ga, who were a constant source of fun and inspiration, and generously shared their time to introduce me to local ways and wisdom.

https://doi.org/10.11647/OBP.0171.03

might be more limited in their lifestyle choices compared to urbanites due to their limited access to cash, the onerous nature of work on the land and the restricted variety of available consumer goods and services. While this disparity has grown in most areas of post-Soviet Russia, the deterioration of the *kolkhoz* system and retreat of the state from peripheral regions in the course of postsocialist transformations have provided people in Chavan'ga with spare time. It has also given them the means to go beyond what is simply given and to invest in things they desire. Remote areas in Russia more generally have undergone cultural and symbolic transformations which made them more attractive to people. In the wake of the fall of the Soviet Union, many rural places took on new meanings, often rooted in values and traditions that the Soviet regime had tried to undermine (Humphrey 2001). These transformations have now offered new possibilities for personal fulfilment.

This chapter develops an idea of lifestyle as manifested in a particular way of engaging with place. It involves using a place's specific affordances in such a way that corresponds to people's values and aspirations, which in turn brings them personal fulfilment and satisfaction. Lifestyle is always creative, if we understand creativity as a universal fulfilling capacity rather than a privileged ability to produce something new and original (Evans & Deehan 1988; Pope 2005: 60–62). It is also intersubjective, in the sense that one's own preferences and inclinations are in a constant dialogue with a world of commonly held ideas and attributes (Jackson 1998: 7). Individual lifestyles of contemporary Chavan'ga villagers are a direct manifestation of wider processes that have taken place during both the Soviet and post-Soviet periods in Russia, and shaped people's aspirations and values.

Most literature on lifestyle speaks of it as a specifically urban phenomenon (cf. Chaney 1996: 100–03), with the exception of research on lifestyle migration from cities to the countryside (Benson & O'Reilly 2009; Hoey 2005). Such literature, however, usually approaches lifestyle from the perspective of affluent urbanites that aspire to a better quality of life in rural idylls, rather than from the rural population itself. A comprehensive recent study of urbanisation and counterurbanisation in contemporary Russia again focuses on the city as a starting point of people's movement to the countryside (Nefedova et al. 2016). Within this approach, former villagers who come back to their rural places of origin upon retirement or young people who return to the countryside after having tried their luck in the city seem to belong outside the realm of lifestyle migration. The two types of migration, however, are similar in nature. Both involve lifestyle choices, as they are an outcome of people's pursuits of certain ideals and aspirations.

Ethnographic research on rural Russia has for a long time remained focused on rural areas as spaces of production rather than on their potential to produce multiple spaces (Shubin 2006: 429): of work and leisure, collective and individual. In the context of strong ideological pressure from the Soviet regime, ethnographers often resorted to "ideologically neutral" areas of study, such as folklore and material culture. The end of the Soviet period opened up the borders for foreign researchers, and brought the overall liberalisation of Russian science itself. While this has introduced a whole array of novel topics, most of research in rural areas focused on political economy and/or resource use (e.g., Gray 2003, 2004; Humphrey 2001; Stammler & Ivanova 2016; Wilson 2016), whereas studies of leisure, popular culture, lifestyle and consumption were mainly reserved for urban areas (Puuronen, Sinisalo & Shvets 2000; Barker 2005), with a few exceptions (e.g. Bridger 1989; Il'in 2015). This chapter contributes to the body of literature that looks at the village as a space for leisure, lifestyle choice and self-fulfilment.

I bring together stories of three individuals from three different generations to explore reasons behind people's deliberate choices to live in the village and to reveal connections between personal decisions and wider processes within Russian society. My protagonists include a woman in her mid-fifties and two men, one in his forties, and the other in his early twenties. I use their real names, with the permission of all three protagonists.

Both men have chosen to live in the village because the rural space allows them to have a high degree of personal mobility. There are different drivers behind these individuals' desire to be mobile. The older man, Andrei, has an inquisitive attitude towards the world which makes him constantly seek for new opportunities to travel. These aspirations have roots in Andrei's Soviet childhood as he grew up in a system that had a strong focus on educational and ideological power of organised tourism and excursions. The younger man, Anton, gave up an advantageous job in the city arranged by his relatives for a lower paid job in the village. He did not like the city job because it submitted him to very rigid timetables and externally imposed regimes. His job in the village, on the other hand, allows him a high degree of freedom to follow his own rhythms and spend a lot of time outdoors. While many adults in the village find such behaviour careless and short-sighted, Anton's choice reflects a current tendency among young Russian people to put a stronger emphasis on finding a job that is close to their aspirations than their parents' generation did.

The third protagonist, Vera, decided to move to Chavan'ga for good after having lived for many years in the city because the village gives her moral and physical strength. Vera's decision to move back to the village is a typical example of a recent phenomenon of urban-rural migration in Russia. After a mass exodus from the village to the city during the late half of the Soviet era, many people now move back to the countryside upon reaching retirement in order to reconnect to their rural homeland and to achieve personal comfort and satisfaction.

Many Chavan'ga residents expressed their content with life in the village. Many of them made a conscious choice to live in the countryside rather than in the city. The three individual stories presented in this chapter are not necessarily representative in terms of the reasons for their choices, as every villager has their own story about the choices they made. However, they are representative in terms of reflecting people's general perception of the village as providing a better quality of life than the city and better opportunities to pursue their lifestyle aspirations. The contemporary Russian rural space allows for certain possibilities for personal fulfilment, such as realising one's aspirations in work and leisure or living up to personal moral values. The lifestyles of all three protagonists are creative responses to these opportunities and to ever changing power dynamics, ideologies, economic developments, and infrastructures.

In what follows, I first comment on the essential role of kitchen table talk as a research tool when conducting fieldwork in the Russian countryside. This section also functions as an initial introduction to Chavan'ga as a place. I provide further details about Chavan'ga in the next section and speak about how its current affordances and limitations have made certain trajectories appealing and certain lifestyle paths possible. In the section after that, I present the life histories of the three protagonists in Chavan'ga and reveal the kind of choices they have made in order to achieve what they think is best for them. In the final section of the chapter, I further develop an idea of lifestyle as a creative way of engaging with place.

Kitchen table talk as a research tool

When conducting fieldwork in Chavan'ga, one should be prepared for various forms of "liquidation of time" (Pesmen 2000: 125). Among them, drinking tea at the kitchen table proved to be the most prominent in my work. When I rented my own accommodation in the village, I would have on average three to four visits for tea and coffee per day. There were days when I had hardly any time to write fieldnotes as I had one visit after another. Visitors were predominantly local youth, with a group size ranging from one person up to half a dozen people. While it was all right for me not to have any food in the house, sufficient provision of tea bags, instant coffee, sugar and sweets or biscuits was my regular concern. A significant proportion of my luggage when travelling to the field consisted of chocolate and other treats, as the range of choice in the local shop was rather limited. I spent an equal amount of time at other people's kitchen tables, our conversations ranging from idle talks to discussions on profound social issues.

Nancy Ries considers talk "an especially meaningful arena of value production and negotiation among Russian-speakers" in late Soviet and post-Soviet Russian society and acknowledges the special status of kitchen table talk: "there, over tea or vodka, people could speak their minds, tell their stories, and spill their souls openly" (1997: 20–21). The situation when "the only places to talk are kitchen tables and analogous ones in workplaces" (Pesmen 2000: 95) has been changing rapidly ever since Russia embraced free market in the 1990s, especially in the city with its proliferation of public places for people to meet and socialise. In the village, however, the role of kitchen table talks in producing and transmitting local values remains very strong.

In a village as small as Chavan'ga there are no places for either eating or drinking out; people's houses are thus the main built spaces where socialising takes place (Nakhshina 2013). Public built spaces where people can interact with each other are limited to the *kolkhoz* office, the social club, the shop, and the helipad once a week. Opportunities to socialise during work are limited because work places are generally scarce, and because many forms of common labour such as hay making or harvesting have virtually ceased to exist. Fishing, which is the main *kolkhoz* activity in Chavan'ga, makes an important exception as it often involves spending long hours collaborating with other people.

Like in numerous rural settlements throughout Russia, there is a social club in Chavan'ga. However, the former role of this institution as a centre and initiator of various social activities has diminished significantly in the course of post-Soviet transformations (Habeck 2011). Chavan'ga social club's functions are currently reduced to hosting celebrations of public holidays such as New Year or Victory Day and local holidays such as the official Day of the Fisherman, and to providing a physical space for people to socialise indoors on a regular basis. The social club is open from Wednesday to Sunday from about 6pm until 1am, after which time electricity in the village is turned off. It is largely up to visitors themselves to organize their activities in the club on regular days. There has been a significant revitalisation of the club's attendance recently when they acquired entertainment and sports equipment such as a pool table and table tennis table. The pool table is the major pull factor that attracts both young people and adults to the club, generating sometimes rather long queues of players. I spent many hours socialising in the social club; yet, the most revealing discussions and soul openings always took place during kitchen table talks.

There are a few methodological implications of the role of kitchen table talk when conducting fieldwork in Chavan'ga. First, I had to allow for much more time for tea drinking than I had imagined, not only because this was the major way of getting local news and gossip, but also because I was actually expected to regularly participate in tea drinking sessions both as a guest and host. Next, tea drinking at the kitchen table was virtually the only space where I could socialise with some people in the village, as there were no other occasions for us to cross. Furthermore, participation in tea drinking was often a way for me to be accepted as *svoia* (one's own), as well as an indicator of such acceptance. Some people in the village never invited me for tea, and they tended to be the people with whom I socialised least, if at all. Last but not least, taking part in kitchen table talks in a village of Chavan'ga's size can be very political. As the place is very small, people usually know whom one visits, for how long and how often. The very houses that one visits often define one's wider social circles in the village and determine instances of further communication.

There is a major difference in the contemporary meaning of tea drinking and kitchen table talk in rural versus urban contexts. Those living in a city might see this "liquidation of time" as an unattainable luxury. In villages on the White Sea coast, however, these idle and profound, joyful and solemn kitchen table talks belong not so much to the realm of leisure as to the tapestry of everyday life.

Ethnographic material in this paper originates mainly from kitchen table conversations and is supplemented by data received through other methods, such as participating in local activities and working with regional newspaper archives. I spent several months in Chavan'ga during different seasons of 2011–2012. My research was part of the team project "Conditions and Limitations of Lifestyle Plurality" carried out by the Siberian Studies Centre at the Max Planck Institute for Social Anthropology (see the Appendix).

(Dis-)empowered by the state: lifestyles of (im)mobility

Life in a small fishing outpost: livelihood and transportation

Chavan'ga is a village on the Terskii Coast of the White Sea coastline in the Kola Peninsula in the northwest of Russia. Administratively it belongs to Terskii Raion (district) of Murmansk Oblast. The Terskii Coast is a historical name of the north-western and northern part of the White Sea coastline: as people from other regions of Russia came in several waves to settle along the White Sea coast over a span of several centuries, different parts of the coastline received their individual names. Settlers' main occupation became fishing and hunting sea mammals, which made them distinct from the rest of the Russian people who were mainly involved in agriculture. Due to their proximity to the sea and a livelihood based on extraction of marine resources, people living in the White Sea area have been traditionally called Pomors, from the Russian *po moriu* (by the sea).

Like many other Russian villages, Chavan'ga has experienced a steady outflow of people to the city throughout the second half of the twentieth century and until now. There were eighty people registered as permanent population in the village at the time of my fieldwork, although the number doubled during the summer when many of those who had moved to cities came to the village on holiday. Chavan'ga's demographic composition is rather typical for the contemporary Russian countryside, with middle-aged and elderly people constituting the population's majority and young people being the minority. Among the rural youth, boys significantly outnumber girls, which reflects a continuing tendency of recent decades when women are more prone to leave the Russian countryside than men (Bridger 1989; Schweitzer et al. 2015: 143–44). This is reinforced by Chavan'ga's main economic activity — fishing, which has been a predominantly male occupation. Salmon fishing allows people to earn much money over a short period of intensive labour, leaving the rest of the year free for other activities.

This makes life in a village like Chavan'ga rather attractive for men. Women, especially young girls, who are usually confined to housework indoors, often prefer the city with its domestic amenities. The situation might be different in other rural parts of Russia where there is a mixed Russian and indigenous population. Gernet (2012: 283) observes that most young indigenous women in villages in central Kamchatka prefer to remain in the village and not migrate to urban areas (as most non-indigenous young women do). From their perspective, the life in the village enables a middle way between an existence in the forest or tundra and existence in the city, as it combines elements of urban infrastructure with proximity to nature (ibid: 284, 286).

Salmon fishing has historically been an important occupation and source of income for the people of the White Sea area. Before the Soviet period, fishing was done mainly by self-organised groups of individuals within a community and by monasteries (Laius et al. 2010). In the late 1920s and early 1930s, the Soviet government eliminated private enterprises and established collective farms (*kolkhozy*) instead. All fishing was now done by *kolkhoz* brigades; individual fishing for salmon was prohibited. Fishing was also supplemented with vegetable and dairy farming. The collective farm in Chavan'ga survived into the post-Soviet period. With currently more than forty employees, the cooperative is the major provider of jobs in the village. The main activity of the *kolkhoz* is fishing which includes inshore salmon fisheries in the White Sea near the village and trawling in the Barents Sea near Murmansk. While the former provides employment for villagers, the latter sustains the *kolkhoz* financially.

Most *kolkhoz* workers are men, whereas women occupy the majority of positions outside the *kolkhoz*: in the service sphere, leisure and education, which have been traditional locations of female labour in Russia since the Soviet period. *Kolkhoz* jobs include an accountant, welder, cleaner, manual workers, truck and tractor drivers, fish processing workers, a chairman, and his deputy. Non-*kolkhoz* occupations include a librarian, social worker, post officer, shop assistant, primary school teacher, social club manager, and telecommunications engineer.

There was no permanent electricity, and no internet or mobile connection in Chavan'ga at the time of my fieldwork. There is no official road to the village and the fastest and probably the most comfortable way to get there is by helicopter that goes once a week from the town of Umba, which is the administrative centre of Terskii Raion. Time in Chavan'ga is counted in helicopters. It is not rare to hear that somebody is going somewhere in two helicopters' time, or that something happened before the last helicopter. The demand for seats on the helicopter outstrips the supply. While the bench style seating results in a certain "flexibility" of ticketing, it is the combined weight of people and luggage that determines the number of passengers. This means that if people have too much heavy luggage, someone might not get a seat on the flight. This makes it difficult for people to plan their travel to and from Chavan'ga.

There is also a ship that comes from Murmansk three times a year during summer navigation. While it can take a very large number of passengers, it is not a very reliable mode of transport. The sea along the Terskii Coast is too shallow for the ship to come close to the shore. Villagers therefore have to come out on small boats to take passengers off the ship. If the weather is bad and visibility is very poor, the ship would not stop at the village and would go back to Murmansk. This again makes Chavan'ga hard to access. Transportation is somewhat easier in winter when people can travel by snowmobiles. Since most jobs in the village that involve driving a vehicle have been traditionally performed by men, the latter are more mobile and less dependent on officially provided transportation as they have skills, knowledge and connections required to get access to means of transport. Women's opportunities to have their own means of transport are limited, which makes them more bound to travel by public transport and more dependent on other villagers who have their own transport.

The main reason why there is no proper road to Chavan'ga is that there is a big river in the way. The official road goes all the way along the Terskii Coast from Umba up to the River Varzuga. There is no bridge across the Varzuga and one has to use a boat or ferry to get across and travel further. This geographical divide is reflected in the way people in villages on two sides of the river refer to the urban centre. In the last village before the river, when somebody goes to town, people say *poekhat' v goroda* (to travel to cities), while in the village after the river people say *poekhat' na bol'shuiu zemliu* (to travel to the mainland); the two villages are only fifty kilometres apart. This verbal distinction shows that people in Chavan'ga might feel isolated, or somehow cut off. There is a rudimentary unpaved road to the village now, which appeared about ten years ago. This makes it possible to reach Chavan'ga by truck during summer but the road is still very challenging.

Individual mobility is not an easily available resource for people in Chavan'ga. One has to have the right connections or invest a considerable amount of effort in order to achieve a high degree of personal mobility. There is a strong desire among people in the village, especially men, to obtain their own means of transport, such as a truck, motorbike, or snowmobile. To have one's own vehicle is a matter or prestige and independence, even if it only allows mobility in the close vicinity of the village. Many male villagers occasionally like to escape to the forest on fishing and hunting trips that can last a few days. Without their own transport, they are confined to the village space. If a young man's parents already have a snowmobile, he would still try to save money to buy his own. If someone regularly borrows a vehicle from others, they might be criticised for not investing in their own means of transport.

A very large part of families' incomes in Chavan'ga goes into procuring transport and fuel to allow travels within the village and Terskii Raion, often at the expense of travels over larger distances. When I asked a girl from Chavan'ga why her family would not go on holiday and get out of the village at least for a short period, her answer was that they cannot afford any travel because their snowmobile broke and now they have to save money for a new one.

Although vehicles are expensive, and official employment opportunities are very limited, many people in the village can regularly obtain cash from informal economic activities. The deterioration of established systems of state management and control in post-Soviet Russia have allowed people in villages on the Terskii Coast to earn extra cash from informal fishing activities (Nakhshina 2012a, 2012b). People either fish themselves or provide tourists with transportation, accommodation and guidance to fishing places. Such informal sources of income can provide people in Chavan'ga with enough money to invest in their own means of transport. It is mainly men who can earn a sufficient amount of money from fishing, partially due to their initial possession of skills, knowledge, vehicles, and other equipment, which reinforces women's dependence on official transportation or on other villagers who have their own transport.

Double twist of (dis-)empowerment

People in Chavan'ga today seem to have more freedom to follow their own regimes of mobility rather than those imposed externally, compared to the situation during the Soviet period. Factors that have allowed for that include growing ownership of one's own means of transport; deterioration of the *kolkhoz* system with its binding working regime; the weakening of state control in rural areas after the collapse of the Soviet state; and the households' ceasing to keep their own cattle that would tie people to the place and restrict their mobility.

At the same time, there are strong limitations to Chavan'ga villagers' freedom to move. First, it is within the village's immediate surroundings and district that people move most. There is not much movement over larger distances, mainly due to the lack of means and insufficient infrastructure. Second, many of those trips that people make are in a way forced upon them because they are caused by the retreat of the state from the area. Many services that used to be available to people in rural areas during the Soviet time are not there anymore, and therefore people have to travel out of the village, usually at their own expense, for things like medical care or various administrative reasons and secondary education (secondary and in some cases primary schools have been closed in most villages on the Terskii Coast). In this light, state policies continue to condition people's mobility to a large extent.

On the one hand, life in Chavan'ga is empowering because people have more freedom to move and follow their own rhythms; on the other hand, it is disempowering because they have to spend a lot on travel for services that the state no longer provides, which in turn means there is less money available for other things, including holiday-making or other leisure activities. This double twist of empowerment and disempowerment is characteristic of life in many villages on the Terskii Coast.

The high degree of freedom to structure one's daily routine has made certain lifestyles possible in Chavan'ga. In the next section, I introduce several individuals with whom I sat at the kitchen table particularly often and spoke about the choices and decisions they made in order to fulfil their hopes and aspirations.

Life histories over "liquidation" of time

Andrei: a curious explorer

I usually visited Andrei's family in the evening when he and his wife were back home from work. I would come with a genuine intention to pop in for an hour, and end up leaving around midnight. Their incredible hospitality never ceased to impress me: every time they would invite me to join them for a family meal, and then magically squash in an extra chair by the tiny table in the very confined kitchen space.

Andrei loves travelling along the Terskii Coast and seizes any opportunity to vanish on his snowmobile or motorbike. He enjoys the beauty of the coast and often takes a camera with him to record a spectacular dawn or a giant pile of foam thrown against the rocks by the storm. Andrei has an extended digital archive of landscape photographs on his computer at home; showing them to me, he would not stop commenting on the beauty of the local landscape and how many interesting places there are in the area. Before marriage, he would often embark upon spontaneous trips, leaving the village unexpectedly, satisfying his impulse to travel. This caused him occasional arguments and complaints from some villagers, he admits.

Fig. 3.1. Tundra selfie. Terskii Coast, Murmansk Oblast, 2010. Photo: Masha Shaw's interviewee (with permission), CC-BY-ND.

Andrei has always been particularly interested in history. He says that his "unhealthy attraction to museums" started after his trip to a pioneer camp in Ukraine at the age of twelve. Participation in regular excursions to cities and fortresses in Moldova, Belarus and Ukraine organised by the camp allowed Andrei to develop a deep aspiration towards visiting historical places and acquiring new information. Since then, the thirst for knowledge has become a decisive factor in Andrei's travelling.

The Soviet state recognised the educational and ideological role of tourism from the very beginning. It established a "Central Museum and Excursions Institute" and a "Scientific Research Institute of Excursions" already in the early 1920s while Russia was still emerging from the civil war (Sokolova 2002: 202). The new Soviet government saw tourism and excursions as an effective method of building socialism. Other goals of state-organised tourist and excursion programmes included the advance of citizens' cultural level, encouragement of communication among peoples of the USSR and promotion of patriotic feelings towards the socialist motherland and interest in local history (cf. Chapter 4 in this volume). A special institution was established in 1970 to coordinate excursion activities of schools, colleges and out of school organisations.

Andrei's school years were in the 1980s, which was the peak period of excursion activities in the USSR (Sedova 2004). Andrei's trip to a pioneer camp in Ukraine was a perfect example of the Soviet tourism factory at work: it contributed to nurturing Andrei's patriotism, interest in local history and desire for knowledge.

Having a curious mind himself, Andrei encourages the same attitude in his children: his five-year-old son once asked him what a zebra is, which made Andrei determined to go on holiday to visit a zoo. Andrei's family has relatives in St Petersburg which determined his final choice of a destination for a zoo trip: "In St Petersburg there are relatives, there is a zoo, although I think probably it would have been better to travel to the zoo in Moscow". Relatives' place of residence often plays an important role in villagers' travel patterns. During the late Soviet period when the transportation system was very affordable, family members travelled thousands of kilometres to visit their relatives in other parts of the country.

Andrei's father comes from the south of Russia and Andrei remembers that throughout the 1980s his family often travelled by plane and train to visit their relatives there. Looking back at those trips today, Andrei says that making those long-distance journeys was absolutely normal for him; it was no more exceptional than to visit his grandma at the other end of Chavan'ga. Regular trips for long distances since childhood have made Andrei fearless towards travel. Andrei dreams of making a trip to Kamchatka one day. He has several cousins from his father's side living there. They have recently resumed their communication via the social networking site VKontakte. Kamchatka is in the Russian Far East and the vast distance is the main factor that prevents Andrei from travelling. However, when I made a joke that it is indeed too far to travel by snowmobile, Andrei replied that where there is a will there is a way, and that it could in fact be possible to reach Kamchatka by snowmobile via Yakutia.

Andrei's freedom to travel has been largely due to his job in a local branch of a big telecommunication company. He worked in the *kolkhoz* as an unskilled labourer before. The *kolkhoz* job was binding and physically demanding, and the salary was too low for Andrei to purchase his own vehicle and fulfil his travel aspirations. After Andrei left the *kolkhoz* for the telecommunication company, he was soon able to save some money and buy himself a motorcycle first and a snowmobile a bit later. Andrei regularly buys second hand vehicles or spare parts and assembles things himself. He has accumulated so many cars and spare parts that a number of them remain unused and stand outside his house, open to wind and precipitation — a fact that has not gone unnoticed by other villagers.

What makes Andrei stand out in the village is his love of travelling just for the sake of it rather than out of necessity. Some people in Chavan'ga find Andrei's investments into vehicles and travel highly unpractical and his spontaneous trips irresponsible. For Andrei, however, such travels are an ultimate expression of his aspirations as they satisfy his inquisitive attitude towards the world and his love of the place he lives in. Andrei says his family were the first in Chavan'ga to take their children on holiday to the seaside in the south. Andrei, his wife and their children regularly go on vacation together: this usually implies travelling over long distances which costs a lot of money for a large family with modest means. Andrei's next dream for a family holiday is to go abroad once their children are a bit older.

Such travelling for leisure is something that very few families in Chavan'ga do. It took Andrei years to persuade his friend in the village to take his family on holiday to a resort in the south of Russia. The reason for villagers' reluctance to go on holiday is not always the lack of means but also a particular attitude that travel has to be utilitarian in order to be considered worthwhile.

One couple in the village finally decided to go on holiday outside Chavan'ga after many vacations spent in the village. Their children advised them to go to a sea resort somewhere abroad. The couple's final choice, however, was a health spa in a town nearby. They rejected the idea of an overseas resort on the grounds that lying on the beach was a waste of money; at least a trip to a health spa allowed them to conduct a useful holiday and ultimately feel good about the money spent. Every time the couple talked about their trip they felt they had to justify their "luxurious" expenditure by stressing its use and health benefit.

People in the city have always been subject to more pressure and incentive to travel for leisure, due to a higher degree of their exposure to media and stories about other people's travels, higher average incomes, and better access to spare money and infrastructure. At the same time, it remains rather an exception for the rural population in Russia to travel regularly for leisure. It therefore requires a particular stance towards travelling to lead a life such as that of Andrei, in a social environment that does not necessarily approve of the choices and behaviours involved. My next protagonist had to put up with even stronger disapproval of his lifestyle choice by the local community.

Anton: a cool ranger

My kitchen table conversations with Anton mainly happened at my place. People in Chavan'ga do not lock their houses during the day, and I was prepared to hear a knock on the door at any time. Anton, like many other young people in Chavan'ga dropped in on a daily basis, sometimes several times a day, for a quick catch up or cup of tea. The spontaneous nature of those visits was something I missed most when I was back in the city.

Anton was born in Chavan'ga in the early 1990s and has lived in the village most of his life apart from a few years in a boarding school in the centre of the *raion*, three years at a vocational school in a regional town, and a few months of employment in a city. The most frequent story that people in the village told me about Anton is that relatives had arranged a good job for him in the city as a mechanic in a big company that cooperates with foreign countries and involves opportunities to earn good money and travel abroad. Anton worked there for a few months and came back to the village for good. He now works in the *kolkhoz*, doing various seasonal jobs. Everybody from whom I heard this story disapproves of Anton's choice not to stay in the city.

Anton says he really likes his current life in the village, where he can go hunting, fishing, or travelling in the forest and tundra with other men. He cannot stay indoors for too long and needs to regularly escape to nature. At the same time, he emphasises that he can move to the city at any time once he has had enough of the village. Anton enjoys the ease and freedom of life in the village. People in Chavan'ga often told me that one needs less money to live a decent life in the village compared to the city. As boys in the village put it, problems start as soon as they arrive in the city: they have to buy more clothes and deal with various bureaucracies. In the village, on the other hand, they can get by with one pair of trousers and live without having to deal with any paperwork for years. Anton is on good terms with the *kolkhoz* chairman, which allows him to enjoy a certain flexibility in his work regime. He is one of very few young men among *kolkhoz* workers, and the chairman encourages his enthusiasm and passion by often assigning him tasks that involve his favourite pastimes.

Fig. 3.2. Adventure calling! Kamenka River, Terskii Coast, Murmansk Oblast, 2014. Photo: Masha Shaw's interviewee (with permission), CC-BY-ND.

Anton believes that a job should be primarily for pleasure and not just for money. He quit the promising job in the city because the schedule was too rigid and because life in the city would not allow him to enjoy the kind of activities he is most passionate about. This speaks to two interrelated phenomena that characterise life in contemporary Russian society: young people put stronger emphasis on finding a job that is close to their aspirations compared to their parents' generation; work and leisure merge into one another as boundaries between them start to blur.

Older villagers often say that young people these days are irresponsible, lazy, and are after easy money. What is not taken into account in these observations is the idea that many young people might in fact be after a job that is close to their heart rather than just any job. To be able to choose a desired job in today's Russia is only partially a structural privilege in Pierre Bourdieu's (1984) sense of people's choices being conditioned by their class positions within the society; it is also very much, and increasingly so, a matter of one's values and aspirations. The ever-growing prominence of the role of leisure in contemporary society might further affect young people's attitudes towards work, making them more fastidious in their job choices.

Leisure and work were not strictly differentiated in pre-industrial society. Leisure as a mass phenomenon emerged as a result of industrialisation towards the end of the nineteenth century, when working days were shortened and workers subsequently had more free time; in this period, work became strictly differentiated from leisure time (Kucher 2012: 45). The last few decades have seen a growing tendency for work and leisure to merge again, albeit on different grounds. In pre-industrial society, life for most people was primarily work, while leisure activities were interwoven into it; in post-industrial society, leisure activities often become a decisive factor in one's choice of work. Increasingly people in Russia take on jobs as a result of choice rather than their structural positions within society; this has further blurred the boundary between work and leisure.

Anton combines work and leisure in a way that brings him satisfaction and contentment. He knows what he wants, what is important for him and is very explicit about it. He settled in the village not because he has adopted "a taste for necessity which implies a form of adaptation to and consequently acceptance of the necessary, a resignation to the inevitable" (Bourdieu 1984: 372). He made a deliberate choice to move to Chavan'ga because it allowed him to pursue a lifestyle he desired. While some adults in the village might not approve of his choice to move back to the village, "at least he is doing something" — as one villager put it — "instead of ruining himself with drink". Always keeping busy is an aspiration of my next protagonist who finds moral comfort and satisfaction in being constantly active.

Vera: active leisure as moral commitment

I visited Vera more than any other person in Chavan'ga. No matter how busy she was, she would always make a break to sit down with her guests: a kettle would be put on and everyone would gather around the kitchen table for a good couple of hours. There was never a shortage of visitors in Vera's house: guests of all manner seemed to feel equally comfortable and welcome.

Vera was born in Chavan'ga and lived there until she was about fifteen when her family moved to Murmansk. After school she went to a college in a big city in the south of Russia and then returned to work in Chavan'ga after graduation. A year later she got married to a man from Moldova and they both moved to his home country. Six years later they came back to Murmansk and lived and worked there until retirement.

Vera tried to come to Chavan'ga at least every other vacation while they lived in Moldova, and then every single year after they moved back to Murmansk. The north had always appealed to Vera and she decided to eventually move back despite an attractive opportunity to live and work in a city in the south with a more favourable climate and better access to fresh fruits and vegetables.

Vera started to think of moving to Chavan'ga for good when her parents died and there was nobody left in the village to look after the family house. It took Vera a few years before she could realise her dream, the main obstacles being her husband's poor health and her young daughter still needing support. She then moved spontaneously when an employment opportunity came up in Chavan'ga. Vera's decision was a shock for many of her friends and relatives. She was already a few years into her retirement; and moving to a harsh climate to live in an old, poorly insulated house in a hard-to-reach place at her age sounded like a reckless idea.

Yet, Vera was prepared to realise her dream. She came back to Chavan'ga in the hope of doing something purposeful for the village. She feels very strongly about preserving Chavan'ga for future generations. She sees a way to do it through preserving her own house and through fostering love towards the village among her own children and grandchildren. Vera firmly believes that for children to love the village, there must be a house for them to come to. The more well-maintained houses there are in the village, the better the chance of a long-term future (Nakhshina 2013: 220–21). Vera took up a job in Chavan'ga to save some money to repair the house — a first step towards realising her goal.

Fig. 3.3. Never an idle moment: crossing the River Chavan'ga on the way to work, 2011. Photo: Masha Shaw's interviewee (with permission), CC-BY-ND.

Chavan'ga has always been a source of moral strength for Vera: simply being there, taking regular walks along the seacoast, seeing familiar objects all take her worries away. If she were going through difficult times, she would often come to Chavan'ga to be healed from her troubles. Chavan'ga serves as both the inspiration for Vera's outlook on life and a means to live it. Vera feels she needs to repay her moral debt to the village by preserving it for the future: Chavan'ga gives her moral and physical strength, and if she maintains her house, then maybe someone else in the future can live there and benefit from Chavan'ga's healing power.

A house in the village requires a lot of work. Whenever I visited Vera for tea, she was never idle. She says she is not used to being at rest and doing nothing. Even during her vacation, she would always work hard. She gets very tired by the end of the day in the village. Yet, when she sits down in the evening, she enjoys this overall pleasant feeling of tiredness, as she feels that she has done something useful: another day has passed with good reason.

Vera has never been on a beach holiday: leisure for her is imbued with moral value and she has to be active even during rest periods in order to feel good and useful. Chavan'ga is the perfect place for such a lifestyle of moral leisure as life in the village requires a lot of work.

Many villagers think that the city, on the other hand, spoils, corrupts and makes one idle and even ill.

For Vera, keeping busy is more than just performing everyday physical tasks: it is a way to pursue her aspirations and moral values. By putting all her free time and resources into the house, which is actually shared between her and her numerous siblings, she lives out her ultimate dream of serving Chavan'ga and preserving it for future generations.

I miss the long cosy hours I used to spend around the kitchen table in Vera's house. Warm and welcoming homes such as hers guarantee that Chavan'ga will indeed continue into the future, as having visited once, people will want to come back.

Conclusion: lifestyle as a creative engagement with place

The limitations of the *kolkhoz* system during the Soviet period, and later the post-Soviet deterioration of provision of state care and services in rural areas accompanied and partially fuelled Soviet urbanisation, which has overall contributed to an unattractive image of life in the countryside in Russia. Able-to-work people who stayed in the village, or left for town and then came back to the countryside, are widely perceived to have somehow failed in life, or reduced their chances to succeed. The idea that those who live in the village — especially young people — have missed out on opportunities that modern life has on offer prevails among contemporary Russian city dwellers.

The life stories presented in this chapter suggest a more optimistic view of contemporary rural Russia. Andrei, Anton, and Vera all hold very strong views on why they have chosen to live in the village and are very explicit about their choices. They deliberately followed their values and aspirations, rather than simply ending up there by default. Chavan'ga has served as both an initial inspiration and ultimate means for achieving their goals. Their lifestyles are manifested in distinct ways of engaging with place, ways that bring them personal fulfilment and satisfaction.

One's strive for self-fulfilment is always creative. This implies a particular understanding of creativity which is profoundly different from a mainstream approach. The latter understands creativity as producing something new and original and thus sees creation as an achievement (result) (for an overview of this approach, see Pope 2005). An alternative view sees creativity as self-fulfilling and therefore understands creation as a process. Peter Evans and Geoff Deehan (1988) refer to the root of creativity in the Greek verb *krainen* (to fulfil). They suggest that "by this definition, anyone who fulfils his or her potential, who expresses an inner drive or capacity [...] may be said to be creative" (Evans & Deehan 1988: 21).

Chavan'ga provides a rich field of dynamic potentialities to its dwellers. Andrei, Anton, and Vera actively use their native place's specific affordances to pursue their values and dreams. Their expressive lifestyles are an outward manifestation of their creativity, as they allow these individuals to follow an inner drive and fulfil their ultimate potential. Lifestyle is often seen as manifested in external attributes, such as appearances or pastimes. But lifestyle can also be expressed in the way someone engages with the place they live in, when this engagement is an articulation of their ultimate values and aspirations.

The choices that Russian rural dwellers are making cannot be understood in isolation from the globalising trends that are transforming Russia as a whole, including its urban populations. The lifestyles of Andrei, Anton, and Vera are intersubjective as they speak to larger processes (Jackson 1998) that have been affecting Russian society and shaping people's aspirations and values: from the Soviet focus on the educational and ideological role of leisure to a more recent trend among younger generations to put more emphasis on finding an occupation that resonates with their aspirations.

Another important factor is the changing nature of Russian remote areas more generally. Caroline Humphrey speaks about new qualities that Russian remote areas have acquired in recent years. Remote places in Russia can now exercise a wide variety of previously hidden or non-existing relations of attachment: to landscape, human and non-human beings, legends as well as relations that open up new possibilities (Humphrey 2014: 9). As the Russian administrative grip has loosened in the wake of the fall of the Soviet Union, many small places have received an opportunity to be more independent in evaluating their own history and determining their future development. Many remote places have now become some kind of reservoirs of all those values that the Soviet machine tried to undermine: traditions, "authentic" ways of life, sacred places, or ancestral graves (ibid: 14–15). These transformations made remote places in Russia more attractive to people as they now offered new possibilities of personal fulfilment.

What brings the stories of my three protagonists together is that their native village allows them to be masters of their lives. It allows them to pursue their true values and aspirations manifested in their distinct lifestyles. There is a common perception that lifestyles happen in the city with its abundance of available goods and services, while the village has far too many limitations in terms of such consumables. At the same time, the life stories of Andrei, Anton, and Vera suggest that a remote place in the countryside can offer unlimited lifestyle opportunities, if we approach lifestyle as a creative process of achieving self-fulfilment rather than as the disposal of final consumable products.

References

Barker, Adele M. (ed.). 2005. *Consuming Russia: popular culture, sex, and society since Gorbachev*. Durham, NC: Duke University Press, https://doi.org/10.1215/9780822396413

Benson, Michaela & Karen O'Reilly. 2009. "Migration and the search for a better way of life: a critical exploration of lifestyle migration". *The Sociological Review*, 57 (4): 608–25, https://doi.org/10.1111/j.1467-954X.2009.01864.x

Bourdieu, Pierre. 1984 [1979]. *Distinction: a social critique of the judgement of taste*, trans. Richard Nice. London: Routledge.

Bridger, Sue. 1989. "Rural youth". In: *Soviet Youth Culture*, ed. James Riordan, pp. 83–102. Bloomington, IN: Indiana University Press, https://doi.org/10.1007/978-1-349-19932-7_4

Chaney, David. 1996. *Lifestyles*. London: Routledge, https://doi.org/10.4324/9780203137468

Evans, Peter & Geoff Deehan. 1988. *The Keys to Creativity*. London: Grafton.

Gernet, Katharina. 2012. *Vom Bleiben in Zeiten globaler Mobilität: Räume und Spielräume der Lebensgestaltung junger indigener Frauen im russischen Norden* [Staying in times of global mobility: spaces and room for manoeuvre of young indigenous women regarding their life decisions in the North of Russia]. Frankfurt am Main: Peter Lang.

Gray, Patty A. 2003. "Volga farmers and Arctic herders: common (post)socialist experiences in rural Russia". In: *The Postsocialist Agrarian Question: property relations and the rural condition*, ed. Chris Hann and the Property Relations Group, pp. 293–320. Münster: LIT Verlag.

—. 2004. "Chukotkan reindeer husbandry in the twentieth century: in the image of the Soviet economy". In: *Cultivating Arctic Landscapes: knowing and managing animals in the circumpolar North*, ed. David G. Anderson & Mark Nuttall, pp. 136–53. New York: Berghahn.

Habeck, Joachim Otto. 2011. "Introduction: cultivation, collective, and the self". In: *Reconstructing the House of Culture: community, self, and the makings of culture in Russia and beyond*, ed. Brian Donahoe & Joachim Otto Habeck, pp. 1–25. New York: Berghahn.

Hoey, Brian A. 2005. "From Pi to Pie: moral narratives of noneconomic migration and starting over in the postindustrial Midwest". *Journal of Contemporary Ethnography*, 34 (5): 586–624, https://doi.org/10.1177/0891241605279016

Humphrey, Caroline. 2001. *Marx Went Away — But Karl Stayed Behind*. Cambridge: Cambridge University Press, https://doi.org/10.3998/mpub.11004

—. [Kerolain Khamfri]. 2014. "Izmenenie znachimosti udalennosti v sovremennoi Rossii" [The changing significance of remoteness in contemporary Russia]. *Etnograficheskoe obozrenie*, 3: 8–24.

Il'in, Vladimir I. 2015. "Daushifting [sic] kak voskhodiashchaia sotsial'naia mobil'nost'" [Downshifting as upward social mobility]. *Sotsial'noe vremia*, 1: 78–90.

Jackson, Michael. 1998. *Minima Ethnographica: intersubjectivity and the anthropological project*. Chicago, IL: Chicago University Press.

Kucher, Katarina (Kukher, K.). 2012. *Park Gor'kogo: kul'tura dosuga v stalinskuiu epokhu, 1928–1941* [Gorki Park: the culture of leisure in the Stalinist epoch, 1928–1941]. Moscow: ROSSPEN.

Laius, Dmitrii L., Anna I. Alekseeva, Aleksei V. Kraikovskii & Yuliia A. Laius. 2010. "Proshloe lososevykh rek: biologicheskie i sotsio-kul'turnye aspekty" [Salmon rivers in the past: Biological, social, and cultural aspects]. In: *Liubitel'skoe rybolovstvo i sokhranenie lososevykh v Rossii*, ed. V. V. Zinichev & Yu. V. Saiapina, pp. 76–87. Moscow: Fond "Russkii losos'".

Nakhshina, Maria. 2012a. "'Without fish, there would be nothing here': attitudes to salmon and identification with place in a Russian coastal village". *Journal of Rural Studies*, 28 (2): 130–38, https://doi.org/10.1016/j.jrurstud.2012.01.014

—. 2012b. "Community interpretations of fishing outside legal regulations: a case study from northwest Russia". In: *Fishing People of the North: cultures, economies, and management responding to change*, ed. C. Carothers, K. R. Criddle, C. P. Chambers, P. J. Cullenberg, J. A. Fall, A. H. Himes-Cornell, J. P. Johnsen, N. S. Kimball, C. R. Menzies & E. S. Springer, pp. 229–41. Fairbanks, AK: Alaska Sea Grant/University of Alaska Fairbanks, https://doi.org/10.4027/fpncemrc.2012

3. *Lifestyle and Creative Engagement*

—. 2013. "The perception of the built environment by permanent residents, seasonal in-migrants and casual incomers in a village in northwest Russia". In: *About the Hearth: perspectives on the home, hearth and household in the circumpolar North*, ed. David G. Anderson, Robert P. Wishart & Virginie Vaté, pp. 200–22. New York: Berghahn.

Nefedova T. G., N. E. Pokrovskii & A. I. Treivish. 2016. "Urbanization, counterurbanization, and rural-urban communities facing growing horizontal mobility". *Sociological Research*, 55 (3): 195–210, https://doi.org/1 0.1080/10610154.2016.1245570

Pesmen, Dale. 2000. *Russia and Soul: an exploration*. Ithaca, NY: Cornell University Press.

Pope, Rob. 2005. *Creativity: theory, history, practice*. London: Routledge, https:// doi.org/10.4324/9780203695319

Puuronen, Vesa, Pentti Sinisalo & Larissa Shvets. 2000. *Youth in a Changing Karelia: a comparative study of everyday life, future orientations and political culture of youth in north-west Russia and eastern Finland*. Aldershot: Ashgate.

Ries, Nancy. 1997. *Russian Talk: culture and conversation during Perestroika*. Ithaca, NY: Cornell University Press.

Schweitzer, Peter, Peter Sköld, Olga Ulturgasheva et al. 2015. "Cultures and identities". In: *Arctic Human Development Report: regional processes and global linkages*, ed. Joan Nymand Larsen & Gail Fondahl, pp. 105–50. Copenhagen: Nordic Council of Ministers, https://doi.org/10.6027/TN2014-567

Sedova, Natal'ia A. 2004. *Kul'turno-prosvetitel'nyi turism* [Cultural and educational tourism]. Moscow: Sovetskii sport.

Shubin, Sergei. 2006. "The changing nature of rurality and rural studies in Russia". *Journal of Rural Studies*, 22: 422–40, https://doi.org/10.1016/j. jrurstud.2006.02.004

Sokolova, Marina V. 2002. *Istoriia turisma* [History of tourism]. Moscow: Masterstvo.

Stammler, Florian & Aitalina Ivanova. 2016. "Resources, rights and communities: extractive mega-projects and local people in the Russian Arctic". *Europe-Asia Studies*, 68 (7): 1220–1244, https://doi.org/10.1080/09668136.2016.1222605

Wilson, Emma. 2016. "What is the social licence to operate? Local perceptions of oil and gas projects in Russia's Komi Republic and Sakhalin Island". *The Extractive Industries and Society*, 3 (1): 73–81, https://doi.org/10.1016/j. exis.2015.09.001

4. Holiday Convergences, Holiday Divergences

Siberian Leisure Mobilities Under Late Socialism and After

Luděk Brož and Joachim Otto Habeck

It is the summer of 2010, and Viktor is walking with a couple of his friends towards one end of a spacious village. They are on holiday in a village called Chemal, a well-known tourist area of the Altai Republic. Chemal has a dam, with a beach where tourists flock when the weather is good, and a connected open-air market and amusement park. Tourists can also try white-water rafting on the Katun' River or visit an Orthodox chapel built on a rock island in the river. Absorbed in such leisurely activities, Viktor and his friends are missing out on visiting another well-known attraction of Chemal: a private museum of Altaian culture. This is the realm of Raisa, an enthusiastic woman in her sixties dressed in a traditional Altaian costume. As she guides groups of visitors through several *aiyl*, traditional Altaian hexagonal houses, Raisa tells them about the native population of the Altai Republic — about traditional means of subsistence, social organisation, and costumes. Visitors can slip on an Altaian coat and take a picture of themselves dressed in it. At the end of the visit, tourists usually purchase some traditional souvenirs and try national food, such as a rock-hard dried cheese called *kurut*.

   https://doi.org/10.11647/OBP.0171.04

This chapter is based on the holiday-making experiences of these two informants, Viktor and Raisa. Their biographies mirror distinct forms of holiday-making in Soviet times as well as the conspicuous changes that have occurred in the post-Soviet decades. One informant is from a big Siberian city, the other from a small village in the "deep" province (*glubinka*). One is Russian, the other of non-Russian ethnic identity. One is a male born in 1963, the other a female born in 1945. Seeking to embed a comparison of our two protagonists' travel biographies within a more general interpretation of changing predilections and patterns of mobility in Siberia over the last thirty years, we approach these biographies through the notion of taste and collectively sustained desires. Noting that not all the journeys our protagonists talked about were made of their own will (and not all of them were experienced positively), we keep our focus to voluntary journeys conducted to a certain destination during weekends, holidays, or summer vacations and then back home again. These journeys are associated with certain positive expectations and motivated by certain desires. Although they are individually held, these desires are crafted and shaped collectively: the idea of *what is to be desired* was and is regimented socially and politically. Such collectively shared desires point to the existence of *communities of taste*. Desires and dreams are products of taste, which itself is sustained by an individual's position in the social space and, vice versa, is what sustains that very position (e.g. Bourdieu 1984). They also reflect personal sensibilities (Chaney 1996; see Chapter 1) and serve as collectively shared motivations for leisure and holiday journeys, which in this chapter we describe as *noble causes*. More so than in many other spheres of life, tourism carries the promise of making dreams come true (temporarily).

Apart from drawing on the concept of *communities of taste* and pointing out the changes such communities have undergone over the past few decades, this chapter explicates how ethnicity has acquired new value not just in making certain destinations more attractive than others, but also as a *noble cause* in the self-perception of the travelling individual. Moreover, we aim to uncover shared spatial imaginaries,[1] expectations, and actual practices of travelling that have shaped holiday-making and leisure mobility in Siberia from late socialist times to the 2010s.

---

1   We owe the concept of spatial imaginaries to Joseph Long, who discusses this term in more detail in the following chapter.

The chapter is arranged roughly chronologically, divided into sections on so-called late socialism (see Yurchak 1997), the 1990s, and the 2000s. To add nuance to the otherwise highly schematic character of such a comparison, for each period we will describe what makes each of our informants typical or unique in his or her social context and what other patterns of holiday-making were in operation in such contexts. Building on this debate, we will then discuss more generally how vacation was framed in terms of rest and exercise in official Soviet discourse; how practices and tastes of holiday-making have developed over the last thirty to fifty years; and how touristic self-exploration in Russia and beyond has been shifting between visions of a unified modernisation project and visions of a particular indigenous magic.

Before we proceed to discuss the travel biographies and practices of holiday-making in Soviet and post-Soviet times, let us briefly introduce our two protagonists:

Raisa was born in 1945 in the Shebalino region of what is now the Altai Republic. Raisa is an Altaian. Due to her late husband's job, she has lived in almost every part of the Altai Republic while working as a teacher. Raisa lives in Chemal on her own, but is often accompanied by her daughter and grandchildren, who spend the whole summer with her every year. Even though she has retired from teaching, she is very active in running her family's small museum and Altaian cultural centre in Chemal. Raisa has two daughters and many grandchildren.

Viktor, born in 1963, grew up in a suburb of Novosibirsk and has lived there all his life. Viktor is Russian. At the beginning of his career, he worked for Novosibirsk's public transport system as a trolley driver and clerk. Since 2006, he has had no regular employment. Between 2011 and 2012 Viktor was involved in commerce and managed to accumulate quite a lot of money. Viktor is single and has neither children nor a permanent partner, but has a large network of friends. He owns a flat and earns his livelihood by renting out two of the three rooms.

Tourism and holiday-making during late socialism

Raisa attended four years of elementary school in her native village before moving to the village of Shebalino, the regional centre, to attend boarding school. After finishing her fifth year there in 1958, the best pupils of the year — including Raisa — were taken by lorry to Gorno-Altaisk, the capital of the administrative unit that is now the Altai Republic, for sightseeing. She remembers details of what they saw very well, as it was the only travel experience of her childhood; she spent all her holidays working with her parents, who were herders. She nevertheless recalls that her mother went to a pioneer camp in the early 1930s, something that the Soviet Union was unable to provide for her war-born generation (see also Zubkova 1998).[2]

After finishing school, Raisa moved to Gorno-Altaisk to attend a pedagogical institute to become a teacher. She was admitted to study foreign languages in the city of Barnaul, but was too timid to go, as she had never been there. In Gorno-Altaisk she met her future husband, an Altaian engineer, who soon became a member of the Communist Party — a "party man" (*partiinyi chelovek*). Their first daughter was born in Raisa's final year of studies. Because the Communist Party sent her husband from one district to the next, Raisa's family often had to change residence and hence lived in many different parts of the Altai region. Raisa's husband was frequently stressed and overworked, yet his position made a crucial difference to the family's holiday-making possibilities. She emphasised that thanks to his managerial status, unlike "ordinary citizens", he was entitled to *putëvki* (holiday vouchers) for two: himself and his spouse.

As a distinct and widespread phenomenon of holiday travel in the Soviet era, it is worthwhile to take a more detailed look at the distribution of *putëvki*. Genealogically, the voucher system goes back to Thomas Cook and his coupon system, yet in the Soviet Union the *putëvka* represented "a nonmarket mechanism for the allocation of the scarce

---

2   The Organisation of Young Pioneers of the Soviet Union (established in 1922) played an important ideological role in socialising children into socialist values. "Pioneers" were children between the ages of ten and fifteen. Membership in the organisation was often preceded by membership in the Little Octobrist/October kids' organisation (for children between the ages of seven and nine) and followed by membership in the Komsomol (the All-Union Leninist Young Communist League). After World War II, Organisations of Young Pioneers were also established in other countries of the socialist bloc. Pioneer camps differed from holiday resorts with permanent structures; rather, they resembled Boy Scout camps. Life in pioneer camps was ideally disciplined, aiming at improving the health, hygiene habits, and ideological loyalty of future socialist — and eventually communist — subjects.

resource of a place on a tour or in a tourist destination. [… T]he economic
organisation of Soviet tourism revolved around the voucher, rather than
disposable income, personal savings, or consumer demand" (Gorsuch
& Koenker 2006: 4). People were most often able to obtain *putëvki* via
the regional branches of the Trade Union (*Profsoiuz*), allegedly based on
the merit of the worker, but in practice *putëvki* were often acquired on
the basis of informal favours known as *blat* (cf. Ledeneva 1998, 2006). In
the late Soviet period, the two main genres of travel — recreational and
educational tourism — were supervised and managed by two different
councils within the overarching structure of the Trade Union. The
Central Council of Health Resorts distributed *putëvki* to spas (*kurort*),
sanatoriums (*sanatorii*), health-oriented vacation centres (*pansionat*), and
recreational centres (*dom otdykha*). The Central Council of Tourism and
Excursions issued vouchers for guided tours and supervised both the
tourist bases and the small number of motels and camping sites. Some
of the vouchers were given for free to exemplary workers in recognition
of their commitment; most vouchers were sold at subsidised prices,
i.e. the Trade Union covered thirty per cent of the nominal cost of the
voucher. A *putëvka* entitled the holder to accommodation and board at
his or her destination; in the case of a tour, it also covered transportation
expenses. Vouchers entitling holders to curative procedures in spas and
sanatoriums had to be paired with a doctor's prescription (*spravka*);
there was also an option to purchase medical treatment on the spot
without accommodation and board, which was called *kursovka* (see, for
example, Noack 2006: 282–85, 302).[3]

---

3   Noack's (2006: 302) statement that "The heavily subsidized vouchers were normally
    sold at 30 roubles" seems to be incorrect. We have heard from several sources that
    thirty per cent of the cost of the voucher was covered by the Trade Union, while
    the rest was to be covered by the travelling individual. Usually, a *putëvka* was valid
    for one person only and the Trade Union would allocate one at a time to each
    lucky worker. Cadres of party *nomenklatura* of Raisa's husband's standing were
    entitled to an additional voucher for their spouse. People in higher *nomenklatura*
    ranks were entitled to even more privileged holiday-making in restricted-access
    holiday resorts and sanatoriums. Special holiday-making regimes were some of the
    numerous privileges enjoyed by the *de facto* ruling class of the Soviet Union (see, for
    example, Andrle 1994: 254–55; Matthews 2011). A famous depiction of a restricted-
    access catering facility for members of the Union of Soviet Writers can be found in
    Mikhail Bulgakov's novel *Master and Margarita*. Figure 5.2 in Chapter 5 shows three
    young women who got to know each other during a *putëvka* to Crimea in 1991; one
    of them is Nastia, interviewed by Joseph Long.

Fig. 4.1. In the spa (*kurort*) of Arshan in Tunka District (Buryatia), the local administration kept track of "the number of patients that underwent treatment in the spa". Since its pre-revolutionary beginnings, the spa claims to have received steadily growing number of visitors. At present, the two sanatoriums of Arshan attract customers with medical treatment, health and relaxation for the whole family (http://kurort-arshan.ru). Photograph by Luděk Brož, 2011, CC-BY.

In the early 1970s, Raisa's husband got a *putëvka* to the well-known spa of Piatigorsk, in the south of the European part of Russia, about 4,000 kilometres away from their home. Unlike her husband, Raisa said she was more interested in sightseeing (*chtoby posmotret'*) than treatment (*lechenie*). In Piatigorsk she was very enthusiastic about places connected to Lermontov's life, while her husband simply wanted to relax. In her words, she always made him see places there. Having obtained the *putëvka*, the couple decided to take their younger daughter with them, as she was often ill (their older daughter spent that summer with Raisa's mother). The *putëvka*, however, was only valid for two people. Therefore, they found private accommodation for their daughter in Piatigorsk in the flat of an Altaian girl who had married there. Their daughter only spent the nights in this flat; the rest of the day she was with her parents and ate in the spa canteen (*stolovaia*) with them.

To improve her rather poor health, Raisa's younger daughter later went to several children's sanatoriums (*detskii sanatorii*),[4] including one

---

4   Similar in function to spas, sanatoriums provided important sites for holiday-making in Soviet — and, to some degree, post-Soviet — times. Their centrality

in Belokurikha, a spa in the piedmont of Altai some 150 kilometres away from Gorno-Altaisk. Their older daughter, on the other hand, once went to the famous pioneer camp Artek as a reward for her good grades in school.[5]

During late socialism, Raisa and her husband were very active holiday-makers, which was rather unusual in Altaian rural areas. Raisa is aware that this is partly due to the fact that her husband was a high-ranking party official; therefore, as previously mentioned, they could enjoy comparatively exceptional access to *putëvka* trips for two people. Raisa nevertheless suggests that an important part of the story was their will to travel, which she associates with professions like teachers, doctors, or clerks of all kinds — in other words, with small-town and rural intellectual elites. In contrast to them, she believes the collective-farm herders largely did not want to travel far on their holidays. They preferred to rest in the mountains at *arzhan suu* (healing springs) and other sacred sites in the region. One of our informants called this *otdykh po-altaiski* ("rest in the Altaian way"), which, among other things, might implicitly classify Soviet holiday-making styles as "Russian".

Raisa went with her husband to Kislovodsk (another spa in the southern part of European Russia) twice, and to Belokurikha three times. Her last trip of that era took place in 1988, after she had received a *putëvka* in recognition of her excellent work performance from her employer, the education department of the municipal administration. She went to one of the Black Sea resorts for a month by airplane. On the way back, she had a lay-over in Barnaul and stayed overnight with her younger daughter, who was studying there at the time. Raisa brought all kinds of presents for her family, especially clothes for her

---

shows that one's holiday, though officially recreational, was often justified by *lechenie* (treatment of illnesses). As Kesküla (2018: 550) has aptly put it, a sanatorium was not a place for "ordinary holiday"; rather, it offered informal sociability in combination with *lechenie*. Raisa and other informants used such expressions as *ozdorovitel'nyi* (convalescence tourism) or *lechebnyi turizm* (medical treatment tourism). Depending on the sanatorium, such treatment could vary from something very close to hospitalisation in a regular hospital to what we might perceive more as wellness hotel relaxation, where the medical aspect is absent. While for adults a stay in a sanatorium meant time off work, children's sanatoriums offered school attendance for their little clients.

5   Youth camps (*molodezhnyi lager'*) and pioneer camps (*pionerskii lager'*), etc., were managed by separate organisations. They deserve a closer analysis, a task that goes beyond the scope of this chapter. Therefore, these forms of holiday travel are mentioned only occasionally here.

daughters. When she landed in Gorno-Altaisk, no one came to meet her; she surmised that her husband must be very busy and made her way back to their flat herself. That evening when he came home, she found out that he had just been instructed by the party to become chairman of a collective farm, which required his family to move to Chemal, 120 kilometres from Gorno-Altaisk. Tearfully, Raisa accepted the last move of her career. This move inadvertently defined the circumstances under which she and her family encountered the breakdown of socialism — in what would later become one of the most touristy areas of the Altai Republic.

Viktor still remembers many details of his first holiday: back in 1969, as a young boy, he went by train in a third-class sleeper (*platskart*) to the famous Black Sea city of Sochi with his mother and an older male cousin. His father could not go with them — Viktor thinks now in hindsight that his father probably liked the opportunity to do his own thing. The journey by train took three or four days. The stay in Sochi was based on informal arrangements. Immediately after their arrival in Sochi, Viktor's mother phoned a female friend, also a holiday guest from Novosibirsk, who helped them find private accommodation for two weeks. They soon settled in lodging provided by a landlady, one of many residents in Sochi who privately let rooms. But their private accommodation had its drawbacks: there was no electricity in the room, thus one could not prepare hot food there. Viktor, his mother, and his cousin went to a canteen (*stolovaia*) for lunch, though not every day. There were quite a few canteens in the city, yet they did not have sufficient seating to cater for all the holiday guests in the city. The queues for these canteens were awfully long — up to two hours. Restaurants did exist, but their prices were rather prohibitive. Those who had received accommodation in one of the hotels or sanatoriums were better off: each sanatorium had its own cafeteria or restaurant where the guests would take their lunch in shifts (this system is still in practice in many sanatoriums). Viktor remembers how impressed he was by the sea, but after two weeks he felt ready to go back to Novosibirsk, where he would see his relatives, neighbours, and friends; he looked forward to telling them so many exciting things.

Our protagonists' early memories of travel mainly fall into the late 1960s and 1970s, a period when recreational travel and tourism experienced rapid development. Noack (2006: 281) states "that the number of Soviet domestic tourists more than doubled between 1965 and 1980" and holiday travel became a mainstream activity — for the urban and educated parts of Soviet society, at least. However, the state-provided sector of infrastructure in tourism and recreation always lagged behind the growing number of travellers and their demands. This made many travellers opt for informal arrangements and practices, which came to be known as *dikii* ("wild") tourism. Raisa's account of taking her daughter to Piatigorsk without *putëvka* and Viktor's account of his trip to Sochi resemble Noack's (2006) description of the interplay of "wild" and organised tourism in Anapa, another important Black Sea resort, in the same period. Their accounts illustrate that in late Soviet times, tourist accommodation, catering, and services were intended to serve the demands and desires of visitors who came via the approval and arrangement of their factory, office, Trade Union, etc., not of visitors who came on their own initiative. Nevertheless, the latter often had to rely on the state-provided tourism infrastructure and used it in informal ways. Occasionally, "wild" tourists even managed to find informal accommodation in a large factory's recreational centre on the shores of the Black Sea.

In 1984, Viktor was declared the "best trolley driver in Novosibirsk" and he was rewarded for his outstanding work performance with a two-week, all-expenses-paid journey to a youth holiday centre (*molodezhnyi lager'*) in Kanev, Ukraine. This part of Viktor's story illustrates the management of social recognition in Soviet society. While only a limited number of workers were granted such a privilege, there was an established mechanism for the allocation of such rewards. The local branches of the Trade Union distributed complimentary tours (along with other forms of recognition; see Habeck 2011). In line with — and as a model for — other socialist countries,[6] the function of the Trade Union in the Soviet Union, where conflicts between employers and employees supposedly no longer existed, was not a form of political mediation. Instead, it involved the distribution of benefits and entitlements to particular forms of consumption.

---

6   In the case of the German Democratic Republic, Görlich (2012) has conducted a study on the history of the FDGB-Feriendienst (the holiday service of the Trade Union); see also Moranda (2006). On the adoption of the Soviet model in socialist Romania, see Light (2013).

In the years to follow, Viktor took a few business trips (*komandirovka*) for professional training courses to cities in the European part of the Soviet Union, but he mainly conducted journeys on his own initiative, investing a significant part of his income into what he described as spontaneous hops by airplane to such cities as Kiev, Khar'kov, Vilnius, Riga, and Leningrad. Thus, while having some experience along the lines of organised and state-provided complimentary travel, Viktor mostly travelled on the basis of individual, informal arrangements.

Precursors and "noble causes" of socialist holiday worlds

As the first part of our comparative travel biography of Raisa and Viktor has shown, leisure mobility under late socialism did have some commonalities with leisure mobility in Western countries, i.e. those on the other side of the so-called "iron curtain". In the 1970s, for example, the seaside resort holiday was a mainstream aspiration in the Soviet Union as much as it was in Western Europe. To a certain degree, the reasons for this could be called historical. Considering English historians' assertions that "the roots of our own recreational practices and beliefs about leisure lie in the nineteenth century" (Lowerson & Myerscough 1977: 1; quoted in Baker 1979: 85), we are tempted to say the same about the leisure practices of Raisa and Viktor. Industrialisation created work "organised as a relatively time-bound and space-bound activity, separated off from play, religion and festivity" (Urry 2002: 19), which was a major change when compared to pre-industrial spatial-temporal divisions of life (see Thomas 1964). In effect, modernity broke up "the 'leisure class,' capturing its fragments and distributing them to everyone" (MacCannell 1999: 37).

Such democratisation of leisure nevertheless posed a challenge: "Viewed from above, leisure constituted a problem whose solution required the building of a new social conformity — a play discipline to complement the work discipline that was the principal means of social control in an industrial capitalist society" (Baker 1979: 82). Hence "In Victorian England, partly in response to a perceived threat of social and political disorder, and partly out of a wish to improve the conditions of working-class life, reformers embraced leisure as a means of educating and edifying the masses" (Parratt 1999: 471). The leisure of the growing working classes therefore became a concern of the upper and upper-middle classes — the patronising, philanthropic idea of "rational recreation" was born (cf. Cunningham 1980; Rosenbaum 2015). Leisure mobility soon became one of the building blocks of rational recreation, enabled — like the spatial-temporal leisure slot itself — by important socio-technological changes of that time.

Without a doubt, Britain was the vanguard of changes leading to the emergence of tourism and organised travel in the nineteenth century. The specific factors behind the trend were summarised by Scott Lash and John Urry (1994: 260) as follows:

> rising real incomes; rapid urbanization with pronounced levels of class segregation; new transportation technologies such as the railway and the steamship; the systematizing of work and the increased regulation of the hours and conditions of labour; novel methods of facilitating and organizing travel; and the development of a number of romanticized 'place-myths' to attract potential travellers. Travel therefore came to be both organizationally possible and desired by large numbers of people, beginning with the more affluent sections of the English working class.

The democratisation of leisure and the consequent rise of leisure mobility pioneered in Britain was soon followed in other European nations and the United States. Imperial Russia was known for its urge to "catch up" with Europe by adopting, among other things, European tastes. Aristocratic and other affluent classes of Russia developed leisure mobility early on; they travelled to European spas such as Baden-Baden or Karlovy Vary, but they also initiated the development of spas and similar resorts in Russia. Although other segments of Russian society mimicked the aristocracy and affluent members of the bourgeoisie, more significant was the democratisation of leisure initiated during the industrialisation and urbanisation of the early Soviet Union. In 1936, the Soviet state even codified the right to relaxation in its constitution (Article 119). Interestingly, as in Britain decades earlier, such development created a concern about the way leisure time was spent, which led to an ideology similar to "rational recreation". In the early years of the Soviet industrialisation and urbanisation process, just like in Britain, members of the upper classes (especially women) voluntarily took on the civilising mission (cf. Parratt 1999; Volkov 2000). Soon, however, the task was taken over by the state.

As the civilising mission was to be accomplished during the workers' free time, in socialist ideology leisure activities were far from being fun for fun's sake. They were bound up with specific noble causes, or sensibilities (Chaney 1996). Prime among these noble causes were physical and mental health. In line with the Marxist thesis about reproduction of labour power, leisure activities were meant to reproduce "physically and ideologically healthy Soviet citizens" (Gorsuch 2003: 761; cf. Rosenbaum 2015). Holiday-making in socialism was characterised by a discourse that in effect "medicalised" what elsewhere would be understood as simply recreation and relaxation. It seems that the word "recreation" was implicitly endowed with some deeper meaning of re-creation of oneself as a good worker, able-bodied to participate in the building of a socialist society. Putting oneself together in terms of health was almost an obligation for the socialist subject while being on holiday.

The hard-core *turizm* "proper" as a kind of outdoor sport officially recognised since the early 1950s was quite a different route leading to the noble cause of physical and mental recreation. It was meant to produce healthy citizens not through medicalised rest, but through *zakalka* — training, extreme exercise, preventive strengthening of the human organism, literally a process of "hardening" as that of metals. It emphasised the agency of the *turist*, expressed through independent muscle-driven locomotion and self-reliance in the wilderness with almost military connotations. *Ozdorovitel'nyi* or *lechebnyi turizm* in sanatoriums or spas and hard-core outdoor *turizm* both thus combined ideological goals with a focus on the healthy body (constructed in each of the two in very different ways).

Apart from the medicalised or athletic recreation of healthy socialist subjects, edification and self-cultivation were noble causes of leisurely travel as well. This type of travel, called *poznavatel'nyi turizm*,[7] primarily cultivated the ideological-educational aspect, mostly omitting the aspects of physical health and the body. Trips to Soviet cities (be they Riga or Samarkand), historical sites (Shushenskoe, the location of Lenin's

---

7   In this context, *poznavatel'nyi* could be translated as "educational", "exploratory", or even "experiential".

Siberian exile, or Yasnaia Poliana, Tolstoi's estate), and picturesque landscapes (the Baltic Coast or Lake Baikal) generally included an appeal to travellers to acquaint themselves with local particularities and the place's contribution to the common Soviet project (cf. Qualls 2006: 167). This principle of unity in diversity (Chapter 8 in this volume) served as a contextualisation of the peculiar against a background of regularities in social and economic development.

All three abovementioned modes — health-focussed recreation, *turizm* as outdoor physical exercise, and tourism aiming at mental self-cultivation — were supported as noble causes of travelling by the state, regional and local administrations, the Youth League (*Komsomol*), the Trade Union, and other official institutions.[8] Motivated by these noble causes of Soviet leisure, such support was further nested in an emphasis on social equality. However, since communism (which was supposed to satisfy all people's needs) was yet to be achieved, needs, including the need for recreation, were allegedly satisfied according to one's merits under socialism. As is already apparent from the examples of Raisa and Viktor, the key instrument of distribution according to one's merits was a *putëvka* allocated by the Trade Union.

To equate the official ideologies of (late) socialism with the actual desires, imaginaries, dreams, or practices of Soviet citizens would be too simplistic; no discourse is "consumed" in the way it is "intended". Alexei Yurchak (2006) has offered what is probably the most sophisticated argument along these lines regarding late socialism in the USSR. Yurchak's thesis about the hegemony of form in this context helps us to understand equality and socialist merit as hegemonic rhetorical forms that were not fully representational of the actual practices of Soviet holiday-making. It was obvious to everyone that there was a limited number of *putëvki*, hotel beds, restaurant tables, and sanatorium facilities, and more generally a limited infrastructural capacity of the entire official tourism sector. It was also clear that one's deservingness, nominally defined as work performance, was in fact often a priority equated with one's position in the state enterprise/institution or party structure, and the recognition of one's claim and actual allocation of

---

8   For children and youth, a similar canon of motivations was in operation, even
     if their destinations, modes of travel, and mechanisms of entitlement partially
     differed from those of adults.

holiday vouchers often depended on the claimant's ability to exploit the network of informal favours (*blat*).

Creative use of the system was not limited to the exploitation of connections to obtain holiday vouchers. If holiday-makers acquired an entitlement for a certain type of holiday, it often did not fit their expectations, desires, or needs; they had to try to shape the holiday accordingly (Noack 2006: 287). The absence of *putëvki* for families was a particular sticking point in the system; anyone seeking to spend a holiday with their spouse and children had to search for ways to do so. "Wild" tourism was the most notable expression of this. Interestingly, though different from state-promoted tourism in many aspects, wild tourism did not differ that strongly in terms of destinations. Surely, numerous wild travellers went to places far off the well-trodden *putëvka* itineraries and far out of the realm of recreation as officially imagined. Nonetheless, our research findings corroborate that a large contingent of wild travellers followed the stream of official tourists, sometimes due to the sheer necessity of arrangements for family members to come along, and sometimes out of the wish to go to places that were featured as "desirable" destinations. Even our two protagonists' travel biographies bear witness to the fact that wild and organised forms of tourism were intertwined, particularly in the most prominent resorts on the Black Sea coast (cf. Noack 2006: 301).

In specific ways, the actual practices of late-socialist holiday-making re-interpreted the official emphasis on social equality and deservingness (see above); moreover, they also re-interpreted the prescribed noble causes for tourism. Intended to recreate socialist subjects physically as well as ideologically, places like Black Sea resorts in fact often worked as hubs where the latest (often western) trends, such as "The Twist" dance and connected fashions, were learnt and taken home (Yurchak 2006: 171). Mountaineering, to give another example, often took place within official structures of organised outdoor *turizm*, yet it worked as a centre of gravity for subcultures (*tusovki*) that were *vne*, i.e. outside of the Soviet ideological world, to use Yurchak's terminology (2006), if not against it outright.

Communities of taste under late socialism differed not only in their preferences, desires, or dreams of leisure travel and how these diverged from those promoted by the socialist ideology; they also differed in ways of fulfilling such desires and in utilising the system for doing so. Compared to many European nations, the Soviet Union was a relative latecomer to the process of democratisation of leisure travel. During late socialism, such democratisation allegedly achieved the ideal of equality and deservingness. In practice, however, within the shared world of late-socialist leisure travel, there were divisions correlating with regional and ethnic identity, level of education, age, and gender.

Considering, for example, Raisa's trip to Piatigorsk and Viktor's childhood trip to the Black Sea, we can see a crucial similarity: the desire to embark on leisure travel with close relatives. Nevertheless, there are some important differences. While the comparatively more highly educated Raisa did not mention a single completely self-organised trip in her narrative, Viktor started his holiday travel narrative with the experience of a "wild" tourist. Wild tourism was a much more widespread phenomenon among urban people and better-educated classes of the Soviet Union. We believe that a certain diffidence and hesitation towards self-organised travel was (and probably still is) typical for rural areas and less-educated people with less study- and work-related travel experience.[9] While Raisa stands out among our informants from the Altai Republic thanks to her account of bringing her daughter on their voucher holiday as a wild tourist, Viktor, who grew up in a large city, may be seen as more representative of informal holiday arrangements, given his experience of travel without a voucher at all.

We also came across divergent interpretations of supposedly universal (i.e. all-union) socialist values in tourism. One of the professional tourism employees in Altai, for example, mentioned the case of a holiday-maker from Uzbekistan who came to Altai on a *putëvka* for a mountaineering trip in the 1980s. Horrified that walking with a heavy pack was considered "recreation", he refused to participate in trekking, explaining this with reference to his dignity. Drawing on different sets of values and meanings, he did not consider this kind of walking appropriate for a person of his status.

---

9   Such experience helps to form what may be called "travel competencies": each kind of travel requires a certain degree of specific skills. See Chapter 2 in this volume.

Divergent travel biographies
in the first post-Soviet decade

The end of the Soviet Union in 1991 catalysed a period of Russian history that is often referred to as a decade of depression and despair.[10] This was a difficult time for most people as extreme insecurity entered their lives; for many of them, the economic transformation of the 1990s meant life at the poverty line — if not below. For Raisa and her family, however, this period was more ambivalent and less bleak. On the one hand, they certainly did not belong to the small number of people who benefited from economic deregulation and consequently could make a fortune during these years. On the other hand, Raisa's husband could be seen as belonging to what Andrle (2001) called the "Buoyant Class" in the context of the post-communist Czech Republic — i.e. the class of people achieving success regardless of the actual political climate and economic circumstances. A senior Communist Party member, Raisa's husband retired in 1993 from his position as chairman of the collective farm, but he subsequently accepted the position of regional director of Altaienergobank in Chemal. At the same time, he became active in the Altaian national revival and was elected as *aga jaisaŋ* (political leader) of the Maiman clan in 1992.[11]

In the mid-1990s, following some health problems, Raisa's husband retired from his position at the bank and focussed fully on what he regarded as "work for people", the results of which would outlive him. He decided to build a museum and cultural centre in the Ongudai region of the Altai Republic, where he had originally come from. Yet at the time, his goal was almost impossible to achieve. He did not have enough resources to contract workers or secure land, and mere social capital was not enough in a time of crisis when people were struggling to feed their families. Resourcefully, Raisa extended their garden in

---

10   This characterisation is supported by more than economic figures and the devaluation of the Russian rouble. During the 1990s, the Russian Federation witnessed an increase in mortality rate "unprecedented in a modern industrialised country in peacetime" (Men et al. 2003: 6), which was accounted for by "changes in mortality from vascular disease and violent deaths (mainly suicides, homicides, unintentional poisoning, and traffic incidents) among young and middle-aged adults" (Men et al. 2003: 1).

11   For more on the Altaian national revival in general, and the function of *jaisaŋ* in particular, see Halemba (2006: 24–27).

Chemal by purchasing two neighbouring plots, and she suggested to her husband that he could bring the timber he had purchased in Ongudai over to Chemal and build the museum in their garden. Those years were certainly hard on the family budget, yet in her story Raisa occasionally spoke about individuals from the Altai Republic's government or important state agencies who had been her husband's peers and helped with money here and there. By the end of the 1990s, Raisa's family had a museum and cultural centre in her garden that consisted of several *aiyl*, with a partially paid mortgage of some 350,000 roubles (almost 13,000 US dollars at the end of 1999).

It is not surprising that Raisa's travels, including holiday travels, were dramatically reduced during the 1990s. At the beginning of the 1990s, she went to the nearby spa of Belokurikha with her colleague during a summer holiday; her husband went there on his own the following year in the autumn. Raisa's husband once also went to a sanatorium in Barnaul to deal with his health problems. Even though his position enabled him to claim two *putëvki*, his schedule as a collective-farm chairman was simply not compatible with Raisa's schedule as an elementary school teacher (where she worked until 2008, including twelve years as a working pensioner).[12] Thus each of them individually used the *putëvka* entitlements that they had obtained via their respective employer. In the later 1990s, the system of *putëvka* practically collapsed. In Raisa's words, there were other pressing issues, especially long delays in receiving salaries and retirement-pension payments. Amidst this complicated situation, Raisa's husband used his social capital not to maintain their comparatively high living standards, but rather to realise his dream.

Nevertheless, there is a link between Raisa's husband's dream and tourism/holiday travel. The first three years of the museum's operation (between approximately 1997 and 2000) were purely non-commercial, i.e. Raisa and her husband did not charge visitors entrance fees. The museum was visited by virtually every class from each school in the Chemal region, as well as by many other classes from schools throughout the Altai Republic. After three years, Raisa said, both the regional administration and local travel agents suggested the museum start charging visitors. The regional administration organised a

---

12 Summer school holidays coincide with the peak season of agricultural work.

seminar for travel agencies at the museum, during which Raisa and her husband performed an exemplary guided tour, gave a lecture, and fed travel agency representatives samples of Altaian meals. The most important result of the seminar was an agreement with participating travel agencies on the price of tickets for the museum's first regular season — fifty roubles per person.

Even though Raisa and her husband resembled their fellow compatriots in the 1990s in terms of decreasing holiday mobility, in their case this was partly caused by voluntarily channelling their better-than-average resources to other ends. At the end of the "horrible" 1990s and the beginning of the 2000s, Raisa and her husband had not only managed to realise her husband's dream of establishing a museum and cultural centre, but also found themselves to be entrepreneurs of tourism in a region destined to boom in the years to come.

Viktor's account of travels in the 1990s is very different from Raisa's. With the end of the Soviet Union, travelling abroad became an option,[13] and Viktor applied for a passport (*zagranpasport*).[14] Germany became his favourite destination for the next twelve years. Every other year, he went to Bremen to stay with a former classmate from school and used this as a secondary home base for short stints in different German cities. He also learned the German language. Vilnius and Riga were no longer on Viktor's travel list.

Viktor's travel experiences in the 1990s exemplify the new, post-Soviet connectivities that emerged when movement and communication across the state border became less restricted. The flipside of this new prospect of journeys to the west was the almost prohibitive level of living costs in western countries throughout most of the 1990s; still, many people from Russia managed to get around on a shoestring. There was also a growing influx of tourists from abroad into Russia, including Siberia (Zuev 2013). Among other factors, the rapid development of the

13 In Soviet times, going abroad was either connected with a business trip or a package tour; in both cases, travellers were considered to be very privileged and expected to be morally steadfast against all forms of (capitalist) seduction (Gorsuch 2006, 2011; see also Natal'ia's memories in Chapter 5 of this volume).

14 In present-day Russia, authorities issue two types of passports: domestic ones, which are obligatory for every citizen aged fourteen or older, and international ones, for those who plan to travel abroad. These two types of passports also existed in the Soviet period (Matthews 2013), yet it was much harder to obtain an international passport than it is now.

Internet facilitated contacts and increased exchange in certain cultural domains.

While the Far Abroad appeared to be nearer, the Near Abroad (the successor states of the Soviet Union) moved away politically and symbolically. If in earlier times, cities like Samarkand or Riga seemed to be just around the corner, and were in fact located in the same political and discursive space, they now became "strange". Living in these places presumably became difficult for Russians as well as for nearly everybody else. Few would wish to travel for a holiday to the Central Asian republics in the 1990s when numerous individuals, ethnic Russians in particular, were trying to leave everything behind in order to migrate to Russia. The Far North and the remote regions of eastern Siberia also turned into a space of withdrawal, but not all of those who dearly wanted to leave the Far North were able to move (Heleniak 2009). For many — probably most — citizens of the Russian Federation, the 1990s were a period when habitual destinations were no longer within reach. Immobility became a primary aspect of social and personal suffering.

The economic turbulence of the 1990s did not affect Viktor that heavily, though for different reasons than in Raisa's case. Even though Viktor's job did not provide a sufficient income, Viktor was privileged inasmuch as he owns a three-room flat and does not have a family of his own; he can let two rooms and combine the revenues with his salary. Despite being very sociable with a large circle of friends, Viktor has always sought to be self-reliant. His mother used to have a *dacha*, but Viktor made it known early on that he was not keen on helping with it. Thus, unlike a large number of urban inhabitants of Russia (Caldwell 2011; Stammler & Sidorova 2015), Viktor does not think of a *dacha* as a place of recreation and self-fulfilment. And unlike many, he does not rely on familial networks of support. Moreover, he generally tries to avoid courtesy journeys to relatives. Viktor's action space, his mobility, and his travel destinations are not influenced by kinship ties, which places him in stark contrast to our other interlocutors.

Here, we have to make a detour to address some important developments of leisure mobility in 1990s Siberia that neither Viktor nor Raisa can help us exemplify. The first trend we will mention is shopping tourism. Even during (late-)socialist times, many — if not the majority of — travellers saw shopping as an important part of their holiday experience, somewhat contrary to official warnings about the "cult of things" (see Oushakine 2014). These items not only included memorabilia connected to the particular holiday destination, but also consumer goods that were otherwise hard to get in the late-socialist economy of shortages. Under late socialism, some people used their leisure mobility to supply their extended family with consumer goods or used these goods to participate in the informal economy of favours, but some also sold them on the black market. In the 1990s, this phenomenon grew considerably larger. People started to travel regularly to the borderlands with Poland, Finland, or China in order to obtain goods and use the revenue from selling them to cover their travel expenses as well as their own shopping. For some, these small side businesses were the beginning of a serious involvement in commerce that resulted in trips of a purely economic nature, rather than leisure (for an analysis of post-socialist border trade, cf. Stammler-Gossmann 2012). The passenger car was a typical commodity that inhabitants of Siberia travelled to border regions to obtain. A whole class of traders grew around the passenger car, which also served as a means of intra-Siberian leisure mobility (see Broz & Habeck 2015).

In the 1990s, Siberia also witnessed a rebirth in package tourism to Europe, luxurious trips to tropical seas, or educational tourism, all offered by newly established travel agents. While Raisa and Viktor did not partake in that segment of leisure travel emerging in the market economy, some of our informants did; its heyday nevertheless came only with the rising economic powers of Russia in the following decade.

Growth of the Siberian tourist industry in the 2000s

The stabilisation of Russia's economy at the beginning of the twenty-first century correlates with a sharp increase in holiday travel by Russia's citizens within Russia and abroad. Not surprisingly, some parts of Russia became booming holiday destinations in the 2000s. This upsurge particularly affected the Altai Republic — Raisa's home region. Parts of the present-day Altai Republic featured as destinations of both state-organised and *dikii* tourism during late socialism. During the decline of the 1990s, and much more markedly in the last fifteen years, the image of the Altai Mountains appealed to Russia's tourist industry. A place of unspoiled natural beauty, Altai started to attract thousands of tourists; nowadays, it receives hundreds of thousands of tourists annually. Some of them simply enjoy typical holiday activities like sauna, barbecue, and drinking surrounded by the scenery (see Broz & Habeck 2015); others "recharge their batteries" through the "energy" of the *genius loci* with a slightly new-age flavour, or use Altai as a playground for extreme sports such as mountaineering, white-water rafting, or paragliding.

Fig. 4.2. Tourists on the rope bridge that connects the village of Chemal with Patmos, a small island with a monastery. Photograph by Luděk Brož, 2010, CC-BY.

Chemal soon became one of the booming tourism spots in the Altai Republic. There are multiple reasons for this: a relatively mild climate; proximity to some of the big cities of south Siberia (Barnaul and Novosibirsk), which makes even a weekend visit by car manageable (Broz & Habeck 2015); and some elements of tourist infrastructure that emerged in late-socialist times. Many inhabitants of Chemal started to rent out parts of their houses or built additional housing facilities in their gardens to host tourists. A sizeable open-air market and an amusement park at the local dam started to form each tourist season. From mid-May to mid-September, Chemal's main street is flooded with visitors' cars, little kiosks offering adventurous trips on off-road vehicles or white-water rafts, and dwellers of Chemal selling their produce.

Even though the actual placement of the museum was an outcome of the circumstances of economic hardship of the 1990s, it could not have been located more thoughtfully.[15] During the summer tourist seasons that coincided with Raisa's summer holiday at school, the museum welcomed individual tourists as well as tourist groups. During the school year, the couple continued to host school excursions and acted as a showcase for visitors hosted by Raisa's husband's friends and supporters, be they politicians or entrepreneurs. The museum has since featured in most tourist guidebooks of the Altai Republic. Raisa also makes sure that leaflets advertising the museum are in wide circulation among travel agents and *turbaza* owners,[16] at least in the Chemal region.

During the 2000s, Raisa, her husband, and one of their daughters extended their involvement in the tourist business by establishing a small farm-like chalet some thirty minutes away by car from Chemal. Ownership of land under Russian law is far beyond the scope of this chapter and the comprehension of its authors, but the law seems to recognise various categories of land, such as "land of agricultural exploitation" as opposed to "land of agricultural destination"; various kinds of (legal) persons, such as Russian citizens or companies with less than fifty per cent of foreign capital; and various types of entitlements that the latter can claim over the former, varying from short-term lease to "ownership proper" (for a comprehensive, book-long summary, see Wegren 2009). For the purpose of this chapter, we will note that land ownership outside urban areas (in the context we are describing) is often emulated by long-term rent, typically for 25 or 49 years. Land

---

15 While the Chemal region is at the heart of tourist development in the Altai Republic, the Ongudai region, where Raisa's husband originally wanted to build the museum, has avoided major streams of tourists until recently.

16 *Turbaza* is an abbreviation for *turisticheskaia baza* (tourist base), an institution that in earlier decades used to cater to hikers and was premised on the understanding that a *turist* (literally, "tourist") is a hiker (see main text above for a more detailed characterisation of the *turist*). In the Altai Republic, our interlocutors used the word *turbaza* to denote an accommodation facility that offers additional services to tourists such as guided tours, catering, etc. It is not always clear what distinguishes a *turbaza* from a hotel, for example. Use of the term seems to deliberately activate connotations of tourism with the Soviet meaning of physical activity, i.e. as a kind of outdoor sport.

that used to belong to (now often defunct) collective farms is subject to leasehold claims by former collective-farm members. The claimant has to prove their eligibility with a certificate of collective-farm membership and identify a plot of land that used to belong to the collective farm and is not already claimed by another former member. The actual process of negotiating a rent agreement is complicated and far from transparent, which leaves lots of space for what is known in Russia as *blat*.[17]

As a former collective-farm director, Raisa's husband got involved in the process as a claimant and succeeded in renting a plot of land with pastures and meadows at the bank of the Katun' River, upstream from Chemal. Just as Raisa's family museum combines activism for the sake of Altaian national revival with creating a commodity in the tourist industry, their small farm project was meant to combine herding with services for tourists, notably an open-air museum with accommodation. However, Raisa's husband's health started to deteriorate in the mid-2000s, and he died in 2008. Their elder daughter is now taking care of the farm, which in 2010 consisted of several unfinished *aiyl* meant for accommodation and exhibits, a small log cabin, and cowsheds. During the site's early stages of development, the farm's main tourist revenue stemmed from renting plots on the riverbank to campers, with some basic services such as litter disposal included in the charge. Raisa did not seem completely sure about the cost-effectiveness of the museum and farm.

In terms of Raisa's own leisure mobility, the 2000s were not that different from the 1990s. During her holidays, she worked at the family museum with her grandchildren and husband, who spent more time at the farm when he was still relatively fit. With the exception of Raisa's husband's several hospitalisations, they spent their time in and around

---

17   As was mentioned in earlier sections, *blat* denotes the practice of informal favours and the networks around them. In places like Chemal, where land in tourist areas became a scarce and precious resource, the atmosphere became very tense at times. People with interest and means — both locals as well as those from elsewhere in Russia — invested in collective-farm membership certificates for "peanuts" during the crisis years, and now they can acquire lucrative plots of land. Many locals in Chemal feel cheated; they have only recently realised the real value of their long-gone membership certificates, or they are facing the fact that while they are still struggling to obtain their rent agreements, professional speculators from elsewhere are effectively receiving rent agreements for the best plots. Some authors understandably describe the general situation in Russia in terms of land grabbing (see, for example, Visser et al. 2012; Ledeneva 2013: 192–93).

Chemal. The only somewhat regular leisure journeys that Raisa made were one-day trips to theatre performances or concerts in the republic's capital, Gorno-Altaisk. As a retired schoolteacher, she enjoyed subsidised transport and free tickets, which the regional authorities distributed to school employees and other interested state employees. Raisa's attendance of concerts and theatre performances is in line with her self-perception as belonging to the "cultured" rural elite.

Viktor, our other protagonist, ceased to travel long-distance after 2006 — partly because his financial situation had changed as a consequence of losing his job as a clerk at the trolley company, and partly because his urge to move around and see how people live in western countries had waned. Viktor was affected by the consequences of economic changes later than others; for him, this led to a reduction of mobility at a time when he was starting to feel jaded by travelling. While many of his friends are still longing to go to Turkey or Cyprus, to Thailand and other "exotic" destinations, Viktor claims he has no need for it. Occasionally, though, he spends a weekend with his friends at Chemal or Aia, another holiday resort in the Altai Republic.

New directions and motivations: post-socialist holiday worlds

Twenty years after the end of the Soviet Union, the diversity of communities of taste has obviously increased; likewise, though not quite in the same way, the range of desirable destinations has become wider. The inventory of noble causes has grown, too. Soviet tastes, spatial imaginaries, and touristic sensibilities have not been fully replaced, but rather augmented. Many communities of taste that exist today are genealogically rooted in Soviet habits of travelling and holiday-making. Raisa's predilection for concerts in the capital of the region where she lives can be seen as a continued exercise and persisting belief in the noble causes of travelling: for her social status and self-esteem, the benefits of edification and cultivation have not lost their importance. In addition to these motivations, new noble causes have emerged: spending time in good company; getting to know new people;[18] self-experience

---

18   This is done, among other means, through "couch-surfing" (Zuev 2013).

through encountering cultural difference; and putting oneself to the test in extreme situations (*ekstrim*). Perhaps somewhat more mundane, and now more openly acknowledged than in earlier years, are holiday purposes such as shopping, sexual encounters, or simply the wish to stay in a luxurious environment. Consequently, new communities of taste have come into being.

The differences in access to fulfil such aspirations have increased as well. In earlier decades, access to touristic resources was determined by personal achievement, privilege, and informal connections, in partial contrast to the principle of deservingness and squarely in contrast to the principle of social equality. In the 1990s, that mission of equality was abandoned altogether. What we see instead are not just newly formulated desires, but also new (mostly commercial) mechanisms of how these desires are fuelled, along with much more blatant financial inequalities in the ways people can try to pursue such desires.

Turning to ethnicity and "local tradition", we first must very briefly assess the symbolic significance of Soviet-era touristic journeys to Soviet non-Russian cities and regions, for example Riga or Samarkand (subsequently, we will turn to tourist destinations in Siberia). Riga, with its Hanseatic Old Town, and Samarkand, with its outstanding oriental architecture, had the flavour of the picturesque and exotic. Surely cities such as Samarkand or Riga were promoted as "unique" in terms of local culture, folklore, and cuisine. However, guided tours and guidebooks always featured the achievements of socialism, presenting with pride the landmarks of socialist architecture, Soviet cultural institutions, and memorial sites in honour of revolutionary heroes. As an intended result of centrally orchestrated urbanisation, Soviet cities came to resemble each other, and the consequent orchestration of the "tourist gaze" (Urry 2002) is evident in the postcard sets that were issued for each large city. Samarkand and Riga were indeed unique, but their uniqueness was partly eclipsed by stories and pictures of modernity and similarity in order to show the integrative power of new Soviet society (in the case of Tallinn, see Gorsuch 2012: 60). Just as the principle of *unity in diversity* governed the symbolic space of the Soviet Union, it also moulded officially legitimate holiday experiences. In her study on tourism in the Soviet Union in the late 1940s and 1950s, Gorsuch (2003, 2012) summarises this experience: "Through tourism, the more 'exotic' parts of the USSR were incorporated into the central circulatory system of the Soviet Union" (Gorsuch 2003: 776). However, she adds, "while promoting tourism to spaces of ethnic and cultural difference might have been intended as 'taming' these unpredictable places and minorities by Sovietizing their spaces for tourist consumption, it is not obvious that it had such an effect" (Gorsuch 2003: 778).[19]

This all-Union dimension of tourism noticeably changed in the late 1980s and 1990s. Not only did the Soviet Union republics break apart from each other, but also, within the Russian Federation, ethnicity acquired a new, "less tame", and sometimes violent dynamic; ethnic diversity came to be seen as a social and political challenge in the early and mid-1990s. When tourism grew again in the early and mid-2000s, the Russian state had regained some of its hegemony to produce iconic forms of diversity; however, the whole arena of negotiating otherness had changed, for three reasons. First, indigenous spokespeople and entrepreneurs had become able — temporarily, at least — to formulate new, allegedly more authentic images of their respective ethnic identities (cf. Kasten 2009). Second, in line with a general tendency to turn ethnic difference into capital, in Russia, too, the display of symbols of ethnic identity gradually underwent a process of commodification (see, for example, Bruner 2005; Comaroff & Comaroff 2009; Greenwood 1977). In Chemal and elsewhere, artefacts and narratives have been refashioned as consumables of culture, endowing hosts and guests of the tourist encounter with different ethnic and cultural qualities, so that a host/guest divide has come into play. Third, as previously mentioned, the range of touristic sensibilities had widened: among the newly emerging noble causes, one can find self-experience through otherness — in this case, ethnic otherness. This requires the highlighting of difference rather than similarity, hence the marked tendency towards exoticising indigenous spaces and livelihoods in Russia over the last fifteen to twenty years. Now, a growing number of tourists — both from within Russia and abroad — come to the Altai Mountains or to Lake Baikal in search of shamans and indigenous peoples supposedly living in harmony with nature. By experiencing "the other", many tourists try to pursue a new way of experiencing themselves.

---

19 For a discussion of depictions of such dilemmas and tensions in Soviet cinematography and literature, see Pattle (2015: 92–94).

Ethnicity and "local tradition" are important drivers of tourism. Though formally conceived as multi-ethnic states with all nations enjoying the same rights, both the Soviet Union and the Russian Federation share an important feature: "Russians never became a nationality like any other", but rather "were increasingly identified with the Soviet Union as a whole" (Slezkine 1994: 443), which arguably only deepened with the creation of the Russian Federation. Standing behind the state as a whole had specific implications for identity politics. While other groups, whose identity was defined along the lines of nationality/ethnicity, had their specific territory regarded as homeland, for Russians such territory was everywhere and nowhere at the same time. Obviously, many ethnic Russians also have a sense of ancestral homeland and regional belonging. We can observe that cities like Yaroslavl', Vladimir, and Suzdal' actively invest in fostering the image of key sites of Russian history and identity. It is nevertheless impossible to single out an area in the Russian Federation that could be turned into a destination intertwined with the idea of Russian homeland at the expense of all other locations. This has important implications for those who moved into countless tower-block districts of various cities during the processes of Soviet urbanisation. While non-Russians kept their default regional belonging, for ethnic Russians it became much easier to drift away from any distinctive local identity.

In any case, while certain small towns and villages in Russia are known to be peculiar and picturesque, and hence serve as destinations for mid-range or local tourism, rurality as such — in contrast to France, Great Britain, and Germany, to name just a few examples — does not seem to feature as an intrinsic touristic attraction. Large swathes of "the province" are of nearly no interest to any tourist. For non-locals, the idea of spending time there would be rather deterring. Local identities thus have very unequal touristic appeal, and places with visible marks of indigenous "non-Russian" culture can generate particular value that distinguishes them from the grey sea of other places. While this is in line with worldwide trends toward commodified ethnicity, what is distinct about post-Soviet Siberia is the rapid speed with which ethnicity has turned into an asset. With the exception of Irkutsk, which serves as a stopover for railway travellers (Zuev 2013), and Vladivostok, located at "the end of the line" and a particularly scenic spot on the Pacific coast,

Siberian cities are rarely considered as destinations for tourism. And with the exception of the Trans-Siberian Railway, sites of technological heritage have not received much touristic attention in Siberia either. Over the last twenty years, there has been a tendency towards depicting Siberia as an exotic and culturally diverse yet fragile place, one that is worth being cherished and protected. By this very tendency, indigenous inhabitants such as Raisa receive positive attention and respect for their innate "alterity". Now their otherness is perceived as a source of vitality, whereas in late Soviet times it was seen as quaint, though ultimately contradictory to the idea of modernity.

Having said that, we are aware that Raisa and her husband actively crafted the indigenous feeling of the village where they live. They participated in the construction of the divide between guests versus "exotic" hosts. This guest-host relationship is characterised by both ethnic and economic difference. The growing stratification of income in Russia throughout the 1990s and 2000s has been accompanied by new forms — and more ostentatious expressions — of social distinction. The guests can afford to travel and "leave" their money in the region (the museum, the village) of the hosts.

More generally and very obviously, new economic inequalities also mean that some citizens of Russia pursue tourism as a form of consumption and mobility, whereas others do not have the financial means even for low-budget tourism. We thus return to the point that leisure mobility in Russia is influenced by household income, gender, and familial status. But in addition, leisure mobility also depends on particular skills, social networks, time constraints, and one's place of residence. Social networks and travel skills enable individuals to travel even on a very minimal budget, as Zuev's (2013) study on couch-surfing in Siberia shows. Such travel arrangements are usually slow and time-intensive. Place of residence is a particularly strong factor in a region where transportation networks are dendritic rather than netlike (see Chapter 2 of this volume). Differences in leisure mobility between big cities and rural settlements had already existed in Soviet times, not just because of the fact that the habit of "going on holiday" initially developed among privileged urbanites, but also because of social and institutional control over individuals' movements (Matthews 1993: 27–35; cf. Burrell & Hörschelmann 2014) and requirements of mutual support, especially in the countryside. Visits to relatives were an accepted cause for leisure mobility, but recreational trips were not on the agenda of *kolkhoz* (collective farm) members before the 1960s. Such trips became available to rural dwellers only in late Soviet times, and we have argued above that their distribution was managed unevenly. Today, rural inhabitants who want to spend a holiday at the seaside are doubly disadvantaged: their average earnings are lower than those of urbanites, and their expenses for getting to a holiday destination are higher because they must travel to the regional capital first, which is now relatively more expensive than it used to be in the late Soviet period.

Both Viktor and Raisa had similar experiences of visiting seaside resorts and spas in the south of Soviet Russia on the basis of combined *putëvki* and informal arrangements. We nevertheless cannot take such a convergence of travel biographies for granted as an inevitable outcome of the official ideology of equality. Quite the contrary, as we tried to demonstrate, the reason that a rural dweller from Altai had similar experiences to someone from the largest Siberian city is due to the fact that Raisa was a representative of Soviet native intelligentsia connected to the political *nomenklatura* through her husband.

The itineraries of our two protagonists started to differ in the 1990s. Raisa continued to pursue the project of self-cultivation on several fronts. On one hand, she continued travelling to attend theatre and music performances, complying with the ideal of culture in the "opera house" sense of the term. On the other hand, she partook in the shift of mood of native intelligentsia towards intensified ethno-national revival. She and her husband established their museum as an institution focussing on the self-cultivation and fostering of Altaian culture and national identity. Combined with the simultaneous commodification of ethnicity, their project gradually assumed an entrepreneurial character, at least to a degree, without losing its genealogical link to certain Soviet ideals of sociality, with the individual gaining importance as part — and *only* as part — of a bigger whole. Over those years, Viktor explored the cities of Ukraine, the Baltics, and later Germany, staying with friends and extending his social networks into Europe. Having left his Soviet professional past and associated ideals behind him, he is an excellent representative of an individualist and hedonist approach to life, one that is nevertheless in continuation of the Soviet ideal of *poznavatel'nyi turizm* (educational/exploratory tourism).

In both biographies, goals and destinations were partly conditioned by economic circumstances; more strongly, however, our protagonists actively pursued certain personal interests and predilections. Both were able to realise their projects. Their comparatively high degree of personal success makes them different from many other interlocutors within our research, who had fewer opportunities to make their dreams and plans come true. We have argued in this chapter that life projects, favourite travel destinations, and tastes have changed from Soviet times to the present: their range has generally broadened, and the role that national/ethnic identity has played in their establishment has become much more acknowledged by various social actors. Simultaneously, the means to practise such tastes are now distributed much more unevenly than three decades ago.

Final thoughts on the future of tourism to, from, and within Siberia

Many of the "old" Soviet destinations are still widely popular today. As a striking example, the city of Sochi has experienced enormous investment in infrastructure in relation to the 2014 Winter Olympic Games, which have enhanced additional flows of tourists to the Russian Black Sea. In recent years, there have been initiatives to promote the popularity of tourist destinations within Russia, both in view of the temporary inaccessibility of previously popular destinations such as Turkey and Egypt (Leonidova 2016) and with the aim to improve the image of tourism-related services and facilities in Russia. As in Soviet times, but to a much lesser extent, there are some work-related entitlements to holiday-making (as of 2017, for instance, employees of the public sector in some Siberian regions may obtain subsidised railway tickets for holidays at the Russian Black Sea coast every second year). Apart from patriotic appeals to domestic tourism, exemplified among other means by the holiday choices of President Putin displayed in the media and certain subsidies for holiday-making within Russia, passport and visa regulations continue to deter elderly people and rural residents in particular from travelling abroad. For the latter, visiting relatives continues to be a noble cause for travelling; if close relatives live outside Russia, this provides an incentive for travelling abroad. For example, after the large-scale emigration of ethnic Germans from the southwestern part of Siberia to Germany in the 1990s (see for example de Tinguy 2003), transnational contact and travel between Siberia and Germany have become more frequent.

Within Siberia, flows of tourists are still highly structured by the dendritic character of transportation and infrastructure (e.g. Kuklina & Holland 2018). Hence the growing popularity of Lake Baikal, for instance, which is facilitated by its proximity to the main Siberian artery of transportation. At the same time, the remotest corners of Siberia have a distinct attractiveness due to their pristine nature and/or local culture, which incites some adventurers to visit them. Their numbers may seem negligible when compared with truly popular destinations, but might be significant when seen in the context of the very low population density of those areas. Importantly, in between these easy-to-reach and very hard-to-reach destinations, there are large sections of Siberia of almost complete insignificance in terms of tourism. Their intermediate position between central and remote, between markedly urban and markedly rural, creates an atmosphere of indifference. Having said that, Raisa's case demonstrates that ethnicity can be an economic asset, especially in a region that offers picturesque scenery and athletic forms of entertainment. While many communities in Siberia may hope to attract more domestic and international tourists in the future, Chemal is in the privileged position of already doing so.

Even privileged destinations in Siberia have to compete with destinations abroad, however. Viktor's case exemplifies post-Soviet individual tourism of the early 1990s, which preceded the mass movement of Russian tourists to seaside resorts characteristic in the 2000s. Indeed, for many travellers, holidays are considered relaxing and satisfying when they are spent at the coast, in the sun, in a comfortable environment. Spatial imaginaries of seaside resorts were already influential in Soviet times and have only increased in attractiveness since the 1990s, as is documented by increasing flows of holiday-makers from Siberia to the coasts of the Mediterranean or to Thailand. As a recent phenomenon, one can discern a certain trend among young urban intellectuals of Novosibirsk to spend several months in Thailand in order to escape the coldest months of the Siberian winter and, to a lesser degree, to save money thanks to smaller living costs.

What we observe, however, is not (only) straightforward competition. Rather, there are strong signs of complementarity and co-existence between tourism from, within, and to Siberia. The weeklong seaside trips of families from Novosibirsk might well have replaced similar trips to Lake Teletskoe in Altai. At the same time, however, the growing automobilisation and improvement of infrastructures enabled a new genre of weekend trips to Altai (see Broz & Habeck 2015) that have been responsible for a striking increase in visitors. In other words, the leisure-travel repertoire of many inhabitants of Siberia is becoming more diverse rather than simply shifting. For a smaller but growing number of people, this also means interest in less mainstream leisure travels to or within Siberia. Their additional or alternative motivations subsume pristine nature and/or culture with the potential promise of physical or spiritual regeneration or extreme athletic activities, conditioned on geographical features such as high mountains or white-water rivers.

With the wax and wane of economic difficulties that replaced Russia's prosperity in the 2000s, we can also foresee the continuation — if not the deepening — of inequalities in terms of leisure mobility across Siberia. Those inequalities are played out not only along emerging class divides, but also along regional (including urban versus rural) and ethnic/national identity divides; they will likely continue to do so. The lesson we can learn from Raisa and Viktor nevertheless reminds us that communities of taste are fuzzy, amorphous entities; and that despite "objective" structural constraints of social, economic, or geographical character, individuals shape their leisure travel biographies through a creative combination of socially shared predilections, familial arrangements, and personal preferences.

References

Andrle, Vladimir. 1994. *A Social History of Twentieth-Century Russia*. London: Arnold.

—. 2001. "The buoyant class: bourgeois family lineage in the life stories of Czech business elite persons". *Sociology*, 35 (4): 815–33, https://doi.org/10.1017/s003803850100815x

Baker, William J. 1979. "The leisure revolution in Victorian England: a review of recent literature". *Journal of Sport History*, 6 (3): 76–87.

Bourdieu, Pierre. 1984. *Distinction: a social critique of the judgement of taste*, trans. Richard Nice. Cambridge, MA: Harvard University Press.

Broz, Ludek & Joachim Otto Habeck. 2015. "Siberian automobility boom: from the joy of destination to the joy of driving there". *Mobilities*, 10 (4): 552–70, https://doi.org/10.1080/17450101.2015.1059029

Bruner, Edward M. 2005. *Culture on Tour: ethnographies of travel*. Chicago, IL: University of Chicago Press.

Burrell, Kathy, & Kathrin Hörschelmann. 2014. "Introduction: understanding mobility in Soviet and East European socialist and post-socialist states". In: *Mobilities in Socialist and Post-Socialist States*, ed. Kathy Burrell & Kathrin Hörschelmann, pp. 1–22. London: Palgrave Macmillan, https://doi.org/10.1057/9781137267290_1

Caldwell, Melissa L. 2011. *Dacha Idylls: living organically in Russia's countryside*. Berkeley, CA: University of California Press, https://doi.org/10.1525/california/9780520262843.001.0001

Chaney, David. 1996. *Lifestyles*. London: Routledge, https://doi.org/10.4324/9780203137468

Comaroff, John L. & Jean Comaroff. 2009. *Ethnicity, Inc*. Chicago, IL: University of Chicago Press, https://doi.org/10.7208/chicago/9780226114736.001.0001

Cunningham, Hugh. 1980. *Leisure in the Industrial Revolution: c. 1780–c. 1880*. London: Routledge, https://doi.org/10.4324/9781315637679

Görlich, Christopher. 2012. *Urlaub vom Staat: Tourismus in der DDR* [Vacation from the state: tourism in the German Democratic Republic]. Cologne: Böhlau, https://doi.org/10.7788/boehlau.9783412215248

Gorsuch, Anne E. 2003. "'There's no place like home': Soviet tourism in late Stalinism". *Slavic Review*, 62 (4), 760–85, https://doi.org/ 10.2307/3185654

—. 2006. "Time travelers: Soviet tourists to Eastern Europe". In: *Turizm: the Russian and East European tourist under capitalism and socialism*, ed. Anne E. Gorsuch & Diane P. Koenker, pp. 205–26. Ithaca, NY: Cornell University Press.

—. 2012. *All This Is Your World: Soviet tourism at home and abroad after Stalin*. Oxford: Oxford University Press, https://doi.org/10.1093/acprof:oso/9780199609949.001.0001

— & Diane P. Koenker. 2006. "Introduction". In: *Turizm: the Russian and East European tourist under capitalism and socialism*, ed. Anne E. Gorsuch & Diane P. Koenker, pp. 1–14. Ithaca, NY: Cornell University Press.

Greenwood, Davydd J. 1977. "Culture by the Pound: an anthropological perspective on tourism as cultural commoditization". In: *Hosts and Guests:*

the anthropology of tourism, ed. Valene L. Smith, pp. 129–38. Philadelphia, PA: University of Pennsylvania Press, https://doi.org/10.9783/9780812208016.169

Habeck, Joachim Otto. 2011. "'Thank You for Being': neighborhood, ethno-culture, and social recognition in the House of Culture". In: *Reconstructing the House of Culture: community, self, and the makings of culture in Russia and beyond*, ed. Brian Donahoe & Joachim Otto Habeck, pp. 55–74. New York: Berghahn.

Halemba, Agnieszka. 2006. *The Telengits of Southern Siberia: landscape, religion and knowledge in motion*. London: Routledge, https://doi.org/10.4324/9780203008102

Heleniak, Timothy E. 2009. "The role of attachment to place in migration decisions of the population of the Russian North". *Polar Geography*, 32 (1–2): 31–60, https://doi.org/10.1080/10889370903000398

Hirsch, Francine. 2005. *Empire of Nations: ethnographic knowledge and the making of the Soviet Union*. Ithaca, NY: Cornell University Press.

Kasten, Erich (ed.). 2009. *Rebuilding Identities: pathways to reform in post-Soviet Siberia*. Berlin: Dietrich Reimer Verlag.

Kesküla, Eeva. 2018. "Oasis in the steppe: health and masculinity of Kazakhstani miners". *Central Asian Survey*, 37 (4): 546–62, https://doi.org/10.1080/02634937.2018.1492903

Kuklina, Vera & Edward C. Holland. 2018. "The roads of the Sayan Mountains: theorizing remoteness in eastern Siberia". *Geoforum*, 88: 36–44, https://doi.org/10.1016/j.geoforum.2017.10.008

Lash, Scott & John Urry. 1994. *Economics of Signs and Space*. Thousand Oaks: SAGE, https://doi.org/10.4135/9781446280539

Ledeneva, Alena V. 1998. *Russia's Economy of Favours: blat, networking and informal exchange*. Cambridge: Cambridge University Press.

—. 2006. *How Russia Really Works: the informal practices that shaped post-Soviet politics and business*. Ithaca, NY: Cornell University Press, https://doi.org/10.7591/9780801461682

—. 2013. *Can Russia Modernise? Sistema, power networks and informal governance*. Cambridge: Cambridge University Press, https://doi.org/10.1017/cbo9780511978494

Leonidova, Yekaterina G. 2016. "Stimulirovanie razvitiia vnutrennogo turizma: otechestvennyi i zarubezhnyi opyt" [Stimulating the development of domestic tourism: insights from the home country and abroad]. *Voprosy territorial'nogo razvitiia*, 2016 (3): 1–9.

Light, Duncan. 2013. "'A medium of revolutionary propaganda': the state and tourism policy in the Romanian People's Republic, 1947–1965". *Journal of Tourism History*, 5 (2), 185–200, https://doi.org/10.1080/1755182X.2013.828780

Lowerson, John & John Myerscough. 1977. *Time to Spare in Victorian England*. Brighton: Harvester Press.

MacCannell, Dean. 1999. *The Tourist: a new theory of the leisure class.* Berkeley, CA: University of California Press.

Matthews, Mervyn. 1993. *Passport Society: controlling movement in Russia and the USSR.* Boulder, CO: Westview Press.

—. 2011 [1978]. *Privilege in the Soviet Union: a study of elite life-styles under Communism.* London: Routledge, https://doi.org/10.4324/9780203815571

Men, Tamara, Paul Brennan, Paolo Boffetta & David Zaridze. 2003. "Russian mortality trends for 1991–2001: analysis by cause and region". *BMJ,* 327: 964, https://doi.org/10.1136/bmj.327.7421.964

Moranda, Scott. 2006. "East German tourist itineraries: in search of a common destination". In: *Turizm: the Russian and East European tourist under capitalism and socialism,* ed. Anne E. Gorsuch & Diane P. Koenker, pp. 266–80. Ithaca, NY: Cornell University Press.

Noack, Christian. 2006. "Coping with the tourist: planned and 'wild' mass tourism on the Soviet Black Sea Coast". In: *Turizm: the Russian and East European tourist under capitalism and socialism,* ed. Anne E. Gorsuch & Diane P. Koenker, pp. 281–304. Ithaca, NY: Cornell University Press.

Oushakine, Serguei A. 2014. "'Against the cult of things': on Soviet productivism, storage economy, and commodities with no destination". *The Russian Review,* 73 (2), 198–236, https://doi.org/10.1111/russ.10727

Parratt, Catriona M. 1999. "Making leisure work: women's rational recreation in late Victorian and Edwardian England". *Journal of Sport History,* 26 (3): 471–88.

Pattle, Sheila. 2015. "'Tourism for everyone': domestic tourism in the USSR during late socialism, 1950s-1980s". Masters thesis, Durham University, http://etheses.dur.ac.uk/11093/

Qualls, Karl D. 2006. "'Where each stone is history': travel guides in Sevastopol after World War II". In: *Turizm: the Russian and East European tourist under capitalism and socialism,* ed. Anne E. Gorsuch & Diane P. Koenker, pp. 163–85. Ithaca, NY: Cornell University Press.

Rosenbaum, Adam T. 2015. "Leisure travel and real existing socialism: new research on tourism in the Soviet Union and communist Eastern Europe". *Journal of Tourism History,* 7 (1–2): 157–76, https://doi.org/10.1080/175518 2x.2015.1062055

Slezkine, Yuri. 1994. "The USSR as a communal apartment, or how a socialist state promoted ethnic particularism". *Slavic Review,* 53 (2): 414–52, https://doi.org/10.2307/2501300

Stammler, Florian & Lena Sidorova. 2015. "Dachas on permafrost: the creation of nature among Arctic Russian city-dwellers". *Polar Record,* 51 (6): 576–89, https://doi.org/10.1017/s0032247414000710

Stammler-Gossmann, Anna. 2012. "'Winter-tyres-for-a-flower-bed': shuttle trade on the Finnish-Russian border". In: *Subverting Borders: doing research on smuggling and small-scale trade*, ed. Bettina Bruns & Judith Miggelbrink, pp. 233–55. Wiesbaden: VS Verlag für Sozialwissenschaften, https://doi.org/10.1007/978-3-531-93273-6_12

Thomas, Keith. 1964. "Work and leisure in pre-industrial society". *Past and Present*, 29 (1): 50–66, https://doi.org/10.1093/past/29.1.50

de Tinguy, Anna. 2003. "Ethnic migrations of the 1990s from and to the successor states of the former Soviet Union: 'repatriation' or privileged migration?" In: *Diasporas and Ethnic Migrants: German, Israel, and post-Soviet successor states in comparative perspective*, ed. Rainer Münz & Rainer Ohliger, pp. 100–13. London: Frank Cass, https://doi.org/10.4324/9780203486276

Urry, John. 2002. *The Tourist Gaze*. London: SAGE.

Visser, Oane, Natalia Mamonova & Max Spoor. 2012. "Oligarchs, megafarms and land reserves: understanding land grabbing in Russia". *The Journal of Peasant Studies*, 39 (3–4): 899–931, https://doi.org/10.1080/03066150.2012.675574

Volkov, Vadim. 2000. "The concept of *kul'turnost'*: notes on the Stalinist civilizing process". In: *Stalinism: new directions*, ed. Sheila Fitzpatrick, pp. 210–30. London: Routledge.

Wegren, Stephen K. 2009. *Land Reform in Russia: institutional design and behavioral responses*. New Haven, CT: Yale University Press, https://doi.org/10.12987/yale/9780300150971.001.0001

Yurchak, Alexei. 1997. "The cynical reason of late socialism: power, pretense, and the anekdot". *Public Culture*, 9 (2): 161–88, https://doi.org/10.1215/08992363-9-2-161

—. 2006. *Everything Was Forever, Until it Was No More: the last Soviet generation*. Princeton, NJ: Princeton University Press, https://doi.org/10.1515/9781400849109

Zubkova, Elena. 1998. *Russia After the War: hopes, illusions, and disappointments, 1945–1957*, trans. & ed. Hugh Ragsdale. Armonk, NY: M. E. Sharpe, https://doi.org/10.4324/9781315701011

Zuev, Dennis. 2013. "Couchsurfing along the Trans-Siberian Railway and beyond: cosmopolitan learning through hospitality in Siberia". *Sibirica: Interdisciplinary Journal of Siberian Studies*, 12 (1): 56–82, https://doi.org/10.3167/sib.2013.120103

5. Spatial Imaginaries and Personal Topographies in Siberian Life Stories

Analysing Movement and Place in Biographical Narratives

Joseph J. Long

This chapter explores paradigms for analysing movement and place in the lives of people in Siberia. Much has been written in Siberian ethnography about place and space, particularly in relation to the cosmologies and practices of indigenous peoples. Movement in this context is largely explored through the phenomenology of landscape in hunting, herding, and ritual practices (e.g. Anderson 2000; Jordan 2011; Miggelbrink et al. 2013). Meanwhile, emerging studies of tourism in Soviet and post-Soviet Russia have shed light on mobility, infrastructure, and the discourse surrounding travel (e.g. Gorsuch 2003, 2011; Koenker 2003, 2012; Gorsuch & Koenker 2006; Randolph & Avrutin 2012), but have focussed less on the lived experience of travellers. This chapter suggests a means to bridging these two bodies of work. Here I suggest how a holistic approach might address multiple relations to movement and place among contemporary Siberians. The choices and practices through which Siberian interlocutors craft and represent their life projects — explored in this volume as lifestyle — are examined here through the representation of movement and place in biographical narratives and photography. In the material

 https://doi.org/10.11647/OBP.0171.05

reviewed here, our interlocutors recounted travel that anchored them in places named as "home" as well as travel that expanded their horizons. Interviewees discussed places designated as sacred in religious cosmology as well as places discovered through tourist brochures and captured in holiday photographs.

The collaborative project reported in this volume employed photo elicitation interviews to explore visual self-presentation and travel biography interviews to investigate mobility in the lives of Siberian people.[1] As the project unfolded it soon became apparent that these elements of lifestyle were closely linked in our interlocutors' accounts of their lives: photos chosen by interview subjects to represent their life stories often featured travel and tourism, while travel biographies often referred to trips discussed in photo elicitation interviews. In this chapter, I therefore explore the relationship between our interviewees' travel trajectories, the places that those trajectories connect, and the images and narratives that give meaning to movement and place.

In doing so, I experiment with theoretical concepts to analyse relationships to movement and place. First, I account for trajectories of movement in relation to "spatial imaginaries" that are variously informed by indigenous worldviews, socialist geopolitics, tourist literature, and popular media. Second, I seek to understand the "personal topographies" made up of significant places in an individual's life and the trajectories of travel and migration that link those places together. I explore how these personal topographies are inscribed through movement, recounted in biographies, and captured in photographic images. Through the voices of our interviewees, I illustrate how the confluence of these practices informs individuals' sense of identity.

Mobility, geography, and topography

Theorists of mobility and travel have explored the enduring need for corporeal travel in a world that is connected by multiple means of

---

1   This project was a collaborative one, with material shared and exchanged between researchers. I draw on material gathered through my own participant observation and interview work in the Baikal region, including the cities of Irkutsk and Ulan-Ude. In order to gain a broader picture, I also analyse shared material collected by team members from across Siberia. Where I do so, I indicate the researcher and location in question.

communication. John Urry (2002) emphasised the need for physical co-presence for a range of social practices: legal, economic and familial obligations; the need to see people face to face; the desire to spend time with people; the wish to experience a place directly; the need to experience a "live" event in person; or to attend to objects, technologies, or documents that are tied to a specific location (Urry 2002: 262–63). Urry's approach provides an impetus to combine studies of tourism with analyses of other kinds of mobility and movement. In line with the literature in this field, the term "mobility" here invokes consideration of the conditions and possibilities for travel in a given context. "Movement" refers to travel in practice — from everyday journeys to exceptional holidays or long-term migration, whether that is from village to city or across national borders (see Urry 2007). The project reported here examined obligations and motivations to travel in the Siberian context, and what unique constraints, possibilities, and meanings for movement are evident in the accounts given to us.

In the contemporary world, international mobility and migration, flows of goods and services, and media and communication technologies mean that the borders of a nation state can no longer be perceived as a boundary to the social relations of most citizens. In this context, theorists such as Arjun Appadurai have called for a "postnational geography" that recognises the complex relations to place and space experienced by contemporary subjects (Appadurai 1996).

In this theoretical context, I employ the concept of a "personal topography" — a constellation of places and routes described as meaningful in the life of an individual.[2] For our Siberian interlocutors the personal topography might include a distant homeland, a sacred ritual site, a university town, a workplace, or a fondly remembered holiday destination — places connected by corporeal movement over the life course. In exploring interlocutors' personal topographies, researchers may learn how movement is influenced by institutional and infrastructural limitations, informed by historical circumstances, and given meaning by collective cultural representations. Furthermore, the accounts presented here describe the interpersonal relationships that are rooted in particular places and experiences of co-presence.

---

2   I have previously written of "shamanist topographies" to describe constellations of sacred places in the Cisbaikal landscape (Long 2013). Here I use "personal topography" to describe significant places in the life of an individual.

Narratives, images, and the spatial imaginary

Travel biography interviews and photo elicitation interviews draw upon two important ways that individuals give form to their experiences and choices of travel — biographical narratives and visual images. Travel biographies have been developed over the last two decades as a method for understanding the motivations and meanings behind travel (Desforges 2000; Frandberg 2006, 2008; Lanzendorf 2003). This is not only reflected in the destinations that a person might choose, but also in forms of movement that are obligatory, expected, or limited by circumstance. Biographical narratives elucidate how senses of identity are constituted through movement, place and the meanings attributed to them. The second mode of representation explored here — visual imagery — accounts for a fundamental way in which movement is anticipated, documented, and memorialised. Photo elicitation is well established as a method of engaging with a subject's visual self-representation (see Collier & Collier 1986; Harper 2002). Here the method is used to explore the relationship between narrative and the images that inform both fantasies and memories of place. Schwartz & Ryan (2003) have noted the role of photography in constituting relations to place: photographic images memorialise particular journeys, visits to culturally or personally significant places, and the social encounters that travel allows to happen. The decision to use photo-elicitation techniques was guided by the previous experiences of ethnographers in our team carrying out fieldwork in Russia: all of us could recount multiple occasions on which we had been handed photo albums to look at and comment on as a common feature of hospitality in Russia.

In exploring how individual subjects anticipate and memorialise movement, I suggest the concept of a "spatial imaginary" as a way of considering how places, routes and landscapes are given meaning in visual media and narrative accounts. The "imaginary" has appeared with increasing frequency in anthropological literature over the past two decades. Taking inspiration from the work of Castoriadis (1997) and Taylor (2002), the term "social imaginary" generally refers to collective representations of social identity. In particular, the imaginary has been deployed to denote shared cultural representations that are not limited to national borders or proximate communities (Appadurai 1996). In anthropological literature, it is common to read of political, religious, and social imaginaries all evoking these — often idealised — social ties.

Noel Salazar's work (Salazar 2010) takes as its focus "tourist imaginaries", describing the way that certain destinations and journeys are fantasised about and given meaning through tourism advertising and media. Moreover, Salazar notes that while tourist imaginaries are built on culturally and collectively created meanings, they are subjectively and individually experienced (2010: 5–7). It is this relationship between the collective imagination and individual experience that our methods explore.

If, as argued above, tourism can be explored within broader practices of movement and place-making, then the more holistic "spatial imaginary" provides some utility for our present purposes. Here the spatial imaginary is employed to connote the combination of discourses, images, memories, and fantasies that inform and reflect travel practice, realised in the personal topographies of individuals.

This is not to suggest that the spatial imaginary or personal topography exist as coherent or objectified wholes in the minds of individuals. Rather, I use the terms heuristically to describe how collective and individual representations are given coherence through the processes of narrative, particularly those narratives elicited in interviews. I suggest these devices as a means to explore how far travel choices are influenced by collective imaginaries, and to explore the relationships between spatial imaginaries and realised trajectories of movement. I illustrate some tentative applications of the approach below.

Both narrative and image are informed by the cultural discourse that influences a subject's travel choices. Both are also mediated by the possibilities for mobility in a given context as well as constraints such as affordability, transport infrastructure, and the state regulation of travel. In Soviet Siberia this included processes of ticket allocation, and regimes of passport and visa provision that were heavily controlled by the state. My aim in the passages that follow is not to give an exhaustive picture of movement and place in Siberia, but rather to illustrate how this approach can reveal patterns in the way that subjects picture and talk about travel, patterns that provide insights into the cultural and institutional contexts for mobility. More in-depth discussion of particular experiences of travel can be found in Chapter 3, Chapter 4, and Chapter 8 in this volume.

Changing spatial imaginaries and possibilities for travel

Tourism in the Soviet Union was largely organised and regulated by state travel agencies, workplaces, and trade unions. Often tourism was undertaken in work collectives or groups assembled by travel agencies. Movement was largely limited to the geopolitical space of the Soviet and East European communist bloc. Moreover, as Anne Gorsuch (2003, 2011) and Diane Koenker (2012) have suggested in their accounts of post-war Soviet tourism, tourist travel was promoted as a way of constituting the communist space as a coherent whole in the imaginations and experiences of citizens. This spatial imaginary was cultivated through advertisements in Soviet journals and newspapers, as well as articles in magazines such as *Vokrug Sveta* (*Around the World*) extolling the merits of Soviet tourist destinations. Official Soviet discourse differentiated between tourism (*turizm*) as purposive, educational, cultured, and even patriotic, and the "rest" (*otdykh*) that took place in sanatoria and tourist bases for health and relaxation (Gorsuch 2011, Koenker 2003; Chapter 4 in this volume). These restful qualities were also associated with outdoor activities such as walking, climbing and camping. Outside of the institutionalised mechanisms for travel, the category of "wild tourism" (*dikii turizm*) denoted leisure travel not undertaken through the organised system of vouchers and travel packages (Noack 2006). Whilst this could imply making one's own travel arrangements in booking trains, flights, and hotels for a pleasure trip, the term often connotes the camping trips, hiking, and fishing that characterised the outdoor health ethos.

The majority of official tourism in the Soviet Union was organised by trade unions and work places, many with their own tourist bases (*turbazy*). Travel vouchers (*putëvki*) were awarded for productive officials to travel from the remotest corners of Siberia to the Black Sea resorts of Ukraine and southern Russia. In different places across Siberia sanatoria functioned according to the nineteenth-century European model where industrial and agricultural workers could take the air, use the steam baths, and undergo restorative treatments. In the late Soviet era, possibilities to travel elsewhere within the communist bloc increased with tourist trips to Bulgaria and Romania promoted alongside cultural trips to East Germany or Czechoslovakia (Gorsuch 2011). Gorsuch's research illustrates very well the promotion of a shared spatial imaginary — a united geopolitical space in which good citizens — that is, good workers — were rewarded with touristic and leisure opportunities. The spatial imaginary of Soviet tourists incorporated Black Sea resorts, the metropolitan cultural centres of European Russia and, in the late Soviet period, partner nations in Europe. Diane Koenker notes an implicit tension in Soviet tourism between the careful control of mobility by the state, with its emphasis on collective travel, and the individual knowledge and self-improvement that tourism was purported to achieve for citizens (Koenker 2012). Attention to biographical narratives and lived experience therefore yields important insights into the way that individual choices and personal development were fulfilled within the regulated infrastructures and cultural expectations of Soviet Siberia.

In Irkutsk, I interviewed Natal'ia (aged 61 at the time of the interview), who worked as an economist in the city's trade centre. Natal'ia had a fairly typical trajectory for those that were able to obtain *putëvki* in the Soviet era: she made her first overseas visit to Romania in 1981, followed by a later trip to Berlin and Dresden in the German Democratic Republic and then to Czechoslovakia. In 1990, shortly before the collapse of the USSR, her *kollektiv* from the trade centre took part in a competition to visit cities of the Soviet Union and were awarded a trip to Kiev, where — in an archetypally Soviet way — they travelled as a group to watch the Ninth-of-May military parades and celebrations. This last competition illustrates very nicely Gorsuch's observation that the state used travel opportunities to cement the idea of a Soviet space.

Soviet travel was highly regulated by a system of internal and international passports, and citizens were required to register with the local authorities in any towns or resorts that they visited. Moreover, when travel was granted to Eastern Europe, several of the Soviet-era travellers that researchers interviewed remembered a high level of surveillance and were even briefed on how to conduct themselves when travelling outside the USSR. Natal'ia recalled her trip to Romania in 1981: "When we went to collect the tickets, they studied us for a long time, checked everything, people from the party talked with us: 'this is not allowed, that is not allowed' and we were under surveillance everywhere!"

Lifestyle in Siberia and the Russian North

As Natal'ia continued: "In 1983 it was still like that [...] but in the 1990s it was already possible to travel peacefully, no one would tell you how to conduct yourself or what to do". In the late 1980s, our informants remembered a growing possibility to visit destinations outside the socialist geopolitical space. Nastia, an interviewee whose experiences I recount below, remembers vividly the joy of getting a *putëvka* to visit Athens in 1988. At that time in Irkutsk, the Soviet tourist agency *Sputnik* was the arbiter of international travel and Nastia — like many of our informants — remembers being turned down from several different destinations:

> At that time, we had Sputnik international travel bureau. We went there to buy travel tickets, that's where they had tickets. But before that you had to get permission from your work, you had to fill in a pile of documents, a form. They would confirm everything, sign it, and then you went [to the travel agent]. It was very complicated [...] I submitted my documents to travel to the FRG [Federal Republic of Germany], but they didn't let me go. They didn't explain. I wanted to go to Spain, but they didn't allow it, they didn't explain why. And they didn't allow me to go to Cuba.

Yet Nastia's desire to travel remained strong and Greece in particular loomed large in her imagination: "To me Greece was really something! We had a saying 'Greece has everything' (*V Gretsii vsë est'*)". The images of Greece as a cradle of civilisation in geographical journals and history books played a part in this as Nastia explained: "Greece was a country that had a high level of cultural development in the first and second centuries BCE — so many millennia and it is generally preserved".

The post-Soviet era has seen an increase in tourist travel and package holidays to destinations further afield. If the spatial imaginary of the Soviet era focussed on the Black Sea and cities of the communist bloc, then the imagery of the post-Soviet era has been of package holidays to the Mediterranean — particularly the affordable destination of Turkey. Where Soviet tourism was imagined through propagandistic journals as cultured and patriotic, by the 2000s the television comedy *Turisty* regularly lampooned the exploits of brash Russian holiday-makers in Turkey. While I was undertaking fieldwork in Irkutsk in 2007, a direct flight to Bangkok from the city's airport was launched with much fanfare. Advertising and media coverage across the city depicted Thailand as a tropical paradise. The images reflected an expanding spatial imaginary, with travel to new destinations increasingly within the grasp of many Siberians. As the post-Soviet appetite for consumption has snowballed, shopping has also become an increasing feature of travel. Shopping trips to China were very popular among my acquaintances in Irkutsk and Ulan-Ude from where a train to the border town of Manzhouli allows Russian consumers to buy cheap clothes, electronics and luxury goods in enormous outlets.

Alongside the broadening imaginaries of foreign travel, regional destinations were, and remain, particularly important in relation to the idea of "rest" (*otdykh*). The Altai mountains in south-central Siberia are a popular place of retreat for city dwellers in Novosibirsk Oblast (see Chapter 4), and Lake Baikal is not only a draw for tourists from across Russia, but remains a popular destination for weekends and day trips from the large industrial cities of Irkutsk, Ulan-Ude, and Chita. Nastia, introduced above, remembers spending much of her summer vacation from university in the early 1980s camping on the shores of Baikal, living for weeks at a time as a "wild tourist". Today in the Baikal region the number of tourist bases on the lakeshore multiplies every year. In the national parks of the Tunka Valley and Alkhanai, Soviet era sanatoria nestle alongside a multitude of new guesthouses and *turbazy*. Students that I interviewed in Ulan-Ude all recounted weekend trips to these destinations with friends, and I have often joined family trips to Baikal while staying in the region. While the collective spatial imaginary is expanding with possibilities to travel abroad, regional places are no less a part of that imaginary, incorporated into physical trajectories of travel in weekend and summer trips.

Institutionalised rites of passage in travel biographies

Around Irkutsk Oblast in the summer of 2011 it was possible to see posters adorned with the simple line "Work in Kamchatka" underscored by a telephone number. These posters were not only visible in the city, but could be seen pinned to the walls of shops and post offices in the countryside. From the late Soviet era onwards people from the region, especially students, have spent summers on Kamchatka Peninsula in the Pacific Far East of Russia working in fish processing plants and factories. Mariia Ivanovna, a 51-year-old lecturer, recalled how her university gathered large work teams to send to the peninsula in the early 1980s:

> Many students went. First, because it was an opportunity to earn money. But most importantly, it was lots of young people all together. A lot of fun. A lot of dating, boyfriends and girlfriends. And there were students from different universities — not just ours. There were technological and agricultural universities of Buryatia, and students also came from all over Russia [...] And even when we went there on the train, for example, the train was full of the work teams — just students on all the wagons. And when we sailed there, the ship was also all students. Imagine how fun it was. Singing songs, getting to know each other. They were very interesting days, of course.

Mariia Ivanovna worked as a cook, catering for the workers, while her course-mates worked cleaning, salting and pickling fish, and cooking fish eggs for caviar. This institutionalised mixture of fun and work represented an important landmark for Mariia Ivanovna as her first long trip away from home, spending two and a half months in the Far East.

While undertaking fieldwork in Buryatia in 2011, I met a number of students and young people who had undergone a contemporary version of this working holiday, spending a summer in the United States of America through a scheme named *Work-and-Travel*. The programme offers Russian students the chance to undertake seasonal, unskilled labour such as waitressing or housekeeping at hotels, and provides visa support for doing so. Both of my travel biography interviewees who were in their twenties had participated in the scheme, and a student interviewee was waiting to hear about his application when we met. Several of our project's interviewees in Novosibirsk Oblast had also spent time in the US through *Work-and-Travel*. My interviewees spoke of their time in the US as formative and important experiences in their life stories. Both picked photos of their trips as images that said something about their lives for the photo elicitation exercise.

Although Russian citizens face far less regulation of travel by their own state than they used to, travellers often face strenuous visa regimes to travel to western countries to work or study. The popularity of the *Work-and-Travel* scheme therefore hinges on the visa support that it provides as much as the experience it offers. I asked Kolia, my student interviewee, why the scheme appealed. Shrugging his shoulders, he replied: "It is a very well-known programme; I had heard a lot about it. My brother went through it. It will be very interesting to visit the United States [...] [I can] have new experiences, see the United States, relax, make money of course, and improve my English". When I asked why, in particular, he wanted to visit the United States, Kolia added: "Because the programme is limited only to the possibility of travelling to the United States. If you do not go on a programme [...] you are left to your own devices, and that seems complicated. For the first time I think it's easier to go through a programme".

For Kolia, access to the *Work-and-Travel* programme — with visa procedures and travel negotiated by the organisers — was a motivating factor for travelling in itself: the spatial imaginary of young people in Siberia today is regulated as much by possibility as by desire.

Both holiday work in Kamchatka and the *Work-and-Travel* scheme constituted something of a rite of passage for my interlocutors — a formative experience personally, but one undertaken by many of their generation. Moreover, the difference between Soviet and post-Soviet travel cannot be characterised as "controlled" and "free" travel: both schemes represent an institutionalised form of travel, regulated by the possibilities afforded by internal and external visa regimes.

I found that possible freedom granted through the regulated *Work-and-Travel* scheme became a point of much discussion in itself among acquaintances in Ulan-Ude, however. Over the course of my fieldwork I talked to several participants who knew of young people who had travelled through the programme but remained illegally in the US. Parents and grandparents whom I know expressed worry that their children might stay in the US, concerned whether they could ever return to Russia if they did so illegally. The spectre of unregulated and illegal movement therefore lay behind this institutionalised rite of passage for many parents. In this regard, the expanding spatial imaginary may be one of fear and trepidation for some as much as it is one of possibility and excitement for others.

These brief snippets from narratives of tourist travel and working holidays offer insights into the way that changing infrastructures and regulation influence the motivations and possibilities for travel over time. Below I look into further ways that these experiences feature in narratives and images of movement and place.

Narratives of discovery

Tropes of discovery were related to travel in many of our project interviews. Sonia, a 25-year-old woman from Krasnoiarsk, picked out a photo of her first visit to Paris in a photo elicitation exercise. Her comments about the memories it invoked typify narratives of travel experiences as pivotal moments in someone's life story:

> When I first went abroad to Europe with my parents, just then I think I learned more about the world […] I was always like a well-read girl — I read a lot. I knew, in general, about geography — I loved it. But, perhaps, at that moment, when you see all this with your own eyes, something changes in your inner world. Because you understand that the world is not only what you have outside your window — your yard, your city. The world is really huge, and there are these places that are not just pictures in books […].

Fig. 5.1. Paris: not just a picture in a book. Summer 2001. Photo: Dennis Zuev's interviewee (with permission), CC-BY-ND.

For Nastia, introduced above, visiting Athens and leaving the USSR for the first time in 1988, the impressions were similarly vivid. As well as remarking on the marble buildings, the cuisine, and climate, Nastia vividly remembered the differences from life in the communist bloc:

> My neck ached from simply opening my mouth and gawping. Why? Because there were so many advertisements, such an abundance of advertising, which we did not have here. For me it was very surprising that so much was stuck up, everywhere things were glued up. There were banners everywhere, advertisements, posters. Everywhere! On every house, on every building!

For Kolia, the student introduced above, even weekend visits to places of interest in Buryatia held such possibilities: "It's about some kind of new sensation, discovering something new. It is possible to go somewhere nearby […] somewhere really near and still discover something new for yourself. It's an interesting, educational sensation for real pleasure".

Narratives of discovery represent the way that the spatial imaginary turns from one of fantasy and expectation to one of experience, embedding memories and significant moments in a personal topography that expands and changes as individuals travel and move.

Movement that anchors: roots and *rodina* in personal topographies

Accounting for movement and place in the lives of Siberian subjects requires attention to travel that anchors identity as much as travel that expands horizons. Such movement may be underpinned by a religious cosmology, an ethical obligation to relatives, or an affective attachment to the landscapes in which someone grew up.

Travel biography interviews began with the question "where do you consider home?" and during the interview we also asked about our interlocutors' travel to visit relatives or return to communities where they grew up. In interviews the term *rodina* (usually translated as "homeland") often appeared as an alternative to an interviewee's current place of residence. A *rodina* may be a country of origin for international migrants, or a home village in the same province for city-dwellers in Novosibirsk, Irkutsk, or Ulan-Ude. The relational nature of the term was evident in its array of uses in interviews.

The late Soviet and post-Soviet periods have seen a city-ward migration from the Siberian countryside. In this context, relationships to the villages in which people were born and raised often appeared in personal narratives. In multiple cases this took the form of an affective attachment to place, in some a nostalgic or idealised vision of the countryside, in other cases that relationship is underpinned by specific cultural practices and cosmologies. Aleksandra, a 34-year-old woman living in Irkutsk, returned every second weekend to the village where she grew up — some four hours away — to visit family. When I asked her if she felt that this was an obligation or a pleasure, she answered firmly that it was the latter: "it's not a duty, it's a pleasure, I simply rest there: my soul rests. You need to leave the city to relax, it gives me strength — the people there, our land. I come back a renewed person!"

This was a sentiment echoed by Vasilii, a 67-year old man interviewed by Habeck in Novosibirsk, who emphasised the generational nature of this feeling: "Those that were born and brought up in the city — they don't have that attachment to the homeland like me, to the countryside. They are very much 'crowded in'. But there [...] I was in fields, I ran around, I went exploring. But what can you do here? The city is the city". With no relatives remaining in the village, and limited opportunities to visit, Vasilii's *rodina* was not a place that he visited often, but it remained an important presence in his personal topography, and a spatial imaginary that reified the countryside as a place superior to the city.

During my field research in Siberia I interviewed a number of Buryats living in the cities of Irkutsk and Ulan-Ude. Most that I interviewed, including those that had been born and brought up in the city, explained how they made returns to their ancestral villages for kin celebrations and ritual events. Buryat shamanists are obliged to return to their family hearth every summer in order to share offerings with the spirits of their ancestors that dwell in the landscape there (Long 2013). Whilst many also returned to help relatives with cutting hay, for family weddings and celebrations, or just to visit, the attachment to their homeland was underpinned by a religious cosmology that emphasised place as the root of identity and relatedness.

For several Buryats that I interviewed, the personal topography retained a strong spiritual element in regarding the homeland as a sacred place. Galsan, with whom I undertook a photo elicitation interview, chose a picture of his ancestral homeland in the mountains as a significant image with which to relate his identity, discussing his genealogy at length. He used the photo to recall a visit in which he returned to "find his strength" and went on to discuss how his own shamanic calling was identified by a shaman there.

This shamanist cosmology underpins the romanticisation of the homeland in Buryat national culture. The song that I most often heard sung in Buryat is *Toonto nutag*, a paean to the home village. The centrepiece of the Buryat National Gallery in Ulan-Ude is a painting with same title. There is a specific Buryat collective imaginary, then, which places cultural importance on the homeland — however personal — as a key place in the personal topography.

As Artem Rabogoshvili demonstrates in this volume (Chapter 8), culturally significant imaginings of the homeland are not just an urban-rural phenomenon but also figure strongly in the narratives, images, and trajectories of diaspora ethnic populations with the former Soviet space. Rabogoshvili's interviews illustrate both the ongoing significance of the homeland and the ideal of returning.

Sites of significance for kin groups, ethnic groups, or religious communities take their place in collective and individual spatial imaginaries as concretely as the holiday destinations or cultural sites do in tourism media. As such, movement is not just a means of expanding horizons, or opening up new possibilities, but also a means of inscribing identity and belonging through physical presence at key places.

Visualising social encounters

In over seventy photo elicitation interviews undertaken for this project, the one answer that interviewers received time and time again when asking why someone had taken a particular photo was *"na pamiat'"* (for the memory). As much as these photographs inscribed memories of significant places, these were often mementos of social encounters and relations.

Thus far I have written of "spatial" rather than "social" imaginaries. However, the photographic material discussed in interviews made literally visible what is increasingly recognised in social science literature — that the spatial and the social are inextricably interconnected concepts, that places as meaningful nodes in the trajectories of subjects are crucial anchors for identity, belonging, and interpersonal relations.

The photographs that our interlocutors chose in order to tell us something about their lives bear testament to the importance of place in memory and the social ties embedded there. Much as movement roots people in their *rodina*, it is not just those places; but the kin relationships and friendships rooted there are depicted in photographs. Nastia picked several childhood images of her family and friends in the village where she grew up, recounting her regular returns to visit relatives and the ongoing significance of the place in her personal topography.

A common feature of the narratives of tourism, travel, and working holidays in Soviet and post-Soviet Siberia seems to be the enduring nature of friendships forged on these trips. Soviet tourist holidays brought together travellers from across the USSR and several of our interviewees described lifelong correspondences with people they met on these trips.

Nastia also selected a picture of a trip to Crimea in 1991 to stay at a Soviet health spa. She travelled on a *putëvka* awarded by her workplace — the Irkutsk branch of the Communist Youth League (*Komsomol*).

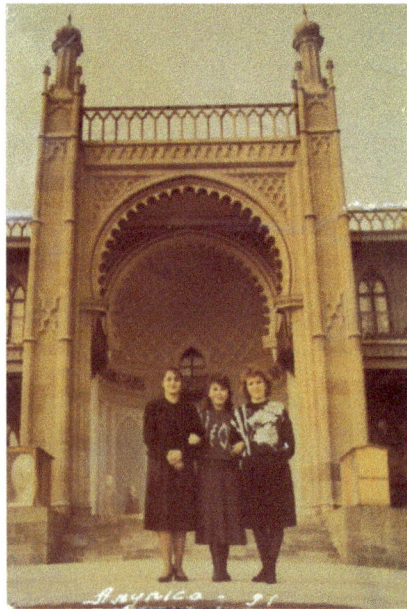

Fig. 5.2. A social encounter on the Black Sea coast. Alupka, summer 1991. Photo: Joseph L. Long's interviewee (with permission), CC-BY-ND.

The picture, of Nastia and her assigned room-mates, was taken by a professional photographer at the Vorontsov Palace in Alupka. It records a particular experience of place; a moment in Nastia's life that she recalls with pleasure; and a social encounter that led to a lasting correspondence. Nastia remembered in detail "such a powerful palace" with its "unique reflection of light", "grand rooms" and "botanical gardens". In a longer discussion of her trip prompted by this photo, Nastia also recalled members of the tourist "team" to which she was allotted to undertake activities — a combination of older men who worked as miners and women of her age. She remembered visits to the fair; bathing and barbecuing on the beach; and being roused at 6am to follow a morning exercise regime. The picture, and the memories that it prompted, revealed much about Soviet tourist sociality. Nastia had travelled alone and been allotted a bed in a room with the two women pictured with her. Recalling her room-mates, Nastia remembered with fondness her friend Sasha from Donetsk. She recalled visiting the fair and bars, and in turn meeting others. She also recounted that "for a time we even corresponded, for a long time we maintained our communication".

Younger interviewees similarly chose to memorialise social encounters as part of their travels. In an age where ongoing communication can easily be maintained through emails and social networking sites, they also kept in touch with people they had met abroad. Darima, a 23-year-old woman from Ulan-Ude, chose several photos of her *Work-and-Travel* summer in Myrtle Beach, South Carolina. She placed particular emphasis on a photo of her with a friend getting ready for a night out: "It's a very important photo for me because she is a person very close to me […] we met by chance […] [but] we constantly call each other, maintain our ties". As Darima went on to explain: "I think maybe I'll never find such a person again in my life […] I have a really good relationship with her".

Sonia, the young woman of 25 whose description of Paris was recalled above, chose to include in her pictures a photo with her friend in Vladivostok to where she had recently moved from her home town of Krasnoiarsk. She chose the picture as she felt it represented her new life, taken only a month after she arrived:

> This is Vladivostok. It turns out, this was only taken in the spring of last year, 2010, when I moved. That's it. And this is my friend, a French

woman, who moved here to be with her boyfriend [...] And I just remember, I did not have any friends here [...] I did not know anyone [...] and it turned out that we got to hang out with one another. It was fun.

Sonia went on to explain how these new social relationships were synonymous with her feelings about her new home and the place depicted in the picture:

> This place is the marina. There is a thing [...] I loved to go walking there, and being photographed. Well, for me it was interesting, all the sea, right? There is no sea in Krasnoiarsk, so all that was connected with the sea was unusual and interesting. So I chose this photograph.

Here, as with the accounts of travel quoted above, Sonia combined a sense of narrative, place, and sociality. Sonia's current life was represented along with the social ties she had formed in her new home.

Urry (2003) uses the metaphor of "facing" in discussing motivations for travel: his categories include, for example, "face the place", "face the event", and "face the person". Acknowledging the dominance of photography as a medium for documenting movement and social encounters, a more accurate formulation might read, "find the place and face the camera". For it is not only through travel itself but also its documentation that places are given significance for individual identity, through the self-image produced in photography.

Returning to the idea of the spatial imaginary, I propose that just as narratives recall the transformation of anticipation and fantasy into experience and memory, photographs play a key role in fixing that memory and building an imaginary of significant places and social encounters in the life of the individual.

Movement as lifestyle

However regulated travel in the Soviet Union and post-Soviet Russia may have been, narratives and memories built around travel often emphasise choice and the desire for mobility despite the bureaucratic processes involved. Nastia's yearning for discovery is striking given the refusals, bureaucratic hurdles, and expense of travelling she described above. As she explained: "I earned 300 to 340 roubles a month but a travel ticket cost 5,000. For that money you could buy a flat. I remember that people said to me 'You'd be better to buy a one-bedroom apartment or a car, why are you going to Greece?' I said: 'But why would I need them? I prefer to go to Greece and see it!'".

For some of our interviewees narratives of movement were integral to the representation of their lives to themselves and others, given its centrality in their life choices. In some instances — particularly in interviews with scholars and culture workers — travel was intricately tied up with professional activities: travelling with performance ensembles, undertaking expeditions, or attending conferences. In these instances travel was emphasised as a core aspect of interviewees' wider vocation.

For Zhanna, a 54-year-old woman living in Novosibirsk, her travel activities and professional identity have long been intertwined. Zhanna's mobility during and after the Soviet times was tied up with her interest in Germany and the German language, an interest that could be mobilised within the communist bloc. As a secondary school student in 1979 she studied hard to win a competition to visit socialist East Germany, where she visited the city of Halle with a group of high-achieving pupils. Zhanna remembers visiting Red Square in Moscow, and Alexanderplatz in East Berlin on her way — sites filled with meaning in the spatial imaginary of communism. Going on to become a German language teacher, and later working in a German culture centre afforded Zhanna many trips over the decades, as she recounted in her travel biography interview. "My travels have been in some way related to my work", she explained, "Contact with the Germans — that's my favourite thing: going to Germany". In the post-Soviet era her cultural work has allowed her to visit more of Germany including Hamburg and the Baltic Coast. In her photo elicitation interview, a photo of Zhanna in Berlin in 2000 was an important part of the self-image that she wished to put across: "This is when I was in Berlin for the first time since [that other] trip long, long before [...] [when] we had been there as students, doing a three-week language practice — that had been generally my first view of the world. I had the same mood [this time]".

Zhanna summarised why she felt travel was important in giving an account of herself: "Well, somehow that's me. I go, I move. And now I still do... it's great". Moreover, Zhanna is very clear that she is more interested in cultural travels than the recent trend towards package

Fig. 5.3. Zhanna's return to Berlin, July 2000. Photo: Joachim Otto Habeck's interviewee (with permission), CC-BY-ND.

holidays: "I have not even once been to Turkey, where all our people go to swim", she asserted.

This rejection of mainstream tourism was striking among some of the most seasoned travellers. Yurii, a 52-year-old man from Novosibirsk took a similar view, explaining with some pride: "I have never once been on a tourist trip — really, in the post-Soviet period I have never travelled like that. Either I travel independently, or I travel for work".

Dennis Zuev's research within the collaborative project focused on the couch-surfing movement in Siberia (cf. Zuev 2013). He describes an alternative to mainstream tourism by individuals that see travel — and the social encounters afforded by reciprocal hospitality — as fundamental to their lifestyle. Yurii was one of Zuev's interviews from this network — a seasoned traveller, and a former sailor. He reflected lyrically upon his own relationship to travel when asked about his most memorable trips:

> Basically, every journey is some kind of jewel. And there have been a lot of them. To somehow choose from them — which is better: a ruby or malachite — it's hard to say. They are all different [...] As for the meaning, well, I somehow [...] that's a question I find hard to answer, because it's like 'what is the meaning of life', and the meaning of life is to live. What is the meaning of travel? In fact, to travel, of course. That is, the process itself is the meaning.

Mobility and travel have become, to Yurii, much more than the need for discovery expressed by our other informants:

> Some time ago, I would have said that I like a change of impressions, some kind of new information. But now a glut has come and I do not feel the value of the new information. I don't need new information. I mean, I even surprised myself with this [...] But the process [...] I have gained the habit that I am comfortable when moving [...] the process of movement. It is impossible to explain this, I think, it is purely reflex. My body needs it, as smokers need to smoke.

Movement as integral to lifestyle is not restricted to long distance travellers or professionals. As Masha Shaw's research demonstrates (Chapter 3 in this volume), mobility in the countryside around very remote villages; knowledge of the local landscape; and an unregulated trajectory of hunting, fishing, and backwoodsmanship is central to the self-image of her interlocutors in the Far North of Russia. The emphasis on choice, and freedom to move, even in a context where travel opportunities at first appear limited, resonates with the narratives of interviewees who place long-distance movement at the centre of their identity. It is among all these interlocutors that movement appears not just at significant moments in a life story, but as a lifestyle in itself.

Conclusion

My aim here has been to suggest ways in which travel biography and photo elicitation can draw out common themes relating to movement and place in the lives of people in Siberia. The emerging narratives reveal the constraints and possibilities that governed mobility in Soviet and post-Soviet Siberia. The predictable trajectories of Black Sea tourist trips, cultural exchanges to Eastern Europe, or mountain sanatoria not only reveal regulated trajectories, but also common spatial imaginaries. Such imaginaries are propagated by mass media and governed by those institutional and infrastructural conditions that make travel possible — or impossible. Moreover, spatial imaginaries are perpetuated in the memories of pleasure, discovery, rites of passage and social encounter that surface in interviewees' stories and they are documented in photographic records. Yet however normative possibilities for mobility are in Siberia, the lived experience of these constraints and possibilities — evoked in the voices, stories, and memories of individuals — reveals the subjective significance of travel and movement in individual life stories. This includes those narratives of discovery and social encounter found in newly experienced places. It also features journeys that, in an era of city-ward migration, anchor a sense of belonging to an individual's homeland.

Whilst I have documented different types of place — the imagined destination, the place of rest, and the notion of *rodina* — these are combined in the life stories of Siberians, together forming the personal topographies of individual subjects. For example, Nastia's personal topography included Athens in Greece and Alupka on the Black Sea, tourist destinations she had memorialised as sites of discovery. It also included Lake Baikal as a place of freedom and her home village with all its social ties and obligations. Both of the latter places are close to her current residence in Irkutsk city, but hold specific memories and are as significant as her foreign adventures. Kolia anticipated with excitement his trip to America, and looked forward to adding the United States to his personal topography, but he also stressed local sites in Buryatia as places of learning and new experiences, traversed at weekends away from university. Sonia used her photographs to situate Paris as a place of formative experience, seeing the wider world for the first time, and also to reflect upon her recent move to Vladivostok, contrasting the maritime city with her home city of Krasnoiarsk. Describing a photograph of her new home led Sonia to reflect on this significant move in her trajectory, and the social relationships associated with a changing personal topography.

The broader aim of our project concerns the ways in which individuals present their life choices through narratives and images to evoke a coherent life project or personal identity — framed here as lifestyle. The methods recounted here do not just reveal existing practices of self-presentation — in photography and narrative — but, through the interview process, elicit moments of reflexivity, self-stylisation, and attempts at biographical coherence relating to movement and place. Among those interviewees for whom movement was central to their sense of self, stylisation was apparent in the rhetoric of seeing movement as an addiction, of journeys as "jewels", and choosing images that portrayed themselves as seasoned travellers. But there are elements of creativity and stylisation in all of the accounts of movement and place reported here. I have tried to preserve elements of our interlocutors' voices and idioms in the snippets of narrative above precisely because they evoke this process of self-presentation. A crucial way in which individuals create a self-image is through memorialising significant travels and places in their life story, evoking a unique personal topography through their particular trajectories of movement.

References

Anderson, David G. 2000. *Identity and Ecology in Arctic Siberia: the number one reindeer brigade*. Oxford: Oxford University Press.

Appadurai, Arjun. 1996. *Modernity at Large: cultural dimensions of globalization*. Minneapolis, MN: University of Minnesota Press.

Castoriadis, Cornelius. 1997. *The Imaginary Institution of Society*, trans. Kathleen Blamey. Cambridge, MA: MIT Press.

Collier, John Jr., & Malcolm Collier. 1986. *Visual Anthropology: photography as a research method*. Albuquerque, NM: University of New Mexico Press.

Desforges, Luke. 2000. "Traveling the world: identity and travel biography". *Annals of Tourism Research*, 27 (4): 926–45, https://doi.org/10.1016/S0160-7383(99)00125-5

Frändberg, Lotta. 2006. "International mobility biographies: a means to capture the institutionalisation of long-distance travel?" *Current Issues in Tourism*, 9 (4): 320–34, https://doi.org/10.2167/cit262.0

—. 2008. "Paths in transnational time-space: representing mobility biographies of young Swedes". *Geografiska Annaler: series b, human geography*, 90 (1): 17–28, https://doi.org/10.1111/j.1468-0467.2008.00273.x

Gorsuch, Anne E. 2003. "'There's no place like home': Soviet tourism in late Stalinism". *Slavic Review*, 62 (4): 760–85, https://doi.org/10.2307/3185654

—. 2012. *All this is your World: Soviet tourism at home and abroad after Stalin*. Oxford: Oxford University Press, https://doi.org/10.1093/acprof:oso/9780199609949.001.0001

— & Diane P. Koenker (eds). 2006. *Turizm: the Russian and East European tourist under capitalism and socialism*. Ithaca, NY: Cornell University Press.

Harper, Douglas. 2002. "Talking about pictures: a case for photo elicitation". *Visual Studies*, 17 (1): 13–26, https://doi.org/10.1080/14725860220137345

Jordan, Peter (ed.). 2011. *Landscape and Culture in Northern Eurasia*. Walnut Creek, CA: Left Coast Press, https://doi.org/10.4324/9781315425658

Koenker, Diane P. 2003. "Travel to work, travel to play: on Russian tourism, travel, and leisure". *Slavic Review*, 62 (4): 657–65, https://doi.org/10.2307/3185649

—. 2012. "Pleasure travel in the passport state". In: *Russia in Motion: cultures of human mobility since 1850*, ed. John Randolph & Eugene M. Avrutin, pp. 235–52. Urbana, IL: University of Illinois Press.

Lanzendorf, Martin. 2003. "Mobility biographies: a new perspective for understanding travel behavior". Conference paper held at Session I, *Moving through Nets: the physical and social dimensions of travel*, 10th International Conference on Travel Behaviour Research, Lucerne, 10–15 August 2003, http://archiv.ivt.ethz.ch/news/archive/20030810_IATBR/lanzendorf.pdf

Long, Joseph J. 2013. "Shamanist topography and administrative territories in Cisbaikalia, Southern Siberia". In: *Nomadic and Indigenous Spaces: productions and cognitions*, ed. Judith Miggelbrink, Joachim Otto Habeck, Nuccio Mazzullo & Peter Koch, pp. 181–201. Farnham: Ashgate, https://doi.org/10.4324/9781315598437

Miggelbrink, Judith, Joachim Otto Habeck, Nuccio Mazzullo & Peter Koch (eds). 2013. *Nomadic and Indigenous Spaces: productions and cognitions*. Farnham: Ashgate, https://doi.org/10.4324/9781315598437

Noack, Christian. 2006. "Coping with the tourist: planned and 'wild' mass tourism on the Soviet Black Sea Coast". In: *Turizm: the Russian and East European tourist under capitalism and socialism*, ed. Anne E. Gorsuch & Diane P. Koenker, pp. 281–304. Ithaca, NY: Cornell University Press.

Randolph, John & Eugene M. Avrutin (eds). 2012. *Russia in Motion: cultures of human mobility since 1850*. Urbana, IL: University of Illinois Press.

Salazar, Noel B. 2010. *Envisioning Eden: mobilizing imaginaries in tourism and beyond*. New York: Berghahn.

Schwartz, Joan M. & James R. Ryan (eds). 2003. *Picturing Place: photography and the geographical imagination*. London: I. B. Tauris.

Taylor, Charles. 2002. "Modern social imaginaries". *Public Culture*, 14 (1): 91–124, https://doi.org/10.1215/08992363-14-1-91

Urry, John. 2002. "Mobility and proximity". *Sociology*, 36 (2): 255–74, https://doi.org/10.1177/0038038502036002002

—. 2007. *Mobilities*. Cambridge: Polity Press.

Zuev, Dennis. 2013. "Couchsurfing along the trans-Siberian railway and beyond: cosmopolitan learning through hospitality in Siberia". *Sibirica: Interdisciplinary Journal of Siberian Studies*, 12 (1): 56–82, https://doi.org/10.3167/sib.2013.120103

6. Something like Happiness

Home Photography in the Inquiry of Lifestyles

Jaroslava Panáková

This chapter explores the potential of the visual material in the study of lifestyles.[1] It revisits one of the two fundamental questions of this volume: what is the mutual relation between changing technology and infrastructure on one hand, and lifestyles as exposed by changing visual forms of self-presentation on the other? The main task is an analysis of photographs that the research team compiled through photo elicitation interviews. The capacity of the photo elicitation method lies in the ways the photographs — concurrently visual records, mnemonic devices, sensory stimuli, representations of the past, and sites of interaction with the researcher — stimulate individuals to consider and narrate their life experience. What will emerge from this analysis is a conspicuous difference between the notion of individual integrity conceived of as happiness and depicted by the photographs, and the expression of incompleteness in the verbal accounts in the process of interviewing. The

1   This chapter was written with support from the public sources of the Slovak Research and Development Agency under the contract No. APVV-14-0431. The author gratefully acknowledges Nikolai Vakhtin's guidance regarding Yupik language. I am indebted to Andrej Mentel for his assistance with the statistical analysis. My thanks also go to Jean-Luc Lambert for his ethnographic insights from Siberia. The author also wishes to thank her numerous informants in Novoe Chaplino and beyond.

https://doi.org/10.11647/OBP.0171.06

impact of changing technology on visual representations of happiness is doubtless; nevertheless, conventions and aesthetic standards have a proven tenacity in the visual characteristics under consideration, such as composition, the size of the face in relation to the overall size of the picture, and the height of the horizon.

On the notion of happiness

> The first image he told me about was of three children on the road in Iceland in 1965. [...] He said that for him it was an image of happiness and also that he had tried several times to link it to other images but it never worked. He wrote me: 'One day I will have to put it all alone at the beginning of the film with a long piece of black leader. If they don't see happiness in the picture, at least they'll see the black.
>
> Chris Marker, *Sans Soleil* (1983: 00:00:42-00:01:14)

In describing the North of Russia, Siberia, and the Far East,[2] outsiders would without hesitation use the word "desolate", while locals would sometimes with sarcasm, sometimes with sincere worries, stick to the word "dull" as in the oft-heard statement, "there is nothing to do there" (*tam delat' nechego*). When it comes to statistics, Siberia seems to be a gloomy place indeed: life expectancy at birth is markedly below the world average; tuberculosis rates are comparatively high; violent deaths (caused by accidents, suicide, or homicide) occur on a regular basis; alcoholism is comparatively widespread and often calls forth or aggravates the phenomena just mentioned. These worrying trends have been documented and discussed in a number of publications.[3]

Such an unsettling image is more likely to be found in rural indigenous communities, but the urban or non-indigenous population is not completely spared of it either. I remember two photos that a local woman showed me, with the words I am paraphrasing here: "Would you reckon that these two snapshots depict the same man?" One photograph portrayed a handsome young Russian soldier during his military service; the other taken about 25 years later, showed an

---

2   For simplicity, I shall use the term Siberia from now on for all three geographic names.

3   Bogoyavlenskii (2008: 14–15); Bogoyavlenskii & Pika (1991); Ettyryntyna & Koryagin (1996: 227); Gray (2005: 204); Istomin (2012); Lester & Kondrichin (2003); Pika (1996); Pika, Davis & Krupnik (1993); Pivneva (2005: 68–70); Vakhtin (1992).

alcoholic who looked much older than he actually was when the photo was taken. "This is my relative. You see how Chukotka has changed him!" Such fragments of personal experience confirm and even surpass the diagnosis mentioned above.

The more I think of my field site, the more names of my informants who died tragically or violently come to my mind. When I think of Zhenia, a Yupik Eskimo woman in her early twenties who committed suicide in 2012, I think of her subtle smile. I have neither the right to speak for her on this occasion, nor do I equate a smile with happiness, but I am sure that despite Zhenia's discomfort with this world, she must have experienced happiness in her life, even if only a tiny ray of it. For the sake of these bits and pieces of good which people sense, define for themselves, reflect, try to remember, and sometimes fail to recall in the critical moments of unease, I shall look at the evidence of happiness in Siberian lives and make sense of it anthropologically. Such an attempt shall not be taken as escapism from the tensions that affect so many people's lives. On the contrary — and here I agree with Barbara Rose Johnston et al. (2012) — it shall reveal how happiness as a sensory force may provoke a transformation of human lives in order to (re-)define, sustain, fulfil, and/or dream of what one should be, wants to be, and can afford (or manage) to be (see the Appendix to this volume).

In this sense, happiness in social terms trespasses on its linguistic origin, the "linguistic world-picture" as Al'bert Baiburin and Alexandra Piir (2009: 218) put it. For instance, the Russian word *schastie* implies three meanings: "the complete fulfilment of someone's wishes" (Dal', in Baiburin & Piir 2009: 217–18), "lucky chance", and a metaphysical "kind fate" (Baiburin & Piir 2009: 218), limited in stock and destined. The word for happiness in Sakha language — *d'ol* — resembles the first two Russian meanings, "the fulfilment of a wish" and "unexpected success" (Afanas'ev et al. 1994: 65), but a broader interpretation includes such word categories as happiness-child, happiness-work, or happiness-love (Yemelianov, 1965: 213); the Central Siberian Yupik language does not contain the term happiness as such but related meanings can be formed from the corresponding roots: *quyallek* — joy (the root *quay* — to be glad), *nunakilleq* — pleasure or satisfaction (the root *nunaki* — to feel pleasure), and *kentalnguq* — someone who is lucky in something, e.g.

hunting or gambling (*kenta* — root for luck and lucky person).[4] The Yupik stories collected by Georgii A. Menovshchikov (1969) clearly show the presence of dreams of happiness. The protagonists wish to have a decent family, good health, capable children, an abundance of food, comfort, security, and social justice. We could go on with the diverse linguistic meanings present in our Siberian field sites; the key categories are similar. However, it is the current social meaning of the term "happiness" which is the focus of our attention.

In a social context, happiness is part of an individual lifestyle project, its "architect" and "companion", and sometimes its ultimate goal. We seek to do what we think will make us happy, even if it does not necessarily end up this way. Happiness is woven into a common braid of meanings with aspirations, expectations, values, and choices that are manifest in individual self-formation. Since self-formation would not be possible without making *personal* choices in a particular *social* setting with all its prospects and limitations, happiness would not be achievable, or at least dream-able, without rendering oneself to the interaction between what one imagines choosing, what choice one actually makes, and what in the given circumstances is affordable to be chosen and, if possible, accomplished at the end of the day.

When people reflect lifestyles, they do so through a prism of a certain *durée*, pointing out at least some adversities and challenges, major turning points, and significant moments. Although the importance of life (as perceived by the individual) does not necessarily equal happiness, the former conditions the latter. While significant moments might be unhappy, full of tension, challenge, and struggle (e.g. failure at university exams, loss of the reindeer herd, marital infidelity, etc.), happy moments *cannot* be insignificant (e.g. the birth of a child, falling in love, successful hunt, etc.).

In this study, I am interested in how people in Siberia define happiness, what is common in the awareness of choice-making which is to sustain the achievement of happiness, and how happiness is expressed in order to transgress individual experience and be shared within the community. I shall examine the phenomenon in the context of social transformation, hence my major concern: how do changing

---

4   Linguistic assistance was kindly provided by Nikolai Vakhtin, personal communication (3 May 2014).

circumstances (social setting, technology, and infrastructure) affect people's understanding of what happiness is all about?

My analysis draws on the photo elicitation interviews conducted for our comparative project (see Appendix). The main study material contains 484 home photographs archived by seventy informants from ten different field research sites accompanied by in-depth photo elicitation interviews.[5] I am specifically interested in the visual portrayal of the individual and the social notion of happiness. The initial assumption is that the snapshots preserved in the home archives are predominantly visual accounts of well-being, not the opposite. In fact, it is double happiness they re-evoke: they contain joyful moments and are visually pleasing.

Without a doubt, private collections also contain unhappy pictures. For example, an informant preserved a photo of her and her beloved man; when they broke up, she cut out his face from the picture. When I asked why she still keeps the picture, which I considered spoiled, she simply replied: "Look, how happy I was back then!" This example shows that happiness is transient; visual and verbal accounts reveal the flickering between the categories "happy" and "unhappy". Most pictures selected by our informants are from happy times. It is only the story which reveals that the moment before and/or after the snapshot was taken, was uneasy. For example, a man tells a story about his son's daughter. A small house was built at the *stoibishche* (camp) for the young family in order to have a place to stay when visiting the parents. The whole family was staying together. But after his son had died, his wife remarried and ceased to come to the *stoibishche* with her daughter. One photo shows the whole family at the *stoibishche* and another portrays Grandpa with his granddaughter. The images depict those happier times.

In addition, I shall analyse the impact of visual technology on conventions of depicting "happiness". The aim is to examine the genres, aesthetic conventions, and visual forms that appeal to our informants and why. I assume that although our informants selected the images primarily according to their content, the visual characteristics of the chosen images are not accidental. I acknowledge that due to failing

---

5   The photographs were not necessarily taken by the informants themselves. In most cases, they were taken by a different person (see below). Seventy interviews were analysed out of the total of 79 photo elicitation interviews conducted by the research team. The nine photo elicitation interviews that were not analysed were transcribed and shared with significant delay, thus preventing their inclusion here.

technology or insufficient competence not all the happy moments of our lives have been captured visually, photographically; some of these, however, may be kept in memories. Oral narratives about the absent images of happiness are therefore also considered.

By confronting social and technological changes of the Soviet and post-Soviet modernisation project with individual perceptions and depictions of happiness, I shall be able to reveal not only how the concept of happiness has been changing in Siberia throughout the last five decades but also to argue how the pursuit of happiness has been changing people's lives. This latter moment is of particular significance if confronted with the harmful, self-destructive practices described in the beginning of this chapter. Making sense of things requires contrast and differentiation. In order to reveal with our informants the different fragments of happiness in their pictures, I shall constantly keep in mind the black strip of tragedies in their communities.

Photo elicitation interviews

In order to answer the above questions, I turned to the photographs as well as the narratives collected during the photo elicitation interviews. In social research, the photo elicitation method has been tested in diverse contexts and in a variety of forms (Bunster 1978; Bunster, Chaney & Young 1989; Collier & Collier 1986; Empson 2011; Harper, 1987, 2001, 2002; Harper et al. 2005; Smith & Woodward 1999; Tucker & Dempsey 1991). The coexistence of images and words in these studies is a vital part of the data collection. The scholars point to the strength of photographs to act on the immediate experience of the interview and to stimulate the personal narratives on this occasion. And yet once the data collection is finished, the images are treated as if they fit the stories as nothing more than illustrations. I shall attempt to rectify this situation by acknowledging the power of the visual (Rose 2007: 35) throughout the entire research process. I shall pay equal attention to the relationship between the images and the words, the images themselves, and those narratives which go beyond the images.

The procedure of the photo elicitation interview went as follows: in each of the ten regions, informants with whom the team members of our research project had had previous contact and with whom, as they assumed, conducting such an interview would be feasible, were chosen. The overall sample contained women and men of different age groups from rural and urban settings and diverse professional backgrounds ("traditional" and "non-traditional" activities, manual-labour professions, intellectual work, etc.). Each informant was asked to choose six photographs amongst all the pictures she or he had access to. The request for a definite number of images was taken as a rough guideline by some informants (some chose more, some chose less) and taken literally by others (one Khanty woman chose seven images in order to avoid "the number six", perceived as unlucky by many Khanty people). The type, genre, and other characteristics of the photos were not restricted.

The photo selection process was stimulated by the researcher's statement: "Please select and show the researcher six photographs that characterise your personality in different periods of your life" (*Prosim Vas vybrat' i pokazat' issledovateliu shest' fotografii, kotorye kharakterizuiut Vas kak lichnost' v raznye periody Vashei zhizni*). The statement was formulated deliberately in such a way to give the informants enough room for their own choice- and self-making. Therefore, the ways in which each informant understood the statement and set the criteria of photo selection were also a significant part of the study (e.g. such motivations as "I'll choose those pictures which show how successful I am", "I'll choose only those pictures which are comprehensible for a foreigner and which can demonstrate to her/him my native culture", "Well, how to respond correctly to this task?", "I have no clue. I'll just choose the first ones that I put my hands on", etc.). In some interviews, the individual researcher's particular topic had an influence on the content of the photo elicitation interview and the choice of photos, as informants anticipated they would speak about a particular aspect of their life. To ask *what*, *how*, and *why* photos were selected or omitted was part of this process. Some of these photo selections were done by the informants in front of the researchers and thoroughly recorded.

Analytical instruments

In each interview, the photographs represented a means of study: the stimuli of a narrative, feedback, sites of interaction, mnemonic devices, tools for the reconstruction of events, and illustrations of some, even abstract statements. In the analytical part, however, the images became the objects of study, the representations. Their three interdependent modes — content, meaning, and expressiveness — are examined by content analysis, semantic analysis, and compositional interpretation respectively.

There is a tendency for social scientists to leave the duty of examining images to art and media specialists. The function of the image is restricted to the following: "[…] photography for social researchers is simply a means to certain ends, which visual methods are able to achieve rather than in terms what photographs inherently are" (Knowles & Sweetman 2004: 6). I suggest that such boundary delineation is limiting. Visual analysis in social research, using the assumption that images are representations, allows each photograph to be considered as "a sight which has been recreated and reproduced" (Berger 1972: 9) and as an "important means through which social life happens" (Rose 2007: xiii). These two aspects, visual and social, coexist and shall be conceived as such.

The effects of the images are entangled with social practices. And yet none of it would be possible if the appearance of the images lacked its own particular significance. Visual analysis, in this case, semantic and component analysis of the images, is important because it is through their very appearance that images appeal to and affect people. Parallel to the analysis of the social setting in which the images are embedded, a visual examination of each image shall be carried out, during which the content and meaning of the images are thoroughly studied.

The study of visual expressiveness is based on the fact that a combination of visual elements reflects organisations of experience and feeling. Plastic and spatial organisation, line, colour, texture, perspective (relationships of size, distance, representation of depth), light modulation, etc. can point to the ways that social settings structure visual conventions as well as to the ways that people conceive their feeling visually. The visual elements or their groupings may function as "visual idioms" (Kepes [1944] 1995) — stabilised visual forms with figurative meaning which can point to a specific visual convention or aesthetic preference.

For example, "the selfie" image, which has become a visual convention in contemporary social networking sites, contains several elements which point to its expressiveness: face size, background quality (blurred, in focus, complementary, etc.), framing (cut out face(s), completeness), space organisation (in the foreground and background or between the subject(s) and objects) and after-effects (arranged by the use of apps or specialised software). Some, like the focus, may refer to technical and aesthetic ability. With the improved image resolution of the latest gadgets, the expected outcome is to produce high definition photographs. Any failure to do so is excused by the fact that the image is an "amateur" one (as opposed to a professional one) and "it will just do". At the same time, a blur, not just a "mistake" but a visual idiom, may refer to the "here-and-now" moment and as evidence of a full, satisfying life.

The sense of visual preference is equally traced through our encounters with the informants, whose competence of talking about the pictures was never called into question. The issue of embarrassment based on some technical imperfections was rarely articulated and did not cause any disruption in communication between the researcher and the informant. Despite researchers' initial doubts, most of the informants were able to verbalise why the particular image had an appeal to them. They have a complex idea of what a photo is, and the agency it can have. People also talk about the effect the images can have; according to them, the images emit a "feeling" or "energy" of the times when the pictures were taken; one informant chose a photo of a coming typhoon because she liked the physicality of the natural phenomenon. The content of the images is not the only concern here; visual representational efficacy is equally at stake. The informants' understanding of the photos follows the existing theory: the images are never merely visual but, in fact, they conjure up synaesthetic and kinaesthetic effects; the visual provokes other sensory responses (Edensor 2005, in Rose 2007: 248).

Images never stand alone. If even one image is singled out, as the introductory quote suggests, something precedes and follows it (e.g. a black strip as a visual idiom of a pause). Similar to Gillian Rose, György Kepes accentuates social relatedness and interdependence as important aspects of visual experience. Both scholars rightly urge us to take a relation-minded stance rather than an object-minded one; in other words, to see in the images not atomically separated objects but order, relatedness, and structure(s) (Kepes [1944] 1995; Rose 2007). In addition to the analysis of the semantics, composition and "visual idiom", another step has to be made. In order to reveal the social categories and patterns hidden behind the visual features and to link them to a broader social setting, the pictures must be examined side by side with the informants' narratives. These data show how people make choices about each image, evaluate its significance, appeal, relevance (to their visual experience, to their life, as well as to the researcher's task) and look for the links which connect the selected images to each other. Some informants tend to organise the images into a collage, some stack them in a pile, some order them in a line. This visual order is closely related to the narrative structure of each informant's story and, again, should not be overlooked in the analytical process of what happiness means in Siberia. Some informants prefer to narrate finished stories, and others engage in an open investigation of their lives.

Basic characteristics of the selected images

Out of all 484 images selected from the private collections, 67 photos were made by a professional photographer (passport portraits, studio photos, wedding images, reportage shots, newspaper scraps) and 417 were amateur pictures, out of which there are eight selfies: five made with the help of a self-timer and three with a so-called "long arm".[6] Eleven photos were developed and printed by the informants in a home darkroom, out of which nine images were also photographed by the informants: one is a selfie made by a self-timer, five represent other people or events, and three are landscape images. The remaining two images portray our informant but were taken by someone else. Most images in the collection were photographed by someone other than the informant, mostly because he or she did not own a camera, or wanted to be depicted in the picture (without having to master the self-timer or the "long-arm" selfie).

What features do the selected images have? Apart from authorship, the selection is quite heterogeneous. There are several styles of visual

---

6   In the last five years, the practice of taking selfies with a "long arm" has become much more widespread; in the collection of photographs compiled for the research project in 2010–2012, it is of rather small significance. See the penultimate section of this chapter for an interpretation. The "selfie stick" is a device that was not popular among our informants at the time of our field research.

appearance and forms of representation. The time span between the oldest and the most recent photograph is over eighty years (1930–2012). The images were produced with the help of diverse equipment and in specific technological settings, from manual single-lens reflex cameras (mostly Lomo, Zenit, or Fed), fully automatic compact cameras (Kodak, Polaroid) instant cameras, digital compact cameras (firstly without, then with HD video recording), to built-in cameras in mobile phones and tablets, etc. As is typical for home photography (and regardless of the camera), a standard all-in-focus imaging prevails, unless technological failure occurs. Only in five pictures is depth of field used for compositional means, which means that the background is blurred and the foreground is in focus or vice versa; however, three out of these images were made by professional photographers.

The images also differ in terms of condition. In each household, there are different ways of archiving: cardboard boxes, scrapbooks, photo album sleeves, or "just in a muddle", CD, USB flash drives, external hard disks, SD cards, or online (directly in an email folder or on social networking sites). Some people prefer to literally dig memories out of the box in a contingent order. Some, by contrast, spend more time ordering their photographs. They make special albums with quotations, hand-made decorations and stickers; they say that they "put their soul" into such pieces of work and, therefore, do it during peaceful vacation time. This time-consuming practice has not ceased even in the digital age. Some of those who possess mostly digital photos have set up a folder on their computer or external hard drive titled "The Best" and, at the same time, they have some experience with the actual printing of digital photos.

Last but not least, in each case the image has gone through a particular social life: it was received as a gift from an army buddy; cut out from a local newspaper dedicated to an exemplary worker (*stakhanovets*, see Fig. 6.1); circulated among several households before it reached the final owner; or "just taken for myself, for good memories". If it was not the photo itself which was exchanged, it was the camera at the time of shooting. For example, one informant explains that when he went on a safari trip, he deliberately exchanged his camera with another visitor: "[…] I was shooting him on his camera, he was shooting me on my camera so that I would get pictures of me and he would have pictures

Fig. 6.1. Mother in the newspaper, Yanrakynnot (Chukotka), 1999. Photo: Jaroslava Panáková's interviewee (with permission), CC-BY-ND.

of himself". This practice shows how travelling can turn into an act of reciprocal exchange. Some photographs receive considerable respect: they are decorated with embroidery, put in a frame, hung on a wall, or placed in the living-room glass cabinet. Some "old" pictures, as the informants call them (usually black-and-white images), exist as a single original and are, therefore considered precious. Such photographs are given to a child who departs for university studies or leaves home after marriage; this is done on a special occasion with heart-breaking words, as some informants claimed.

Regardless of whether the photographs were selected in chronological order, each image signifying an important life period, or drawn from one folder made in the same year, the overall visual data set is indeed diverse in terms of the (visual) experience it represents; a single question asked by an interviewer stimulated the informants to think of their lives through images and resulted in a photo collection which covers a broad range in terms of content, meaning, expressiveness, and social context.

Is it possible to reveal a pattern in such a mix of (visual) experiences? Can the features of visual representation be adequately cross-examined and linked with verbal data, having compiled such a hodgepodge of photographs? Beyond any doubt, there is a common strand in the data, both visual and verbal. It consists of three main elements: *personal biography* narrated along with the chosen pictures, which reflects how modern institutions influence the way people conceive of themselves; *modern institutions*, taken in a broad sense, which manage people's possessions, intellectual and physical capacities, relationships, and self-perception, including the sense of "being happy"; and *the visual* itself, as a result of technological and institutional developments, which have the expressive power and social dimension to be an effective instrument for self-presentation.

Let's start with the visual. The focus in this study is on the selection of the visual rather than visual production. The pattern of visual preference in connection with the notion of well-being, not the skill or competence, is what is being examined. The informants might not know about all of the technological details that went into making the photos (or how photos are made *per se*), but they do make a choice about the image that will represent a significant fragment of their life, and they insist on preserving it. There are cases when the informant changed his or her decision and selected a new image. All of these choices were made consciously, and what is even more important, thoughtfully. One can argue that the selection was done simply on the basis of content. For instance, an informant would like to show his devotion to his mother, select a photo related to her and narrate a story about her. What photo does he choose? Most likely, in accordance with the visual convention related to the representation of persons in a particular cultural setting (I shall return to this convention in the analysis of portraits), he selects a portrait of his mother. Here comes the complexity of his choice: there are, let's say, at least two pictures of his mother in his collection. Which one does he choose? The one in which she is younger and, as he thinks, prettier? The one where the size, light, colour, and texture are more appealing? Does he prefer the photo where he is pictured with her or just a single portrait of her? These and many more questions arise.

Despite the entanglement of many factors present in such a choice, there is a high probability that within a particular sample such selection is based on at least one pattern of aesthetic preference; in several studies it has been shown that a visual idiom such as composition, particularly expressed by the height of the horizon, is linked to a degree of the analytical or holistic affordance of the individual (Masuda & Nisbett 2001, 2006; Miyamoto, Nisbett & Masuda 2006; Istomin, Panáková & Heady 2014). Other scholars point out that another visual idiom related to proportionality — the golden section rule — has an impact on aesthetic preference (Benjafield & Adams-Weber 1976). In the sections to follow, the correlation between the compositional parameters (height of the horizon, perspective, and face size of the subjects) and the origin of the images (time, location, authorship) will be examined.

Aside from the visual itself, the images provide the narrated biography with rich material. The selected images are not atomic units, they are in some cases loosely, and in others tightly linked to each other; yet, all are tied to the biographical stories of the seventy individuals. The narratives told along with the photos provide insights into the mediation of the meaning between anthropologist and informant of what it takes "to live a life" and, if possible, "to live a happy one".

The interplay of the personal accounts, selected photos and the immediate experience of the photo elicitation interviews serve to place subjective experience in the context of lifestyles, which themselves are produced and reproduced within complex supra-individual, traditional and modern institutional frameworks. Not only does the network of possibilities configure individuals' choices and actions (Bourdieu 1990), it also frames the personal awareness of people's lives as if they were individual projects of self-making (Giddens 1991: 1).

Susan Sontag identifies visual media as a key feature of the "modern": "[...] a society becomes 'modern' when one of its chief activities is producing and consuming images, when images that have extraordinary powers to determine our demands upon reality and are themselves coveted substitutes for first-hand experience become indispensable to the health of the economy, the stability of the polity, and the pursuit of private happiness" (Sontag, [1977] 2005: 119). If the institutional setting influences the ways in which individuals structure, organise, reflect, remember, and represent their experience visually, the selected photos together with the narratives are likely to show a particular pattern of the structuring. The organising principle of the visual can then be linked with a specific institutional framing, e.g. foregrounding obedience and conformism in a well-ordered, symmetrically arranged school group portrait.

The institutional dimension is present in the sample through the diverse visual conventions which have evolved over time. In relation to the research questions, this shall be an advantage. My aim is to confront the changing institutional framing of the personal perception of happiness with the changing preference of a particular visual convention. The very nature of photography stems from the capacity to trace, frame, and preserve the time; not only does each image portray a moment in history, but the series of images from different time periods manifests the technological and institutional changes ("technological" in terms of the capacities to create an image, whereas "institutional" in terms of what is desirable to be depicted and in which way). Particularly, one cannot leave unnoticed how the time flow, *durée*, is materialised in the different visual qualities.

Let me give you one example. The visual property which is most notably linked to the time change as a result of industrial and technological progress is texture. As Kepes wrote, neither the unaided eye nor a machine could follow all the surface qualities and visual properties of the newly developed materials: softness, hardness, roughness, smoothness, etc. Photography, however, with its optical, visual, and technical qualities had indeed the capacity to capture textures (Kepes [1944] 1995: 150). In this sense, texture is a technological change inscribed directly in the photographic image. Texture has also become the only visible sign indicating spatial relationships and organisation (ibid: 151). It does not only portray the time span, it preserves it: whereas colour (with its particular features such as hue, brightness, and saturation) can fade and cease to be a marker of time (the photos in our sample made in the 1990s look older than those from the 1980s), texture persists. Regardless of whether they are analogue, digital, or digitally manipulated, the texture of the portrayed objects reveals the kind of visual and social life the picture has gone through.

Now, apart from the visual qualities, there are other visible elements in each picture which point to the changing institutional framing over time: (i) the style of the subjects (posing, body arrangement, clothing, hair style, etc.); (ii) the occasion which was considered worth photographing; and (iii) the visual appearance of the photograph. For instance, the photographs show self-stylisation through clothing: work outfits or school uniforms (in pre-1990s photos), ethnic costumes (in the Khanty-Mansi Autonomous Okrug, Irkutsk, and Buryatia), trendy fashion (urban residents in Novosibirsk or rural youth in Sakha, Chukotka, and the Khanty-Mansi Autonomous Okrug) as a manifestation of being "contemporary" and "knowledgeable", or "anti-glamour" garments in the reactions of some middle-class youth in Novosibirsk to the dominance of mainstream fashion trends.

Modernity the Siberian way

David Chaney (1996: 159) considers the precondition of lifestyles to be modernity. Although he writes about lifestyles in the context of capitalist countries, they are equally developed in centralised economies. The modernisation project, which started in the Russian territories in the nineteenth century, has further evolved under dramatic historical and political conditions: Bolshevik revolution, Civil War, War Communism, New Economic Policy, Stalinism, etc. The legitimacy and thus persistence of the regime was dependent on several successful flagship projects; and the transformation of Russia's vast and remote periphery, Siberia, was one of them.

The sovietisation process in Siberia followed the same pattern as elsewhere, and yet with a decade-long delay and higher inconsistency (Ssorin-Chaikov 2003) due to the geographical and climatic specifics of the region. The small, scattered settlements and nomadic camps of the native Siberian peoples were gradually conglomerated into larger villages with *kolkhoz* or *sovkhoz* farms as part of the amalgamation policy (*politika ukrupneniia*) over a period that started in 1928 and extended into the 1980s.[7] Standardised modern institutions for education, medicine, local administration, industry, and agriculture were established throughout the Soviet Union. "Culture" turned into social obligation; cultural workers were to stimulate the natives to become culturally and morally "true" Soviet citizens. The intensification of industry reached the major Siberian centres in the 1950s and 1960s. Factories and mines were built in tandem with urban settlements, encouraging the gradual urbanisation of the population. Large-scale industrial projects tended to be built and run by Slavic incomers who migrated to the new industrial towns. In the late 1960s, the achievements and

---

7   For instance, Novoe Chaplino came into existence in 1958 by putting together the
     people of Staroe Chaplino (Ungaaziq, at that time this hamlet already included some
     Yupik clans from other places, e.g. Siiqlluk) with some other Yupik settlements (e.g.
     Avan, Kivak, Aslliq) and moving them to the shore of Tkachen Bay.

accoutrements of the "golden" five-year plan[8] arrived to Siberia: apartment houses, refrigerators, television sets, the *Smena-8M* photo camera, and Soviet tea with an elephant on the packaging. Nikita Khrushchev made some palpable ideological concessions in regard to the consumption of material goods in order to legitimise socialism in geopolitically difficult times (Crowley & Reid 2010: 14). Initially, the regime had given the utopian promise of material pleasures in some "later" historical period (ibid: 3). However, in the 1960s such pleasures became real. As a result, people of different ethnic origins who had already learnt to identify with the Soviet project, additionally came to submit to consumerism. Without proper infrastructure in the rural territories, however, only a trip to Moscow (or the regional capital, to some degree) could satisfy the consumers' needs; hence, the origin of shopping travel (*poekhali zakupat'sia/otovarivat'sia*), which persists even today.

The two dimensions of well-being, Soviet citizenship and consumerism, fell apart under the political and economic circumstances of the 1990s. The withdrawal of people, resources, and services was so massive that in some places such as Chukotka (at that time a part of Magadan Oblast), even after the recuperation period since 2000, the highest numbers of the Soviet era have not been reached. Those people who stayed (mostly the native population) found themselves without jobs, transportation, adequate pensions, and in some cases even heating and hot water in the middle of a Siberian winter. Extensive new investments in the 2000s, aimed at renewing the extraction of natural resources, led to the return of consumerism. Similarly, since 2000, recentralisation has fostered identification with the Russian state, demonstrated among other things by the obligatory military-patriotic youth education programme (*voenno-patrioticheskoe vospitanie molodezhi*) (Laruelle 2008; see also Chapter 11 in this volume) and youth and children organisations such as *Nashi* (Ours) or *Mishki* (Teddy Bears) with high loyalty to the state (Baiburin & Piir, 2009: 252; Hemment 2015).

---

8   The five-year plan for 1966–1970 proved to be the most successful (GNP increased by thirteen per cent) and therefore is referred to as the "golden" one. Kosygin's reforms introduced a series of new economic strategies, e.g. producers' interest in gaining revenue, which stimulated the state-directed economy.

Home photography in Siberia

The first traces of photography in Siberia date back to the beginning of the twentieth century. As home media, however, photography was introduced into everyday life during Khrushchev's peak era of Soviet modernisation. While reporters and professional photographers recorded the state's achievements in the sphere of construction and production, along with the life of the institutions (workers' communes, workplaces, and schools), people used photography as a reminder and evidence of their well-being. Although visually, home photography in Siberia is a Soviet cultural product, socially it is primarily a phenomenon of modernity: mechanical reproduction (Benjamin 1977) turns the visual into consumer products and photographing into a testimony of tangible well-being. As to Siberia, the question then is whether distinct local patterns of visual representation entered the general Soviet model. In other words, is there a particular and preferred photographic image of Siberian happiness?

Siberian home photography shows two dominant features: on the one hand, it follows the standard middle-brow aesthetics, which can be labelled "Soviet"; on the other, there is a set of qualities that emerged from the eternally unfinished and thus provisional state of existence. In order to cope with the institutional and infrastructural incongruities, *bricolage* (Lévi-Strauss 1966; de Certeau [1974] 1984) seemed to be a handy approach. Triggered by the uneven and inconsistent influx of people, material, finances and technology to Siberia, *bricolage* became a way of patching missing elements through the assemblage and re-assemblage of the existing ones. *Bricolage* is "the purest notion of variation on a theme by mere recombination" (Friedman 2001: 47); this technique has also been applied to home photography.

Bricolage

The following examples refer to *bricolage* as a way of representing significant and/or happy moments without disturbing the visual convention imported from the urban environment. The status photos of any Soviet citizen in front of monuments such as statues of political leaders, the eternal fire, or war memorials can be found in large numbers in the Siberian collections. However, pictures in front of the statues of famous writers or painters are less common. The established standard in the city, still alive today, is altered by recombination. For instance, the Pushkin statue on the Ploshchad' isskustv in St Petersburg, a common place where a local middle-class couple would take their wedding photo to emphasise their status, is altered by the Siberians with another object or place, more likely to be a status marker recognised in the province. While visiting the city, village people often pose in front of the building of a Ministry or novelties of the "civilised world"; for example, men take pictures of themselves standing in front of an expensive motorbike, a trendy car, or with the latest model of a rifle in the hunter's shop, while women pose in new fashion releases in the shopping malls.

Fig. 6.2. Christmas celebration in a private living room, Altai Republic, 2004. Photo: Luděk Brož (with permission), CC-BY-ND.

Another form of recombination is found in the photographic memorabilia of one's achievements: here anything of a respectful or rare character that the protagonists put in front or behind themselves can be viewed as a trophy. Hunting and tourist trophies prevail. And yet, in the Far Northern regions, where grapes or watermelons are rare, a fruit can easily become a trophy. Another example of *bricolage*, in this case an imperfect imitation of the urban convention, is a group portrait (mostly family or communal gatherings) in the living room with a display cabinet or hanging carpet in the background (Fig. 6.2). Such display refers primarily to the cohesion of and "happy moments" in the family (see Bourdieu et al. [1965] 1990 for a similar case in France from the 1960s) but may relate to any other reference group. In the Siberian arrangement, however, the Russia-wide standard of home decoration is contrasted with the traditional household. Members of local intellectual elites arrange their homes to the standards they themselves perceive as Russian-like, and they prefer to present their reference groups, such as families or church groups, through such portraits with the carpet in the background. In this way, they define "happiness" by the capacity to show their homes as cultivated places, which would confirm their support for the Soviet civilising mission.

The principle of *bricolage*, as mentioned above, echoed a spatially disproportionate availability of different (visual) technologies as well as an uneven distribution of specialists and supplies. Centrality and peripherality have a direct impact on the ways in which technical innovations come isolated to the settlement and are appropriated in a hit-or-miss way. The time delay of the incoming novelty usually had an impact on how, if at all, it was appropriated and could result in any visual convention. What is peculiar about the remote regions of Siberia is the fact that new technological devices would usually be introduced as "lone" items (e.g. brought from the city centres during business trips, studies, or vacations), i.e. taken out of the proper context. For instance, an analogue compact camera would be purchased in the city without having a facility, a film lab, in the native village to retrieve the pictures from the film. It could take up to two years, until the next allowed vacation leave, when the person could go to the city to have the film developed and photos printed. To give another example, local amateur photographers who learnt during their studies in the city how to make their own black-and-white prints often encountered shortages of chemicals and other supplies in their home village.

Similarly, the opening of the borders initiated a new round of the inconsistent spread of technology, this time from abroad. Instant cameras, incompatible with anything there was on the market before or after, reached Chukotka in the early 1990s when the local Yupik people started visiting their relatives across the border in Alaska. Just for comparison, the popular use of these cameras in the United States dates back to as early as 1972 when Polaroid introduced its *SX-70* followed by Kodak, which in 1976 entered the instant market with its

Kodak *EK4*. The use of this technology in Chukotka was limited literally by the number of visits abroad, because at home no proper supplies, such as cartridges, were available. Such a camera became for locals a mere "gimmick" (*dikovinka*), a first exemplary product of a throw-away approach to things, very markedly in contrast to the compulsive hoarding of Soviet times.

All of these examples may seem to refer to photographic production only. However, they directly point to the absence of any distinct convention in aesthetic preference. The cases show that numerous technological novelties in photography could not be widely adopted in Siberia, since infrastructure, long-term occurrence, and camera owners' active experimenting with aesthetic forms were lacking. In such conditions, neither a shooting style, nor any distinct aesthetic preference can be easily established. The technology which becomes obsolete so fast fails to generate any lasting visual standards. More importantly, however, these incongruities lead to a specific framing of reality. Technology and infrastructure condition and limit the ways local people are able to, or even dare to see and visualise their lives preserving the instants and spells of well-being.

Aside from its *bricolage*-like nature, Siberian home photography abides by middle-brow standards. Formal school education, the introduction of technology from/by major Soviet centres, and centralised management of artistic activities through the Houses of Culture (Donahoe & Habeck 2011) directly contributed to middle-brow aesthetic preferences. Majority aesthetic standards (be it Soviet or contemporary Russian ones) endure in the most remote Siberian regions with a degree of variation.

Pursuing the golden section rule

Let us consider one of the key visual characteristics: the composition of the image. This parameter can be quite broad and analysed in many ways; I will focus on the height of the horizon. Its most common manifestation in middle-brow image production is the golden section rule, which envisages a relation of 61.8 to 38.2 per cent as aesthetically most pleasing. The horizon displayed on the image should be located at approximately 61.8 per cent or approximately 38.2 per cent of the image's height (counted from the bottom margin). As there are both vertically (175) and horizontally (309) oriented pictures in the collection, the horizon was counted as the percentage relative to the height of the photo. Out of 484 images, there are 375 which show an identifiable horizon (N=375, out of which 250 are horizontally and 125 vertically oriented).[9] I was also interested in whether the sample revealed any changes in the composition throughout the decades.

The results show that there was almost no change in the height of the horizon throughout the decades. A very slight change between the 1960s and 1980s as well as between the 1960s and 2000s can be observed. It seems that in the 1960s, the height of the horizon was lower but the values are insignificant. Overall, the height of the horizon has remained relatively stable over more than four decades.

What is intriguing, however, is the fact that the stable value of the mean height of the horizon as measured from the bottom margin in the vertically oriented photos approaches the value of the golden section rule (about 38 per cent from the bottom margin), while in the horizontally oriented images it tends towards the midpoint (about 44 per cent).[10] This once again proves that the aesthetic preference in Siberia in regard to photography complies with imported visual standards.

The question is whether the standard aesthetic rule is equally applied in the rural and urban environments. In the selection of all photos provided by the urban informants, the height of the horizon increases in each decade towards the present, i.e. from about 27 per cent (in the 1950s) to about 46 per cent (in the 2000s), whereas the selection of the rural informants shows the opposite: a decrease in the horizon from about 57 per cent (in the 1950s) to about 44 per cent (in the 2000s). As the distribution is uneven and old photos are not sufficiently represented, the power of the effect and the statistical power of the test are low. The differences may be accidental and, therefore, further research is necessary. Nevertheless, it is evident that the photographers

---

9   Out of 109 photos, in which the horizon is not identifiable, there are 59 horizontally and fifty vertically oriented images.

10   The standard notion of what is visually appealing also explains why most of the selected pictures are taken at eye level (364 pictures) and without any particular compositional perspective (382 pictures). They have a linear perspective accentuated by a narrowing element (e.g. a corridor or road) or a diagonal perspective (delineated, for example, by a staircase inclining from one corner to another).

of the images taken in the research project's rural settlements in the 1950s, 1960s, and 1970s, were professionals or amateur photographers schooled in the city. In the urban environment, authorship was much more diverse from the 1950s onwards. Both rural and urban backgrounds have produced uniform images from the 1980s towards the 2000s: the compilation of photographs from those decades reveals a preference for horizontally oriented images, in which the horizon divides the scenery into halves.

The data seem to support my initial assumption that Siberian home photography is regarded as pleasing, and thus evokes positive emotions when it follows the standard aesthetic rule of the golden section. It is possible to conclude that practices of photographing and practices of selecting photographs for display to others (in this case, researchers) follow acquired aesthetic conventions that seem to eclipse any differences in individual perceptual style. In other words, it is not possible to detect spatial or temporal dynamics in the height of the horizon; what emerges instead, is a certain uniformity in the way photographs are designed and selected by the beholder. This standard appearance of the Siberian photographs assures common visual experience that is taken as pleasing. Consequently, it is only the content of the pictures and the accompanying individual stories which can prove the diversification and differentiation of the understanding of what happiness might be.

Biographical narratives: consistencies and ruptures

After this description of the social settings and the aesthetic and technological contexts in which the visual emerges, it is now time to turn our attention to the stories of and along the photographs.

The biographical moment which allows the photos and the narratives to intermingle also reveals contradictions. Firstly, the photos might seem to portray happiness and can be described as such by their owners, even if the reality at the time of photographing was perceived as gloomy. In other words, unhappy reality can nevertheless produce happy pictures: for example, an image of the tundra landscape or a portrait of the informant sitting on a hill and contemplating the landscape, both photographed during an escape from the humdrum of the quotidian. Secondly, although the photograph usually stimulates a rich narrative

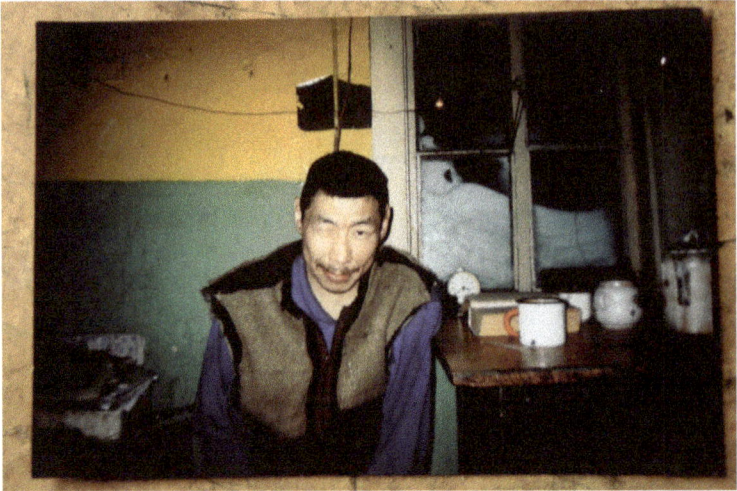

Fig. 6.3. In memory of the deceased son, Novoe Chaplino, 1990s. Photo: Jaroslava Panáková's interviewee (with permission), CC-BY-ND.

which goes well beyond the content of the picture, occasionally there are images which result in silence. Most of these recall some absent person and thus represent absence itself: for instance, the father who presents the only remaining portrait of a deceased son (Fig. 6.3), or the son who shows a newspaper image of his working-hero mother (Fig. 6.1) and feels guilty for not being able to pursue her legacy. Thirdly, there are stories along images that do not exist; such absence of images may be caused by their loss, ruin (through fire), or deliberate destruction and deletion (images in which "I do not look well", images of "the people with whom I broke up", "the whole school album because it looked awful", and similar cases) or by the fact that these images were never made (the camera broke, the moment occurred so unexpectedly) but are "well remembered".

It is worth mentioning that a whole series of images might be missing in home archives: for instance, photos of everyday life before the 2000s are rare, as the devices would not allow easy and quick handling. This means that working days were portrayed only through official images, while home cameras recorded the days or hours off work. It stands in contrast to the abundance of today's mobile phone snapshots of virtually any moment of one's life. Although present in the home archives, in the photo selection made for the photo elicitation interview, there are no images of toddlers, portraits of oneself as a bride, or pictures of nightlife. There is but one portrait from a Christmas celebration and two from a birthday celebration. Even though the home archives are surely full of these, the informants did not find them relevant for the given purpose. Interestingly, there is one portrait of a man while he is photographing — a sort of a reflection of the subject in the mirror.

These possible absences of photographs exemplify potential ruptures of the biographical narratives. They urge us to ask ourselves about the universe of people, things, and places that the interviewees draw upon for self-presentation, and their particular preference for one image over another. What part of life do they try to keep hidden and what part of life are they open to talking about? What does the interviewee try to tell the interviewer when they shift in their narration from the selected images to the non-existent ones? In the appreciation of the absent or fragmentary, anthropologists come to resemble archaeologists. The truly missing images or words keep reminding us of the fact that all the photographs and memories point to moments which are already gone. The patterns hidden in such data may yet reveal transitions in time.

"Collective and individual"

Socialism was a social experiment which arguably took on even more experimental traits in Siberia than in any other region of the country (cf. Kotkin 1995; Ssorin-Chaikov 2003). In Soviet times, "experiments with happiness" (Baiburin & Piir 2009: 221) were part of the grand social project; they depended on, and were products of, the personal, societal, and ideological design (Balina & Dobrenko 2009: xvii). Although we encountered a variety of personal trajectories, the common, ideologically approved standards of happiness that structure the lives of our informants can be observed across the data. The institutional criteria of "having a happy life" were reduced to the assigned, collective good. If the state-promoted ideology imposed the standard of happiness at the same time as the state machinery severely punished the disloyal, then to be happy (the standard way) was *obligatory* (Baiburin & Piir 2009: 226). The transition to the post-Soviet period was marked by the absence of the controlling gaze of the state, while responsibility was delegated to the individual; now it is the individual who is responsible for being happy.

My aim in this section is to show how biographical and institutional aspects intersect in the collective and individual concepts of happiness and how they are manifested by the images in the informants' selections. Higher levels of individualism or self-independence in a given community are linked with the tendency towards analytism in the visual representation (Kitayama et al. 2003; Markus & Kitayama 2003). In other words, object-focused images prevail; in photography, these may be singular portraits, selfies, or images of things in the foreground. On the other hand, collectivism or self-interdependence correlate with perceptual holism, which is manifested by the field-focused representation; in the images, the background tends to be equally important as the foreground (e.g. tourist group portraits at a tourist site and landscape images). In fact, if a group of persons and things is present, it is well distributed over the composition, so it creates the field itself. I shall look at the individualistic and collectivist traits in the collected Siberian photos. It will be possible to see whether the social experiments in Siberia, together with the adoption of the Russian (Soviet) photographic visual standards in photography, led to the object-focused representation of happiness. Let me first focus on a descriptive analysis of the photos and then turn to the interpretation of the images along with the narratives.

Firstly, the photo selection can be sorted by the simple characteristics of the pictures into group portraits and portraits of a single person. In both categories, we have images in which the informants are depicted and those pictures in which the informants are absent. The presence of the informant in the image prevails. In the given sample, the ratio of images in which the informants themselves are depicted to those in which another subject is chosen is 381 to 103. It is true that the phrase of the given task included the words "your life" and "yourself", which the informants could have taken literally, despite the fact that they were specifically instructed to choose *any* image with *any* subject in it. There can be a simple logic behind the informants' choice: "when I am asked to tell 'my' story about 'my' life, why shall I restrict myself to being in the image 'myself'?" Or: "it is 'I' who is experiencing the happy moments and it is 'I' who shall, therefore, be present in the visual evidence".

In most of the regions, independent of sex and age, informants chose predominantly images with themselves (with or without other subjects).

Out of seventy informants, 37 individuals selected images that *all* show themselves in the picture, with or without someone else. The remaining 33 informants included more than sixty per cent of the images in their individual photo sets which depict themselves (again with or without someone else). In Novosibirsk and Chavan'ga, each photo set has a roughly equal number of images that include the interviewee versus those that do not include the interviewee (half and half). In the Khanty-Mansi Autonomous Okrug and in Buryatia, the share of photographs showing the interviewee is roughly one third. The Republic of Sakha and Chukotka are remarkable in this respect: in Sakha, one female informant did not choose a single picture with herself; in Chukotka, there are three such cases, two men and one woman. One individual selection in Sakha (an urban resident) and another four in Chukotka (all villagers) contain significantly less than forty per cent of pictures with the owner (16.7 per cent in Sakha and 23.5, 14.3, 38.5, and 18.18 per cent in Chukotka). Most informants in Chukotka are older than forty and the limited range of photographs they could choose from may be the reason for such particularity; and yet, a 34-year-old woman (urban resident) and a 28-year-old man in Sakha (who had recently become an urban resident) as well as a thirty-year-old man in Chukotka (a villager) acted similarly. In all these selections, each informant decided to show their life through another subject or object. Within the total selection of 484 images, there are eighteen cases of identification through an object, 29 through one significant person and 56 through a group of persons.

When it came to individual versus collective depictions, almost half the images (45.5 per cent) depicted a single person of object: 174 single portraits of the informants themselves (Table 6.1 on p. 254), eighteen images of objects, and 28 single portraits of other persons (a "significant other", Table 6.2 on p. 255). The remainder is constituted by images of a couple or a group, with or without the informant, who are enjoying life collectively. The presence of the informant accentuates his or her relationship with the collective. No matter to what degree and in which way the informant dominates the group portrait — be it by gesture, size (standing closer to the lens), or posing — it is a collective wherein everyone shares a portion of happiness with the informant.[11] Although

---

11   The Russian word *dolia* translates as both "share" and "fortune" (Baiburin & Piir 2009: 218).

the individual and the collective may seem to oppose each other semantically and divide the selection quantitatively into two halves, the data, in fact, support the idea that an underlying trope in the self-presentation of our interviewees from Siberia is neither just self, nor a collective, but self-in-a-collective.

Even in portrait photographs in the strict sense, we are made aware of the fact that someone was standing behind the camera; the sharing of the moment was then happening as a dialogue while photographing rather than as a session of being photographed together. Some home photos taken by analogue cameras occasionally show a blurry thumb on the margin — the evidence of an (unskilful) photographer.

There is also an effect of the observer's view meeting with the view of the portrayed individual; it happens especially in those images that represent a subject who is looking directly at the camera. It is one of the most powerful visual sources of dialogue: namely, the encounter of a portrayed subject with someone who is looking at her or him in physical reality — the photographer (in the process of photographing) or the spectator (in the process of sharing and discussing the photos). Such gaze, as David MacDougall writes, "evokes one of the primal experiences of daily life — a look returned by a look — through which we signal mutual recognition and affirm the shared experience of the moment. [...] In a Lacanian sense, the self is reaffirmed and mirrored in these comparatively rare direct glances from the screen" (MacDougall 1998: 100). In other words, although the portraits may manifest very intimate spheres of the informant, their hidden feelings and desires, they also depict the experience of a dialogue with someone else in the physical (who is photographing me?) or mental space (who will be watching me in the picture?).

"Reading" the narratives along the photographs

Now let us look more closely at these images along with the narratives. Semantically the happiness of self-in-a-collective is expressed through images of two key social institutions: family and work. This can often be traced in the narratives of indigenous informants regarding their sense of home. On the contrary, happiness understood as a personal pursuit braided with a series of transformations and restatements of self-integrity is most fervently manifested by the portraits of self and significant others as well as by travel photos of non-indigenous informants.

Fig. 6.4. Portrait from kindergarten times, Tegi (Berezovskii Raion), 1992. Photo: Ina Schröder's interviewee (with permission), CC-BY-ND.

Work and education

In Soviet ideology, the paradigm of happiness was twofold: on the one hand, it was universal, the transcendent happiness of the Soviet citizen, characterised, besides anything else, by honesty, work ethic and appreciation of the Soviet Union; on the other hand, it was happiness in personal life (*schastie v lichnoi zhizni*), to use the term that became popular under Leonid Brezhnev (Baiburin & Piir 2009: 223). Immediate material well-being was to be deferred to a rather distant future and, therefore, happiness was linked with sacrifice and struggle. The self-realisation of the Soviet citizen took place through work understood as a moral deed; work was considered a personal commitment to the benefit of the community. Moral satisfaction is a criterion mentioned by the informants whose careers were launched during Soviet times.

Be it a teacher, scientist, bus driver, accountant at the *kolkhoz*, or reindeer herder — nearly all of our older informants defined work with enthusiasm. The retrospective narratives allow us to identify some categories that were eclipsed, or at least were not pronounced, during Soviet times: the informants imply that the capacity to perform a certain profession does not depend solely on the institutional context or personal effort but includes an irrational category of destiny, fortune or talent. The images that evoke narratives about work are restricted to several types: the collective portrait with co-workers (emphasising collectivity), portraits in uniform or work outfits at the workplace, e.g. school, forest, *kolkhoz* (indicating status and affiliation), and depictions of award ceremonies (documenting symbolic reward).

In addition, women tend to talk about their professional career along and in line with the images of their family or children. The ideal of a woman who manages to combine the roles of excellent worker and true citizen, loving wife and caring mother is regarded with respect; it stands for achievement reached through sacrifice. Some women think of themselves as having performed poorly or having "failed"; but their personal criteria are so intermingled with the institutional framing that they do not realise that "their" concept of happiness was, in fact, institutionally given. Self-reflection, however, happens in the description of the social changes in the 1990s. Here the informants contrast the personal responsibility of the true Soviet citizen to the paternalism of the state broadly understood as a false understanding of collective responsibility for other individuals.

Those of our younger informants, who reached adulthood in the 2000s, understand responsibility as self-reliance, self-sufficiency, or even self-containment; in their narratives they accentuate self-perfection, self-fulfilment, and self-improvement. All of these expressions evoke intensive self-centredness. Work has to be meaningful for the person, only then can it bring a true reward (see Chapter 3 of this volume). The photographs related to these narratives of young informants represent the workplace, e.g. office (status and affiliation), graduation and similar ceremonies of award conferment (symbolic reward), as well as goods that were bought from the money earned, usually clothes, hobbies, or tours (material reward). The main difference between Soviet and post-Soviet careers is the shift from socialisation towards the acquisition of

Fig. 6.5. First day at school (*pervyi zvonok*), Khanty-Mansiisk, 1 September 2008.
Photo: Ina Schröder's interviewee (with permission), CC-BY-ND.

material well-being, from work for dignity to work for consumption, from toil to hedonism. This pronounced self-centredness does not necessarily mean that people look only inward and have fewer social contacts; in fact, our data show that the sphere of socialisation might have moved from work to leisure time, during which the enjoyment of things (clothes, food) or places (travelling) in good company is of prime importance.

No matter what their age, all our informants tended to display themselves through social institutions interwoven in their individual biographies. Such images show conventionalised initiations, which are inherent to Soviet and post-Soviet times alike. The particular institutions mark turning points in the chronology of people's lives:

- registration of a newborn at the registry office;

- kindergarten (standardised, official individual or group portrait, see Fig. 6.4);

- school (annual group portraits; images of the initiation ceremony called the "First Bell" (*Pervyj zvonok*), see Fig. 6.5; photos of the last day of school and closing ceremony (*Poslednii zvonok*); images of the graduation ceremony (*Vypusknoi*);

- university graduation;

Fig. 6.6. Army pledge, near Rubtsovsk (Altai Krai), 2006. Photo: Ina Schröder's
interviewee (with permission), CC-BY-ND.

- military service (portrait of a recruit giving the pledge, see Fig. 6.6);

- work collectives (including Soviet *kolkhoz* work teams, groups of teachers, reindeer herders, contemporary office life, and corporate meetings).

While most of these images are standardised and taken by a professional photographer, the school and university images include some spontaneous snapshots. However, everyday life in such institutions is very rarely portrayed. The number of such images may increase in the upcoming years with the technological development of built-in cameras in mobile phones.

Sense of place

The sense of place is perpetually (re)confirmed by movement, which produces personal "topographies", and by the images and narratives that accumulate in the stock of "spatial imaginaries" (see Chapter 5 in this volume). As the photo selection proves, the informants convey their biographies as interwoven not only with essential encounters and "decisive moments" (Cartier-Bresson 1952) which are not to be forgotten, but certainly with meaningful places as well. The images documenting people's movement (or dwellings), including such a pervasive genre as tourist photography, would deserve a separate chapter. Here I restrict myself to the aspects I find most important in relation to happiness.

There are 208 images that clearly depict a place or movement in the exterior. Most of the images manifest a dialogue between the person(s) and place, except for sixteen images[12] which do not contain any person at all: eleven of these photographs feature a landscape; three of them, a building or an urban object; and two of them, a still life. Together with the chosen photos, the informants produce elaborate narratives of the sense of home on the one hand, and "distant hereness" (Kirshenblatt-Gimblett 1998) on the other.

Overall, the number of home sceneries is lower than expected, taking into account the fact that a majority of the urban residents offer rich narratives of their hometowns and most of the rural residents claim an intensive emotional link with the land. The home geographies imply quotidian connectedness with the places. The latter ensure people's well-being by nurturing them; we repeatedly encountered informants' stories about their getting reconnected with nature by embracing a tree or lying on the ground (see Fig. 6.7). The notion of the "power/energy of the place" (*energetika mesta*) is articulated. The significance of a specific place is explained through its distinct features: it may be the cluster of the "right" trees (e.g. birch), a hub for communication with the spirits, or the home of ancestors; it may provide memories of the past as well as one's own subjective experience, rest, and peace for the soul, and an assemblage of senses (mostly visual, haptic, and olfactory). For these informants, place is considered a meta-term for a happy life.

---

12   There are two more images in the photo selection which lack a person in them. They represent objects related to people's hobbies but have no connection with the topic of place or movement.

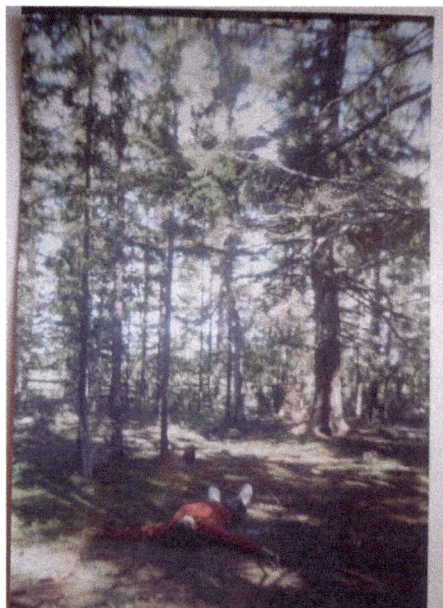

Fig. 6.7. Self in unity with nature, near Yakutsk, summer 2006. Photo: Eleanor
Peers' interviewee (with permission), CC-BY-ND.

Representations of homeland

In the narratives of the indigenous informants, it is the homeland
where the dialogue with self is possible. The reason for this is the
understanding that personhood is not attainable without taking into
account the system of kinship, communal ties, environment, and a
cosmology that transcends every person. All of these elements are
highly charged with emotional energy. In fact, humans, animals, and
spirits exist as endless mimetic doubles of one another (Willerslev 2007)
and many of our indigenous interviewees share such a view at least
in some situations. In most Siberian cosmologies, human beings have
their individual selves, but at the same time they *are* also their ancestors
who have returned to this world through the process of name-sharing
(Nuttall 1992; Willerslev 2007).

In visual terms, indigenous informants abide by the visual standards
of presenting themselves through place, while being depicted in the
place themselves. The image of place itself is not sufficient to refer to

the informants' relationship with it. Thus, people record the places as part of events involving themselves and other people. In the prevailing number of images, the place is visually associated with the self-in-a-collective mode of experiencing happiness.

"Distant hereness" as a device of self-expression

By contrast, the non-indigenous informants present contemplative moments about their vision of who they are and who they aspire to become at places that are distant from home (Fig. 6.8). This nature of the photos is at first overshadowed by the otherness of the sites where they were taken. They evoke a sense of "distant hereness" (Kirshenblatt-Gimblett 1998) — a special relationship with the exotic landscape, which despite its otherness is expected to be accessible for "touring" (Cartier & Lew 2005; Bagdasarova 2012). As opposed to geographies at home, which are "used" and to which a person is affiliated, tourist destinations are to be explored, consumed, gazed at, and documented. Whereas home landscapes are associated with people who enroot their sense of home through their sense of being in a collectivity, in the imagery of travel individual portraits at the tourist site prevail.

There are no images of any encounter of a tourist and the hosts; in other words, the type of relationship which is constitutive of tourism (cf. Chapter 4 in this volume) is remarkably absent. There are portraits of other tourists as well as the self and other tourist companions together, but their total number is still less than that of the portraits of the travelling self. The informants present themselves through photos as if they were in a unique position: "It was *me* who was *there*". The appropriation of a place through visual imagery is individualised as it is limited to the depiction of self at the site without any other person. At the same time, it is aesthetically standardised: in the series of photos from one and the same person, we observe a change of background, whereas the individual posture seems the same; in the series of photos of different owners from one site, what changes is the face but the background and the posture remain the same (e.g. the images of the person's profile looking at the sea). The backgrounds and foregrounds are in the end interchangeable and lose their representational efficiency.

Fig. 6.8. Contemplative moment near a lighthouse in Japan, 2011. Photo: Dennis Zuev's interviewee (with permission), CC-BY-ND.

In addition to the first impression given by the sense of "distant hereness", there is another characteristic trait, more important in terms of the sense of happiness. In fact, informants do not focus much in their narratives on exoticism or otherness. There is no sign of "ethnotopia" — a shorthand for the visual and epistemological conquest inspired by the fascination of other (Nichols 1991: 218). Rather, these images are often poor evidence of the trip, lacking sufficient details, diversity of events, and contrastive views. What these images manifest is an initiation into another understanding of what one should be, wants to be, or can afford to be through displacement. In most narratives, people define the precise moments during travel in which they could recognise the sensory force, which has, as they feel, changed them; whether it was confirmation of family unity, conviction of "true love", change of work, or moving out from their parents' home, all of these informants regard their trips as meaningful due to its transformational nature. The primary significance ascribed to the travel photographs does not result from the fact that they are evidence of exoticism, leisure, or economic status; rather, they are memorabilia of self-transformation and the regaining of self-integrity.

For the sake of the family

A major part of home photography is dedicated to family. It is the main purpose of the home media to portray family and provide evidence of a "happy collective". In our informants' selection there are family gatherings, leisure time (travel, hobbies), and studio family portraits (Fig. 6.9). The purpose of this section is to show some particularities inherent for the studied region and to find out how a family in Siberia experiences their happiness.

Fig. 6.9. Family portrait taken in a professional studio in Kemerovo, 1983. Photo: Artem Rabogoshvili's interviewee (with permission), CC-BY-ND.

The photographs seem to be an important part of people's relationships with *some* but not necessarily all of their relatives. Women, unprompted to do so, quickly talk about their children. Some select portraits of themselves with their child(ren) (Fig. 6.10). Most mothers, however, choose pictures of their children, including either a single child, several children or children in a group with other persons (Fig. 6.11). They document the moments of their children's coming of age. The difference between the images of the mother and child together as opposed to the images of children alone may be substantial. In the former choice, it is as if the informant was saying: "These are my children and me together". She emphasises well-being as a collective enterprise. In the latter choice, another phrase resonates: "Look, this is my child"; the happiness seems to be externalised. The informant prefers to be giving rather than sharing: "I am happy for my daughters to be together on the beach" or "I am happy for my son to have fun with his friends". In each case, it is a parental comfort when children are well taken care of. In social terms, the woman is credited the most when she succeeds in the role of a mother and protector of the heart of the family (*khranitel'nitsa semeinogo ochaga*). Our female interlocutors seem very much aware of this image. It can also be interpreted as: "first them, then me".

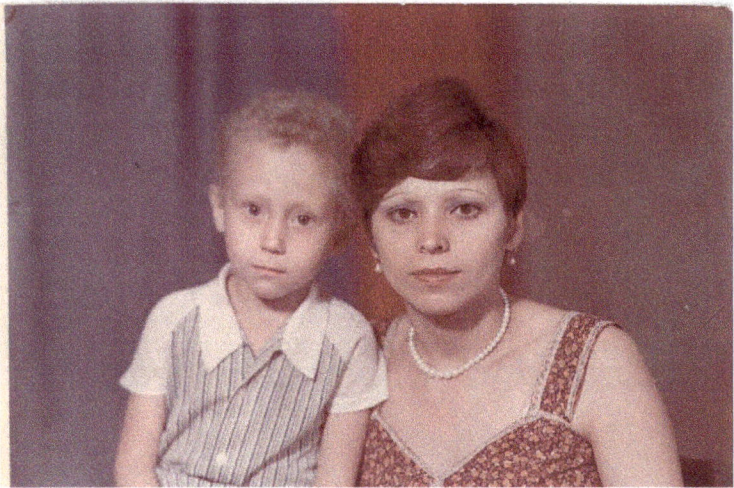

Fig. 6.10. Self as mother with son, Sochi, 1983. Photo: Ina Schröder's interviewee (with permission), CC-BY-ND.

This position — of treating one's own demands as less urgent than those of other family members — is not rare in Siberia. However, it does not necessarily imply a "complete" nuclear family. Many women give birth to a child "for themselves" (*rodit' dlia sebia*) without planning to establish a full family or without expecting the father to support the woman and child. Some of the divorced or abandoned women among our interlocutors just fleetingly mentioned the break-up with their partner and never returned to it in their narrative. Even if they enjoy being together with the husband/father in a full family, many women will implicitly restrict their happiness to the children's or grandchildren's self-fulfilment; they interpret the category of "family happiness" in terms of children and tend to overlook the category of "personal happiness" in a strict sense of self.

Fig. 6.11. Achieved motherhood manifested through images of children. Here it is accentuated by the capacity to finance a holiday journey to China (early 2000s). Photo: Eleanor Peers' interviewee (with permission), CC-BY-ND.

The photo selections of male interviewees also relate to family; but they differ from the women's images in one essential way: men like to see the family *together*. We came across several cases when the informant made the image himself: he preferred to portray his family including himself and since there was no one around to take the picture, the self-timer was used. The majority of the selected images portray the family around a festive table. Prosperity and completeness are the basic characteristics of the happy family according to men. They prefer the image of a full family even if the actual family has ceased to exist (because of separation, divorce, etc.). Whereas women choose not to hold on to the "broken" relationship and instead focus on children, men tend to perpetuate the notion of integrity. At the same time, however, they cultivate an image of another significant group — their male friends and peers (whom they know from the army, the workplace, or some leisure activity).

Celebrating collectivity at home: the wall carpet

Many of the family photos are dedicated to gatherings at a festive table (*zastol'e*) or picnics. Solemn passport photos or photos of official gatherings (manifestations, award ceremonies) contrast with these photos of the celebrations and leisure as if "the happy" moments (or rather moments of individual, private happiness) occur during days off. In fact, in the Soviet times each official holiday had its continuation in the private space, amongst family, colleagues or friends. This is also the case today. For example, in Novoe Chaplino, Chukotka, the Day of Indigenous Peoples is celebrated in two parts: the official programme takes place in the House of Culture or on an open-air stage and is supported by the district administration; the ceremony is then followed by family gatherings at home. Photos taken during such festive days exhibit two features of happiness significant for our informants: the comfort of the home as well as collectivity in the particular, extraordinary moment.

The object that most tellingly unites these two is the wall carpet, tangible proof of how the individual understanding of aesthetics can submit to the collective concept. Industrially made hanging carpets spread massively under Khrushchev's rule. Although they are widely associated with Soviet quotidian design, including home design (*sovok, sovkovskii byt*), they are still found in many provincial Siberian homes. Khrushchev denied Stalin's synthesis of the beautiful and useful, denigrating high ceilings and stucco mouldings as "extravagant". Functional five-storey buildings, mostly with either two-room apartments (forty square metres) or one-room apartments (18 square metres), known by everyone in Russia as *khrushchevka* (wooden houses) were introduced in 1948, and from 1959 onwards were constructed on a massive scale (cf. Reid, in Balina & Dobrenko 2009: 133–60).[13] In Siberia, the urban population could enjoy a built-in winter refrigerator, separate toilet and bathroom, running water, and central heating. To the Siberian province, this type of housing arrived much later, and often without urban amenities. Notwithstanding the government's policy of making nomadic households sedentary (which started around 1935 and lasted well into the 1970s), it was not until the 2000s that rural indigenous inhabitants had the occasion to make use of running water or sewage systems. In either case, the poor thermal and sound insulation of the *khrushchevka* led to the massive use of wall carpets as a functional yet

---

13   From 1959 to 1965 more than 300 million square metres of accommodation were built. The construction of this type of house stopped only in 1985 (Crowley & Reid 2010).

decorative element (Panáková 2014). As a result, the carpet is widely used as a background in the family photographs. Thus, group portraits in front of the carpet combine two key elements of the collective happiness framed by the private space: the material comfort of the functional Soviet home and the special occasion of the holiday.

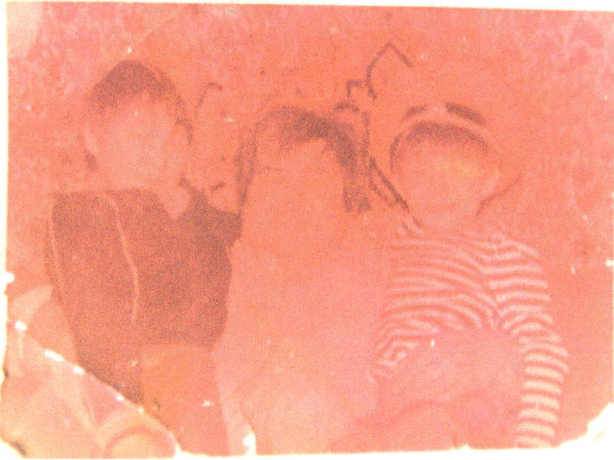

Fig. 6.12. Picture from childhood with father and brother, Yanrakkynnot (Chukotka), 1990. Photo: Jaroslava Panáková's interviewee (with permission), CC-BY-ND.

The basic composition of a "happy family" has the following features: family members gathered around a table, and/or sitting or otherwise posing on a couch covered with a quilt (decorated as much as the carpet) in front of an ornamental carpet (Fig. 6.12). The scenery may be completed by the ubiquitous television set covered with a tablecloth, a cupboard decorated with photos and diplomas, and photos on the walls (such photos are present in the collected home archives but not in the informants' selection). The seasonal house of a nomadic reindeer herder does not contain these elements, although the act of gathering around a table is still an important genre of a family portrait (Fig. 6.13). The contemporary population in large urban centres tends to implement "modern" designs in their flats and houses, which implies the rejection of the carpet as an outdated *sovok* element (Fig. 6.14). Moreover, some of our urban informants preferred to demonstrate their abundant life through a different setting, namely in a restaurant. These photos, however, lack the sense of collective enjoyment: the individuals appear to be slightly lost in the frame (Fig. 6.15) or the photos resemble a still life of the objects of individual hedonism (Fig. 6.16).

Fig. 6.13. Family picture in a reindeer herder' cabin, Numto, 2006. Photo: Ina Schröder's interviewee (with permission), CC-BY-ND.

Fig. 6.14. Group portrait taken by auto-timer in auntie's flat, Barnaul 2010. Photo: Joachim Otto Habeck's interviewee (with permission), CC-BY-ND.

Fig. 6.15. Enjoying a dinner with a relative, Ulaanbaatar (Mongolia), 2009. Photo: Artem Rabogoshvili's interviewee (with permission), CC-BY-ND.

Fig. 6.16. A moment in a newly opened Italian restaurant in Krasnoiarsk, 2011. Photo: Dennis Zuev's interviewee (with permission), CC-BY-ND.

In other words, the high moments are not necessarily enjoyed inside the family circle. Moreover, the significance of the moment goes beyond the phenomenon of the festive holiday. The diversity of leisure activities during days off has increased: in addition to old (Soviet) and new (Russian) holidays, days at the *dacha* and picnics, recent images document travelling, hobbies (playing games, creative projects, horse-riding, dancing etc.) (Fig. 6.17; cf. Chapters 9 and 10 in this volume). In addition, voluntary work in cultural organisations (festivals, costume making, debating) continues to be fairly popular and has attained new forms (cf. Chapter 8). There is one more tendency worth mentioning. Due to technological innovations it has become much easier to take spontaneous pictures rather than having people pose. This change has not only led to a diversification of images in terms of themes but also to a different understanding of what a "decisive moment" actually is. Significance is equally ascribed to instances of being quotidian. "Being there", no matter where and in what role, has become a major subject of recent images.

Fig. 6.17. Scene from a live-action role play near Miass, Cheliabinsk Oblast, 2011. Photo: Tatiana Barchunova's interviewee (with permission), CC-BY-ND.

"Significant other"

Some of our informants, when prompted to choose photos which best describe their lives and themselves, included portraits of people with whom they identify or to whom they relate. Such sense of attachment was a suitable way for the informants to describe themselves.

Both women and men showed their affiliation with their partners to the same extent (women selected two images of men, men selected three images of women, one man chose an image of his gay partner).

The informants also chose images of themselves with their siblings (both sexes selected three such images). The number of such images is low in comparison to other family pictures. In the case of the images depicting couples who are dating, at their own wedding, or married, the number is even lower. Although the strategies of finding a partner are articulated in the informants' stories, visually this issue seems to be insignificant. It is fair to assume that both women and men prefer to choose a family photo of the couple with children rather than without children. The child-centred sentiment seems to be overwhelmingly strong for both women and men. In other words, the visual representation of a family implies the presence of offspring, presumably as a marker of continuity.

Having mentioned above the frequent cases of the self-presentation of women as mothers, here is the other side of the coin — informants choose pictures of their own mother to point to motherhood as a significant source of their own well-being. If the informants desire to emphasise their ties with ethnic traditions, they usually select an image of their grandmother rather than their mother. The narrative then has a double plot: the first is to show how Granny ensured the integrity of the family in times of crisis, i.e. during the 1990s. The happy time of the informant's childhood is contrasted with a description of terrible decline in the village, town, or the whole country. Granny, however, is depicted as someone who has the capacity to surpass these unpleasant memories; her significance lies far beyond the place. Thus, while the female interviewees focus their narrative on the traditional skills (splicing, fur treatment, sewing, embroidering) and the legacy (moral values, healing capabilities) which Granny passed on to them, i.e. on continuity, the male interviewees accentuate that Granny taught them orderliness and reliance; this is partially because of gender differentiation (the boys learn their duties and skills from the men). The second plot in the story develops around Granny's death. The denouement of the story, illustrated by supplementary images, shows the informants ensuring the continuity of the family: they are posing in ethnic costumes and with their family, organising a cultural festival, practising traditional handicrafts, and being in close contact with the Siberian landscape. Here well-being is understood as the awareness and fulfilment of the ancestors' legacy.

Some of these photos are actually portraits of a significant person alone; many are regular passport photos (seven passport photos come from Chukotka, one from Novosibirsk, all made in the 1980s). In a rural province, such as Novoe Chaplino, a passport photo is oftentimes the only available photographic depiction of a person from the past; such genre then represents the only visual memory at hand.[14] Some of the informants who selected passport photos also possessed other pictures of themselves, e.g. a group photo in front of the *kolkhoz* headquarters; but still, these informants decided to choose passport photos. It may be assumed that this preference follows the Soviet (and European) standard, according to which a single portrait expresses the nuances of the personality in the most plausible manner.

Portraits of self

More than one third of all selected images (36 per cent) represent single portraits of our informants. Despite the different representation of age groups, the distribution shows that people aged between 21 and thirty chose the largest number of portraits (49.8 per cent of the total number of images, out of which only two images were made in the 1990s; the remaining 101 images were taken in or after 2000). The data show that whenever the informants (no matter what age) decided to choose a portrait of self, they would look for it among the most recent photos of the 2000s (133 images or 27.5 per cent). In order to understand the nature of these photographs, I attempt to reveal major visual traits and, thus, conceive the visual paradigm that dominates the sample. I will link this dimension with the narratives in which the reading of the term *self* carries an *emic* nature. I shall also show instances of individual happiness.

In our study, what, how, and why a photo was selected (or, on the contrary, omitted) was part of the *process*; it was not necessarily an easy

---

14   There is also a possibility that some indigenous peoples of Siberia reject completely the faculty of photography to preserve "the past" in some specific contexts; in particular, when the image is related to a deceased person and used in the funeral ritual, it must be destroyed. In a discussion with Jean-Luc Lambert (CNRS), I learned of such cases both in West Siberia and among the Nanai people. This practice may give new insight into memory and permissible forms of its preservation. Such instances did not occur in this project.

process. The presence of the researcher stimulated the informant's engagement in the course of ascribing significance to a particular portrait over another. What is the informant who is looking at his or her picture like? How does she or he wish to be seen? Mikhail Bakhtin's concept of a mirror ([1929] 1994) resembles this process of reflection and selection. It is not the self who can be viewed in the picture; it is the person (appearance of the person, mask) who is to be shown to others. The choice is inevitably accompanied by the anticipated reactions of others to this face as well as one's own reaction to the reaction of others (Bakhtin [1929] 1994). Taking into account the fact that a photographic image is made as the selection of an infinite number of possible shots, the choosing of the representative portrait, i.e. the selection of the selection, is not an easy exercise. People's choices as well as arguments for these choices tend to vary.

Within the selection of 174 single portraits of the self (Table 6.1 on p. 254), thirty photos were taken by a professional photographer.[15] Except for four pictures that were shot by recording the protagonist in action, all of these photos show the depicted person in a deliberately arranged setting (as in Fig. 6.18): the face occupies most of the picture (except for one full-length studio portrait), while additional props are arbitrary.

The remaining portraits of self are true home snapshots. They include a specific mode — the self-portrait. There are six selfies, all made by men, of which three were shot with the use of a self-timer (in 1971, 1974 and 2009) and another three that were taken with a long arm (two in 2010, one in 2011). Although our sample consists of 43 young informants (in their 20s and 30s) who are the most likely to choose such genre of photography, only two such photos were shot with a "long arm" in this category. According to my observations, however, this visual canon is well established in the youth culture in Siberia and also

---

15   These include a) four arranged photos taken in a certain institution, out of which two were taken during the informants' military service in the 1970s, one in military service in 1985, and one in kindergarten in 1994. (Other images are taken in institutions but in a rather informal style: one in military service in 1969, one in the 1990s and two portraits at graduation ceremonies in the 2000s); b) four passport photos, one of which was taken in the 1970s and three in the 1980s; c) nine studio portraits, of which two were made in the 1970s, three in the 1980s, and four after 2010; d) ten arranged portraits in the exterior (all were taken after 2010; they also represent a current trend as opposed to the old-time studio portraits with decorations and hanging draperies); and e) three photos for reportage purposes (all taken in the 2000s).

Fig. 6.18. Studio portrait of himself on his birthday, Novosibirsk, 1985. Photo: Joachim Otto Habeck's interviewee (with permission), CC-BY-ND.

in communication on social networking sites. The recent popularity of a "selfie stick" and lens enhancement (close focusing mode, better light-gathering ability and higher sharpness) in light hand cameras and built-in cameras (mobile phones, tablets) allows the production of selfies in which the "long arm" is not even seen; such images are, however, absent in our data collection.[16]

Some portraits of self may have been made in post-production. This is mostly done by cropping out the other persons from the group portrait. In our data, there is a curious case of such omitting of the collective: one informant wished to present his life just through the pictures of himself but did not have enough portraits of himself which would satisfy him; thus, he simply took group images and cut out the other depicted persons from the pictures and presented them as portraits of himself (e.g., Fig. 6.19). His selection is generally self-centred: there are four portraits of self, two portraits are self-cropped out of a group portrait

---

16   This trend might have appeared in the studied locations after the year 2012 when our data collection was ended.

Fig. 6.19. Cropping out the collective. Business meeting in a café in Paris, 2009. Photo: Joachim Otto Habeck's interviewee (with permission), CC-BY-ND.

and one picture captures himself with another person. The informant justified his choice of the latter image as follows: "Because we look alike, everybody thinks that we are brother and sister. This photograph symbolises to me that we are very close friends still [...] and therefore I did not crop her out. She looks fine here. Every image is a certain part of life, which doesn't exist anymore" (Fig. 6.20).

This story is interesting for another reason: it shows a particular relationship towards the photo object. I mentioned above another example from my field site when a woman cropped a man's face out of the photo. While the woman disrupted the integrity of the analogue photo by literally cutting out the person who betrayed her, the young man transformed digital images in order to present his life as a series of self-contained events (in Russian, there is an expression *dlia sebia liubimogo* — "for himself beloved"). The different treatment and lifetimes of analogue and digital photos are evident in other cases. At least two

Fig. 6.20. "We are very close friends still": dinner in a hotel in Novosibirsk, 2010. Photo: Joachim Otto Habeck's interviewee (with permission), CC-BY-ND.

informants admitted that they deliberately destroyed analogue images. In contrast, two informants refused to spoil the "true photograph" (the analogue, printed-out image) but had no problem with deleting the digital images. Another two informants talked about an unexpected loss of their photographs: one man lost his home archive of analogue photos in a fire, while a young woman suffered the loss of digital images due to a computer virus. Thus, the technological underpinning of the photo production has an impact on the life of each photograph.

Even when taken by non-professionals, the portraits of self often lack the spontaneity of home snapshots. They reflect the studio-like behaviour of getting ready for the image. Although the act of photographing occurred in a real-life situation, the informants pose for the camera: in front of an exotic place or a monument (portraits at the seashore or a lakeside are common), at home (on a sofa, in front of a hanging carpet or at the *stoibishche*), with their favourite object (car, food, pet, computer) and in the midst of some kind of action (working on a project, engaged in a hobby or sport, celebrating, travelling, hunting, or hiking). These are all staged snaps for memories (*na pamiat'*). A few informants also mentioned the practice of getting together with friends, dressing up and photographing each other. This kind of self-fashioning seems to be an experimentation with a cover-girl look; it imitates analogical practices in the business of fashion and media, in particular in glossy magazines.[17]

As mentioned above, in the 21–30 age cohort, almost half of the selected images (49.76 per cent) are single portraits of self. In contrast to older informants, these young people talk about photographing consciously for themselves. Photography enables the reflexive process of self-realisation, both by recording the moments of one's life and by offering the terrain for structuring, and the control and demarcation of oneself from others. There is also a certain appeal to observing oneself. Even if the photos are from one period, the informants can clearly point to what they have achieved. The meaning of life, which they consider to be the key element of self-fulfilment, is "to do things for themselves". Self-progress seems to be significant to them: "My achievements are who I am". Education, the ability to travel, and the satisfied desire for material goods are common indicators of improvement.

In the 1970s and 1980s, because of the visual canon as well as the absence of a camera at home, most of the portraits were done in a studio, with individuals stiffly posing in front of a painted decoration or draped fabric. The photographer gave specific instructions on how to pose and did not encourage people to smile, but rather to look serious. The convention of a sombre look in the representational photograph was widespread in the Soviet Union and survived until the mid-2000s. The off-day or everyday life photos, in contrast, could show emotions. The act of going to the studio was a significant life event in its own right (birthday, anniversary, etc.). The moment of taking the photo was thus as important as the result. This is also true for some home photos, e.g. an image of a birthday person, and yet, there is not the same solemnity in the preparation, arrangement, organisation, and payment as in the old-time studio portraits. Considering the whole set of photos of the informants aged 51 to 60, it is clear that a temporal order is used to present the self as a person changing in the course of time.

The informants in the 31–40 age cohort assume the possibility to present their lives through their own portraits in a fourth of the cases (24.6 per cent). Others, in the 41–50 and 51–60 age cohorts, do so in a

---

17 Some of the informants aged 51 to 60 also chose to present themselves through portraits. Among these are men who are active on dating sites, on which the genre of a portrait is perceived by many as a must. Nevertheless, along with recent photos, the informants chose almost a third of portraits in which they are young.

third of the cases (33.3 and 29.8 per cent respectively). Whereas most informants up to the age of forty prefer recent pictures, the others distribute the "significant moments" within different time periods as if life was a series of events. The strategy to present themselves as diverse personalities (*pokazat' sebia raznym*) is perceived by the two age groups of informants differently. The informants in their twenties and thirties chose different events and places squeezed into a few years; they used a "here-and-now" mode or a continuous present tense. The older informants have naturally a broader timeframe within which they can select the photos. What is significant, however, is that they selected the type of images which were equally present in their personal archives, but not in the selections of the young informants; namely images of "the person I was but I am not anymore". Some of these informants preferred to line up the photos in chronological order; they literally made historical albums with the aim to preserve their memories, to remember "how it was". Nevertheless, it is also a kind of ongoing self-making based on references to the past.

Our informants in their twenties and thirties preferred to present their life through significant moments experienced *individually*, as opposed to the informants in their forties and above who contextualised their happiness in a *collective* (a couple or a group). We are not suggesting that the experience of happiness itself is becoming individualised throughout the generations, but what seems to be true is that the forms of self-presentation have become increasingly self-centred. The size of the portrayed face in relation to the overall size of the picture is one piece of evidence for a more subject-focused visual representation. In the data set, there are several cases of an extremely large face (occupying more than eighteen per cent of the surface). This is most common among recent portrait photography. The seven such images made in the 2000s are portraits of the informants, out of which three were made by a professional photographer (two arranged portraits, one passport photo), three were taken deliberately at an amateur photo shoot (of these, one is a selfie and two were used for an online dating site) and one represents an informant in a significant moment (graduation ceremony). The largest face in the portrait made in the 2000s takes half of the surface of the image. There is but one portrait of an informant with an extremely large face made in another time period, namely the 1970s.

The face in this case takes up about one sixth of the size of the image. A large face also appears in three photos from the 2000s that fall under the category "the informant depicted in the company of someone else". There is also one photo from the 2000s and one from the 1980s depicting the large face of another person — a portrait of the informant's own child. The other extreme cases come from the 1980s. The largest face in these images occupies approximately 24 per cent of the surface of the image. These are mostly passport photos of the informants themselves and a "significant other" (seven passport photos come from Chukotka, one from Novosibirsk). The genre of the passport portrait explains the extremely large size of the face in these images.

Despite these several extreme cases, however, the face of the informant in most portraits from the 2000s actually does not occupy more than nine per cent of the surface, while the face of another person does not take up more than six per cent of the surface. In fact, the largest relative size of the face is observable in photos from the 1970s (approximately thirteen per cent of the surface) and 1980s (approximately twenty per cent of the surface). This is due to the fact that the prevailing genre of this period was a studio portrait focusing solely on the person (the drapery only suggests a complementary atmosphere) whereas the recent photo set includes numerous everyday-life, snapshot-like portraits in which the person is placed in context (place, activity, background, etc.).

So while it may be assumed that the more recent the photo, the larger the face, this is not supported by the data. Nevertheless, there are several facts that support the assumption of a pronounced self-centred representation in recent photography regardless of the age of the informant: 36 per cent of the images reflect the way people prefer to see themselves. Their personhood is also expressed through objects which matter to them (3.7 per cent of the images); in group portraits which include the informant, the largest face (mostly the face of the informant her or himself) is on average larger than any face in any portrait photograph which does not include the informant; the face of the portrayed informant is on average larger than the face of any other person in the group portraits; and the position of the informant in the group portraits is mostly dominant and central. These aesthetic traits of the photos complement the narratives of recent times which are based on the personal pursuit of happiness. The concept that happiness is a portion of the collective fortune limited in stock seems to be overwhelmed by the hedonistic drive. Similarly, the Soviet idea of deferred well-being is challenged by the "here-and-now" approach. Personal happiness seems to flourish along with the collective; it does not have to be necessarily nurtured from the collective and for its own good.

Conclusion

In anthropological theory, there is a common notion that images themselves do not tell any stories. Supposedly, they are silent. They might even be uninteresting in themselves. What is important, are the memories and stories people tell around them. I disagree with this position. The image is "a sight which has been recreated and reproduced" (Berger 1972: 9); it is a serious thing to be taken seriously. As MacDougall writes (1997: 292), it is a means of communicating understandings that are barely accessible verbally. The notion of happiness is such a phenomenon.

This study represents an attempt to analyse those elements of photographic representations and narratives which point to the evidence of happiness in Siberian lives. Because of their temporal specificity, photographs tend to imply the transient nature of the depicted moments. Thus, in regard to happiness, they may be easily mistaken for an instantaneous agitation preceded and followed by oblivion. Careful analysis of the images along with the narratives, however, has enabled me to reveal the patterns which reoccur within certain time periods, regions, and social conditions. At the same time, a diachronic perspective (including over half of a century) helped me to convey how happiness defines, constructs, and stimulates people's lifestyle projects. What interested me the most was the question of how happiness as a sensory force can stimulate change in human lives.

In order to reveal how changing visual technology and social conditions relate to happiness — which is one of the constitutive elements of the individual lifestyle project — I considered institutional, biographical, and visual characteristics relevant to the Siberian context. The biographical or personal is linked to modalities of what one wants to be, should be, would be, or could be. The social settings imply the modalities in which the personal values arise and choices can be made;

thus, the possibilities, impossibilities, contingencies, and necessities of social institutions have a direct impact on what is understood as happiness, which visual and narrative imaginaries nourish the *emic* concepts of happiness, how (if at all) happiness can be pursued, and how it refines people's lives.

The photo selection of 484 images is structured around those "decisive moments" which are perceived by our seventy informants as meaningful in terms of their self-formation. The prevailing themes include family, education, and work, and sense of place. The collective condition of happiness expressed by the group portraits on one hand, and the personal pursuit of happiness manifested by single portraits on the other hand, are acknowledged to an equal extent. And yet, self-centred photographs are accompanied by elaborate narratives of sharing decisive moments with others while the group portraits mostly include the informants themselves. Thus, although the photo selection is divided quantitatively into two halves, both visual and narrative representations manifest a syncretic trope of happiness in Siberia: happiness is pursued neither just by the self, nor by the collective, but within a *self-in-a-collective*.

People's connectedness, affiliations, and ties are not contrasted to personal aspirations. Self-making is enabled by the collective: family, friends, an employee's collective, or interest group. The collective's inability to accommodate the potential of the individual, however, is the subject of the verbal accounts of the 1990s. In this regard, only the family ties remain a strong reference in the self-making project. The affective and meaningful dimensions of the quality of life comprise achievements in work and education (promotion, graduation, and award), bonding with the family or another collective, and leisure activities (hobbies, travel). Meaning is commonly preferred over meaninglessness; the latter is a notion which arises in the stories of social change (e.g. the 1990s) or in personal tragedies (the death of a relative, loss of a herd, etc.).

At the same time, there are observable differences in the understanding of happiness in the context of Soviet and post-Soviet middle-brow ideologies of taste. In the photographs and narratives of the Soviet times, the individuals were well aware of themselves, of their personal aspirations, motivations, and wishes. However, they interpreted their self-realisation as the capacity to contribute to the collective good. The immediate well-being of each individual should be sacrificed for moral deeds beneficial for the collective, whether it is a family, community or the "Motherland". By contrast, the recent concept of happiness is more focused on self-realisation as well as a hedonistic experience of the world. This distinction is clear in the self-presentation of women as mothers. Motherhood is perceived to be significant by all women in the relevant age range. In Soviet times, motherhood — when achieved — implied that a woman could "do it all", i.e. could reconcile career and family. However, today mothers often accentuate their ability to "provide it all", including material goods such as travel and leisure activities. There is a gender difference in how family is perceived: while women associate family happiness with images of/with children, men like to see the family in unity and abundance, symbolised by gatherings at a festive table. While the cosy home has been a popular representation of material well-being throughout the decades, in recent photos, prosperity is equally defined by the leisure time spent outside the home (picnics, hobbies, travel).

There is a distinction in the self-presentation of the informants in their twenties and thirties as opposed to the older informants. While the young informants present the "here-and-now" concept of life, the informants older than forty convey their life as a series of events starting from childhood to the present. Although there is a tendency to convey life as a chronological, linear trajectory, some informants of these age cohorts emphasise the meandering and and unpredictable nature of life events. By providing images of different periods of their lives, these informants wish to present themselves as changing beings. By contrast, young informants show their diverse personalities by changing the context: events, places, and activities.

The research was based on the assumption that home photography preserves double happiness; people do not just portray well-being, they also document it by the means that provide for a satisfying appearance. Therefore, part of the study aimed to find out the aesthetic standards that are conveyed as visually pleasing and how they have been changing under the influence of evolving technology. It was revealed that the dominant approach in Siberia is *bricolage*, implying a recombination of the aesthetic standards, prevailing themes, and technological capacities imported from the centres (Moscow, St Petersburg) and then adapting them to the local urban or rural environment. Because of the geographical and infrastructural specificities, there has been a disproportionate availability of different (visual) technologies, specialists, and supplies. This means that some aesthetic conventions — those which rely on technology — were adopted only partially.

This is not the case of the golden section rule that is well-established in Siberian home photography; it is considered especially pleasing in the vertically oriented images. In most of the horizontally oriented images, the horizon line breaks the portrayed reality into equal halves. Until the 1980s, there was an aesthetic divide between Siberian urban and rural home photography; since then, both backgrounds have adopted a preference for horizontally oriented images with a horizon line in the middle.

Another parameter, the size of the portrayed face in relation to the overall size of the picture was measured in order to determine whether the increasing self-containment present in the narratives was mirrored in the increasing tendency of the self-centred depiction in recent photography. Our data failed to confirm this suggestion. Nevertheless, there are other visual elements that support it: a high percentage of portraits of the self within the photo set (these are made by different methods, such as by a timer, as a selfie snapshot, or by cropping out the group); conscious self-fashioning in the photos; the dominant, central posture of the owner of the photo; and the comparatively large size of the informant's face in the group portraits. There is no evidence that the experience of happiness itself is becoming individualised through the change of the generations, social regimes, or time periods. Yet it is clear that people (regardless of their age) tend to contextualise their happiness more strongly in a self-centred manner and less strongly as being "dissolved" in a *collective*. Recent technological changes have also led to a shift in understanding of what a "decisive moment" actually is; images of self in the everyday context have gradually become equally significant as images of the unusual, unique, or exoticised.

Methodologically, this study shows a specific dynamic between visual and narrative representations, between photo stimulation and biographical narratives. The photo elicitation technique is acknowledged for lengthy narratives evoked by a single visual record. However, the relationship between the images and words is more complicated. The images described as "happy" may well be accompanied by narratives of hard times, personal unease, and social decline. A vast number of narratives were stimulated by the images which were presumably taken but are now missing. In fact, loss plays a significant role. There are images which do not stimulate any narrative whatsoever. The portraits of people who are missed and mourned for evoke silence; all-telling silence — the black strip which makes the "happy" images stand out.

In Russia, Lev Tolstoi's words are often quoted: "Happy families are all alike; every unhappy family is unhappy in its own way" (Tolstoy 2001: 1). Our account of the Siberian experience elucidates that not only the representations of happiness vary but also how exactly these variations emerge from the particular institutional setting. The commonalities we discovered draw our attention to the forms that challenge the usual patterns, emerge unexpectedly, and surprise us by their novelty. Although the images are held to make a series, the happy images may not always link together. The immediate experience behind the images varies profoundly. Put together, the photographs cannot make up a happy life; they are only fragments, intermingled with ruptures and incongruities. And yet, the photographs have the ability to indicate the ways in which people are able to, or even dare to see their life. It takes courage to recognise happiness; whoever fails to do it, may at least see its absence.

Summarising the findings, our study shows that even though the stories around the images may be diverse in terms of emotional load mingling the positive and negative sides, the images tend to show the better (nicer, more pleasing, and more harmonious) parts of people's lives. The photographic framing removes the historical setting from its own context and transforms it into a transient moment of individual (hi)stories. The perception of "good times" varies, however. So do the strategies of how to attain happiness and how to recapture it. As Gordon Mathews and Carolina Izquierdo write: "There is no unambiguously single pursuit of happiness, rather there are multiple pursuits of happiness" (2009: 1).

In this study, I also wished to show how happiness can be a stimulating force in people's lives. Despite the diverse understandings of happiness in Siberia, our informants manifested awareness of their choice-making, self-reflection, and the ability to pursue well-being. They could recognise the ways in which particular events, actions, and relationships are significant to them. There was a common understanding that happiness, even if taken as a personal category, is part of a larger social context. Thus, happiness does not affect individuals alone: the changing self is mirrored in changing others, whether it is in the family, work collective, or village. The ability of people to relate to each other proves to be crucial whenever happiness is to become a transformational force.

References

Afanas'ev, Pëtr S., Pëtr A. Sleptsov, Gavril V. Popov, Vladimir I. Likhanov et al. 1994. *Sakha tylyn byhaaryylaakh kylgas tyld'yta* [Short explanatory dictionary of Sakha language]. D'okuuskai: Bichik.

Bagdasarova (Panáková), Jaroslava. 2012. "Sense of distant hereness: making and unmaking oneself at home (case of Chukchi and Yupik)". In: *The Reshaping of Space and Identity: proceedings of the international congress, 29 September–1 October 2011*, ed. E. Filippova. Moscow: Russian State University for the Humanities, pp. 185–97.

Baiburin, Al'bert & Alexandra Piir. 2009. "When we were happy". *Forum for Anthropology and Culture*, 5: 217–53. (Special issue: Soviet culture in retrospect).

Bakhtin, Mikhail M. 1994 [1929]. *Problemy tvorchestva Dostoevskogo* [Questions about the oeuvre of Dostoevskii]. Kiev: Next.

Balina, Marina & Evgeny Dobrenko (eds). 2009. *Petrified Utopia: happiness Soviet style*. London: Anthem Press, https://doi.org/10.7135/UPO9781843318170

Barthes, Roland. 2004. *Mytologie*, trans. Josef Fulka. Prague: Dokořán.

Benjafield, John & Jack Adams-Weber. 1976. "The golden section hypothesis". *British Journal of Psychology*, 67 (1): 11–15, https://doi.org/10.1111/j.2044-8295.1976.tb01492.x

Benjamin, Walter. 1977. *Das Kunstwerk im Zeitalter seiner technischen Reproduzierbarkeit* [On the work of art in the age of its technical reproducibility]. Frankfurt am Main: Suhrkamp Verlag.

Berger, John. 1972. *Ways of Seeing*. Harmondsworth: Penguin.

Bogoiavlenskii, Dmitrii D. 2008. "Narody severa Rossii: demograficheskii profil' na rubezhe vekov" [Peoples of the North of Russia: demographic profile at the turn of the centuries]. In: *Vliianie global'nykh klimaticheskikh izmenenii na zdorov'e naseleniia rossiiskoi Arktiki*, ed. B. A. Revich. Moscow: The UN Office in the Russian Federation, pp. 14–17.

— & Aleksandr I. Pika. 1991. "Nasil'stvennaia smertnost' u narodov Severa (na primere Kamchatki i Chukotki)" [Violent death rates among the Peoples of the North (on the example of Kamchatka and Chukotka]. *Geografiia i khoziaistvo*, 4: *Raiony prozhivaniia malochislennykh narodov Severa*, ed. A. I. Chistobaev. Leningrad: Geographic Society of the USSR Press, pp. 162–82.

Bourdieu, Pierre. 1990. *The Logic of Practice*. Stanford, CA: Stanford University Press.

—, Luc Boltanski, Robert Castel, Jean-Claude Chamboredon & Dominique Schnapper. 1990 [1965]. *Photography: a middle-brow art*, trans. Shaun Whiteside. Cambridge: Polity Press.

Bunster, Ximena. 1978. "Talking pictures: a study of proletarian mothers in Lima, Peru". *Studies in the Anthropology of Visual Communication*, 5 (1): 37–55, https://repository.upenn.edu/svc/vol5/iss1/

—, Elsa Chaney & Ellan Young. 1989. *Sellers and Servants: working women in Lima, Peru*. New York: Bergin & Garvey.

Cartier-Bresson, Henri. 1952. *Images à la Sauvette* [Images on the go]. Paris: Verve.

Cartier, Carolyn & Alan A. Lew (eds). 2005. *Seductions of Place: geographical perspectives on globalization and touristed landscapes*. London: Routledge, https://doi.org/10.4324/9780203645796

Certeau, Michel de. 1984. *The Practice of Everyday Life*. Berkeley, CA: University of California Press.

Chaney, David. 1996. *Lifestyles*. London: Routledge, https://doi.org/10.4324/9780203137468

Collier, John Jr & Malcolm Collier. 1986. *Visual Anthropology: photography as a research method*. Albuquerque, NM: University of New Mexico Press.

Crowley, David & Susan E. Reid. 2010. "Introduction: pleasures in socialism?" In: *Pleasures in Socialism: leisure and luxury in the Eastern Bloc*, ed. David Crowley & Susan E. Reid, pp. 3–51. Evanston, IL: Northwestern University Press, https://doi.org/10.2307/j.ctv43vtgm.4

Donahoe, Brian & Joachim Otto Habeck (eds). 2011. *Reconstructing the House of Culture: community, self, and the makings of culture in Russia and beyond*. New York: Berghahn.

Empson, Rebecca. 2011. *Harnessing Fortune: personhood, memory, and place in Mongolia*. Oxford: Oxford University Press, https://doi.org/10.5871/bacad/9780197264737.001.0001

Ettyryntyna, Maya I. & A. Koryagin. 1996. "To live or die". In: *Anxious North*, ed. Aleksandr Pika, Jens Dahl & Inge Larsen, pp. 227–31. IWGIA Document, 82. Copenhagen: IWGIA.

Friedman, Jonathan. 2001. "The iron cage of creativity: an exploration". In: *Locating Cultural Creativity*, ed. John Liep. London: Pluto Press, pp. 46–61, https://doi.org/10.2307/j.ctt18fs9q6.7

Giddens, Anthony. 1991. *Modernity and Self-Identity: self and society in the late modern age*. Stanford, CA: Stanford University Press.

Gray, Patty A. 2005. *The Predicament of Chukotka's Indigenous Movement: post-Soviet activism in the Russian Far North*. Cambridge: Cambridge University Press.

Hall, Stuart. 1980. "Encoding/decoding". In: *Culture, Media, Language: working papers in cultural studies, 1972–79*, ed. Stuart Hall, Dorothy Hobson, Andrew Lowe & Paul Willis. London: Hutchinson, pp. 128–38, https://doi.org/10.4324/9780203381182

Harper, Douglas. 1987. "The visual ethnographic narrative". *Visual Anthropology*, 1 (1): 1–19, https://doi.org/10.1080/08949468.1987.9966457

—. 2001. *Changing Works: visions of a lost agriculture*. Chicago, IL: University of Chicago Press.

—. 2002. "Talking about pictures: a case for photo elicitation". *Visual Studies*, 17 (1): 13–26, https://doi.org/10.1080/14725860220137345

—, Caroline Knowles & Pauline Leonard. 2005. "Visually narrating post-colonial lives: ghosts of war and empire". *Visual Studies*, 20 (1): 4–15, https://doi.org/10.1080/14725860500064862

Hemment, Julie. 2015. *Youth Politics in Putin's Russia: producing patriots and entrepreneurs*. Bloomington, IN: Indiana University Press.

Istomin, Kirill V. 2012. "Once again on the problem of alcoholism and suicide among the indigenous peoples of the Russian North: can attribution style be a factor?" *Sibirica*, 11 (3): 1–19, https://doi.org/10.3167/sib.2012.110301

—, Jaroslava Panáková & Patrick Heady. 2014. "Culture, perception, and artistic visualisation: a comparative study of children's drawings in three Siberian cultural groups". *Cognitive Science*, 38 (1): 76–100, https://doi.org/10.1111/cogs.12051

Johnston, Barbara R., Elizabeth Colson, Dean Falk, Graham St John, John H. Bodley, Bonnie J. McCay, Alaka Wali, Carolyn Nordstrom & Susan Slyomovics. 2012. "On Happiness". *American Anthropologist*, 114 (1): 6–18, https://doi.org/10.1111/j.1548-1433.2011.01393.x

Kepes, György. 1995 [1944]. *Language of Vision*. New York: Dover.

Kirshenblatt-Gimblett, Barbara. 1998. *Destination Culture: tourism, museums, and heritage*. Berkeley, CA: University of California Press.

Kitayama, Shinobu, Sean Duffy, Tadashi Kawamura & Jeff T. Larsen. 2003. "Perceiving an object and its context in different cultures: a cultural look at new look". *Psychological Science*, 14 (3): 201–06, https://doi.org/10.1111/1467-9280.02432

Knowles, Caroline & Paul Sweetman. 2004. *Picturing the Social Landscape: visual methods and the sociological imagination*. London: Routledge.

Kotkin, Stephen. 1995. *Magnetic Mountain: Stalinism as a civilization*. Berkeley, CA: University of California Press.

Laruelle, Marlène. 2009. *In the Name of the Nation: nationalism and politics in contemporary Russia*. New York: Palgrave Macmillan, https://doi.org/10.1057/9780230101234

Lester, David & Sergei Kondrichin. 2003. "Research note: suicide and homicide in Siberia". *Sibirica*, 3 (1): 103–07, https://doi.org/10.1080/1361736032000168058

Lévi-Strauss, Claude. 1966. *The Savage Mind*. Chicago, IL: University of Chicago Press.

MacDougall, David. 1997. "The visual in anthropology". In: *Rethinking Visual Anthropology*, ed. Marcus Banks & Howard Murphy. New Haven, CT: Yale University Press, pp. 276–95.

—. 1998. *Transcultural Cinema*, ed. and with an introduction by Lucien Taylor. Princeton, NJ: Princeton University Press.

Markus, Hazel R., & Shinobu Kitayama. 2003. "Culture, self, and the reality of the social". *Psychological Inquiry*, 14 (3–4): 277–83, https://doi.org/10.1080/1047840X.2003.9682893

Masuda, Takahiko & Richard E. Nisbett. 2001. "Attending holistically versus analytically: comparing the context sensitivity of Japanese and Americans". *Journal of Personality and Social Psychology*, 81 (5), 922–34, https://doi.org/10.1037/0022-3514.81.5.922

—. 2006. "Culture and change blindness". *Cognitive Science*, 30 (2): 381–99, https://doi.org/10.1207/s15516709cog0000_63

Mathews, Gordon & Carolina Izquierdo. 2009. *Pursuits of Happiness: well-being in anthropological perspective*. New York: Berghahn.

Menovshchikov, Georgii A. 1969. *Eskimoskie skazki i legendy* [Eskimo tales and legends]. Magadan: Magadanskoe knizhnoe izdatel'stvo.

Miyamoto, Yuri, Richard E. Nisbett & Takahiko Masuda. 2006. "Culture and the physical environment: holistic versus analytic perceptual affordances". *Psychological Science*, 17 (2): 113–19, https://doi.org/10.1111/j.1467-9280.2006.01673.x

Nichols, Bill. 1991. *Representing Reality: issues and concepts in documentary*. Bloomington, IN: Indiana University Press.

Nuttall, Mark. 1992. *Arctic Homeland: kinship, community and development in northwest Greenland*. London: Belhaven Press; Toronto: University of Toronto Press.

Panáková, Jaroslava. 1996. *Anxious North: indigenous peoples in Soviet and post-Soviet Russia*. Copenhagen: International Work Group for Indigenous Affairs.

—. 2014. "Vec, fotografia a socializmus: príbeh koberca" [The object, photography and socialism: the history of the carpet]. *Národopisná revue*, 24 (1): 46–59.

Pika, Aleksandr, Eugenia W. Davis & Igor' I. Krupnik. 1993. "The spatial-temporal dynamic of violent death among the native peoples of northern Russia". *Arctic Anthropology*, 30 (2): 61–76, https://www.jstor.org/stable/40316338

Pivneva, Elena A. 2005. *V poiskakh sebia: narody Severa i Sibiri v postsovetskikh transformatsiiakh* [Searching for oneself: the Peoples of the North and Siberia in times of post-Soviet transformations]. Moscow: Nauka.

Rose, Gilian. 2007. *Visual Methodologies: an introduction to the interpretation of visual materials*. London: SAGE.

Smith, C. Zoe & Anne-Marie Woodward. 1999. "Photo-elicitation method gives voice and reactions of subjects". *Journalism & Mass Communication Educator*, 53 (4): 31–41, https://doi.org/10.1177/107769589805300403

Sontag, Susan. 2005 [1977]. *On Photography*. New York: Rosetta.

Ssorin-Chaikov, Nikolai. 2003. *The Social Life of the State in Subarctic Siberia*. Stanford, CA: Stanford University Press.

Tolstoy, Leo [Lev Tolstoi]. 2001. *Anna Karenina*. New York: Viking Penguin.

Tucker, Susan A. & John V. Dempsey. 1991. "Photo interviewing: a tool for evaluating technological innovations", *Evaluation Review*, 15 (5): 639–54, https://doi.org/10.1177/0193841x9101500507

Vakhtin, Nikolai B. 1992. *Native Peoples of the Russian Far North*. London: Minority Rights Group.

Williamson, Judith. 1978. *Decoding Advertisements: ideology and meaning in advertising*. London: Marion Boyars.

Willerslev, Rane. 2007. *Soul Hunters: hunting, animism, and personhood among the Siberian Yukaghirs*. London: University of California Press, https://doi.org/10.1525/california/9780520252165.001.0001

Witkin, Herman A. & John W. Berry. 1975. "Psychological differentiation in cross-cultural perspective". *Journal of Cross-Cultural Psychology*, 6 (1): 4–87, https://doi.org/10.1177/002202217500600102

Yemelianov, Nikolai V. 1965. *Sakha öhün khohoonnor unkhomuura* [Anthology of Sakha sayings and proverbs]. Yakutsk: Yakutknigoizdatel'stvo.

Films

Marker, Chris. 1983. *Sans Soleil*. 100 minutes. Neuilly: Argos Films.

Table 6.1. Single portraits of *self* – distribution according to age, year of production, and overall photo selection

Age group and sex distribution	Total number of interviewees	Number of interviewees with at least one portrait of self	Year of the production of portraits of self					Total number of single portraits of self	Number of other images	Percentage of single portraits of self
			2000s	1990s	1980s	1970s	1960s	174 (86f / 88m)	310	35.95
20s	**33**	**31**	**101**	**2**	**0**	**0**	**0**	**103**	**104**	**49.76**
Female	19	18	61	1	0	0	0	62	54	52.54
Male	14	13	40	1	0	0	0	41	50	45.05
30s	**10**	**5**	**17**	**0**	**0**	**0**	**0**	**17**	**52**	**24.64**
Female	6	3	8	0	0	0	0	8	28	22.22
Male	4	2	9	0	0	0	0	9	24	27.27
40s	**10**	**7**	**9**	**11**	**9**	**3**	**1**	**31**	**62**	**33.33**
Female	5	3	2	2	1	3	0	8	43	15.69
Male	5	4	7	9	6	0	1	23	19	54.76
50s	**9**	**7**	**4**	**1**	**3**	**9**	**0**	**17**	**40**	**29.82**
Female	4	2	4	0	2	1	0	7	21	25.00
Male	5	5	0	1	1	8	0	10	19	34.48
60s	**7**	**3**	**2**	**1**	**0**	**1**	**2**	**6**	**50**	**10.71**
Female	5	1	1	0	0	0	0	1	43	2.27
Male	2	2	1	1	0	3	2	5	7	41.67
70s	**1**	**0**	**0**	**0**	**0**	**0**	**0**	**0**	**2**	**0.00**
Male	1	0	0	0	0	0	0	0	2	0.00

Table 6.2. Single portraits of the "significant other" — distribution according to age and year of production

Age group and sex distribution	Total number of interviewees	Number of interviewees with at least one such portrait	Total number of such portraits	Time periods of the photo production				
				2000s	1990s	1980s	1970s	1960s
		20	28					
		10f / 10m	21f / 7m					
20s	**33**	**1**	**1**	**1**	**0**	**0**	**0**	**0**
Female	19	1	1	1	0	0	0	0
Male	14	0	0	0	0	0	0	0
30s	**10**	**4**	**4**	**4**	**0**	**0**	**0**	**0**
Female	6	2	3	3	0	0	0	0
Male	4	2	1	1	0	0	0	0
40s	**10**	**4**	**18**	**4**	**4**	**8**	**2**	**0**
Female	5	3	15	3	3	8	1	0
Male	5	1	3	1	1	0	1	0
50s	**9**	**7**	**0**	**0**	**0**	**0**	**0**	**0**
Female	4	2	0	0	0	0	0	0
Male	5	5	0	0	0	0	0	0
60s	**7**	**3**	**4**	**0**	**3**	**1**	**0**	**0**
Female	5	2	2	0	1	1	0	0
Male	2	1	2	0	2	0	0	0
70s	**1**	**1**	**1**	**0**	**1**	**0**	**0**	**0**
Male	1	1	1	0	1	0	0	0

7. Soviet *Kul'tura* in Post-Soviet Identification

The Aesthetics of Ethnicity in Sakha (Yakutia)

Eleanor Peers

This volume uses the concept of lifestyle to investigate social change in a very specific regional setting — the Russian Federation, the largest country in the former Soviet Union. As David Chaney's work shows particularly clearly, the concept of lifestyle can help us investigate the interrelation between social differentiation, and the varying patterns of aesthetic and ethical values that can be observed in contemporary mass societies (Chaney 1996). However, like other theorisations of lifestyle, Chaney's discussion is explicitly concerned with Euro-American capitalist societies, which have broadly conformed to consumerist forms of production throughout the twentieth and twenty-first centuries. A crucial difference between the development of western European and Soviet social practice was the presence in the Soviet Union of a consistent mobilisation of state resources into promoting expedient forms of cultural production, incorporating a particular notion of the nature and function of aesthetics, in addition to aesthetic and ethical values. How, then, can the trends Chaney describes have emerged in Soviet or socialist societies, where the possibilities for performance and expression were shaped to a much larger extent by a socialist state

 https://doi.org/10.11647/OBP.0171.07

ideology and policy, rather than capitalist consumer production? How could Soviet-era configurations of aesthetics, ethics, communication, and social differentiation be affecting those of the present day? To what extent is a body of theory generated in the capitalist west applicable to former Soviet societies, and what can it show us?

This article takes the national revival of the Sakha people in Sakha Republic (Yakutia), in north-eastern Siberia, as a case study, to examine the extent to which the Soviet legacy is influencing post-Soviet patterns of expression, value, and community — thus evaluating the significance the lifestyle concept has for the former Soviet Union. As this chapter will show, perceptions of cultural difference were a key target of a complex Soviet policy, which utilised a range of artistic and aesthetic forms. Contemporary identification and identity politics in the Russian Federation continue to revolve around cultural production. Hence, the Sakha national revival can reveal the impact of Soviet policy on contemporary formations of community and aesthetic values — and, particularly, those existing in the Russian Far North and Siberia.

The first section describes the forms of expression and value that are linked to the Sakha national revival. This description is structured around an account of the *Yhyakh*, the Sakha people's most important yearly festival, and it includes a discussion of a pattern of aesthetic value and community formation that differs from the cases Chaney describes. It will re-focus the questions posed above towards a particular community within the former Soviet Union — contemporary Sakha society — and the Sakha patterns of social differentiation that involve notions of cultural difference. In doing so, it will explicate Chaney's theory, and its implications for understanding contemporary social differentiation in the west. The second section describes the configuration of aesthetics and community that emerged within Soviet-era authoritative discourse, and, in particular, through state-sponsored cultural production. It also explores the unintended effects these policies had on community formation during the late Soviet period. The third section shows how the Soviet policies that concerned non-Russian ethnic groups incorporated the authoritative aesthetic, and the forms of cultural production it encouraged. The chapter's conclusion will draw links between the specificities of contemporary expressions of

Sakha identification and their aesthetics, and the trajectory of Soviet-era aestheticised social differentiation.

Lifestyle, Aesthetics, and Identity Politics in Sakha (Yakutia)

What's in a coat?: taste and identity politics at the *Yhyakh*

Sakha society has transformed rapidly over the twentieth and twenty-first centuries, as have the nature of its hierarchies, and their values. There are many aspects of present-day Sakha that conform to the post-modern, capitalist social realities Chaney's theory concerns; however, there are features of Sakha values and aesthetics that are distinctive, as this section will describe. The following discussion of lifestyle in Sakha (Yakutia) focuses on the values and aesthetics of the Sakha national revival, and their integration into Sakha's social differentiation. It is structured around an account of the Sakha people's contemporary *Yhyakh* festivals, and the different patterns of community, value, and expression that can be observed on these occasions.

Sakha (Yakutia) is unusual, although not unique, among Russia's federal subjects, in that its titular ethnic group, the Sakha people, is numerically dominant over the Russian population: according to the 2010 census, 49.9 per cent of the population are Sakha, while 37.8 are Russian (*Vserossiiskaia perepis'* 2010). The Sakha, like many other non-Russian peoples of the former Soviet space, experienced a nationalist revival of their religious and artistic traditions during the 1990s, initiated by members of the political and intellectual elites. This revival is occurring against the backdrop of a Russian colonisation of the region beginning in the early seventeenth century, and the Soviet-era social engineering discussed in subsequent sections.

The impact of this revival is evident from the current popularity of one of its flagship events, the summer *Yhyakh* ritual. This event is rooted in the Sakha people's shamanic heritage: the pre-Soviet *Yhyakh* was an opportunity to offer fermented mare's milk, or *kumys*, to the higher nature spirits and gods in the Sakha shamanic pantheon. These rituals both praised the gods for the coming of summer, and asked for prosperity in the future. The festival was banned in some parts of Sakha (the then Yakutian Autonomous Socialist Soviet Republic) during the Soviet period. Soviet *Yhyakh* organisers would frequently omit the shamanic prayers and libations that were the event's original pretext, replacing them with the official speeches that occurred at most Soviet public events (cf. Lane 1981) — thus making the *Yhyakh* indistinguishable from the many other Soviet state holidays. Key members of the Sakha nationalist intelligentsia staged prominent *Yhyakh* festivals during the early 1990s, and since then the *Yhyakh* has become one of the republic's most important holidays. Hundreds of thousands of people now attend the republic's largest *Yhyakh*, put on by the municipality of Yakutsk, the republic's capital; every other Sakha settlement in the republic holds its own *Yhyakh*, as do many of the republic's larger institutions, private businesses, and family groups.

The *Yhyakh* can take innumerable forms, depending on the agenda and means of its organisers — however an *Yhyakh* generally includes the ritual feeding of the upper spirits and gods, followed by a communal circle dance, the *Ohuohai*; eating, drinking and relaxing with family, friends, and colleagues; performances of Sakha folk and pop music and dancing; and competitions in traditional Sakha sports. The larger, state-sponsored *Yhyakh* festivals last for a couple of days, interspersed with a ritual greeting of the sun on one of the mornings. Yakutsk's *Yhyakh* incorporates several sound and concert stages, food stalls, a sports area, horse racing, fashion shows, and a market selling Sakha art, crafts, clothes, jewellery, and souvenirs — in addition to areas where individuals can receive their own shamanic ritual cleansing, healing, and advice. A large part of the festival site is taken up with a series of small enclosures, in which individual organisations and regional administrations host their own rituals, exhibitions and parties.

The photograph below, Figure 7.1, was taken at a private banquet in one of these enclosures, at a large *Yhyakh* organised by the administration of a region close to Yakutsk. An extended version of the ancient wooden Sakha summer accommodation (*urahai*) had been built to house the banquet; the guests were seated at wooden tables around its edge, eating a selection of traditional Sakha foods as they listened to each other's toasts and speeches.

Fig. 7.1. *Yhyakh* participants at a banquet. Photograph by Eleanor Peers, June 2012, CC-BY.

Two out of this group of high-level government officials and businessmen are wearing Sakha national costume — this is the dark grey coat, studded with metal that they have on over their European white shirts and ties. Noticeably, the man facing the camera, a high-ranking regional politician, is not Sakha, even though he has invested in an expensive Sakha national costume. He is sitting between a Russian in a conventional European shirt, and a Sakha man, also in European dress. Sakha national costume is clearly not obligatory at this occasion even for ethnic Sakha, despite the emphatic visual and culinary signals that define the event as Sakha — such as the wooden pillars carved to look like traditional Sakha horse-tethering poles, or the bottles of *kumys* on the tables, rather than wine or vodka.

These signals also highlight indigenous Siberian tradition *per se* as a locus of meaning and value — as does the fact that the banquet's important guests have taken the trouble to wear Sakha national costume. The politician's decision to wear Sakha national costume was clearly made with reference to the complex of meaning and value surrounding contemporary Sakha identity, so evident at this festival. In fact, he was carefully displaying his commitment to Sakha cultural particularity, in order to consolidate his relationship with the region's Sakha population — as a high-level Russian official in a political context conditioned by the Putin administration's emphasis on the supremacy of ethnic Russian interests and traditions, within the Russian Federation as a whole. Sakha government officials also have to manage their expressions of cultural affiliation, depending on their position and context: it is not always appropriate for them to wear national costume, as the smart white shirt on the Russian's Sakha neighbour shows.

All these men are using their dress as a means of visual expression, which, in this occasion's specific circumstances, enables them both to display their own position with reference to the subtle play of value, power, and community at this event, and to act within it. They are employing the repertoire of conventional local tastes into both communication and action — and, in particular, the spectrum of common visual and gastronomic tastes and values, as they choose their clothes and their food. (For instance, does the Russian politician tuck in to the boiled reindeer tongue, which is not commonly found in European Russia — or does he avoid it, thus drawing attention to his ethnic origin, and the tense colonial relationship between Russians and Sakha?) Their behaviour shows how social relationships, power differentiation, and community formation are embedded in sensory experience and value. If aesthetic responses are understood to concern "the qualitative effect of stimuli upon the senses", following Howard Morphy (1996: 258), then they are clearly integrated into the negotiation of power relationships in Sakha (Yakutia), as they are throughout the world.

Lifestyle: aesthetics in action

This section will use Chaney's discussion of Euro-American lifestyle to expand on the role display has within contemporary mass societies, and on its implications for the interrelation of aesthetic and ethical value, and action. In line with other influential writers on the concept of lifestyle, Chaney (1996) places the development of a "culture of spectacle" in the modern capitalist world at the heart of his discussion. He argues that the anonymity of contemporary urban space, the development of cultures of consumption, along with mass advertising and fashion, and the fracturing of pre-modern hierarchies have led to a new emphasis on visualisation in the formation and negotiation of social structuration and identity. Chaney defines lifestyles as "'any distinctive, and therefore recognizable, mode of living'" (1996: 11), following Sobel (1981: 3). He contends that they are "'expressive' behaviours" (Chaney 1996: 11; see also Chapter 1 of this volume). Chaney further describes these expressive behaviours as "characteristic modes of social engagement, or narratives of identity, in which the actors concerned can embed the metaphors at hand [...] lifestyles are creative projects, they are forms of enactment in which actors make judgements in delineating an environment" (1996: 92).

As this quotation suggests, lifestyles are the way that individuals can assimilate the symbols available to them into habitual expressive practices, which orientate them with respect to the changing communities and hierarchies among which they live — and, in doing so, also reproduce these dynamic and yet structured social groupings. Lifestyles signal "patterns of affiliation" or "sensibilities" — groupings of aesthetic and ethical values, which form the terrain of social differentiation in today's societies (Chaney 1996: 11). Lifestyles are therefore the means by which social structure both emerges and is negotiated in contemporary societies, characterised as they are by increasing and destabilising flows of people, information, symbols, technologies, and consumer products. Chaney's elaboration of lifestyle links the notion of the "social imaginary" that Joseph Long presents in Chapter 5 to social structuration. If social imaginaries refer to "collective representations of social identity", Chaney's account points out the work these representations do in the negotiation of power.

As Chaney seeks to emphasise, the expression within these lifestyles relies heavily on the visual: "visualisation has become the central resource for communicating and appropriating meaning" (1996: 101). He points to the increasing preponderance of "visual clues" in contemporary urban environments: "The combination of the inherent anonymity of urban crowds, allied with mass retailing, industries of mass leisure and entertainment and the provision of public information for those seeking guidance in alienating spaces all work to create an insistent chatter of visual imagery" (ibid.). Furthermore, he suggests that the prominence of fashion and design in contemporary societies exhibits a material culture that revolves around a popular capacity to reflect on the distinction between the form and function of material objects; this reflection acts to invest these objects with meaning through incorporating them into different performative demarcations of sensibility. Styles of, for example, clothing, interior decoration, or smartphones express both the values and intentions associated with their particular aesthetic, and the reflexive process of inscribing meaning to physical objects — a process which itself acts to relativise aesthetic judgement. The management of visual cues, or, as Chaney puts it, "surfaces", is thus integral to the process whereby individuals acquire identity and agency through their capacity to navigate the shifting spectrum of taste and value that constitutes social differentiation.

A widespread recognition of the relativity of both aesthetic and ethical values is of course a central part of the lifestyle phenomenon Chaney describes. This relativity extends to the nature itself of the ethical and aesthetic, and their interrelation, through the reflexive awareness of the activity of investing different material forms and sensual stimuli with meaning and expressive power. The process through which individuals communicate and act within social reality invokes ethical and aesthetic values, as part of a spectrum of alternative ethics, aesthetics, and expressions. Social differentiation in contemporary consumer societies therefore occurs through forms of communication that incorporate habituated patterns of aesthetic and ethical value, while also rendering these patterns provisional.

The contingent and dynamic nature of ethical and aesthetic values, within multiple and overlapping instances of lifestyle expression, makes possible a shift in the relative position and nature of the aesthetic and ethical, such that the aesthetic becomes both a means and an end. The invocation of a specific aesthetic response becomes part of the expression of both ethical and aesthetic sensibilities. For example, the extent to which an individual foregrounds the care with which they have coordinated the shapes, textures, and colours in their new kitchen is part of the lifestyle choice it manifests, along with the ethical and aesthetic values this choice implies. It is therefore possible to imagine "the aesthetic" as providing the means for a variety of expressive interventions into the social environment, rather than as the passive experience of the beautiful. Particular patterns of aesthetic response can incorporate understandings of functional aesthetics, which can be mobilised in the service of a given spectrum of lifestyles, and their underlying intentions and sensibilities; as part of this, perceptions and notions of the aesthetic become intermingled with ethical considerations.

To give an example, technological products made by Apple are geared towards individuals who take pride in the beauty of their material accoutrements. The recognition that aesthetic value can and should be incorporated into everyday technologies is the conduit and signal for further systems of ethical and aesthetic sensibilities: the minimalist shapes and hard, polished textures both echo and emphasise the placing of value on capitalist technological development, efficiency, and empirical science. At the other end of the scale, those wanting to signal their disassociation from free-market capitalism and the spread of communication technology can subvert the assumption that everyday technologies should also carry an intrinsic aesthetic statement, by covering their Apple Mac with stickers, for example. Their Mac becomes a vehicle for their personal self-expression, rather than a beautiful object in itself. These examples occur in juxtaposition with one another, even if there is no direct contact between the people involved. Both will have an awareness that alternative aesthetic expressions exist, along with the aesthetic and ethical sensibilities they manifest: their expressive intervention into the social environment is therefore perpetually relative to these alternatives.

Finally, these two aesthetic decisions will be accompanied by many others, which together enmesh these individuals into a variety of overlapping communities they have recognised through their ability to "read" the aesthetic choices of others. Hence, someone in a dark, well-cut suit sits on an urban underground train, engrossed in their iPad, next to another person with body piercings and strikingly dyed hair, listening to an iPhone in a black and red striped case. The people sitting opposite them can while away the journey in imagining their houses; their political views; their life partners; or their pets, in the awareness that others may be doing the same with them. A reflexive awareness of alternative aesthetic expressions is thus built into the way we apprehend the social environment, and the way we engage with it through "performing" our own aesthetic and ethical sensibilities and alliances. The result, in many Euro-American capitalist societies, is a plethora of overlapping appearances linked to lifestyles, which map on to what are recognised as the more stable differentiating characteristics, such as gender, ethnic background, and age, to constitute shifting systems of social structuration, community, and identity.

Sensibilities of ethnicity at the *Yhyakh*

Attending an *Yhyakh* shows clearly that similar combinations of sensibility and expression also serve to demarcate communities and actors within the social reality of Sakha (Yakutia). The Sakha identification is strong enough for most Sakha people to conceive of themselves as belonging to a discrete community within the Russian Federation. And yet the Sakha population is large enough (466,500 people, in 2010) and sufficiently integrated into the Russian Federation's wider social context for social differentiation to occur within it, according to shifting patterns of sensibility and value. For example, an observer familiar with Sakha (Yakutia) would immediately conclude that the men sitting at the *Yhyakh* banquet in Figure 7.1 above are members of the elite, and, therefore, are likely to be managing their expressions of national affiliation very carefully, regardless of their real sympathies.

A survey of the *Yhyakh* at Yakutsk shows some important patterns of sensibility in Sakha (Yakutia), the way they are expressed, and hence the recognisable lifestyle choices that have become both markers and conduits for social differentiation within the Sakha community. Many of the values and preconceptions that inform these sensibilities concern the meaning of Sakha identification, and an emphatic public commitment to the Sakha people and cultural heritage has become a widespread convention among Sakha intellectual, political, and business elites, as Figure 7.1 shows. However, the public celebration of Sakha cultural heritage sits in an uneasy tension with Sakha (Yakutia)'s politically subservient position within the Russian Federation. Visitors to the republic constantly encounter a worry that others may perceive the Sakha people and their culture as primitive, irrelevant, on the verge of dissolution — and, even worse, that this perception could be correct. The massively increased exposure to global technologies and cultural products brought about by the cessation of the Soviet administration has in some respects exacerbated the worry about Sakha culture and its value, while providing opportunities for individuals to adopt or create new forms of Sakha identification (Ventsel 2004a, Ventsel & Peers 2017).

Yakutsk's *Yhyakh* is shot through with the ambiguity that surrounds a Sakha identification, whether manifested through the occasion's political communication, cultural production, shamanic spirituality, commerce, or individual decisions about how to enjoy the holiday. Its main didactic purpose is the cultural establishment's effort to encourage Sakha people to respect and value their cultural tradition; this is also a key motivation within the current revival of the Sakha shamanic tradition, which, again, is supported by many members of the cultural and intellectual establishments. Among these communities, a desire to pursue an interest in Sakha shamanism is associated with a commendable love and respect towards one's native Sakha culture; this in turn is taken to signal an appreciation of higher values, a love of nature and mankind, and an openness towards an engagement with positive, spiritual forces. The contemporary practice of Sakha neo-shamanism is therefore a way of expressing a set of sensibilities, and in doing so marking oneself out as an intellectual, idealist, or creative person (*tvorcheskii chelovek*) — as someone who is drawn to the pursuit of life's mysterious, complex, and creative dimensions, for its own sake.

This set of values is so deeply integrated into the Sakha social context that individuals can refer to them through signals as small as brief asides in a conversation — or as far-reaching as adopting what in some cases can amount to a lifestyle, in Chaney's sense. Some people devote a great deal of their time, energy, and money to attending shamanic lectures, for example, or visiting important ritual sites. These people come to Yakutsk's *Yhyakh* to receive spiritual cleansing, as part of engaging with their pre-Soviet cultural tradition. They may pay particular attention to the *Yhyakh*'s main ritual, undergo private shamanic healing ceremonies, or attend the greeting of the sun — or they may themselves be helping to administer the various different forms of Sakha shamanic ritual. These people are likely to see the *Yhyakh* as an occasion that enables them to engage with and articulate their deepest religious and moral convictions, and thus as one of the year's most important events. Their values to some extent coincide with those expressed by the republic's leading intellectual and cultural figures, and hence put them on the side of Sakha society commonly held to be discerning, enlightened, and elite. In fact, the majority of the people I have encountered who espouse this set of values are from the professional classes, with a level of education that would facilitate their seeking meaning and value in learning about cultural tradition.

However, a large proportion of *Yhyakh* attendees — likely to include many of those who appreciate the *Yhyakh*'s spiritual aspect — are there as consumers of the various attractions provided by both state and commerce. The willingness to appropriate foreign cultural forms, which Chaney (1996) contends is characteristic of modernised, capitalist social contexts, sits in Sakha (Yakutia) with a characteristically modern, capitalist consciousness of an individual's right to seek their own happiness, pleasure, and trajectory of development, through their power to consume (Giddens 1990). In the Sakha context, the directions this consumption can take are inflected by the uncertainty about the value of a Sakha identification, mentioned above. On the one hand, the demonstration that one is "up to speed" with the rest of the world, through one's ownership of prominent foreign brands of clothes, mobile telephones, or computers, is regarded by many as a commendable action. On the other, the healthy market in specifically Sakha crafts, jewellery, art, national costumes, and fashion testifies to a widespread desire to demonstrate that one is not only up-to-date, but proudly Sakha: many decisions, expressive actions, and lifestyle choices are shaped by a felt need to establish the Sakha people's right to regard itself as bearing one of the world's valuable cultures. The *Yhyakh* provides a valuable opportunity both to trade in and celebrate contemporary Sakha fashion, cultural production, and art. Sakha designers and artisans can exhibit their products to potential customers, while individuals have a chance to display their Sakha national costumes and jewellery.

Those who are unable or unwilling to buy expensive Sakha artefacts still have the opportunity to enjoy and display their Sakha affiliation through their consumption of Sakha popular music; the various concert and sound stages at the *Yhyakh* are packed with listeners, many of whom spend the entire night dancing or socialising. The Sakha popular music industry has mushroomed since the 1990s, and now encompasses a variety of genres and performers, each of which addresses and manifests the ambiguities posed by the nature of contemporary Sakha identity (Ventsel 2004a, 2004b, 2009). Many Sakha pop singers use their performances to showcase Sakha fashion designs, which on occasion can incorporate elements taken from Sakha national costume, and traditional art.

On the other hand, Sakha rap artists emphasise their enthusiasm for foreign music genres by adopting hip-hop fashion and style wholesale, in common with their generally young, urban fan base. However, even the Sakha hip-hop fans who stride through the *Yhyakh* in skinny jeans and hi-top trainers are demonstrating their adherence to Sakha hip-hop, in particular. They may not be about to have anything to do with Sakha national costumes and traditionalist shamanism, but they are, nonetheless, a new incarnation of the Sakha people — as their eagerness to participate in the Sakha-language pop and rap scene shows. Sakha-language pop and rap lyrics frequently concern the dilemmas that a Sakha identification can entail for young people, even if the singers and rappers themselves dress, move, and dance like American pop artists (Ventsel & Peers 2017).

As the description of contemporary Sakha fashion and pop indicates, visual display and spectacle have become very important in the contemporary Sakha context, in common with the western capitalist cultures Chaney describes. People can signal their affiliation with the *Yhyakh*'s spiritual meaning by, for example, buying and displaying amulets, or the sacred Sakha horse-tail whips (*debir*). They can demonstrate their pride in their Sakha identity by simply wearing traditional Sakha earrings, if they are women, or a horsehair headband, if they are men — or, at the other end of the scale, by creating their own elaborate national costume. The different perceptions and values surrounding Sakha identification and culture therefore emerge as juxtaposed patterns of expression, which enable individual Sakha people both to identify and to situate themselves among the changing communities within Sakha society. People use combinations of dress, ornament, and behaviour to mark their own priorities, within Sakha (Yakutia)'s familiar spectrum of aesthetic and ethical value — whether they are committed to reviving the Sakha shamanic tradition, or to showing the world that Sakha people can rap and breakdance.

Traces of the Soviet in Sakha shamanic art

The intersections of ethical and aesthetic value, expression, and social differentiation at the *Yhyakh* therefore correspond to some extent with Chaney's description of lifestyle in the west. However, the visual expression at the *Yhyakh* also reveals the influence of Sakha (Yakutia)'s Soviet heritage. As is the case all over the former Soviet Union, contemporary cultural production bears a strong resemblance to Soviet-era cultural production — and understandably so, since many of the people who train and direct cultural workers received their own training at the end of the Soviet era (cf. Habeck 2011a). The *Yhyakh*'s main shamanic ritual is therefore accompanied by complex displays of choreography, which clearly belong to the same aesthetic tradition as the dances staged during Soviet-era public holidays (cf. Lane 1981; Rolf 2009). The majority of Sakha national costumes meanwhile conform to patterns that were recorded and reproduced by Soviet-era ethnographers.

The presence of Soviet-era visual forms reflects a striking repetitiveness within the *Yhyakh*'s visual expression. It is noticeable that the same visual formulae are reproduced in very different contexts, and, as part of this, have become assimilated into the expression of contrasting spectrums of sensibility and community. For example, depictions of Baiaanai, the spirit guardian of the forests for both past and present generations of Sakha people, crop up in a surprising variety of contexts — while also conforming to a stable set of visual conventions. As Figure 7.2 shows, Baiaanai is shown as an old, good-natured Sakha man, with high cheekbones, long hair and a beard, surrounded by wild animals. The representation combines realism with naïveté, and Baiaanai is often merged with the wild animals and landscapes he is portrayed against.

The picture in Figure 7.2 hangs on the wall of a centre for shamanic healing and education, in Suntar', the main settlement of Suntar' region. This establishment, like its equivalents all over Sakha (Yakutia), aims to revive Sakha shamanic practice, and, in doing so, to re-educate Sakha people about their ancient beliefs and values. This picture is part of a series of representations, designed to remind Sakha people about their own sacred traditions; it asserts that area spirits are alive and well, and that they should be respected and revered as sacred beings. As such, it has its own elevated moral value, as does its creator and exhibitors: as I have explained above, a reverence for what is regarded as Sakha tradition signals a praiseworthy commitment to higher ideals. This picture and its presentation therefore are directed towards, and appreciated by, the

Fig. 7.2. A picture of Baiaanai at a shamanic temple in Suntar' Region. Photograph by Eleanor Peers, March 2011, CC BY.

Sakha individuals who espouse the value of reviving Sakha shamanism, along with its concurrent attitudes towards the natural environment.

The carving in Figure 7.3 is also regarded as a highly valuable, original art object; it was on sale at a fair of traditional Sakha arts and crafts, in Yakutsk in 2010.

Again, Baiaanai has a long beard, a good-natured expression, and is fused into the rivers and animals that surround him. And yet this representation is being sold as an art object, rather than displayed as a sanctified reference to the Sakha people's ancient spiritual tradition. The circumstances of its display invite the viewer to admire the artistry of the carving, as much as Baiaanai's intrinsic meaning and value. It is being presented as a work of art, and perhaps also as a patriotic status symbol, within a nexus of value that does not include the assumption that Baiaanai himself should be an object of worship, along with his living environment. One can imagine its eventual buyer as a well-off

Fig. 7.3. A carving of Baiaanai, on sale at a fair in Yakutsk. Photograph by Eleanor Peers, November 2010, CC-BY.

individual who is proud of their Sakha identity and heritage, but who does not necessarily also invest significant resources into pursuing the Sakha shamanic revival. An image that in one context is used to remind the Sakha people of one of their most prominent spiritual entities is used in another to create an attractive household ornament.

Figure 7.4 shows a depiction of Baiaanai on a large, wooden "tree of life", put up as part of the *Yhyakh* celebrations at the town of Mirnyi in 2011. This tree of life refers to the Sakha *Aal luk mas*, a giant tree that unites the shamanic cosmos.

This depiction of Baiaanai is more naïve than the others, although the central elements are the same: we see a Sakha man with a long beard, merged into the landscape, his generosity symbolised by the stream of fish coming from his lap, as in the carving. And yet this representation of Baiaanai is part of a much more overt political statement than the previous two, addressed to an audience of varied ethnicity, rather than the Sakha community. Mirnyi is one of the industrial mining towns built after World War II, according to the Soviet Union's centralised

Fig. 7.4. A representation of Baiaanai at *Yhyakh* in the town of Mirnyi. Photograph by Eleanor Peers, July 2011, CC-BY.

economic planning. These towns grew rapidly, developing primarily non-Sakha populations, made up of industrial workers and specialists who migrated into Sakha (Yakutia) from around the Soviet Union. It remains a predominantly non-Sakha town; as a result, the large *Yhyakh* at Mirnyi in 2011 had to manage relationships between Sakha and non-Sakha residents, and attitudes towards Sakha communities within the wider Russian Federation. The company that runs Mirnyi's diamond mine, ALROSA, also used the event to demonstrate its commitment to both the Sakha people and Mirnyi's multi-ethnic population.

Therefore the "tree of life", like the rest of this particular *Yhyakh*, aimed to mix recognisably Sakha and non-Sakha motifs within a nominally Sakha cultural form. The other panels on the "tree of life" included representations of Russian folktales, of Orthodox Christian motifs, and of different ALROSA settlements, with the name ALROSA itself written along the bottom. This picture of Baiaanai therefore is integrated into a statement, firstly, of the importance and value of Sakha culture to ALROSA, and, secondly, of the capacity Sakha culture has to

welcome and incorporate foreign traditions. Baiaanai himself has very
little relevance to the message, other than as a reference to ALROSA's
respect for the Sakha people's traditional love of nature — and as an
attractive, exotic Sakha cultural form for the *Yhyakh*'s many non-Sakha
attendees.[1]

These three illustrations show how similar visual forms — in this
case, a stylised representation of Baiaanai — can be incorporated into
very different expressive statements, addressed towards a wide variety
of audiences. It is possible for a large diamond corporation to incorporate
a sacred Sakha figure into its public representation, and, conversely,
for an image used in a company's public relations to appear as an art
object, and a visual evocation of core Sakha values and spiritual beliefs.
The same visual forms are of course reproduced in contrasting contexts
all over the world. However, what is striking about Sakha (Yakutia)'s
patterns of aesthetic expression is their lack of reflexivity. None of
the three images above, or their presentation, makes any reference to
the alternative meanings and references to Baiaanai, with which they
co-exist. ALROSA is happy to present a sacred Sakha figure next to
idealised images of its mining settlements, without alluding to the fact
that Baiaanai is more than a pretty story, for many Sakha people.

Meanwhile, the shamanic centre does not feel the need to foreground
a sense that their treatment of Baiaanai may be more respectful of
his value and power than other representations — by, for example,
experimenting with different visual styles and techniques. In contrast,
visual presentations in Euro-American settings can be constructed
under the assumption that viewers will see the repetition of an image
as a deliberate part of the representation as a whole, itself acting as a
reflection on the original source. A classic example is Andy Warhol's
1962 painting *Marilyn Diptych*, which incorporates a still from the
Marilyn Monroe film *Niagara* into a visual comment on celebrity culture.

None of my Sakha interlocutors have ever noted the ease with
which the same visual forms are transferred from setting to setting,
becoming incorporated into fundamentally different expressive acts.
The widespread practice of reproducing a stable set of visual forms is
accompanied by a willingness to accept highly conventionalised forms

---

1   The environmental impact of ALROSA's diamond mining is an extremely difficult
     issue in the areas immediately concerned, as Susan Crate describes (2003, 2009).

of visual cultural production and fashion, to the extent that copying or adapting another person's artwork is not regarded as problematic, or even worthy of comment. The carved figure of Baiaanai in Figure 7.3 is treated as an original art object, for example, even though it incorporates a well-used motif and style. These factors indicate that patterns of aesthetic response take a distinctive form in Sakha (Yakutia), and, therefore, that the interrelation between the expression of sensibility and social differentiation also differs from the patterns one can observe in Euro-America. The Soviet-era origin of so much of Sakha (Yakutia)'s cultural production suggests that the region's distinctive treatment of visual aesthetics also has its roots in the Soviet period. Could Soviet government policy therefore have generated a specific perception of aesthetic value? How did this perception influence cultural production, the expression of sensibility, and, finally, the emergence of social differentiation? How could the trends initiated by Soviet-era policy be influencing the contemporary Sakha lifestyles described above?

Soviet policy, *kul'tura*, and lifestyle

As the introduction to this chapter indicated, the whole spectrum of activities devoted to negotiating and expressing meaning and value in the Soviet Union — be they involved with the education system, cultural production, recreation, or mass media discourse — was heavily and consistently influenced by strategic state policy. The essentially modernist nature of the Soviet project meant that normative conceptions of aesthetic experience and value were deliberately incorporated into the array of expressive forms that manifested officially legitimate patterns of sensibility, along with the forms of social differentiation they generated. Official representations matched the perceptions and values they were seeking to promote with a series of expressive practices, much in the way that the lifestyles Chaney describes "perform" the clusters of sensibility that unite social groupings. As the historical literature on the Soviet Union shows, and as this section will explain, the Soviet population was encouraged from the mid-1930s onwards to adopt a changing spectrum of tastes and styles, which could include, for instance, a predilection for white tablecloths, silk lampshades, and curtains (Volkov 2000: 221).

The Soviet political elite therefore hoped to effect the "rebuilding" of Soviet citizens by offering them the possibility of taking on a new "lifestyle", in Chaney's sense — complete with the patterns of expressive behaviour that would enable them to signal their new incarnation and identification as members of the Soviet community. Successive Soviet administrations generated their own "cultures of spectacle", which incorporated specific forms of aestheticised communication — even if the various ways of reproducing and responding to this communication that developed over time eventually enabled it to signal patterns of sensibility the early Soviet government had not intended, as will be explained below. Later, I will return to the way official Soviet strategy played out within the government's handling of cultural difference.

Morality in cultural production: the meaning of Soviet *kul'tura*

The historical literature on the Soviet Union testifies to the hegemony the Soviet government was able to exert over all forms of public discourse, a hegemony that had huge implications for almost every aspect of daily life (cf. Boym 1994; Dunham 1990; Pesmen 2000). This hegemony did not and could not have existed as a straightforward imposition by one powerful elite over the rest of the population — in common with mass societies across the modern world, the size and complexity of the Soviet state meant that most of its citizens were co-opted in some way into the state's overriding interests.[2] Large proportions of Soviet citizens regarded the various norms, conventions, and values generated by state practice as inherently meaningful and worthwhile, as part of a broader personal commitment to Marxism and its ideals, if not also to the Soviet state itself (Yurchak 2006; Grant 1995). In addition, Soviet state policy, although generally produced as an instruction delivered by the central government to the entire Soviet territory, was of course realised in different ways and to differing extents, according to the varying

---

2   Work on the anthropology of the state has emphasised the difficulty of distinguishing between "state" and "citizen", given the extent to which state institutions and infrastructures emerge out of the collectively held practices, values, and understandings of the people who run them (e.g. Gupta 1995; Mitchell 1999). Nikolai Ssorin-Chaikov has made good use of this literature in his analysis of Soviet governmentality (2003).

circumstances, territories, cultural communities, and personalities that fell within its remit (İğmen 2011; Kotyleva 2004).

Yet the overall effect of the Soviet Union's configuration of power relations and state practice was an unusually consistent, repetitive, and omnipresent system of authoritative discourse, which, as Bruce Grant (2011) suggests, constitutes an important distinguishing characteristic of Soviet modernity. The strength of the Soviet Union's centralised power structure afforded a high cohesiveness between the different strands of state activity. Policy goals related to state building or industrialisation, for example, could also inform the ubiquitous state-sponsored cultural production — thus generating an authoritative discourse that encompassed all these different public spheres of action.

Cultural production was only one activity within the huge network of institutions and activities devoted to the Soviet state's culture. The Russian word *kul'tura* itself came to refer to a complex but nonetheless recognisable set of attitudes, aspirations, and practices over the Soviet period, to the extent that, as Grant notes, Soviet society seems to have been unique in knowing what the term "culture" meant (2011: 264–65). *Kul'tura* in fact came to stand for the process of both assimilating and signalling dominant Soviet patterns of value and community: it became a key paradigm within a process of social differentiation that bears resemblance to Chaney's description of the lifestyle phenomenon, in that it took place through the expression of particular sensibilities. Like the different modes of lifestyle expression Chaney identifies, the ideas and practices associated with *kul'tura* incorporated a reflexive philosophy of the aesthetic, which emerged via an emphasis on a person's engagement with cultural production as both demonstrating and enabling their formation as a "good" Soviet citizen.

As Vadim Volkov (2000) describes, the word *kul'tura* and its derivatives came into use during the late nineteenth century, in the context of the liberal intelligentsia's efforts to transmit education and enlightenment to the peasantry. Within this movement, *kul'tura* came to refer to "a kind of value that could be accumulated, purposefully transferred to and acquired by wider groups of the population" (Volkov 2000: 212). The meaning *kul'tura* acquired during the Soviet period drew from this tradition: the Bolsheviks took on the mantle left by the Tsarist intelligentsia, aiming to transfer Marxist-Leninist enlightenment to the population. As time went on, the attainment of *kul'tura* came to be understood as dependent on an individual's self-motivation, in addition to a collective philanthropic mission towards the uneducated. Over the 1920s and 30s, an important aspect of *kul'tura* referred to the internal transformation of the Soviet Union's population — the creation of Soviet man — which was to accompany the recreation of their economic system and society. By the end of the 1930s, a person's *kul'turnost'*, or level of culture, was understood to manifest the extent to which they had worked on improving their inner moral consciousness, through studying both the Bolshevik political literature, and cultural works from around the world (Kotkin 1995: 181; Volkov 2000). A *kul'turnyi chelovek* (cultured person) had to be acquainted with a range of subjects as varied as the geography of Africa, classical music, the history of the Stakhanovite movement, and specific œuvres of the literatures of Russia, England, and France (Volkov 2000: 224–25).

The dissemination of *kul'tura* via cultural production was heavily influenced by the Soviet government's conviction that the conversion of the population to Marxism-Leninism also entailed the reformation of such basic aspects of human communication and experience as language, and aesthetic value. As historians of the early Soviet Union describe, creative and academic workers of all kinds experimented with new forms of art, music, cinema, architecture, and language during the 1920s — even though this experimentation was explicitly subject to the Communist Party's overall project (Fitzpatrick 1970, 1992; Mally 2000; Stites 1989). The process of apprehending the qualities of sensual stimuli was itself under examination, as artists, musicians, writers, and architects strived to establish the indices of aesthetic experience appropriate for building a communist society. Right from the beginning, a reflexive notion of the aesthetic was understood to be inseparable from the transmission and manifestation of communist values — while the concept of *kul'tura* mingled ethical and aesthetic norms.

This experimentation was to generate some highly original *avant-garde* modernist art, music, cinema, and architecture — but Iosif Stalin's accession to power brought with it a strict assertion of state control over cultural production (Papernyi 2007), limiting the cultural forms and genres cultural workers could safely use. From the mid-1930s onwards, the Soviet Union's art, literature, drama, and film were to have the function of representing the contemporary socialist reality, and therefore all cultural production had to be Socialist Realist in style (Slezkine 2000). The Stalinist regulation of cultural production was nonetheless also based on the premise that a specific appreciation of sensual experience and its meaning had to be inculcated into popular aesthetic values, as part of the new social order.

By the 1940s and 50s, aesthetic values were supposed to be based on the laws of "objective science". Simple, harmonious representations of the Soviet Union's Socialist reality, designed to cheer and encourage the population in its building of the communist world, were deemed beautiful. This notion of the aesthetic led to an emphasis on conventional, unchallenging shapes, colours, sounds, figures, and words, which remained present in Soviet cultural production throughout the later decades of the Soviet era (Dunham 1990; Papernyi 2007). Given the predominantly European provenance of both the Bolshevik leaders and Marxist-Leninist ideology, it is unsurprising that "harmonious" aesthetic experience was also presumed to occur within the parameters of European cultural genres and forms (Habeck 2011b: 65–66).

The primacy of the Marxist-Leninist project meant that aesthetic value was also conditional on the importance of cultural production to a person's moral formation, mentioned earlier: an exposure to "good" art, music, theatre, architecture, film, and literature was regarded as essential to the process of developing an enlightened, *kul'turnoe* society and individual consciousness. Sensual experience therefore also gained its meaning in relation to the search for moral perfection understood to be central to the lives of those devoted to communism. Perceptions of the beautiful became bound up with an idealised, personal quest for moral value, in such a way that by the late Soviet period the notion of *kul'tura* "represented an elusive, ideal world outside the practical necessities of daily life: a dream of beauty, purity, and romance, of leisurely, endless conversations about the meaning of life, or of a happiness and wealth that would always remain out of reach, and whose very desirability perhaps depended on it remaining unattainable" (Nielsen 1994: paragraph 17).

This mingling of the beautiful with a personal quest for moral worth became a key paradigm within the process of Soviet cultural production, influencing both the nature of state-sponsored cultural institutions, and the ways individuals perceived and practiced art, music, literature, and theatre. For an activity to be regarded as aesthetically pleasing, it had to index in some way a yearning for pure, abstracted ideals; in itself, it had to model the victorious transmission of *kul'turnost'*. A particular philosophy of the aesthetic had become an integral part of the functioning of Soviet society, generating the paradigms through which sensory experience was to be integrated into the formation and signalling of appropriate patterns of sensibility and value.

A dedication to producing or appreciating a conventionalised quality of sensual experience — one that conformed to dominant notions of the beautiful, and hence could be categorised as "aesthetic", or as "culture" — came to be associated in authoritative discourse with a desirable spectrum of personal morals. It was possible to demonstrate one's commitment to *kul'tura*, and hence one's status as a *kul'turnyi chelovek*, through a myriad of different behaviours, or exhibitions of taste. In doing so, a person could signal their acceptance of the values associated with *kul'tura*, and hence their allegiance to the collectives expressing similar sensibilities. Mentioning one's love of Shakespeare, for example, would also demonstrate a deeper preoccupation with elevated values and ideals, such as a selfless commitment to the common good. The aesthetic practices that constituted and displayed *kul'tura* encompassed much more than visual experience, as the previous example illustrates. The practice and demonstration of *kul'tura* did, however, rely to a large extent on visual forms — whether these consisted of cultural genres that specifically address visual experience, such as art, film, or theatre, or the stylisation of one's personal appearance or living space. As Volkov notes, official discussions of *kul'tura* in the mid-1930s placed an especially heavy emphasis on the importance of a neat and tidy appearance, and carefully designed, "cosy" (*uiutnyi*) living arrangements (2000: 221); these ideals persisted throughout the Soviet period, albeit in attenuated and complex forms.

The plays and performances of *kul'tura* in Soviet community

Aleksei Yurchak (2006) describes in detail the shifts that occurred in authoritative discursive practice over the late Soviet period, and which caused authoritative discourse to lose its literal meaning, as it became incorporated into practices of community formation that the Soviet political elites had not envisaged. After Stalin's death, authoritative discourse — whether communicated directly as propaganda, or via state-sponsored cultural production — consisted increasingly of repeated poetic and aesthetic forms, rather than substantive messages (Yurchak 2006: 13–14, 44–47). The importance of reproducing the correct verbal or visual forms and sounds came to take precedence over transmitting arguments, ideas, or information. The production of authoritative discourse became the performance of a number of clear and well-understood formulae. As part of this, cultural production became so conventionalised that artists would produce portraits of Lenin according to a series of set poses, each with its own number; for example, a "sixer" (*shestërka*) showed Lenin in his office, while a "sevener" (*semërka*) was Lenin sitting on a tree stump (ibid: 55).

As the relevance of the substantive content of authoritative discourse decreased, the various performances and conventions its production entailed became assimilated into both signalling and establishing the communities and relationships that constituted Soviet society, and enabled its members to act within it. As Yurchak describes, when the members of a Komsomol organisation were asked to vote on a resolution they knew had to be passed,

> [...] they collectively responded not to the constative meaning of this question ("Do you support the resolution?") but to its performative meaning ("Are you the kind of people who understand that the norms and rules of the current ritual need to be performatively reproduced, that constative meanings do not necessarily have to be attended to, who act accordingly, and who, therefore, can be engaged in other meanings?") It is this latter address that the audience at the meeting recognized with an affirmative gesture and that therefore brought into existence the public of *svoi* [ours] [...] (2006: 117)

Authoritative discourse and its rituals thus became incorporated into a set of expressive practices that shaped communities of complicity: their members knew what the official agenda was in relation to their own, and how to balance a degree of conformity, mutually supportive cooperation, and the resources their own positions offered, in order to achieve their ends. These communities of "ours" (*svoi*) did not necessarily correspond to the working collectives that officially constituted Soviet institutions; rather, they formed the complementary networks that were integral to late Soviet social differentiation, agency, and morality. Individual Soviet citizens could formulate and express their personal values and ideals through these relationships, as well as using them for more strategic purposes, such as furthering their careers.

As Yurchak describes, the cohesiveness of *svoi* communities intensified in the larger population centres during the 1960s, 70s, and 80s, creating small networks of people who sought to emphasise their detachment from mainstream Soviet culture (2006: 126–57). These small groups were able to exploit the Soviet system in order to create the time and resources they needed to interact with each other, pursuing activities that could often be self-consciously idealistic, and external to everyday Soviet life — such as researching ancient history, foreign systems of writing, literature, or religions (ibid: 151). Yet the influence that mainstream Soviet culture — and, in particular, *kul'tura*, with its specific configuration of ethics and the aesthetic — could exert is evident from this choice of pursuit. The intention to seek knowledge, values, and ideals existing in separation from the Soviet world by studying unfamiliar histories and cultural traditions resonates with the motivation to attain *kul'turnost'* through moral and intellectual self-improvement. The configuration of the aesthetic and ethical that underpinned authoritative discursive practice is also in evidence in the implied assumption that positive sensual experience occurs in juxtaposition with a search for ideals.

The emergence of these small communities can be regarded as an instance of the way social differentiation could occur via the expression of a set of sensibilities — amounting in some cases to recognisable lifestyle choices — in the late Soviet context. Notably, the type of expression — and the sensibilities themselves — were conditioned by ideas, perceptions, and practices that were circulating within authoritative discourse regimes. Specifically, these were the sets of ideas associated with *kul'tura*, aesthetics and cultural difference, and the practices of community formation that both utilised and reacted against authoritative Soviet convention.

Yurchak's account describes the more extreme cases of this type of expression, contending that they were symptomatic of a broader shift occurring within Soviet society. For example, he presents the group of Leningrad artists known as the Mit'ki, who exaggerated their detachment from mainstream Soviet culture into the absurdly minimalist ways of life that in themselves constituted their art (Yurchak 2006: 238–43). The Mit'ki did the minimum amount of work, for the minimum amount of pay — one shift per week in a boiler room, for seventy roubles a month — and spent the bulk of their time telling stories about themselves and their lives, in a highly stylised form of social interaction (ibid: 239). The social trends Yurchak describes would have occurred in many different forms, in the Soviet Union's highly variable local contexts: the attempts to carve out a space for communal and individual self-expression within Soviet discursive systems would have occurred alongside other forms of expression, and their corresponding sensibilities, creating patterns of social differentiation within Soviet society. However, no matter how ingenious, witty, shocking, or absurd these demonstrative practices were, and no matter how limited the Soviet elite's capacity to influence citizens' actions had become, the display of personal sensibilities always had to take place with reference to the assertive presence of authoritative discourse and its aesthetic — even when denying them. Hence, the sensibilities that formed the backdrop to this social differentiation always implied an attitude towards authoritative discursive practice — whether detachment, conformity, resistance, or approval.

The influence Soviet state policy exerted over the expression of sensibilities also took the form of reducing the range of both consumer goods and cultural products, through the strictures exerted by the planned economy, and the state's attempts to limit the circulation of foreign goods. Therefore, to signal a love of western rock music and fashion was also to demonstrate that you were the kind of person, with the kind of values, who was willing to sidestep state restrictions and look for unofficial modes of consumption and self-expression (for example, by obtaining foreign goods on the black market). The restricted resources, in combination with the prevalence of authoritative discourse, would also have both reduced and homogenised the "insistent visual chatter" Chaney describes as an integral part of contemporary urban experience. This is perhaps why groups such as the Mit'ki made their comment on the Soviet Union's social reality primarily through caricaturing their way of life, integrating the aesthetic and the ideal within a grotesque parody of "the everyday". On the one hand, the centrality of a specific and prominent aesthetic, expression, and sensibility is likely to have reduced the everyday experience of the relativity and reflexivity of the aesthetic and ethical. On the other, it encouraged some members of the population to channel their desire for alternative forms of expression, value, and community into plays on the semantics of the available and well-known objects and visual forms, rather than the semantics of sensual experience.

Kul'tura and the emergence of ethnicity

As this section will show, the Soviet policy relating to cultural difference is a good example of how the ideals of Marxism-Leninism — unity, harmony, and peace — converged with the practical requirements of governing the Soviet territory, to generate a strand of official discourse that referred not only to Soviet institution-building and the values behind it, but also to the ways individuals were encouraged to perceive and express themselves, their identities, and their values. The huge cultural variation among the populations of the Tsarist Empire complicated the task of orientating these peoples towards the building of a communist society. The Soviet government believed the solution to this problem was to inculcate the values, practices, and institutions that would enable their transition to communism — or, as the Bolsheviks understood it, to modernise its undeveloped citizenry, removing the attitudes that hindered their progress. As part of this, the Soviet state aimed to re-form popular perceptions of cultural difference, and the social differentiation associated with it — which, as the following paragraphs will show, required the generation of new understandings of culture, community, and personal identification. *Kul'tura* and cultural production had an integral role in this initiative, and its consequences.

Soviet ideological discourse described its modernisation as the "liberation" of the non-Russian peoples from Tsarist colonisation, which had prevented them from reaching their full potential — thereby distinguishing the benevolent Soviet policy from exploitative capitalist colonisation, in an attempt to gain non-Russian support (Hirsch 2005: 14; Martin 2000: 353; Vihavainen 2000: 80). This "liberation" also entailed the public celebration of non-Russian cultures, despite its incongruity with the Soviet government's primary intention to disseminate a Marxist-Leninist worldview, and in doing so to eliminate cultural difference. The contradiction was resolved through the Soviet establishment's understanding of cultural production as consisting of European art forms, mentioned earlier. The Soviet state claimed to be guiding its non-Russian peoples into bringing out their own national cultural and academic achievements, as part of their modernisation (Slezkine 2000: 335). It would provide non-Russian peoples with the intellectual and material resources they needed to produce their own European-style operas, ballets, literature, art, and academic research, and to record their traditional dances, songs, and oral traditions for future generations. This process also involved adapting these traditional art forms to fit a Europeanised understanding of "folk" cultural production.

As the vital role cultural production played in the Soviet Nationalities Policy indicates, the effort to re-mould notions of cultural difference into the appropriate paradigms was one aspect of the wider reformation of social differentiation and sensibility, described in the previous section. The perception and practice of *kul'turnost'* occurred in a wide variety of different ways, reflecting the size and complexity of the Soviet Union, and its various communities. Nonetheless *kul'tura* became a central paradigm within both authoritative discussions of value and personal morality, and individual expressions of dominant sensibilities. As such, expressions related to *kul'tura* provided the means by which different patterns of community and social differentiation could emerge, as individuals and associations responded in different ways to the opportunities and restrictions the practice of *kul'tura* presented. And as part of this, the aspect of *kul'tura* that related to the "folk" cultural genres mentioned above provided a framework for expressions of cultural difference that served to anchor the peoples involved into the overarching Soviet community, despite the essentialised perceptions of ethnic identity that remained dominant throughout the Soviet period (Hirsch 2005; Shanin 1989; Slezkine 1994). Adaptations of the cultural forms deemed specific to the Soviet Union's different ethnic groups were integrated into the repertoire of *kul'turnoe* cultural production.

As might have been expected from the importance of systematised learning within *kul'turnoe* personal development, the practice of Soviet folk culture was closely connected to academic ethnography (Hirsch

2005; Slezkine 1994). The Soviet Union's corpus of ethnographic work identified each officially recognised ethnic group with a series of cultural forms, which fell into neat folkloric categories. The ethnographic literature re-framed non-Russian cultural practice using the Marxist-Leninist paradigms that underpinned Soviet academia as a whole, creating a "family" of Soviet peoples, each with their own set of dances, songs, folk stories, applied art, and national costumes. The more expedient cultural forms would be emphasised and adapted to suit the overall genre, while other practices were excised. For example, Soviet-era Sakha "folk dances" combined costumes and shapes inspired by the Sakha decorative tradition with Russian dance steps, melodies, and instruments such as the balalaika. Meanwhile, the circle dance that for centuries has formed a vital part of Sakha shamanic practice, the Ohuohai, was officially only permitted to take place within carefully controlled dance competitions, if it was allowed at all (Crate 2006; cf. Vitebsky 2005: 232).

As time went on, these sets of cultural forms became codified through the process of disseminating ethnographic work into popular knowledge. Informative books on non-Russian cultural practice could set out a given ethnic group's various "traditional" cultural forms, while explaining their relationship to the people's pre-Soviet way of life and religion. Non-Russian cultural practice was thus a priori either an anachronism or undergoing a process of transformation, since it referred to the historical period that had given way to the advance of a communist society. At the same time, the non-Russians who were producing European cultural forms were encouraged to incorporate their own "national" culture into their work, thus creating their ethnic group's first classical operas, for example, or ballets, or sculpture. The first Sakha opera, *N'urgun Bootur*, was staged in 1947, and is based on a story recorded from the Sakha epic tradition, the *Olongkho*.

In this way, non-Russian cultural practice was assimilated into cultural forms that coordinated with the prevailing and officially acceptable aesthetic, along with the pursuit of *kul'tura*. Positive official representations of specific ethnic cultural forms could afford them a similar abstracted moral dimension to the Soviet Union's classical European cultural production. This abstracted dimension was only enhanced by the apparently out-of-date pre-Soviet worldview that had generated this cultural production, and which prevented it from having a direct relevance within everyday life.

Thus, a television film about traditional Sakha culture made in 1970 could assert that Sakha folk cultural production inevitably reflects the talent and goodness of Sakha craftsmen.[3] The artistic achievements of Sakha artisans are inseparable from their personal moral worth. Meanwhile the film shows this generalised Sakha artisan along with their morals to exist in an ambiguous and abstracted temporal dimension: the action is apparently taking place in the present, as the film company records it, and yet it consists of the Sakha practices that were rapidly fading out of contemporary life, as the film's makers and viewers would have known perfectly well. The Sakha dancers, craftsmen, and housewives, resplendent in their national costumes, exist in an archaic present, infused with a timeless celebration of beauty and artistic endeavour. The point of the film is that the Sakha people have their "own" *kul'tura* that is beautiful not only in the harmonious shapes, colours, and sounds of Sakha art, music, and song, but also in its association with abstracted moral value.

Many contemporary Sakha citizens might well have been more excited by the prospect of obtaining a motorcycle or telephone line than a traditional wooden goblet — and yet the existence of their national cultural production endowed them with a repertoire of practice and value that enabled them both to express and to perceive an affiliation with dominant state aesthetics and patterns of sensibility. There was nothing to prevent a Sakha person — though fully conscious of the essential Sakha-ness that distinguished them from the European peoples — from signalling their own pretensions towards *kul'turnost'*.

The Soviet Union's different ethnic artistic traditions became increasingly codified into sets of dances, songs, folk stories, and crafts, as part of the increasing formalisation of authoritative discourse Yurchak describes. Likewise, the Soviet-era awareness of cultural difference played its role in some of the forms of expression and sensibility that took shape against the background of authoritative discourse, during the 1970s and 80s. Those who empathised with the mainstream practice of *kul'turnost'* could carry on attending and producing concerts of

---

3   I would like to thank Sakha (Yakutia)'s State Film Archive in Yakutsk for sharing this footage with me.

different folk dances and songs, or building up the new non-Russian canon of classical art, music, and literature. Those who were drawn to the values and ideas they imagined in realms beyond the Soviet everyday could research the different ethnic-specific cultural traditions — as did some Sakha intellectuals, who since have become shamanic spiritual specialists.

Shamanism became an especially prominent theme in Sakha theatre and art during the 1980s and 1990s, as a small coterie of enthusiasts emerged through the cultural and intellectual establishments. In fact, the constant depiction of non-Russian culture in authoritative discourse as existing in an idealised, ambiguous temporality, external to the flow of Soviet reality, could perhaps have made ethnic cultural tradition an especially attractive subject for those seeking to reach beyond everyday Soviet life, especially for non-Russian populations such as the Sakha.

Finally, those interested in political reform could articulate their democratic leanings through raising the banner of national autonomy, leading to the "national revivals" that paved the way for the transformation of the Soviet Union. The Sakha national revival, led by a small but determined group of Sakha intellectuals, cultural workers, and politicians, was the vanguard of a sudden mushrooming of interest in Sakha history and culture among the general population, as the contemporary *Yhyakh* testifies. The early Soviet intervention into identity and social differentiation had produced some very unexpected results: the expressions and sensibilities surrounding *kul'tura* had broken loose from their Bolshevik moorings into systems of value that identified a new social formation — the Sakha nationalists.

Conclusion: Soviet aesthetics and the *Yhyakh*

Returning to the Sakha communities one can identify at the *Yhyakh*, I can now suggest the connections between their characteristic sensibilities and expression, and the Soviet heritage. For example, traces of the *kul'tura* concept and its history are evident in the assumption that a commitment to reviving the Sakha people's shamanic heritage also manifests a praiseworthy attunement to higher values, morals, and ideals. Contemporary Sakha shamanism increasingly combines concepts of an abstracted realm of higher value, with experiences of the real presence and agency of area spirits and deities. An interest in engaging with spiritual forces is nonetheless often couched as a yearning for higher ideals, within a lexicon that also derives much from post-Soviet Russian mysticism, and new-age religion (Peers & Kolodeznikova 2015).

Most importantly, a look at Soviet policies, and the forms of expression, sensibility, and community they generated, can shed light on the distinctive repetition of visual forms, discussed earlier. The ways communities of *svoi* expressed and maintained their cohesion depended more on the presentation of fixed forms within precise configurations of community and context, than on reflection and variation within the forms themselves. This close attention to the community who witnesses the expression, and their probable response, rather than to the content of the expression itself, correlates with Yurchak's description of the highly conventionalised cultural production and public discourse of the Brezhnev era. It seems to be the reason why similar visual forms can be incorporated without comment into very different expressive acts, acquiring multiple meanings with reference to varying communities.

Aesthetic expressions of sensibility seem to be formulated with a greater awareness of the response of the sympathetic viewer, in the Sakha context, rather than alternative configurations of expression and sensibility. This suggests that the power of aesthetic expression to articulate and create social differentiation depends much more on the individual viewer's response, rather than the process of reflecting on the forms of everyday objects. Thus, the people who regard the shamanic temple's picture of Baiaanai as a sacred representation are the people who belong to the community of shamanic revivalists, since they share and support this community's sensibilities. Meanwhile, those who perceive ALROSA's tree of life as a beautiful manifestation of Sakha (Yakutia)'s cultural richness are the people who either belong, or aspire to belong, to the political and commercial establishment. As the lack of acknowledgement of contrasting sensibilities within these representations implies, the people who do not perceive these expressions in the way their creators intended are clearly not part of *svoi*, and are thus external to the communication — in the way that those who found the Mit'ki incomprehensible and ridiculous were simply alien to the movement. Alternative patterns of sensibility, and the communities who express them, are a relevant aspect of the context of these representations — however, their presence is less integrated into the process of the expression itself. Hence the artists at the shamanic temple do not consider a cubist evocation of Baiaanai, for instance, to contrast their appreciation of Baiaanai's real nature with the simple, realist representations produced for tourists and politicians.

The theoretical literature on lifestyle, and Chaney's work in particular, can certainly enhance the analysis of value, power and social differentiation in contemporary Russia. It can be applied to the case of the Sakha people's national revival, and this relevance could increase, as migration and information technology integrate Sakha communities further into the wider world. However, the characteristics of Sakha lifestyles, and their aesthetic expressions, show that the twentieth-century incorporation of cultural production and aesthetic response into sovietisation has had an effect on the interplay of community formation and expression in Sakha (Yakutia). Patterns of sensibility and expression do not correspond exactly to the cases Chaney describes. The differences, however, usefully indicate a certain exclusivity about social differentiation within the Russian Federation, both manifested and perpetuated by an exclusive orientation of expression towards fellow members of *svoi*.

References

Bourdieu, Pierre. 1984 [1979]. *Distinction: a social critique of the judgement of taste,* trans. Richard Nice. London: Routledge.

Boym, Svetlana. 1994. *Common Places: mythologies of everyday life in Russia.* Cambridge, MA: Harvard University Press.

Chaney,   David.   1996.   *Lifestyles.*   London: Routledge,   https://doi. org/10.4324/9780203137468

Chulos, Chris J. & Timo Piirainen (eds.). 2000. *The Fall of an Empire, the Birth of a Nation: national identities in Russia.* Aldershot: Ashgate, https://doi. org/10.4324/9781315200392

Crate, Susan. 2003. "Co-option in Siberia: the case of diamonds and the Vilyuy Sakha". *Polar Geography,* 26 (4): 289–307, https://doi.org/10.1080/789610151

—. 2006. "*Ohuohai*: Sakhas' unique integration of social meaning and movement". *Journal of American Folklore,* 119 (472): 161–83, https://doi. org/10.1353/jaf.2006.0019

—. 2009. "Viliui Sakha of subarctic Russia and their struggle for environmental justice". In: *Environmental Justice in the Former Soviet Union*, ed. Julian Agyeman & Yelena Ogneva-Himmelberger, pp. 189–214. Boston, MA: MIT Press, https://doi.org/10.7551/mitpress/9780262012669.003.0009

Donahoe, Brian & Joachim Otto Habeck (eds.). 2011. *Reconstructing the House of Culture: community, self, and the makings of culture in Russia and beyond*. New York: Berghahn.

Dunham, Vera. 1990. *In Stalin's Time: middleclass values in Soviet fiction*. Cambridge: Cambridge University Press.

Fitzpatrick, Sheila. 1970. *The Commissariat of Enlightenment: Soviet organization of education and the arts under Lunacharsky, October 1917–1921*. Cambridge: Cambridge University Press, https://doi.org/10.4324/9780203130018

—. 1992. *The Cultural Front: power and culture in revolutionary Russia*. Ithaca, NY: Cornell University Press.

— (ed.). 2000. *Stalinism: new directions*. London: Routledge.

Giddens, Anthony. 1990. *The Consequences of Modernity*. Cambridge: Polity Press.

Grant, Bruce. 1995. *In the Soviet House of Culture: a century of perestroikas*. Princeton, NJ: Princeton University Press.

—. 2011. "Recognizing Soviet culture". In: *Reconstructing the House of Culture: community, self and the makings of culture in Russia and beyond*, ed. Brian Donahoe & Joachim Otto Habeck, pp. 263–76. New York: Berghahn.

Gupta, Akhil. 1995. "Blurred boundaries: The discourse of corruption, the culture of politics, and the imagined state". *American Ethnologist*, 22 (2): 375–402, https://doi.org/10.1525/ae.1995.22.2.02a00090

Habeck, Joachim Otto. 2011a. "Introduction: cultivation, collective, and the self". In: *Reconstructing the House of Culture: community, self and the makings of culture in Russia and beyond*, ed. Brian Donahoe & Joachim Otto Habeck, pp. 1–28. New York: Berghahn.

—. 2011b. "'Thank You for Being': neighborhood, ethno-culture, and social recognition in the House of Culture". In: *Reconstructing the House of Culture: community, self and the makings of culture in Russia and beyond*, ed. Brian Donahoe & Joachim Otto Habeck, pp. 55–73. New York: Berghahn.

Hirsch, Francine. 2005. *Empire of Nations: ethnographic knowledge and the making of the Soviet Union*. Ithaca, NY: Cornell University Press.

İğmen, Ali. 2011. "The Emergence of Soviet Houses of Culture in Kyrgyzstan". In: *Reconstructing the House of Culture: community, self and the makings of culture in Russia and beyond*, ed. Brian Donahoe & Joachim Otto Habeck, pp. 163–87. New York: Berghahn.

Ingold, Tim (ed.). 1996. *Key Debates in Anthropology*. London: Routledge, https://doi.org/10.4324/9780203450956

Kotyleva, Irina. 2004. "The role of Soviet ideology in the transformation of the Komi traditional holiday culture in the 1920s". *Pro Ethnologia*, 17: 128–48.

Lane, Christel. 1981. *The Rites of Rulers: ritual in an industrial Society — the Soviet case*. Cambridge: Cambridge University Press.

Mally, Lynn. 2000. *Revolutionary Acts: amateur theater and the Soviet state, 1917–1938*. Ithaca, NY: Cornell University Press.

Martin, Terry. 2000. "Modernization or neo-traditionalism? Ascribed nationality and Soviet primordialism". In: *Stalinism: new directions*, ed. Sheila Fitzpatrick, pp. 348–67. London: Routledge.

Mitchell, Timothy. 1999. "Society, economy, and the state effect". In: *State/Culture: state formation after the cultural turn*, ed. George Steinmetz, pp. 76–97. Ithaca, NY: Cornell University Press.

Morphy, Howard. 1996. "Presentation for the motion, 'Aesthetics is a cross-cultural category'". In: *Key Debates in Anthropology*, ed. Tim Ingold, pp. 255–60. London: Routledge, https://doi.org/10.4324/9780203450956

Nielsen, Finn Sivert. 1994. "Soviet Culture — Russian *kul'tura*: culture, ideology and globalization in the Soviet Union and thereafter, as compared to similar Western phenomena …". Paper presented at the Research Seminar "Continuity and Change in Post-Soviet Societies", Skibotn (Norway), October 1994, http://www.anthrobase.com/Txt/N/Nielsen_F_S_02.htm

Papernyi, Vladimir. 2007. *Kul'tura Dva* [Culture Two]. Moscow: Novoe literaturnoe obozrenie.

Peers, Eleanor & Liubov Kolodeznikova. 2015. "The post-colonial ecology of Siberian shamanic revivalism: How do area spirits influence identity politics?'" *Worldviews*, 19: 245–64, https://doi.org/10.1163/15685357-01903003

Pesmen, Dale. 2000. *Russia and Soul: an exploration*. Ithaca, NY: Cornell University Press.

Rolf, Malte [Mal'te Rol'f]. 2009. *Sovetskie Massovye Prazdniki* [Soviet mass festivities]. Moscow: Rossiiskaia politicheskaia entsiklopediia.

Shanin, Teodor. 1989. "Ethnicity in the Soviet Union: analytical perceptions and political strategies". *Comparative Studies in Society and History*, 31 (3): 409–24, https://doi.org/10.1017/s0010417500015978

Slezkine, Yuri. 1994. *Arctic Mirrors: Russia and the small peoples of the North*. Ithaca, NY: Cornell University Press.

—. 2000. "The USSR as a communal apartment, or how a socialist state promoted ethnic particularism". In: *Stalinism: new directions*, ed. Sheila Fitzpatrick, pp. 313–47. London: Routledge.

Sobel, Michael E. 1981. *Lifestyle and Social Structure: concepts, definitions, analyses*. New York: Academic Press, https://doi.org/10.1016/C2013-0-11518-8

Stites, Richard. 1989. *Revolutionary Dreams: utopian vision and experimental life in the Russian Revolution*. New York: Oxford University Press.

Ssorin-Chaikov, Nikolai. 2003. *The Social Life of the State in Subarctic Siberia*. Stanford, CA: Stanford University Press.

Ventsel, Aimar. 2004a. "Sakha pop music and ethnicity". In: *Properties of Culture — Culture as Property: pathways to reform in post-Soviet Siberia*, ed. Erich Kasten, pp. 67–86. Berlin: Dietrich Reimer Verlag.

—. 2004b. "Stars without the money: Sakha ethnic music business, upward mobility and friendship". *Sibirica*, 4 (1): 88–103, https://doi.org/10.1080/13617360500070897

—. 2009. "Sakha music business: mission, contracts and social relations in the developing post-socialist market economy". *Sibirica*, 8 (1): 1–23, https://doi.org/10.3167/sib.2009.080102

— & Eleanor Peers. 2017. "Rapping the changes in northeast Siberia: Hip Hop, urbanization and Sakha ethnicity". In: *Hip Hop at Europe's Edge: music, agency, and social change*, ed. Milosz Miszczynski & Adriana Helbig, pp. 228–48. Bloomington, IN: Indiana University Press.

Vihavainen, Timo. 2000. "Nationalism and internationalism: how did the Bolsheviks cope with national sentiments". In: *The Fall of an Empire, the Birth of a Nation: national identities in Russia*, ed. Chris J. Chulos & Timo Piirainen, pp. 75–97. Aldershot: Ashgate, https://doi.org/10.4324/9781315200392

Volkov, Vadim. 2000. "The concept of *kul'turnost'*: notes on the Stalinist civilizing process". In: *Stalinism: new directions*, ed. Sheila Fitzpatrick, pp. 210–30. London: Routledge.

Vserossiiskaia perepis' naseleniia 2010 [All-Russian Census of Population 2010], http://www.gks.ru/free_doc/new_site/perepis2010/croc/perepis_itogi1612.htm

Yurchak, Aleksei. 2006. *Everything Was Forever, Until it Was No More: the last Soviet generation*. Princeton, NJ: Princeton University Press, https://doi.org/10.1515/9781400849109

8. Ethnicity on the Move

National-Cultural Organisations in Siberia

Artem Rabogoshvili

As in the previous chapter, devoted to the development of ethnic cultural production in the period from the Soviet era to post-Soviet Russia, the subject of the discussion here will be the relationship between ethnicity and lifestyle of the diverse peoples in Siberia. However, apart from changing the geographic setting from the Sakha Republic (Yakutia) to the more southernly located Irkutsk Oblast and the Republic of Buryatia, I will shift the research focus away from describing the more general aspects of cultural production in the former Soviet Union to analysing specific forms of human behaviour, arising from the regular involvement of people in the activities of ethnicity-based organisations ("national-cultural organisations").

Drawing from the results of my fieldwork in the administrative centres of the two regions — the city of Irkutsk and Ulan-Ude respectively — throughout the year 2011, I attempt to provide a brief introduction to the history of ethnic diversity in the Baikal region and the interconnection of the concept of lifestyle and ethnic activism. Further, I seek to demonstrate how the complex changes in post-Soviet Russia have affected the members of such organisations, broadening or reducing the existing disparities between them, setting certain boundaries for their activism in purely geographic terms as well as making symbolic self-presentation an integral part of their lifestyle.

 https://doi.org/10.11647/OBP.0171.08

Ethnic diversity in the Baikal region

Located in the southern section of East Siberia, Irkutsk and Ulan-Ude are the political and economic centres of two separate, but neighbouring administrative units: Irkutsk Oblast and the Republic of Buryatia, lying on the two opposite shores of Lake Baikal (henceforth both units are referred to as "Baikal region"). As it manifests itself through the names of the regions, the Republic of Buryatia is a nationality republic with a population of 970,000 people, in which its titular nationality, the Buryats, constitutes roughly one third of the republic population, and equals to about half of the Russian population of Buryatia (Census of 14 October 2010). As a result of the Bolshevik nationalities policy, the Buryats were granted a territorially bounded autonomy of their own, which initially covered much of the region around Lake Baikal, but in the 1930s was divided into what is today the Republic of Buryatia on the eastern side of Lake Baikal and Ust'-Orda Buryat Okrug in Irkutsk Oblast on the opposite side (see Chapter 5 in this volume). Today in Irkutsk Oblast, with its almost 2.5 million inhabitants (2010), the Buryats constitute an even smaller fraction of the population, numerically dominated by ethnic Russians, who started to settle in the region from the seventeenth century onwards. In the subsequent centuries of the Tsarist era, the local ethnic diversity was considerably enhanced through both voluntary migration and state-directed relocations of ethnic minorities from the central and westernmost parts of the Russian Empire to Siberia. As a result of the Tsarist relocation policies, the region saw a gradual arrival of the Tatar, Belarusian, Ukrainian, and Chuvash people from the more poverty- and famine-stricken parts of the country and the foundation of their settlements across Siberia, especially in proximity to the then built Trans-Siberian Railway.

In the later periods (notably, from the 1930s to the 1980s), the number of ethnic communities inhabiting the region tended to rise even more as the territory was to become a destination for the deported Lithuanian and Polish people as well as for voluntary workers and Komsomol youth from the Soviet Union's nationality republics who were willing to take part in the construction of large-scale industrial projects in Siberia. Particularly noteworthy here is the building of Baikal-Amur Railway, north of lake Baikal in East Siberia, which came to mobilise ethnically diverse peoples from different Soviet republics who were made responsible for the construction and maintenance of particular railway stations or settlements. Last but not least, ethnic diversification in the Soviet era was considerably facilitated through educational and professional mobility of the population as well as military rotations throughout the Soviet Union. In this chapter, I will use the term "old-time residents" when speaking about these ethnic groups who arrived in the region in Tsarist times, and also to those who came during the Soviet period. Following the democratisation reforms (*perestroika*) in the Soviet Union in the 1980s, and especially with the formation of the Russian Federation in 1991, ethnic minorities of the country were allowed by the new legislation to establish their cultural organisations, designed to promote their national culture and language. Under these circumstances, "national-cultural organisations" (henceforth — NCOs) came to be set up by ethnic minority activists throughout the country. As Siberia was no exception in this process, its old-time residents began to perceive the establishment of NCOs as an important leverage for articulating their relationship with their original homeland both through symbolic means and physical movement.

Starting from the 1990s and even more so in the 2000s, the ethnic makeup of Siberia got even more complex, as the region became a destination for migrant workers and their households both from the independent states of the former Soviet Union (in particular, economic migrants from Uzbekistan, Kyrgyzstan, and Tajikistan) and some other labour-sending countries outside the post-Soviet space (such as China and Vietnam). For example, by the end of the 2000s, the cities of Irkutsk and Ulan-Ude had an increasing community of residents originating from Kyrgyzstan. As most of them — predominantly, male persons — have been involved in retail trade on the city markets, working seasonally for a number of years, it has been not uncommon for the members of their households (including wives and children) to move to the same locations in Siberia and settle there as permanent dwellers. As a result of household migration to Russia, a considerable number of these people would find themselves nostalgic of their ethnic home, while the younger generation had to be socialised at Russian schools and universities. This in turn has been an important factor that motivated migrants' families during their sojourn in

Siberia to attend seriously to the issues of establishing their national-cultural organisations. In contrast to the "old-time residents", I will conventionally refer to this group of population as "newcomers" in the chapter.

Ethnic activism and lifestyle: paradigms of research

In my view, the case of ethnic activism is valuable for the analysis of lifestyles in present-day Russia for a number of reasons: first, activism as a social phenomenon has been uniting a considerable number of ethnically diverse people, who by virtue of their commitment to the collective cause, have pursued common practices and engaged in similar interactions. Considering the formally voluntary and non-commercial character of NCOs, most of their members have not been rewarded financially for their contribution from any external sources. Rather, members have had to resort to investing their own resources to keep their organisations functioning. Indeed, while the involvement in the activities of ethnic organisations in Russia has been underpinned by certain patterns of spending and consumption (such as buying material accoutrement for staging an ethnic performance), a great number of NCO members still agreed to the expenditures, considering them as either justified or inevitable.

Second, the problem of choice as "a fundamental component of day-to-day activity" (Giddens 1999: 80) has been underlying most of the routine activities of ethnic activists in Russia. The necessity to make practical decisions, choosing the most efficient way of securing the required resources, has been underpinned from a broader perspective by the personal choice to join the organisation and sign up to its cause. The particular strategies employed by the activists in the process of making important or consequential decisions have been commonly based on the narratives of self-identity, turning the process of decision-making into an individually meaningful enterprise. I would point here to the importance for ethnic activists of "sensibilities", defined by David Chaney as "a perceived affiliation for an identifiable group with certain ideas or values or tastes in music, food or dress" and presumably governing their major decisions (Chaney 1996: 126; see also Chapters 1 and 7 in this volume).

In what follows, I am going to focus on the ethnic sensibilities of individuals — those centring on their original homeland or by contrast those relating to their current stay in Siberia. The former relationship has most clearly manifested itself through the mobility of NCO members, whose sense of nostalgia and attachment to a particular ancestral location have not only motivated them to visit the places associated with their origin (further referred to as their "original" or "ethnic home"), but have also presented them with certain dilemmas as to whether to return or stay in the current place of residence (referred to as their "new home"). The latter relationship in turn could find expression through multiple social engagements and events which have enabled ethnic activists to display and emphasise their ethnicity during their stay in Siberia. In this sense, the reproduction and stylisation of ethnicity by NCO members during public festivals in urban areas have been likewise based on certain choice-making, involving the narratives of one's "self". As my data suggest, both traveling and visual self-presentation practices have been equally important to the ethnic activists in Siberia, presumably, constituting the core of a specific lifestyle.

Moreover, the involvement of NCO members has been underpinned by certain disparities and divides among different groups of activists — conditioned *inter alia* by their social status, gender, and the centrality/peripherality of their location — which in turn have provided them with an agenda for collective mobilisation. Using the assumption that the complex infrastructural changes that took place in Siberia — and more broadly in Russia — over the last years (see Chapter 2) had unequal circumstances for different cohorts of arrivals and therefore accentuated the existing disparities among them, I am going to address the issue of ethnic activism in Russia as an institutionalised phenomenon. I emphasise the centrality of NCO members' attempts to diminish such disparities and to equalise their social status.

In this respect, some further elaboration of the difference between "old-time residents" and "newcomers" is required here. Indeed, in the context of Russia, the boundary between the two groups has been particularly fluid, given the complex history of population mobility on its territory over different periods. More precisely, just as the influx of newcomers to Siberia has led to the crystallisation of "new" ethnic communities, so too most of its "old-time residents" today represent either the first generation of socially integrated and locally settled migrant people or their descendants, trying to re-establish lost ties with their ethnic homeland. From this perspective, my research has been about the consecutive stages of a typical migration process with its logics and constraints on different generations of people.

Based on the migration paradigm, the comparison of the two groups might not only lie in the diachronic aspects of their relative arrival in Siberia, but also in the synchronic analysis of how the past and current changes — both infrastructural and technological — have affected the opportunities of people for maintaining contacts with their original homeland and consequently limited or facilitated their lifestyle choices in a particular period. Contrary to what might be expected, the breakup of the Soviet Union did not solely mean economic turmoil and closure of transportation routes; rather, the new circumstances made possible diverse forms of relating with home and living between two regions or countries. Transnationalism as a form of migration, by which individuals retain strong connections with the place of exodus, has recast the character of ethnic activism in Siberia, making the issue of reaching out to one's ethnic homeland less of a problem (Glick Schiller, Basch & Blanc-Szanton 1992; Appadurai 1996; Ong 1999; Vertovec 2009). The role of NCOs in this process has been to respond to the needs and aspirations of its members by serving either as a facility to reach out to the country of origin or conversely as a condition of staying away from "home".

At the same time, both "old-time residents" and "newcomers" can be juxtaposed in the light of the ethnic minority paradigm as members of their respective ethnic communities in their "new home". Indeed, a particular lifestyle of ethnic activists has also found expression through their willingness to maintain certain material manifestations of their ethnicity (dress, craft, cuisine, etc.) and to display some of them during public events or festivals. NCOs have in turn provided an institutional platform to those residents of the region who have made a choice to uphold their "sense of difference" and assert it in public. The arrival of newcomers to Siberia has made it possible for the latter to resort to the same symbolic resources as the old-time residents, notably through the public display of ethnicity on special occasions. In the context of Russia, however, the need to respond to the challenges associated with ethnic-minority status, such as xenophobia and mistreatment in public spaces, has evidently been a factor discouraging potential activists from more active modes of engagement. For this reason, to many activists, public displays of ethnicity presumably evolve into acts of asserting their sense of "equality" rather than of "difference". NCOs could be used by their members as a facility for this task.

Divides and disparities among ethnic activists in Siberia

In this section, my aim is to show how the peculiar lifestyle of ethnic activists in Siberia has been conditioned *inter alia* by certain divides and disparities among them. To this end, I will first dwell upon the intensity and degree of people's involvement in the activities of NCOs, outlining the existing modes of their engagement. Further, I will also elaborate on the issues of gender and rural-urban divides between ethnic activists and show their unequal significance for the long-term residents and newcomers to the region.

Intensity and degree of engagement

For the sake of analysis, I refer to the following categories of participants, as enumerated by political scientists Passy & Giugni (2001) and including: "subscribers" (those staying formally outside the organisation, but contributing to its activities financially), "adherents" (members who are active on an irregular basis), and "activists" (members who are regularly active in the organisation) (Passy & Giugni 2001: 132). Schematic as the division between the three categories might be, it nonetheless provides us with an opportunity to define more precisely the role played by different stakeholders engaged in the organisation's activities.

"Subscribers" have been defined by me as non-members who are sympathetic with the cause of the organisation and tend to provide support to its members. Indeed, most of the collective efforts of a relatively small number of ethnic activists in both regions have relied on and appealed to the sense of ethnic solidarity that unites people sharing a particular ethnic identity. Establishing ties and connections with the ethnic fellows, standing high on the social ladder or having some economic leverages, has been key to the success of their most important ventures, while the presence of individuals (notably, ethnic entrepreneurs) who feel called upon to provide help or assist in getting things done has constituted an important form of social capital for the activists of NCOs. Of course, the clusters of relationships, based on ethnic solidarity, extend far beyond the formal membership in ethnic organisations and, as such, have been characteristic not only of ethnic activists in Siberia. Rather, ethnic identity — overlapping in some cases with religious identity — has been an important form of social capital, which could be well converted into certain material benefits by the leaders of the organisations, acting to motivate other members and secure some external funding at the same time.

"Adherents", or those affiliates of NCOs active only on an irregular basis, have probably constituted the most numerous and heterogenous group of members. To some, their membership came as an initially unintended event as they were invited by someone else to attend the organisation's meetings. But even having become a member, most of them, confronted with certain time and money constraints, would tend to stay outside active modes of engagement with the organisations' matters and pursue some other economically more rewarding activities. Partly for this reason, the younger generation, represented mainly by students of local universities, figure prominently as adherents of NCOs.

"Activists", those performing daily chores and taking up responsibility on a regular basis, have constituted the backbone of NCOs. Indeed, the voluntary and non-paid character of work pursued by these people, has required them both certain emotional commitment and material contribution, translating into a specific lifestyle. The chapter is therefore primarily about NCO "activists", while the stories that follow are provided to illustrate their lifestyle. It seems natural that NCOs should be run by "activists" (rather than "adherents" or "subscribers"), yet as my data suggest, leadership positions have not always been claimed by the more "active" personnel, as these positions are in some cases a merely formal or honorary duty. Drawing on my own fieldwork data, I would provide the following schematic classification of NCO "leaders". First, I would refer here to "figureheads" as those formal leaders vested with high symbolic status, but whose everyday input into the organisation's matters remains limited. Second, I would point to a special category of "cultural brokers" as individuals actively engaged in the process of interpreting or renegotiating the ideas of a group's ethnic identity. Normally, these individuals come from educated backgrounds and are often employed as academic researchers, teachers, librarians, or art workers. As members of ethnic minority organisations and, notably, their formal leaders, these people commonly aim to ensure "ethnic revival" among their peers or act as formulators of the organisation's intellectual agenda. Third, I would also mention "managers", i.e. ethnic activists mostly engaged in the resolution of practical questions or addressing the immediate issues of the respective community. Indeed, as my observation suggests, most of the organisations of newcomers have been led by individuals with a background in law or of running their own businesses in the region — those who can either afford to rent an office in the urban area or provide their own premises as a possible meeting place.

Gender divide between activists

Gender status is one of the basic parameters determining the mode and intensity of people's engagement in the activities of NCOs. The issue of gender inequality and, in particular, the persisting domination of men over women in many settings of the public sphere in Russia has been addressed in previous research, but the reverse situation in which women dominate men as formal or non-formal leaders of public organisations or any other collectivities has been rarely dealt with by scholars (Kay 2007; Kulmala 2010; Vladimirova & Habeck 2018). Indeed, the available ethnographic material from Siberia not only provides us with ample evidence of women's regular involvement in the functioning of ethnicity-based organisations, but also reveals the specifically gendered distribution of roles inside them. Thus, in many cases men numerically prevail as the leaders or "subscribers" of organisations in Russia, while women are obviously predominant as rank-and-file activists and adherents, responsible for the bulk of the work, which in turn might reflect a more general social trend characterising the functioning of other "cultural leisure" institutions in Russia (cf. Habeck, Donahoe & Gruber 2011).

Considering the gender divide among the NCO members, my assumption is that those ethnic communities whose cultural imperatives of patriarchal society have generally discouraged public participation of women in the political sphere, could have a similar bias against their formal leadership as part of ethnic organisations abroad. The recent trend for the feminisation of economic migration, which has affected Russia among other countries, not only brought about a rising number of women moving to Siberia from such countries as Uzbekistan, Kyrgyzstan, or Tajikistan as part of their households, but also led some of them to join cultural organisations in Siberian cities. Having established themselves as members of the organisation (frequently as relatives of the male activists), women have mostly engaged themselves in the activities of these organisations as rank-and-file cultural performers or backstage assistants, excluded from the actual decision-making process. At the same time, for many women, leadership positions came to be accessible following the elevation of their status from "newcomer" to the "old-time resident". Indeed, my observation is that those women who run NCOs, catering to the newcomers, have the advantage of being either a long-term resident, sometimes more advanced in age (such as *apa*, or senior lady, among Turkic peoples), or enjoying higher educational qualifications than the rest of the members. Despite that, the possible pressures on the female leaders could be still high enough, also given that the incessant influx of their ethnic fellows to the region has constantly intensified competition between the old-timers and newcomers. As one of the female leaders of a Kyrgyz organisation in Siberia once privately remarked to the author, her leadership position in the organisation had been occasionally contested by some of her country-fellows on the grounds of her being a woman. The result was the formation of a second Kyrgyz organisation, set up by newly arrived people. Despite that, she has retained her post as a well-educated lawyer and a person who has stayed in a Siberian city for a long period.

Rural-urban divide between activists

The ability of people to pursue different activities as NCO members has been also dependent on the centrality/peripherality of a particular location and the availability of roads and transportation connecting remote locations with the administrative centre. In practice, we can, probably, distinguish between two distinct types of organisations: one corresponding to urban areas (*gorodskaia organizatsiia*) and the other corresponding to rural districts (*sel'skaia organizatsiia*). As I will show further below, the two distinct types of locations presuppose strikingly different capacities in terms of ethnic activists' access to material and social resources, which in part explains different scopes of the organisations' activities. Living thousands of miles away from their original home, many of the ethnic activists in Siberia have never been outside their current region of residence, but still maintain family histories and try to transmit their ethnic culture to the younger generation. To some extent, activism of people in rural areas has also been kindled by the presence of historical sites or institutions, including museums and temples, which require collective efforts to be maintained or repaired. This task in turn has been possible in many cases through the support of city-based organisations, which have commonly been able to use the centrality of their location to secure material assistance and information. Of particular importance in this process are the attempts of urban activists to cross the space between the diverse geographically remote locations across Siberia and thus to reach out to the rural communities. Given the vast territorial dimensions of the region and the dramatic difficulties in transportation services in past years, this task has been rather costly and time-consuming; it depended not only on the availability of vehicles, but also on the strong commitment of people.

While for the long-term residents of Siberia, travelling across the region has been part and parcel of their lifestyle within NCOs, the issue of mobility has had quite a different twist for the newcomers. Attracted by the economic opportunities of the city, a bulk of them has been engaged in diverse activities in the urban (rather than the rural) area, working on trade markets or in the service industry. The lack of incentive for visiting the countryside has been countered, however, by the relative importance of other mobility patterns.

Original home and mobility

In this section, I intend to show how the physical mobility of ethnic activists has presented itself as a ground for making lifestyle choices, and how NCOs are seen by their members either as a facility to reach out to the place of origin or conversely as a condition of staying away from the ethnic home. Previously, I have pointed to the importance for those people who wish to emphasise their ethnicity to make the decision to engage in certain patterns of consumption and participate in the activities of ethnic organisations. Covering large geographic distances as part of their activities in NCOs, a great number of people have been ready to invest considerable material resources (such as, for example, their own savings) into their leisure activities, which are viewed by Chaney as being "increasingly experienced by individuals as the basis of their social identity" (Chaney 1996: 112).

Based on a comparison between the destination country (Russia) and the place of current residency (e.g. Central Asia), spatial imaginaries (cf. Chapter 5 in this volume) have played a crucial role in shaping people's decisions to move. In this respect, rational choice theory that explains human decisions exclusively by pragmatic or economic motivations, cannot fully account for the choice of those ethnic activists who may decide to stay in economically less favourable locations or spend personal means on collectively significant trips. The state of in-between, which arises from the double allegiance of many migrants and the perception of home as something malleable, depends considerably on their emotional attachments and moral obligations, in which both representations of Siberia and that of their original homeland figure prominently. The life stories that follow in this section belong to the "old-time residents", since the issue of mobility seems to be of greater concern for this group. Despite that, I am aware of the outlined dichotomy and try to refer to "newcomers" whenever possible.

Repatriation

All in all, those non-native inhabitants of Siberia, to whom maintaining a continual relationship with their original homeland remains a matter of particular concern, have been left with a number of options, or models. The most straightforward and in a sense "radical" option for them would be to leave the place of current residence and return for good to their homeland. In this sense, repatriation has a considerable overlap with other forms of mobility both in terms of the crucial role of social imaginary for the potential travellers as well as the impact of individual economic circumstances on one's personal decision to return — yet at the same time repatriation has its own distinctive character. First of all, much more than with other forms of mobility, return to the historical homeland is in many cases "justified" by the narratives of ethnic identity, emphasising emotional affiliation of the person to their ancestral land. This is, of course, not to say that a person's ethnic identity is the prime criterion for making such a choice: rather, it is frequently contested by other concerns. Thus, for many long-term residents, making such a move would be quite a risk, and would require considerable personal commitment. It may seem easier to stay put due to a lack of accurate information about the original homeland or simply because of their personal inertia. Among the old-timers, repatriation as an option has been therefore more suitable for the relatively mobile younger generation of people while their membership in NCOs in some cases ha facilitated their choice to leave.

The mobility patterns associated with the repatriation of non-native ethnic minorities of Siberia (such as the Russian Jews, Germans, or Ukrainians) to their ethnic homeland were generated with the opening of the Soviet/Russian border at the beginning of the 1990s and since that time have tended to ebb and flow. Even though NCOs have not always been directly involved in the administration of repatriation programmes, they have been in many ways instrumental in this process, working closely with their managers (for example, Jewish cultural organisations and the Jewish "Sokhnut" repatriation agency) and providing those eager to leave with the necessary credentials of one's ethnic background, the required information about the destination country, and a better command of its language.

In this respect, the story of Andrei, a young activist of the Ukrainian cultural centre in Irkutsk, is rather representative. At the time of field research, Andrei (aged 20) was one of the youngest and most active members of the Ukrainian cultural centre of Irkutsk. He joined the centre in 2008 after having been invited to one of its public events and since then has been investing his time learning and teaching the Ukrainian language as well as participating in most of the ethnic festivals organised by the centre. Possessing some Ukrainian background and having been to the Ukraine only as a small child, Andrei became gradually interested in that country and his membership in the local Ukrainian cultural organisation catered to his ability to travel there once again. As a university student, Andrei tried to seize every opportunity to discover new places, despite his time and money constraints. Moreover, although he likes Irkutsk, he was determined to leave the city after the completion of his studies and ultimately to emigrate from Russia. Andrei's decision to emigrate seems to have been shaped by different facts of his professional career. After joining the Ukrainian cultural centre, he got to know about the repatriation programmes for ethnic Ukrainians in Russia and then assisted with their implementation in the region. His knowledge about emigration opportunities continually grew as he was communicating regularly with his peers on social networking websites and regular travels as part of the organisation. My interview with Andrei touched upon his plans for the future and let him voice his attitude towards the issue of emigration:

> Artem Rabogoshvili: Would you like to leave for Ukraine?
>
> Andrei: This is one of my plans for the future.
>
> AR: For permanent residency?
>
> A: For permanent residency.
>
> AR: Why? Because life is more convenient there or because your roots are there?
>
> A: Because I don't like this country…
>
> AR: What about Ukraine?
>
> A: In Ukraine it is much easier. People have a more easy-going mindset there. They are kinder and there is no trouble-making on every occasion there. I appreciate that
>
> AR: Do you have many friends willing to go abroad for permanent residency?
>
> A: Quite a lot. And many of them are taking some concrete steps in this direction.

AR: Where do people want to go?

A: Mainly, Eastern Europe — Lithuania, Ukraine, Serbia, Poland.

AR: Why do they choose [the countries of Central] Eastern Europe?

A: Well, difficult to say. [Central] Eastern Europe is developing rapidly now and many see its prospects. Or maybe it is easier for them to learn a Slavic language. Some of my friends have emigrated to Poland or Czech Republic. They have found Czech or Polish men or women and are doing well there.

Making occasional trips to the original home

More often than not, however, occasional travels outside the region have been to a greater or lesser degree possible for the majority of activists, which I mark here as the second possible option. Like in the case of the first option (permanent relocation), this model has been in many ways associated with crossing national or regional borders, while the ability of people to make such trips has varied considerably depending on the individual circumstances of activists. Trip-making to destinations outside Siberia among ethnic activists is based on quite a number of combined reasons and motivations, including a feeling of nostalgia or homesickness, a desire to visit relatives or friends, and the need to maintain business contacts or attend conferences or workshops. Diverse motivations of NCO members, based on their unequal social and citizenship status, have been conducive to the rise of different strategies and plans concerning their relationship with their country of origin or ancestry. We can distinguish here between two types of outbound travels: those within the Russian Federation and those outside its borders (depending on where the person's historical homeland is), which in turn partly overlaps with the division between "long-time residents" and "newcomers" to the region.

Even though trip-making within the state's borders can be seen as easier and less expensive in contrast to international mobility, the frequency of such travels for the members of NCOs depends heavily on the social background, economic circumstances, and the actual degree of their motivations and commitments, all of which are subject to change with people's age and life experience. In general, the involvement of the old-time inhabitants of Siberia in the work of NCOs has facilitated their mobility across the country through the allocation of funding for their trip or through information about travel opportunities.

To illustrate this situation, I would like to provide below the story of Gulnur, who is one of the oldest and most enthusiastic members of the Tatar-Bashkir cultural centre of Irkutsk. Although in her sixties now, she is not only actively contributing to the activities of the organisation today, but also regularly travels across Irkutsk Oblast for different cultural events and occasionally to Tatarstan — her native region. Gulnur's travels started at the end of the 1950s, when her parents from Tatarstan were allocated housing in the Siberian city of Kemerovo, from where she later moved to Irkutsk to continue her studies. From that time on, she travelled quite extensively throughout different parts of the then Soviet Union, both alone and together with members of her family, either as part of well-organised tours or as an independent traveller. With the start of *perestroika*, and following the breakup of the Soviet state, her family found itself constrained financially. As a result, as an acting scholar and university professor, she had to cease attending academic conferences outside the region at that time. It was in this period at the beginning of the 1990s that Gulnur joined the recently established Tatar centre in Irkutsk. In her words, membership of the Tatar organisation has enabled her to share life experience and knowledge of Tatar culture with other Tatar people born outside Tatarstan but feeling interested in their family background.

By the 2000s, the economic conditions improved for Gulnur, affording her more opportunities to travel. The most memorable trips that she made in the past few years were those to Tatarstan and in both cases she was travelling as a member of the delegation of the Tatar-Bashkir cultural centre of Irkutsk. She recounts:

> In the year 2005, I went to the 1000th anniversary of Kazan'. The travel expenses for us, members of the Tatar ensemble, were assumed by the Tatar centre as a kind of reward for our active involvement. So, we bought a travel voucher at our own expense and the travel costs were borne by the centre. It was my first trip, really a big trip, which was paid for by the centre. But when in Tatarstan, we were somewhat frustrated that we couldn't stop at all these familiar places due to the time constraints, so that my sisters and I swore that we would come here the following year. So

we did. Also, [in] 2010, Mintimer Shaimiev, President of Tatarstan, made up his mind to convene all the women who have made an important contribution to the development of Tatar culture in the country. Out of the total number of participants, 85 persons came from the former Soviet republics and 22 persons from the regions of Russia. There were two of us from Irkutsk Oblast. And this year, I was granted another reward trip, this time to Yekaterinburg for attending the federal Sabantui [see below] festival.

International mobility of ethnic activists has been to a great extent underpinned by the permeability of national borders and the existence of specific mechanisms enabling border-crossings. Visa-free travelling to most of the post-Soviet states (including Belarus, Ukraine, Kazakhstan, Kyrgyzstan, and Tajikistan) and the emergence of new transportation routes has made it possible for some of them to cross the border with just their internal passport, while complicating matters for those originating from countries requiring a visa for entry (such as the Baltic states, Georgia, or Turkmenistan).

At the same time, the issue of making occasional trips home appears in an entirely different light for the newcomers. Indeed, the economic practices in which many of the recent arrivers have been engaged require a regular movement between countries (the practice of transnationalism), which has been an important factor of change in the region itself. Based on economic stimuli, the Baikal region came to be well-connected (both through air flights and bus lines) to the major destinations from which most economic migrants originate. Following the establishment of regular transport connections, most of the newcomers have found themselves in a comparatively favourable position, sometimes having better chances than the long-term residents of Siberia for maintaining physical ties with their ethnic homeland. Under these circumstances, NCOs would rather come up as institutions facilitating people's temporary stay by renegotiating the concept of home, rather than as a facility enabling physical movement.

Renegotiating home locally

The third possible option for those feeling nostalgic, but yet not ready or unable to change their place of residence is to stay in touch with "home" through purely symbolic means, reproducing the familiar cultural surroundings and seeking a sense of togetherness with fellow members of their ethnic group locally. Contrary to what might be expected, this model of relating with the place of origin has not been solely a hallmark of those already more enrooted in the region or less mobile individuals — rather it has been universally shared by most ethnic activists, including newcomers. However, the significance of this model has not been equal for all; given that for most of the newly arrived individuals, being outside their ethnic home often meant just a short interval before returning, while for those who were born in Siberia it frequently entails a once-in-a-lifetime trip. In both cases, membership of an NCO has offered people a chance to obtain support and carve out an existence away from their place of origin.

The story of Oleg, the leader of the Belarusian national-cultural organisation (*Tovarishchestvo Belorusskoi Kul'tury*), demonstrates how travelling within the region (in contrast to repatriation) has evolved into a marker of the specific lifestyle of ethnic activists in Siberia. I have known Oleg from the very beginning of my fieldwork in Irkutsk. Even before I came to the city, he had invited me to visit some of the cultural events organised by his centre. Born in Belarus in 1969, Oleg graduated from a military school in Tiumen' and was subsequently commissioned as a military officer to Irkutsk. Having retired from military service, he stayed on in this Siberian city, where in 1996 he founded the Belarusian organisation and then started to make regular ethnographic trips to the Belarusian villages throughout Irkutsk Oblast. One of the reasons why I decided to interview Oleg was his rich experience of traveling across the Oblast and his ample knowledge of the region. Today, his organisation incorporates twelve local branches of the regional Belarusian cultural organisation across Irkutsk Oblast which have been functioning as a unified whole largely thanks to Oleg's extensive travels even to the most remote places and villages, populated by Belarusian settlers or their descendants.

However, his commitment to the cause of his organisations has been frequently at variance with his actual ability to reach those locations, given the vast territory of the oblast and Oleg's dependence on the public transport. With the collapse of the Soviet-time transportation system at the beginning of the 1990s and the establishment of his organisation he found it particularly challenging to get to some places, lying away from the railroad and major bus lines. In the passage below, he described the situation with infrastructure in Irkutsk Oblast at the beginning of the 1990s:

> My first trip to Tarnopol' village in Balaganskii District was just after our association had been established in 1996. I remember my travelling there at my own expense after I had learned that there is a Belarusian village in that district. It was at that time the first Belarusian village that I happened to visit in Irkutsk Oblast. To get there, first I reached Zalari village by train, and then went to search for the bus station there and to ask the locals how to get to Tarnopol'. Those folks told me: "oh... you need to go to Balagansk first..." I asked them how to get to Balagansk, but they said: "oh... there won't be any bus today... the next bus will be on Monday" [once per week]. [...] So, I had to cover about 130 kilometres, [hitchhiking and] changing transportation. For the first thirty kilometres I rode a motorcycle, sitting in its back seat, but I finished the journey sitting in the back of a lorry together with some local fishermen. Those guys asked me: "Where are you going?" saying *kudi* instead of *kuda* [where?]. At that moment, I realised at once they were from Tarnopol', as they spoke with a Belarusian accent. I was happy to follow them and finally got to the village.

As the transportation infrastructure of Irkutsk Oblast started to change with the rise of mini-buses (*marshrutki*) at the beginning of the 2000s, Tarnopol', like many other small and remote villages, became better connected with Irkutsk. To some extent, possessing a car would be a solution for many of those ethnic activists frequently traveling across the region and aiming to reach out to the small communities of their ethnic fellows in the rural area. In Oleg's words, today he always has to arrange his trips with others, or to buy tickets in advance, but he has been reluctant to buy a vehicle, concerned with the possible expenses and preferring to spend money on his organisation instead. In any event, travelling across the region has evolved into a part of Oleg's routine; while visiting localities associated with Belarusians, has to some extent offered him an alternative to returning to his original home for the permanent residence.

As we can see, the issue of maintaining relations with one's historical home figures prominently in the lives of ethnic activists in Siberia. This relationship can be maintained in different ways: by travelling locally to the places associated with one's ethnicity (as in Oleg's case), by making regular long-distance trips to the original place of birth (as in Gulnur's case) or by changing one's place of residence (as intended by Andrei). The three possible strategies, provided by the above-mentioned biographies, often intermingle (especially when it comes to occasional visits "home" and travelling locally), and are well-suited to demonstrate how the change of transportation infrastructure in Siberia in the post-Soviet period has affected ethnic communities in manifold ways.

New home and visual self-presentation

In this section, I seek to demonstrate how the involvement of ethnic activists in the public acts of displaying ethnicity reveals a certain lifestyle dimension. I also show how NCOs allow their members not only to claim cultural distinctiveness from the rest of the population, but also to foster ethnic equality and social inclusion in the new surroundings. As I stated above, non-native ethnic activists in Siberia — the protagonists of this chapter — can be optionally referred to as migrant people (with the *proviso* that there are those who have just arrived and those settled for years) or as the country's ethnic minorities, united by their membership in NCOs. The latter perspective shifts our concern from the issues of relating with the original homeland and physical movement back to the subject of ethnic diversity of East Siberia and the problem of maintaining a specific cultural identity there.

Ethno-cultural festivals, held in most Russian cities to demonstrate "unity in diversity" — discussed by Eleanor Peers in the example of Sakha Republic (Yakutia) (Chapter 7 in this volume) — have been seen by many ethnic activists in the Baikal region as a means of reinvigorating and asserting their people's cultural identity in contrast to other ethnic groups. Geared either towards members of their own ethnic group or towards the by-standing audience of diverse ethnic backgrounds, such festivals have commonly relied on the practices of visual self-presentation, as their participants have used "traditional" ethnic clothes, singing, dancing, or cuisine for the show. While the preparation for the public appearance has been more often than not underpinned by certain patterns of spending and consumption (such as buying the material accoutrements for staging an ethnic performance), a great number of NCO members still agreed to the expenditures, considering them as either justified or inevitable. Indeed, the investment of time and money on the part of NCO members has been countered by their sense of contribution to the process of ethnic revival and the importance thereof to their own self. By the same token, a great number of ethnic activists are likely to view public occasions as an opportunity to claim their own equality symbolically and derive personal meaning from this process. In this sense, there has always been a certain interplay between people's aspiration to express their distinctive cultural identity ("sense of difference") and their attempts to maintain unity and the sense of community with other people ("sense of equality"). Both orientations can be found among the ethnic minority activists in Siberia, underpinning their specific lifestyle as active members of NCOs. At the same time, the relative importance of these two orientations have arguably been not identical for the one who has just arrived and the one who can already be counted as a long-term resident.

Sense of difference: comparing two ethnic festivals

Further, I am going to focus on two festivals — Sabantui and Nooruz (the first being associated by me with long-time residents, and the latter with newcomers) and trace how since the rise of NCOs in Siberia the pursuit of difference through symbolic means has been a part of ethnic activists' lifestyle. In many ways the Soviet period saw the formation of a specific culture of celebrations, in which ethnicity was to be framed in terms of Soviet nationality politics and as such utilised for the purposes of the state (Rolf 2006). Echoing Don Handelman's metaphor of "mirrors", held up by the state to its citizens through the modern spectacle and designed to provide "an incisive vision of themselves as they should be" (1997: 396), I would point here to the typically taxonomic organisation of Soviet festivals, celebrating the communal Soviet identity of ethnically heterogeneous people and frequently referring to the trope of the "friendship of peoples". Indeed, as described by Peers in Chapter 7, the very logics of the trope made it necessary for the state authorities to foster the spread of such visually expressive genres as national dances, songs, folklore, poetry and many others — familiar to those attending the festival events in the Soviet cities — and by corollary expect their participants to demonstrate something on the stage that would stand for his or her nationality. As the post-Soviet Russian state inherited much of the Soviet-era experience of dealing with nationality issues, participation in public festivals has become central to the activities of NCOs, while the reproduction of ethnicity for public display has evolved into an important mechanism through which local authorities have provided recognition to cultural organisations in their respective regions.

The establishing of ethnic organisations in Russia at the turn of the 1980s and 1990s was accompanied by a resurgence of interest in "folk tradition" among ethnic activists, who attempted to secure "ethnic revival" in their regions through the reinvention of holidays, seen as moribund in the Soviet era. For example, Sabantui, held annually by the Turkic-speaking population of the Volga region to celebrate the end of the ploughing season, had been particularly associated with Tatar people's culture in the rest of the country, and as such was seen as almost entirely abandoned by the Tatars in the Soviet era. The rediscovery of the festival and its come-back to the public sphere at the end of the 1980s was seen by local officials and the Tatar activists of the region as the beginning of a Tatar cultural revival. Since a considerable number of Tatars inhabited the rural areas of Ust'-Orda Okrug and, apart from the Russians and Buryats, had their villages scattered across the territory, the first Sabantui celebrations were staged in Ust'-Orda in 1987, attracting an audience from the neighbouring city of Irkutsk and other urban centres. Moreover, this event facilitated the consolidation of the urban Tatar intelligentsia and gave impetus to the establishment of the first Tatar organisation in the city of Irkutsk.

While the return of Sabantui to the public sphere dates back to the end of the 1980s, the staging of Nooruz, yet another festival of the non-native ethnic minorities in Siberia, has had quite a different trajectory, receiving an impulse for development with the influx of economic migrants from the states of Central Asia towards the end of the 1990s. Even though celebrated by a wide range of Iranian and Turkic peoples, my focus here is on the Kyrgyz case (hence its spelling reflects the Kyrgyz word), considering a rising number of Kyrgyz people coming to the region. As with Sabantui, NCOs have served as a facility for those Kyrgyz activists in Siberia who have cared for the cultural distinctiveness of their people.

Bearing a somewhat Soviet-style name, "Druzhba" ("Friendship") is a Kyrgyz cultural organisation located in Irkutsk. At the time of writing

Fig. 8.1. Sabantui Festival held by the Tatar national-cultural organisation of Ulan-Ude. Photograph by Artem Rabogoshvili, 2011, CC-BY.

it normally relied on the help of non-professional staff, combining their cultural and educational initiatives with other more economically rewarding activities on the market. Beishen, in his forties, is one of the organisation's leaders. He always emphasised to me the importance of Kyrgyz culture in Siberia. From the very start, he saw Druzhba as essentially a cultural organisation. Indeed, Beishen had lived in Irkutsk for more than twenty years after he left Kyrgyzstan at the beginning of the 1980s and made his way to Khabarovsk to study at a police school. After school, he moved to Irkutsk to work as a police officer, and soon grew into a person of authority among his country fellows in the city. Beishen was one of the founders of Druzhba and a regular organiser of Nooruz festival for the Kyrgyz community of Irkutsk.

By the standards of Kyrgyz migrants, Beishen is now a long-time resident, but most of his activities are centred around and for the newcomers. Importantly, while the staging of Sabantui in Irkutsk has relied on the well-established community of Tatar intelligentsia, local entrepreneurs, and state authorities (as well as external support from Tatarstan), the organisation of Nooruz has been dependent on the joint efforts of fewer individuals, including Beishen. Now twenty years after the first public Sabantui was held by the members of the Tatar NCO in Irkutsk Oblast, the festival grew into a highly institutionalised event, supported by both the local authorities and those of the Republic of Tatarstan and celebrated by the activists from urban and rural locations. This has hardly been the case of Nooruz, as organised by Kyrgyz activists in Irkutsk, who lacked the external support (in contrast to Tatar activists) and who lived mainly within the urban boundaries. I still remember asking Beishen why he was so concerned with staging the festival, on which he had to spend such considerable efforts. The reply was: "I feel responsible for my people, as they come here and start to forget who they are. Somebody has to do it, so this is my choice".

The sense of difference, encapsulated by Beishen's words, has been shared by many ethnic minority people, whose own residing away from their ethnic home has led them to join an NCO. To others it has been as important to extend their sensibilities about cultural distinctiveness to the whole ethnic community. It is no surprise, then, that those activists who represent the communities of newcomers also try to reach out to their ethnic fellows arriving in the region. Beishen seems to be that type, as he has claimed responsibility for maintaining Kyrgyz culture under the new circumstances and used Nooruz as an opportunity to reproduce the familiar ethnic surroundings for Kyrgyz people abroad.

The key point here is to what extent and why ethnic activists would rely on expressing their sense of difference in public before the wider audience, rather than organise the celebration in private. The interesting thing about Sabantui is how the social imaginary, associated with this festival in Siberia, impelled local Tatar activists to put considerable efforts into its reconstruction and popularisation among their ethnic fellows as well as the general public. In his book on the "festive state", David Guss examines the changing meaning and organisation of cultural performance as it is interpreted and claimed by individuals in the service of local, national, and even global interests. He argued that cultural performances can be recognised as sites of social action where identities and relations are being continually reconfigured, new social imaginaries are being produced, which can be in that capacity appropriated by the state (Guss 2000: 12). The organisation of ethnic festivals in Siberia has been closely linked with the discourse of modernisation and development of the region. Reflecting the social imaginary of the region as provincial and economically backward, yet promising in terms of its strategic location and cultural attractiveness, the public discourse in Buryatia and Irkutsk Oblast aimed at legitimising festival activities, turning them into an important driver of development both through the "active" promotion of tourism, foreign investment, and the "passive" soliciting of funding from the federal budget from Moscow for the organisation of such celebrations.

Still more important, however, is the way in which the festive forms have been used and manipulated to mobilise the local community for collective action. In this sense, aspirations have been prominent among ethnic activists to be "modern" and "global", but at the same time to refashion their traditions as compatible with "local" conditions. This in turn has motivated ethnic activists — members of NCOs — to adapt their festivals to the gaze of the external audience, including tourists, placing a high priority on the visuality during the expression of ethnic identity through clothing and other accoutrements. While reproduction and stylisation of ethnicity during public festivals — through dress, consumption of ethnic cuisine, and artistic performances — have constituted a part of the lifestyle for many rank-and-file members, their efforts have been underpinned by the cultural brokerage of their leaders attempting to secure public recognition of the festival and its wider proliferation. In a sense, the tendency for the public demonstration of one's ethnic culture reached its apex through the use of modern technological innovations, including the internet. Thus, due to the efforts of the local Tatar activists, the interested audience could also enjoy watching Sabantui online as it was being held in the suburbs of Ulan-Ude.

In many ways, the workings of this globalising tendency are reminiscent of Aleksandr Pika's concept of "neotraditionalism", which in his opinion can well be applied as an alternative to the opposition between the concepts of "ethnic" and "modern" (Pika 1999). As Pika's research on indigenous small-numbered peoples of Siberia revealed, "the new 'traditionalism' does not mean a return to the past. It is a forward-looking development, though one which attends to the specific nature of northern regions and peoples" (1999: 23). Like small-numbered indigenous peoples of the north, activists of the non-indigenous cultural organisations of Siberia do not just gravitate towards a revival of the past, but see their ethnicity as an integral part of the present-day world.

As my evidence suggests, Nooruz, as an ethnic festival organised by the activists of NCOs, has largely remained an event for the

Fig. 8.2. Nooruz Festival organized by the Kyrgyz national-cultural organization
of Irkutsk. Photograph by Artem Rabogoshvili, 2011, CC-BY.

insiders — individuals originating from the Muslim states of Central
Asia and Transcaucasia. The relative closedness in holding Nooruz
can be explained by its "international" character (no particular ethnic
community could claim possession of the festival), but also by the
character of the respective communities. First, as most of the newcomers
are busy settling in the new place or preparing to leave for their place of
origin, most of the festival organisers had to act primarily as "managers"
(rather than "cultural brokers"), renegotiating individual roles and
duties. Second, even though Nooruz has been well established and
widely popular in places inhabited by Muslim groups (including other
parts of Russia), its proliferation in the Baikal region has been largely
associated with newcomers and as such lacked the required popular
support or attention. Despite that, in the light of the same tendency that
has propelled the openness of Sabantui, Nooruz is still likely to become
a more public and tourist-oriented event in the future.

Sense of equality: recognition in a transnational setting

The staging of public celebrations in the city landscape has been usually
underpinned by the rhetoric of interethnic peace and tolerance. Indeed,
NCOs have commonly been seen by local authorities as contributing

to the prevention of possible interethnic conflicts, while their leaders have been recognised by the state authorities as contact persons in charge of representing the respective ethnic communities. Importantly, the authorities tried not only to localise the activities of ethnic activists in time and space (the House of People's Friendship in Ulan-Ude as a network hub and the place where the NCO activists are based is the best example here), but also to impose certain standards as to the outward appearance of the people during festivals. At the same time, as my data suggest, visiting some urban areas, including those assigned for public festivals, is often associated by members of ethnic minorities with a certain danger and the risk of being exposed to mockery or even physical assaults on the part of xenophobic groups. Such anxieties are associated not obligatorily with peripheral and poor neighbourhoods (where xenophobic sentiments among the locals are supposedly stronger), but in some cases, not unreasonably, with central areas; hence why some members of ethnic minorities are wary of visiting such places, let alone demonstrating their ethnicity in a deliberate manner. For this reason, a great number of ethnic festivals (such as Nooruz) are held within a smaller community of insiders, rather than displayed to the wider audience.

Apart from staging a performance before the public, onerous by itself, the involvement in a festival also requires its participants to attend to a number of details, including the securing of the necessary paraphernalia. Indeed, the capacity of ethnic activists to get involved or to organise public festivals has rested on their ability to resolve certain routine difficulties and to tap human and material resources. Thus, the planning of Sabantui or Nooruz, like any other ethnic festival organised by ethnic-minority activists in Siberia, has been not only about getting hold of ethnic paraphernalia, but has also involved a plethora of other pragmatic questions as to who is responsible for what.

My position is that even though those newcomers who are active as members of NCOs could find themselves more vulnerable as possible presenters on the stage, their decision to get involved in the public activities seems to reflect a certain lifestyle dimension, provided they are fully aware of the existing risks and predicaments. The vulnerability of newcomers in turn seems to arise out of their current *liminal* status, as not yet fully settled in the new region. The liminal position, as Victor

Turner suggests, is often associated with "the members of despised and outlawed ethnic and cultural groups" who "play major roles in myths and popular tales as representatives or expressions of universal-human values" (Turner 1969: 369) such as equal treatment of people regardless of their background. Indeed, the Turnerian reference to "small nations" as upholders of religious and moral values is in good agreement with the state policies in Russia, recruiting members of NCOs for the display of ethnic diversity. At the same time, the imperative of seeing no status difference between ethnic groups or declaring equal opportunities for all the nationalities has imparted such festivals with the spirit of *communitas*. According to Turner, *communitas* as a special "modality of social relationship" is distinct from the "area of common living" as a relatively unstructured formation (Turner 1969: 360). The spirit of *communitas*, as reinforced through the surrounding anonymity and joyful atmosphere, has been shared by both old-time residents and newcomers attending the festival. At the same time, I argue, it is the newcomers who potentially benefit more from this spirit, as it might provide them with a sense of equality and consolidation, of which they usually are in greater need than the permanent inhabitants of the region.

Acquiring a particular lifestyle as ethnic activists, the newly arrived individuals will not only benefit from the interaction with their peers, but will also contribute to the success of the collective enterprise. As my own data demonstrate, activists of ethnic organisations have been largely non-professionals when it comes to the reproducing of "their nationality's" culture (understood here in the Soviet fashion as a constellation of visually expressive genres). Yet, while the organisations, representing mainly old-time inhabitants, have been in a comparatively advantageous position drawing human resources from the local intelligentsia and highly educated urbanites, most of the newcomers' organisations (even though commonly having "managers" at their core) have to rely on people from rural areas, who are often manual workers. The lack of personnel qualified in the sphere of cultural production has been to some extent an important mobilising factor, making the organisations' activists use their social networks to find adequate ethnic fellows who are, speaking literally, able to sing and dance on stage.

At the same time, it would probably not be totally justified to contrast "old-time residents" and "newcomers" in terms of their educational background and cultural level, since these parameters have considerably varied among individuals. As an example, I sketch out the story of Mirlan, a Kyrgyz man who works as a salesperson on one of the trade markets in Ulan-Ude and became involved in the activities of the local Kyrgyz cultural organisation. Mirlan, 34 years old at the time of writing, was born in a small town near Batken in southern Kyrgyzstan. As a student of the arts college in Batken he was taught music and choreography as well as the Russian language. Mirlan's career progressed steadily as he was employed at the local university and then promoted to the position of vice principle, responsible for the cultural work of students. Despite his success, he wanted to further improve the material well-being of his family; so when his elder brother, working in Ulan-Ude, offered him a job at the local trade market, he agreed to move to Russia for some period.

Mirlan's daily routine in Russia came to be focused on his job in the market, where he spent up to six days a week. In addition, his professional qualification as a musician and a performer of the Kyrgyz epic *Manas* proved an important asset for him, as he was regularly invited to demonstrate his skills on the stage and before the camera. In this way, he not only publicly represented the Kyrgyz nation in Siberia, but also evoked the feeling of respect from his peers in the market. Mirlan was proud to be part of the team of the local Kyrgyz activists and happy to attend the cultural events, yet due to family commitments he had to return to Kyrgyztan one year after his arrival and give up his cultural activities in Russia.

Mirlan's case is both unique and typical in a number of ways. It is unique because it was by some serendipity that — as a professional cultural worker moving outside his country for manual work — he found his cultural expertise in demand in his new home, unwittingly validating the understanding of culture as a kind of "toolkit" that migrants take on their journeys (Vertovec 2009). But his case is also rather typical in that his decision to return to his place of origin was determined by the economic strategy of his whole household — a fact that unites him with many other seasonal migrants and temporary residents. In any event, representing the local Kyrgyz community was an important motivation for Mirlan to spare some free time and attend the public festivals in the city, even though he was not permanently settling in Siberia. The sense of equality and pride, underpinned by a certain elevation of one's social status, has been an important incentive for those newcomers who would make a choice to go public. True, there have never been too many ethnic activists among newcomers, and Mirlan's case seems to be one of the few. Yet, even though a great many newcomers are busy with menial jobs, their membership in an NCO — temporary as it might be — would enable them to do what they think their life "should" involve (rather what they actually do), carving out a particular lifestyle during their stay.

Before his departure, Mirlan featured as a character in a movie about the Kyrgyz community in Siberia, shot by the local television station, and performed *Manas* before the camera. As he was unable to watch the movie on television, he asked me to secure a DVD copy for him that he could bring home as a memory. In this respect, the case of Mirlan is also indicative of the specific role of visual self-presentation for the lifestyle of ethnic activists and the particular emphasis on "surfaces" — to use the term by Chaney — in their activities (Chaney 1996: 99; cf. Chapter 1 in this volume).

The practice of collecting photos and videos of one's performances during the festivals has been common both among the long-timers and newcomers. The collected audio and video material may be used as evidence of one's personal involvement or as part of the organisation's official portfolio. In the latter case, most of the information has been either stored on data storage devices to be presented on special occasions or uploaded online for public display. In recent years, with the spread of the internet in Siberia an increasing number of NCOs came to set up their accounts on social networking sites (such as the Russian VKontakte) or their own websites, not only serving as a profile of the organisation, but also containing abundant visual information on the past activities of its members. Needless to say, the presented materials have not only been meant for internal consumption, but also to produce a positive image of the organisation for the general public.

Most ethnic activists have largely perceived visual self-presentation as part of their mission to sell "their" cultural heritage to outsiders. Thus, the regular involvement of ethnic activists in the festivals has not only presented them with an opportunity to recruit new members among their ethnic fellows, but also to claim a "superior" position among their peers, especially when it came to the public contest for the "best" NCO.

While the spirit of *communitas* during the festival has in general made possible informal contacts among the performers and the audience, a good self-presentation may secure ethnic activists the required patronage among local decision-makers or enable them to produce some income out of small-scale commercial activities and trading with some of their hand-made goods, such as food or craft items. In summary, all these formal and informal activities during the public events serve as a means not only of claiming cultural distinctiveness, but also of accentuating the sense of equality and reinforcing self-consolidation among the members of the group.

Conclusion

In this chapter, I have endeavoured to demonstrate how the complex changes in post-Soviet Russia have affected the inhabitants of East Siberia, facilitating or reversely limiting their opportunities for maintaining and expressing their ethnic affiliations. Focusing particularly on the activists of ethnicity-based organisations ("national-cultural organisations"), my overall contention has been that membership in NCOs constitutes a specific lifestyle in its own right. But then what can the particular case of ethnic activists in Siberia tell us about the character of lifestyle as a concept?

First and foremost, as the available material suggests, most of the members of NCOs desire to express their ethnic belonging, even though it involves considerable effort, time, and expense on their part. In this sense, the degree of people's involvement and their commitment to the cause of the organisation can be considered as a certain marker of "lifestyle". It is not my intention to downplay the importance of "subscribers" and "adherents", yet their input to the functioning of NCOs seems to be less significant as compared to those of "activists". Indeed, in most of cases, it is NCO "activists" who not only take on the overall responsibility, but also derive personal meaning from their contribution and connect the progress of their mission with their own self. The theme of coming to terms with certain difficulties or overcoming the existing disparities has been dominant among the members of NCOs and as such has been common to both "long-term residents" and "newcomers", sharing common ethnic sensibilities. At the same time, I have shown that the capacity of different individuals to pursue a specific lifestyle as an NCO activist is conditional upon a great number of factors, including their economic circumstances, gender status, and geographic location. "Lifestyle" is viewed here as a specific phenomenon that cross-cuts social classes, rather than being confined to the more prosperous middle class (Bourdieu 1984).

The second conclusion of this chapter has to do with the role of choice in maintaining a particular lifestyle. Depending on our perspective, we might define "lifestyle" either as a flexible phenomenon, providing individuals with a certain leeway, or as a rigid formation, with little or no variation in terms of practice. Drawing from my research on NCOs, I would adhere to the former view, as the issue of relating with the original home, integral to the lifestyle of ethnic activists in Siberia, has been based on a number of options among which they could choose. As I pointed out earlier, the range of possible options for those individuals staying away from home and feeling nostalgic has varied from physical contacts with one's place of origin (through occasional visits home or repatriation) to the symbolic renegotiation of home (in some cases including local travel). In this sense, NCOs have served as a facility to reach out to the country of origin or conversely as a condition of staying away from home. The relative importance of these options, or models, is different for those non-native activists whom I have designated as "long-term residents" versus "newcomers".

Clearly enough, repatriation as a distinct model of relating with the original home has been an option for those inhabitants of Siberia who were born or spent most of their lives there. However, even though NCOs have in general assisted their members in reuniting with their ethnic home, repatriation has been quite a radical option and as such been mainly suitable to the younger generation of activists. The more moderate option — occasional trips home — has mostly been chosen by the middle-aged generation of locally settled activists, with their NCOs funding such trips. Finally, the third model of relating with home is based on symbolic (rather than physical) movement as the activists could renegotiate "home" locally by visiting certain localities associated with their ethnic community, or by emphasising their cultural distinctiveness. Even though this model has been universally shared by both the long-term residents and newcomers, for the former it often meant being settled unilocally in Siberia while for the latter it implied leading a translocal life between the country of origin and country of current stay.

Recapitulating the workings of social imaginary on different groups of the population, I would contrast old-timers and newcomers, as the former could presumably imagine their original home in a more idealised vein (looking to the past for positive memories), while the latter's experience of it might conversely be more matter-of-fact and even dramatic (hence their decision to leave their country of origin).

The third conclusion about the nature of lifestyles as presented in this chapter, is concerned with the degree and importance of their outer expression, or what Chaney referred to as "surfaces" (Chaney 1996: 99). Several theoretical questions are raised here: how many individuals at minimum should be around to constitute a distinct "lifestyle"?; do these individuals tend to form close-knit communities or rather loose collectivities?; and what is the role of the external audience and its potential feedback towards the observed practices? The data from across the volume show that the size of the collective can vary from a number of disparate individuals with their own peculiar ways (see Chapter 3 in this volume) to a virtually countless number of people in proportion to the whole population (see Chapter 7). Perhaps, my own research case represents a middle ground, as activists of NCOs have never been too many among the inhabitants of Siberia. Rather, activists' affiliation with particular organisations and by virtue of this with particular ethnic communities has made their lifestyle mediated by their belonging to a finite number of "groups" within the urban area. This in turn has necessitated a greater emphasis for their part on "surfaces" as a way to distinguish one group from another, thereby intensifying a sense of difference which culminates during ethnic festivals (e.g. it would almost surely be an offence to confuse a person's ethnicity, as he or she is wearing ethnic dress during the festival). As I pointed out, the pursuit of difference has been more characteristic of long-term residents, concerned with their cultural distinctiveness and less of an issue for the newcomers.

Concerning another theoretical issue — the interrelation of a lifestyle group and the outsiders — the available material attests to the existence of relatively self-reliant and semi-closed groups (see Chapters 9 and

10). These groups also emphasise the visual aspects of their practices, but with less focus on the external audience. By contrast, members of NCOs are not only commonly expected to demonstrate their cultural specificity during public events, but mostly perceive it as part of their mission to "sell" it to outsiders. The ethnic activists' emphasis on "surfaces" serves to consolidate the members of the group while also accentuating their sense of equality with other ethnic groups. In this respect, it is the newcomers (rather than long-term residents) who usually seek to establish themselves as equals at their new place of residence or use NCOs as a facility to foster their social inclusion in the new surroundings.

References

Appadurai, Arjun. 1996. *Modernity at Large: cultural dimensions of globalization.* Minneapolis, MN: University of Minnesota Press

Bourdieu, Pierre. 1984 [1979]. *Distinction: a social critique of the judgement of taste,* trans. Richard Nice. London: Routledge & Kegan Paul

Chaney, David. 1996. *Lifestyles.* London: Routledge, https://doi.org/10.4324/9780203137468

Giddens, Anthony. 1991. *Modernity and Self-Identity: self and society in the late modern age.* Stanford, CA: Stanford University Press.

Glick Schiller, Nina, Linda Basch & Cristina Blanc-Szanton. 1992. "Transnationalism: a new analytic framework for understanding migration". *Annals of the New York Academy of Sciences,* 645 (1): 1–24, https://doi.org/10.1111/j.1749-6632.1992.tb33484.x

Guss, David M. 2000. *The Festive State: race, ethnicity, and nationalism as cultural performance.* Berkeley, CA: University of California Press.

Habeck, Joachim Otto, Brian Donahoe & Siegfried Gruber. 2011. "Constellations of culture work in present-day Siberia". In: *Reconstructing the House of Culture: community, self and the makings of culture in Russia and beyond,* ed. Brian Donahoe & Joachim Otto Habeck. New York: Berghahn, pp. 138–60.

Handelman, Don. 1997. "Rituals/Spectacles". *International Social Science Journal,* 49 (153): 387–99, https://doi.org/10.1111/j.1468-2451.1997.tb00031.x

Kay, Rebecca (ed.). 2007. *Equal or Different? Gender, equality and ideology under state socialism and after,* Basingstoke: Palgrave, https://doi.org/10.1057/9780230590762

Kulmala, Meri. 2010. "'Women rule this country': women's community organizing and care in rural Karelia". *Anthropology of East Europe Review*, 28 (2): 164–85, http://scholarworks.iu.edu/journals/index.php/aeer/issue/view/79

Ong, Aihwa. 1999. *Flexible Citizenship: the cultural logic of transnationality.* Durham, NC: Duke University Press.

Passy Florence & Marco Giugni. 2001. "Social networks and individual perceptions: explaining differential participation in social movements". *Sociological Forum*, 16, (1): 123–53, https://doi.org/10.1023/A:1007613403970

Pika, Aleksandr (ed.). 1999. *Neotraditionalism in the Russian North: indigenous peoples and the legacy of Perestroika,* ed. in English by Bruce Grant, with a new afterword by Boris Prokhorov. Edmonton: Canadian Circumpolar Institute; Seattle: University of Washington Press.

Rolf, Malte. 2006. *Das sowjetische Massenfest* [Soviet mass celebrations]. Hamburg: Hamburger Edition.

Turner, Victor. 1969. *The Ritual Process: structure and anti-structure.* Chicago, IL: Aldine, https://doi.org/10.4324/9781315134666

Vertovec, Stephen. 2009. *Transnationalism.* New York: Routledge, https://doi.org/10.4324/9780203927083

Vladimirova, Vladislava & Joachim Otto Habeck. 2018. "Introduction: feminist approaches and the study of gender in arctic social sciences". *Polar Geography*, 41 (3): 145–63, https://doi.org/10.1080/1088937x.2018.1496368

9. "We Are not Playing Life, We Live Here"

Playful Appropriation of Ancestral Memory in a Youth Camp in Western Siberia

Ina Schröder

This chapter starts with an episode of a live-action role play organised by Mansi educators (the Mansi being one of the indigenous groups of West Siberia) for the youth of the village Saranpaul' and its neighbouring villages. In August 2011 during the summer camp *Man' Uskve* (in Mansi northern dialect, "Small Town"), I played a bride who was meant to be chosen by one of the Mansi warriors. I and the other brides stood in a line barefoot, in newly made dresses, beautified with traditional Mansi braids, nervously anticipating who will be our "husband" for the next two days of the play. The warriors with the highest status such as the tribe's chief, his son, and uncle were allowed to choose first. They had the best chances to choose the bride they wished, before she was taken away by someone else. When a warrior made his choice, the bride and the bridegroom told each other their play-names in the Mansi language and the girl followed her guardian to his tribe and stood behind him. The solemn ceremony was observed and orchestrated by one of the educators of the summer camp — a woman aged around fifty — and

  https://doi.org/10.11647/OBP.0171.09

recorded by a few camp's own journalists on a video camera. As a result of the ceremony, I "got married" to a fifteen-year-old adolescent.

This scene is an episode from the role-playing game called the *Time of Singing Arrows* performed near Saranpaul', a rural settlement in the Khanty-Mansi Autonomous Okrug — Yugra. We came here together for one week to get immersed into the glorious past of Mansi history. The play is integrated into a larger frame of summer camps for children and youth, designed by indigenous activists and pedagogues to transmit indigenous knowledge to the next generation. This initiative, along with many other educational, juridical, and cultural institutions of indigenous activists, is a product of the post-Soviet indigenous revival movement that has been active since the late 1980s. The ambivalent Soviet nationalities policy led to the reaffirmation of national identities and an uprising of national resurgence movements (Bassin & Kelly 2012). The process of making the summer camp possible requires considerable bureaucratic, financial, and social skills from the side of educators, who each year have to apply for public money on the basis of a competitive grant system in Khanty-Mansiisk. Since the beginning of the revival movement, they perceived ethnic tradition as the source for spiritual and economic revival of indigenous peoples. Especially the young generation is often seen as needing to be grounded in traditional values and practices.

My intention is to show how the medium of play reflects social transformations in post-Soviet Russia as they find an expression in multiple discourses on tradition, gender roles, and a normative lifestyle. It shows how in the logic of the role play, the boundary between what is framed as real and imaginary, secular and sacred, authentic and spurious comes to be blurred and is being continually renegotiated by educators and participants. In his analysis of lifestyle Chaney refers to "Western" metropolises where stylistic expressions become apparent. This ethnographic case study — along with other chapters in this book — is to illustrate that aesthetics as a means of communication and display of particular aspects of identity cannot be limited to urban centres: rather, their use is also widespread in so called "remote" regions of post-Soviet Russia.

In this chapter, I will begin by situating the shared sensibilities of indigenous spokespeople in the socio-political context of the research region. Then, I will discuss the emic and etic meanings of "style" and in what way the participation in the summer camp can be understood as "lifestyle" in its own right. Following from that, I will deal with the secular and sacred dimensions of the role-playing game; and how the Soviet legacy of military games was translated into indigenous symbols and practice. I will also discuss how gender roles were rendered and legitimated in the role-playing game and how female and male players responded to that. In doing so, I hope to demonstrate how play — with its ambiguous nature — became a ritual with the intention to transform the gendered identity of girls and boys, while at the same time allowing them to manoeuvre between its secular and sacred interpretations.

Shared sensibilities: taking charge of local youth

At the beginning of the 1990s, village-based activists and urban indigenous intellectuals responded to a broad range of problems that afflicted indigenous communities such as loss of land use, poverty, decline of indigenous languages, low life expectancy, lack of family care for children, and the alienation of young people from their cultural roots. These activists were women who in the course of the Soviet educational programmes for native women received higher educational degrees than native men. During the Soviet period, women played the central role in the formalisation of ethnicity through literacy of indigenous languages, schooling, and scholarly activities. Subsequently, by the end of the Soviet Union, they also came to lead the discourse on native revival (cf. Ssorin-Chaikov 2003).

Their concerns can be understood through David Chaney's notion of "sensibilities" (see Chapters 1 and 7 in this volume). The term denotes a set of responses to social processes, discourses, and changes that appear in modern societies and become expressed in particular ethical and aesthetic practices which in their turn engender new social dynamics (Chaney 1996: 6, 128). The sensibilities of indigenous spokespeople were responses to environmental pollution caused by oil extraction, social disintegration of indigenous communities in the Russian Far North, and economic problems mentioned in the same breath with cultural survival and "ethnic purity" (cf. Ssorin-Chaikov 2003: 172). In that respect, representatives of indigenous spokespeople started to look to their own moral values and knowledge as a reaffirmation of their cultural difference.

In their response to societal transformations, native women organised leisure spaces during summer vacations and social patronage for children in need. The main target group for the summer camps was indigenous children and youth from so-called "unfit" families (in Russian, *neblagopoluchnye sem'i*). These are families affected by alcohol abuse, domestic violence, lack of social care, and families with orphans or half-orphans. Such families are under state surveillance and eligible for different kinds of state financial help (cf. Khlinovskaya Rockhill 2010). Some parents have been deprived of their parental rights. The "unfit" status is changeable and parental rights may be regained when the court considers a family or one parent to be able to resume their responsibilities. Due to a high mortality rate (accidents, lethal illness at a relatively young age, suicide) in the *raion* (district), some children and young people have only one biological parent, others are adopted by relatives or live on their own with the support of relatives and friends (cf. Ulturgasheva 2012). The kin solidarity to integrate children and adolescents of alcohol-dependent parents into networks of support does not happen automatically. Although people say that "here almost everyone is related to everybody", this is no guarantee for social care.

Berezovskii Raion — where the protagonists of the study live — is the least populated and urbanised region in the Okrug. The accelerated urbanisation process in the Khanty-Mansi Autonomous Okrug — Yugra — has taken place alongside the oil and gas extraction routes since the 1950s. Today around 96 per cent of the Okrug's economy is based on petroleum production (Wiget & Balalaeva 2011: 267). However, not all districts of the Okrug are equally involved in the fuel economy and the share of its revenues. Saranpaul' with its 2,575 inhabitants (as of 2010) is legally designated as a "remote and hard-to-access settlement" (Zakon 2004). Back in the Soviet period the village was famous for its reindeer-herding state farm (*sovkhoz*) as well as state geological enterprise in the Northern Urals. Saranpaul' was the most convenient reloading point for helicopters, which needed to reach mining parties and reindeer herders in the Ural Mountains. In the post-Soviet period, the former state enterprises were privatised and new ones were established to extract gold, quartz, and coal, but these operations provide very few employment opportunities for the male part of the local population. The reindeer-herding farm is still in state hands, but due to lack of funding and logistics shrunk dramatically.

The transport system relies on water, air, and winter road transportation and is highly dependent on weather and seasonality. From Saranpaul', trips to the *raion* capital Berezovo and onward to the regional capital Khanty-Mansiisk by bus or by car are possible only by winter roads (from mid-December to March). Air transport, monopolised by the Utair company and subsidised by the district, is expensive and does not satisfy the demand. The daily life of people in Saranpaul' — the food supply, medical treatment, visits of relatives, and funerals — all depend on the availability of transportation. People often say "we live like on an island: you can't get here, but when you are here you can't leave again". Digital communication technology, such as mobile phone connection, arrived in 2007. Internet access is also relatively recent, and virtual mobility is still restricted by the slow connection speed.

Saranpaul' is a multi-ethnic village that consists mainly of Komi, Mansi, Nenets, and Russians. When the Soviets came to power, administrators favoured Russians and Komi, allotting them positions of privilege. The inter-ethnic hierarchies intensified after Mansi were resettled from small native villages to larger modernised settlements such as Saranpaul' towards the end of the 1950s. Mansi children were disadvantaged at school compared to Komi and Russian children. Towards the end and after the breakdown of the Soviet Union, poor living conditions, unemployment, and alcohol abuse turned the previously latent conflicts between these groups into outbreaks of open violence. However, the post-Soviet policy of benefits for indigenous peoples reversed the ethnic hierarchies. Komi, as they did not belong to the "small-numbered peoples of the North" (*korennye malochislennye narody Severa*), were not eligible to receive the state benefits that Mansi could claim. This policy again refueled the animosities. The inter-ethnic tensions have weakened over recent years, however. Today inter-ethnic marriages between Mansi and Komi are very common and if fights between people happen after a party in the social club, in a bar or just on the street, they are usually not ethnically motivated.

The camp educators in Saranpaul' try to bridge the gap of social care for children and youth in need, not only in the summer time, but also during the school year. In Saranpaul', as in many other places in Russia (King 2009: 153 ff.), indigenous activists are worried about the disorientation of the young generation as to their sense of belonging, low level of confidence, and education. Young people are perceived to have a sense of meaninglessness about their life, which is reflected in the high rate of suicide among young people in the *raion*.

However, the educator's practice and strategies should not be understood in terms of resilience and coping only, as they are also inspired by visions and aspirations for the young to have a better life than their parents. Summer vacations are seen by indigenous activists as a window in which to organise, control, and channel the leisure time not only of school pupils, but also of young people far into their twenties. The House of Culture, an institution that in Soviet times facilitated extracurricular education and a "leisure to a purpose" that "contrasted with 'idle' forms of pastime and alcohol consumption" has partially lost its primacy in cultivating morally responsible citizens (Habeck, Donahoe & Gruber 2011: 146). The diversification of leisure services since the early 1990s in Saranpaul' offers alternative spaces for children and young people. New services comprise a "National Art School" that incorporates teaching in Mansi music instruments, piano, singing, theatre playing, and painting, a Youth Centre with handicrafts and sports courses as well as summer camps. The authority of the House of Culture has been questioned in Saranpaul' especially by some Mansi activists, who perceive the staged ethnic performances as not authentic. Discourses on "authentic" and "spurious" culture dominate the scene of cultural production and identity building not only among native people in the district, but also in other parts of Russia (e.g. King 2009: 145–47).

Summer camp as a lifestyle

To immerse children and young people into the great past of their ancestors, the summer camp embraces many different events and activities such as music making, handicrafts, hiking tours, different kinds of games, and theatre playing.[1] In the opinion of the educators, the embodiment of ethnic identity should not be just a formal (spurious) exercise, but linked to the spiritual worldview and experiences as connected to the exploration of one's "real self".

The leisure activity in the summer camp constitutes for many children and youth a significant place to craft their (ethnic) identities and to work on themselves (Schröder 2017). The camp draws together youth of different social orientations and ethnic backgrounds, such as Mansi, Khanty, Komi, Nenets, and Russians, the so-called "active" youth and the dropouts, high school, and university students as well as the unemployed. In that sense, youth who would not necessarily communicate and meet due to (relative) geographical distance and/ or generational and social differences are able to develop a sense of community. For participants who repeatedly join in every summer vacation, young camp leaders and educators create a distinct lifestyle which is meaningful to them. As Chaney points out, we need to look at how people use their resources at hand to create a distinct pattern of living and how it makes sense for them in their particular contexts (Chaney 1996). After the camp season, players wait for the next summer and communicate with each other on the Russian network site vKontakte and via mobile phones. Young camp leaders have created a social network group *Man' Uskve* where participants can upload their pictures, videos, and songs, and write comments, wishes, and poems. The group is steadily growing from 177 members in 2013 to 420 in 2018. Participants talk about decisive emotional moments in the role-playing game and heroic deeds long after the camp has finished; and some girls even cry when they vividly recall their memories.

The objective of educators is to improve the social situation of socio-economically marginalised children and youth in a remote district and to raise the social status of Mansi. To express their position in the

---

1   The camping season generally encompasses three distinct events or sessions, which in Russian are called *smena* (shift): the first *smena* at the beginning of July targets the youngest participants, mostly aged between eight and fourteen, and has a particular focus, for example theatre, handicrafts, music, or games; the second *smena* in the last half of July is dedicated to mountaineering in the nearby Ural Mountains and is open to participants starting at the age of fourteen; and the third *smena*, starting in the first week of August, has as its focus the role-playing game *The Time of Singing Arrows*, which is likewise open to participants from ages fourteen or older.

contested field of cultural production educators employ various means, one of which is the process of self-stylisation. The conjuncture of style and ethnicity goes hand in hand with public expressions of identity in Russia and other parts of the world (Eward & O'Hanlon 2007). I understand style by referring to Chaney as "'languages' of social identity" that "reflects or expresses in some way distinctive attitudes or values that are themselves part of a broader outlook or life-world" (Chaney 1996: 129, 128). That is to say people reflect upon aesthetics and employ them to voice and to challenge their social position in modern society (see also Chapter 7 in this volume). Public visibility of ethnicity is conjoined with different, contesting political, social, and cultural agendas of social actors. The discriminating power of indigenous intellectuals over symbolic meanings competes against other powerful presentation strategies of ethnicity, such as folklore displays for regional image purposes at the occasion of the World Chess Olympiad in 2010 or the Biathlon World Championship in 2003 and 2011 in Khanty-Mansiisk.

Ethnic self-stylisation as a matter of identity choice and aesthetic taste takes place in relation to another process: the objectification of culture. In the course of Soviet social engineering, ethnic culture was secularised and reified in recognisable forms of "high culture" known from Russian and European contexts, such as dance, theatre, instrumental music, material objects, and poetry. In the post-Soviet period ethnic culture became once again an object of action as a property and heritage that should be saved, remembered, written down, and called into life again (Donahoe & Habeck 2011). In the context of the summer camp, style — as expressed in role-play paraphernalia, traditional dresses, dances, and choreography — is one of the main semiotic devices to convey a set of values to young people and to channel their conduct (cf. Holland et al. 1998: 35ff). Cultural designers select the "best elements" of Mansi culture as pedagogical tools to boost self-cultivation among members of the young generation. Despite the clearly Soviet influence of the way in which ethnic culture is understood and presented, this process is a complex matter, which draws upon people's affinities, intuition, different forms of knowledge, and sensibilities.

Drawing upon the normative sensibilities of indigenous spokespeople, I differentiate between the discursive use of style and stylisation by them and the analytical term proposed by Chaney. In the emic perspective, "stylisation" (*stilizatsiia*) is a pejorative term that refers rather to spurious representation of culture (e.g. performed by many folklore ensembles), emptied of its spiritual meaning and detached from a particular regional or local grounding. Such performances need to satisfy the taste of an official jury during public festivals and national festivities, and also stand for the commercialisation of ethnic symbols for tourists. In some respects, this "traditionalist" discourse echoes the processes which Chaney detects in mass-consumption society, where style "comes to supersede substance" (Chaney 1996: 151), always shifting and thus indifferent to fixed meanings. Responding sceptically to this "postmodern" play with forms and their references in the field of ethnic symbols, indigenous intellectuals carefully observe and direct the usage of traditional symbols in the summer camp and the meanings they bear.

This happens by teaching participants to do traditional handicrafts and by appropriating visual technologies. The interpretation of the activities' meaning and the selection of meaningful moments takes place in the camp's own "Press Centre", which consists of older participants and produces daily news (called *Man' NEWSkve*) about how the common activities in the camp and the role-playing game are unfolding. They are shown daily to all players after breakfast. Documentation, editing, and watching endorses the dramatic character of the whole process and accords the event an official and serious tone. Besides that, the use of material objects, inseparable from the process of their crafting and performing, constitute a normative path to a "good life" and morally heightened personality. The emphasis on crafting traditional objects oneself expresses anti-consumerist values in the camp and criticism against mass production of objects with ethnic stylisation. Sewing one's own dress for a young woman necessitates particular social actions that are incorporated into the larger outlook of how a harmonious society should function. Thus, young people's sense of a real self is imagined to be intertwined with an ethnic identity that should be shown and lived in an authentic way.

Play and self-cultivation

The role-playing game *Time of Singing Arrows* in *Man' Uskve* is intended to awaken the "spirit of a warrior" in each of the participating boys.

Camp participants refer to this play as a "battle" (*bitva*). The basic scenario of the play is a battle between two mediaeval Mansi tribes in order to win a bride referred to as the "Mansi beauty". One tribe is local and is hiding in a fortress. The other one is coming from a foreign territory and wants to steal the Mansi beauty. Male players have braids that are tightened with a scarf on their heads. The "killing" of an enemy requires tearing off the braids from the head of the other. When none of the male players of one tribe has got braids anymore, they have lost. The martial spirit — so the hope of the educators — should help especially males to face challenges in their daily life, to stand up for their values, and to fight for what they are striving for.

The role-play idea has been derived from the Soviet military game *Zarnitsa* (literally, "summer lightning") that was introduced in Soviet para-military summer camps in the mid-1960s (Kuebart 1989: 106; cf. Barchunova & Beletskaia 2009–2010). During the Cold War, patriotic education became a constitutive part of school and extracurricular programmes. *Zarnitsa* was intended to teach boys and girls aged between ten and fourteen to be ready to defend their motherland against imperialist enemies. Pupils were trained to develop physical strength, team spirit and other military related skills (Kuebart 1989: 106).[2] The transformation of the game *Zarnitsa* to the *Time of Singing Arrows* is, on the one hand, in continuity with the Soviet legacy, but on the other, it shows how ideological practices are changing as they are loaded with new scenarios, symbols, and meanings.

Similar to pioneer camps that served as arenas for *Zarnitsa* performances, new summer camps provide pedagogical spaces for organised and controlled "serious leisure" for children and youth.[3] Games like *Zarnitsa* stand in the legacy of the discourse on progressive human development. As Brian Sutton-Smith points out, in the "rhetoric of progress" play is rationalised as a way of building

---

2   The rules of the game cast two teams as opposite parties. The teams fight for a particular status symbol, e.g. a flag they have to steal from their enemy. Epaulets on players' shoulders symbolise life. When their epaulets are torn off, players have to leave the game. *Zarnitsa* was a popular motif in Soviet cinematography of Pioneer camps.

3   In contemporary Russia games of a similar genre are used by military-patriotic clubs (*voenno-patrioticheskie kluby*) that are mostly based in youth centres or Houses of Culture (Habeck 2014).

children's development and socialisation (Sutton-Smith 1997: 18). Play in this interpretation has no value in itself, but has to point to a particular use that is external to play. Especially games with a motif of *agon* (competition) have been theorised as "a source and expression of power" and "civilizing force" (Lindquist 2001: 15). Following that logic, the Soviet self-cultivation narrative and patriotic education through competitive play were part of a progress-oriented understanding of self and society.

Nourished by ideas from the Enlightenment and the construction of socialism, culture work became one of the main vehicles to carve out the "new man" (*novyi chelovek*), the ideal person for life in a society teleologically oriented toward communism. The "new man" should incorporate the imperative of constant self-cultivation and improvement based on the Soviet concept of *kul'turnost'* (culturedness) which played the central role in the Soviet mission to civilize the masses. According to my observations, many practices and discourses of indigenous leaders, who instigate the importance of ethnic culture as a source of a meaningful life today, are imbued with Soviet understandings of culture and its normative meaning (see Chapter 7 in this volume). To illustrate this point, I would like to quote the camp director, who once responded to a male participant, who said that his main motivation to come to the camp was to "relax": "Don't say you came here to relax! We don't come here to relax! If any of you say you came here to relax, you will work a lot!" Camp participants are expected to work on themselves in the camp, so as to purify their language from vulgar words (*mat*), to be polite, to have good manners, and to be honest. As scholars on post-Soviet Russia have argued, the idea of "working on oneself" constitutes the most powerful moral discourse and ethical practice in today's Russia (cf. Zigon 2011). Active self-cultivation of participants was the main premise of the moral education in the camp.

Despite the historical continuities, the indigenisation of *Zarnitsa* clearly departs from Soviet idealised notions of gender equality. Through selective appropriation of history, creating objects, and establishing a role-play scenario, boys and girls were to be shaped in their essentialised identities. The indigenous meanings that were given to the objects and the embedding of the game in the local landscape coloured the image of masculinity and femininity as a way of reinventing Mansi tradition

(Hobsbawm & Ranger 1999). Thus, in the role-playing game boys and girls were to cultivate gender specific qualities. For girls these were her sewing skills, tidiness, patience, modesty, taking care of her beauty, and listening to men. For boys these were fairness, courage, virility, physical strength, responsibility, respecting, and protecting women.

The emergence of the summer camp and the role-playing game the *Time of Singing Arrows* stands in the interstice between past and new symbolic connections of present-day Russia. As the camp pedagogues shared with me while they were familiar with Soviet education practices, the *content* of what ethnic culture consisted of was an unknown signifier for them. In the next section, I will show that a locally grounded spiritual worldview, which nonetheless had also been transformed in the course of Russification and Sovietisation, plays the central role in forming another way of framing reality in the camp and in the role-playing game.

Indigenisation of *Zarnitsa*: retrieving one's ancestral memory

The re-stylisation of *Zarnitsa* takes place by building connections to Mansi spiritual ways of seeing the world. The role-playing game in its contemporary shape is being created by accumulated and interweaved knowledge and practices of many different actors involved. The camp staff consists of people from several generations, aged between eighteen and seventy. They are teenagers, students, teachers, scientists, craftspeople, representatives from the settlement's administration, and retired elders. All of them have a different approach to "native culture", depending on their biographies, age, gender, ethnic background, and education. Older educators and young leaders negotiate the meta-communication language, symbolic connections, rules, and meanings of the role play. What is central in the re-imagination of *Zarnitsa* is the process of post-Soviet desecularisation of ethnic culture and imbuing it with spiritual meanings (cf. Luehrmann 2005).

Play-theorists (Sutton-Smith 1997; Bateson [1972] 2000; Lindquist 2001) see play as an ambiguous action and as a paradox because it is and is not what it appears to be. Here I use the notion of "frame" by drawing on Gregory Bateson's model of meta-communication in play.

Bateson suggests that it depends on communication partners to send each other signals to frame their communication in such a way that what they do is understood as "play" (2000: 185). The battle is understood by educators and players as a game and as a feigned signifier for war. Yet, the ambiguity of the play allows multiple frames of communication; as Galina Lindquist argues, "frames nest within or braid with other frames, carrying competing or constructing messages" (Lindquist 2001: 18). André Droogers' definition helps here to understand the paradox of play as "the capacity to deal simultaneously and subjunctively with two or more ways of classifying reality" (2012: 81). Droogers refers to Victor Turner's usage of the "subjunctive" as an "as if" mode of doing things in contrast to the "indicative" way of "as is". He suggests that especially religion is the field where humans apply ludic capacities. I argue that in the role-playing game actors are constantly moving between the subjunctive and indicative frames.

Many practices incorporated in the role play and their interpretations by players suggest that the battle has a semi-religious connotation, where authentic tradition is getting revived. As one player had sad: "Maybe it is not just a game. Maybe we resurrect here something, what used to be at this place. We show it in the game" (Maxim, aged 22 at the time of interviewing). Preparations for the role play, the "playground" and play paraphernalia gain their legitimacy by being linked to the past and ongoing beliefs. Thus, the battle carries multiple framing, in which the distinction between what is playful and real is blurring. Elderly educators give young people lectures about the origin of the world, initiation, local spirits, dances and music. They serve to "immerse" young people into the Mansi worldview and to prepare their emotional state for the battle. The knowledge sources of lecturers are manifold: they draw on their own memories and observations, scholarly activities with informants, and ethnography books. Two lecturers tried to reconstruct war craft strategies and martial arts of the ancient Mansi people by looking at Mansi dances and historic literature on war craft.

Stylistic elements borrowed from religious practice are playfully inscribed into participants' body fashioning. To refer to Droogers again, playfulness is an intrinsic feature of religion: "play has potential for the sacred, a serious play — but play" (2012: 25). The crucial symbols in the game are braids, which shift the life-containing substance from epaulets in *Zarnitsa* to the players' bodies — the hair. Participants and educators connect braids to Mansi tradition, where they are a symbol of life and strength. Ethnographic research by Russian scholars provides evidence of scalping practices in the war craft of Khanty and Mansi (Sokolova 2009: 256). The hair used to be seen as the site of one's reincarnated soul: cutting the enemy's hair and scalping was equal to destroying the soul (Sokolova 2009: 254). Soviet ethnographer V. N. Chernetsov described a boy's game related to scalping: players were divided into two teams and representatives of each team met for a wrestling competition. The winner took a knife and cut a piece of hair from the head of the "enemy" (quoted in Fedorova 1988: 89). In pre-Soviet times, both men and women used to plait artificial braids into their hair, a fact that was not known to most participants of the summer camp. Some of them mentioned that when seeing old family photographs, they mistook their male relatives for women because of their hairstyle. Tightening one's own hair into braids is also supposed to provide protection against evil forces trying to enter one's head. Mansi women inserted metal rings, animal figurines, and coins into their artificial braids. Having dreams about hair or teeth falling out was a sign of the imminent death of a relative. This symbolic connection is still alive among some young and older people I have met, although none of boys grow long hair anymore.

In the role-playing game, boys' braids are tightened on their head with a scarf, but in the case of girls they are plaited into their hair. The braids were crafted by female elders when the game was designed. The incorporation of braids into the game turns girls' preparation for the performance into a laborious endeavour, since it requires time and skill. The meaning and value of style is generated in the "right" action. Authentic bearers of tradition produce objects for the game and offer advice for the proper usage of the objects. Elders help girls to sew their dresses and to plait braids into their hair. Educators stress the idea that culture is alive only if crafting and usage of objects are interlinked, thereby implicitly critiquing the fact that self-made ethnic objects are often made merely for exhibition purposes.

According to lecturers, life in the camp and the role play should awake "genetic memory" (*geneticheskaia pamiat'*) or "ancestral memory" (*pamiat' pokolenii*) in young people. That would make them aware of the life of their ancestors, ideally all the way down to the mythical beginnings. Educators believe they see the utterance of ancestral memory in young people in different situations: when the boys fight, when they look after the fire, and when the girls sew their dresses. This implies that the summer camp as an educational space and the role play are seen as merely a framework for young individuals to reveal their "true selves", to activate the immanent knowledge that is thought to be manifest in them by the heritage of their ancestors.

Such discourse on genes appears in Russia also in other contexts where identity claims are crucial (Brož 2009). Apart from primordial ethnicity claims, I suppose that the discourse on "genetic memory" is also fed by local beliefs of reincarnation of souls. A newborn baby is not seen as a psychological *tabula rasa* — free to be sculpted for the good of the society, as it was thought in the Soviet Union (cf. Khlinovskaya Rockhill 2010: 316) — but contains a soul of a dead relative, who therefore affects the character and predilections of the person during their entire life. Even if birth rituals are not performed anymore, the reincarnation beliefs continue to exist. Some young participants are named after their deceased relatives, assuming they have been reincarnated. However, the (cyclical) trope of "ancestral memory" is seemingly in conflict with the (progressive) narrative of self-cultivation, since it dismisses a conscious and rational effort of children and youth to improve themselves. From the "ancestral memory" point of view, the characteristic tendencies of a person are already embodied in their self and revealed in particular time and space.

Educators suppose that ancestral memory wakes up in the "traditional environment": in the forest or some ancestral village, since these places are believed to be inhabited by various spirits and deities. The safety and good fortune of the camp depend on the local protecting spirits. Elderly women — grandmothers — conduct a ritual and feed local spirits at the start of the summer camp season. The spatial location of the role play therefore has an important symbolic significance.

The camp is located at the confluence of two mountain rivers, Khulga and Mania, ten kilometres upstream from Saranpaul', next to the old Mansi village of Yasunt. The village consists of several households and is almost uninhabited throughout the year. In the course of the Soviet consolidation policy in the 1950s and 60s, the entire working population of the district was relocated from small villages into larger settlements.

Today, some camp participants own houses in the village where their grandparents used to live and where their parents grew up. The old cemetery in Yasunt, where the dead are buried exclusively according to native beliefs, is also still in use. Some of them consider Yasunt as their "home" and have acquired new land there, although the actual time they spend in the village is only a few days or weeks in the summer. There are remains of an ancient settlement next to the village in the forest, presumably from the Middle Ages.[4] There have been no excavations of the settlement and local leaders want to prevent any archaeological engagements at the site. For the role-play purposes a wooden fortress has been reconstructed right next to the ancient settlement in the taiga, providing players with the historical ground for building connections to their ancestors and triggering their "ancestral memory".

As I could observe in the camp and also in everyday life in Saranpaul, Mansi who continue to practice religious rituals find themselves in a grey zone of being uncertain about the "right" and "wrong" form of ritualistic actions in relation to spirits (cf. Halemba 2006). Besides that, people dispute and negotiate which elements of "culture" are "allowed" to be disembedded and displayed for outsiders. One reason for the disputes is fear of serious consequences for their own and their relatives' well-being if a staged performance and/or religious ritual dissatisfy the spirits.

Although in the pre-Soviet past Mansi could consult male or female community members who would be specialised on different spiritual issues, today there are no strong religious leaders who can provide guidance on how to communicate with invisible forces. Sometimes accidents or suicides are interpreted as a consequence of social misconduct (that may reach back to their ancestors) towards spirits, but often without knowing where the infringement of rules happened and what can be done to re-establish an equilibrium between human and non-human beings. Thus, playful and creative attitudes in designing a role-playing game exist alongside, or within a spiritual sphere of influence; and as a consequence, they may have positive but also negative transformative effects on practitioners. Elders also may ask local spirits for help to assist one or the other tribe to win the role-playing game.

---

4   Personal communication with Valentina I. Semenova, archaeologist and specialist on Ob-Ugric ethnography.

The religious connotation of the role play is not only revealed in the spirituality of the place and the symbolic meanings of play paraphernalia, but also in the way that the game is interpreted as an initiation ritual. It is seen as an enactment of the long-forgotten initiation of Mansi boys. When during the game one 22-year old participant broke his finger while rushing into the fortress, he was celebrated afterwards as a man who just had passed the liminal phase of adolescence and reached adulthood. The Mansi folklorist Svetlana Popova, one of the educators and advisors of the camp, published a book on initiation rituals in traditional Mansi culture (Popova 2003) where among other life-long *rites de passage*, she specifically paid attention to the initiation ceremonies for boys and young men. She argues that initiation rituals can be reconstructed from folklore material such as songs, folktales, and especially from the oral repertoire of the bear ceremony. The bear is believed to be the sacred animal among Khanty and Mansi, who used to dedicate the bear a feast with long epic songs, dances, and theatrical plays, which took several days. This feast is traditionally performed mainly by men. Although there are attempts to revive the bear feast today, there is a lack of male performers who would know the sacred songs, especially with the sacral speech that was used in the bear cult.

In the camp, particular elements from the bear feast are decontextualised and now serve new purposes. For example, to raise the warriors' spirit, one sacred male dance was disembedded from a bear ceremony and made suitable for the game. In a process of negotiation among educators, the movements were simplified and religious clothing removed lest to offend the spirits. The transformation of the dance's style carries the message to the spirits to be "fake", i.e. it does not imply dialogue between the human and the non-human world. Nevertheless, even if the warrior dance is desacralised, it still may contain a spiritual power and links to invisible forces.

Thus, the dance continues to be an exclusively male performance, as in the original context. During the spirit-raising exercise, girls are not supposed to watch the boys dancing. In this context, old and new elements are intermingled, and the transformed dance exerts a novel magical power on the dancers. One male leader told me: "I sent the girls into the hut. I think girls should not watch a martial dance. I don't know why. But it's better to be cautious. You don't know what might happen". He based his decision mainly on his intuition and intended to protect the girls from male spiritual energy. These actions reflect an interplay between religion, play, and power.

What I see at the core of this endeavour is the constant shifting between the secular and the sacral, between the subjunctive and indicative frames, the real and imaginary. Play is here a way to dive into the unknown: to explore one's own indigenous roots via trial and error and to create a bricolage of different forms of knowledge and historical legacies.

Gender norms, roles, and experiences in the role-playing game

The vignette at the beginning of the chapter and the emphasis on the initiation ritual for boys show how important educators take gender issues. While the Soviet *Zarnitsa* was played by girls and boys alike, the *Time of Singing Arrows* excludes girls from fighting and limits their roles to "wives" and "beauties". In fact, naturalisation of gender roles plays the main role in the reimagining of *Zarnitsa*. The agency of girls and boys and their relationships are mediated through rules. The beautification of women in the role play and the emphasis on masculinity of boys serve the purpose to accentuate gender differences and sharpen their moral values. The retro-gender turn in the play resonates with current political discourses in Russia, asserting the role of the family as "the main site of social regeneration and enculturation" (Povoroznyuk, Habeck & Vaté 2010: 21) but contrasts concurrently with social distress in the everyday family life of many young people. It seems that camp educators internalised widespread discourses and media rhetoric in Russia that "[t]he 'emasculation' of men, their loss of responsibility and power within the family [...] led directly to high levels of male alcoholism, poor physical and psychological health, apathy and indifference to their wives and children" (Kay 2006: 20).

As the afore-mentioned studies on gender shift in the Russian North have shown, Soviet social engineering of such societal institutions as family and marriage and also post-Soviet socio-economic ramifications have resulted in a widespread discourse about the crisis of the conventional male role of breadwinner and protector. Evidence from my own ethnographic study shows that a comparatively large number of indigenous women have a higher level of formal education and take leading positions in the community, while men often work outside the village, e.g. for the mining companies in the Ural Mountains. The discrepancy between the conventional male roles and the factual cases are discussed by women and men alike. Frequently, men complain about lack of employment possibilities and women about the unreliability and alcoholism of their husbands. The low economic status of reindeer husbandry in the *sovkhoz*, and tough jobs in private mining companies and on the construction sites in Saranpaul' leave men with few and rather unattractive occupation options. The high percentage of suicide and death accidents among indigenous men finds various emic explanations and one of them refers to the "weakness" of men when it comes to facing difficulties in life (cf. Kay 2006: 19ff).

Up until the 1950s or 60s, before the whole Mansi working population was forcedly relocated from small villages into large settlements, Mansi married generally among themselves. Today inter-ethnic marriages are most common and native women with higher education normally leave rural communities for the city and/or marry a non-indigenous partner. Female educators respond to the socio-economic marginality of Mansi men with resurrection of gender roles that supposedly existed in "traditional Mansi society". Their strategy is to make boys more masculine, that is responsible for their future family, physically strong and handy, capable of taking initiatives and leadership, and therefore more attractive for girls. These particular sensibilities of educators exemplify the paradoxical situation that has been also observed in other parts of the Russian North (cf. Ssorin-Chaikov 2003: 172ff.): the fact that the revival and re-invention of tradition is headed by indigenous women in the first place, contradicts the naturalisation of female domestic roles in the role-playing game.

Female educators reflect upon their own role in respect to their leadership positions. For instance, one sixty-year-old scholar questioned whether she was entitled to teach boys, since in "tradition" the transmission of knowledge was assumedly gender-specific. Recently however, she found an answer in some folklore research publications arguing that in ancient times, Ob-Ugric peoples used to live in a matriarchal society, until men took over power at a certain moment.

These findings released her tensions of not being authorised to pursue the task of supervising boys' education as warriors. These considerations show that although women try to reinforce patriarchal family relations, nevertheless they back up and legitimise their own leading position by discovering matriarchy as an ancient state of Mansi society.

The separation of gender roles echoes the old Mansi view that male and female components complement each other in the cosmological order of the world. Both sexes have different ritual responsibilities and their movement in space is also regulated. A man is associated with the upper world and is entitled to communicate with territorial and regional protection spirits and to conduct a bear feast. A woman is especially subjected to higher control of behaviour and regulation of movement during her period and while she is of child-bearing age (Fedorova 2000: 396–97). For example, girls are not allowed to climb to the loft or go behind the right-hand corner of a traditional Mansi house, since these are held sacred. In the camp only a limited set of traditional rules about men's and women's behaviour are in force.

Female educators foster the role of boys in the camp because of their important role in the ritual life of Mansi. However, their traditionalist approach is a "selective representation of the past" (Linnekin 1992: 251) that should provide a solution to contemporary sensibilities and political agendas. One young educator shared with me a story that his grandfather had told him, about how during a bear feast, men could not beat a physically strong woman in a playful competition. When I asked him whether they could consider involving girls in the role play in the same way, he replied after some silent moments of consideration, that now they live in a different time. Women have to give birth to children, raise them, and not fight. Taking also safety reasons into consideration, girls should employ their "female" side of influence.

Young women made into wives and sisters

In the warfare scenario, girls are supposed to turn the camping site into a working household: they cook for their "husbands" and serve the warriors food and drink whenever they have a moment to rest. In a similar vein they paint their husbands' faces to make them look more frightening for their enemies. During the attack in the fortress, all girls have to hide themselves in the earth hut built for them, so that they do not disturb the warriors, stay safe, and protect the Mansi beauty from being robbed. The supposed agency of a woman lies in her accuracy to sew her clothes and fulfil her responsibilities with dignity and attentiveness. Recently a new rule was introduced, that women cover their faces with a self-made Mansi scarf in the selection of brides at the beginning of the game, so that warriors choose a bride for her ability to sew and decorate her clothes rather than for her pretty face. The incorporation of the headdress in the role-playing game resonates with the pre-Soviet practice of Mansi women of concealing their faces from older relatives of their husbands. Moreover, this rule leads back to the past, where the value of a woman supposedly depended on her ability to sew clothes for the whole family, her accuracy in making invisible stitches, and ultimately her responsibility for survival and comfort in the harsh northern environment. The materiality of clothes was connected with the spiritual meaning of ornaments that had a protective function. Therewith the woman's field of responsibility was different, but at the same time not of less importance than that of a man.

Yet certain rules have been challenged by some girls, who complain about not being able to even watch male players fighting. The feeling that girls are bored while boys have fun has been discussed in common meetings between educators and players more than once. Girls were urged by educators to take the situation of war in the game seriously and to fulfil themselves in their roles as wives. Ironically, in their daily life educators and young leaders of the camp do challenge the normative patriarchal gender contract through their own practices and comments on other people's relationships. Thus, a woman can be the head of the family and the main breadwinner.

Although artificial braids and scarfs follow a "traditional" model, girls are more or less free to play with the style of their dresses out of the limited resources brought to the camp. The crafting of an authentic traditional dress is a time-consuming activity that cannot be done during the few days of preparation for the battle. Another consideration of designers is that the mediaeval dress of women was different from the contemporary Mansi dress. The research on the "authentic" historical dress model is on-going; in the meantime, all girls get a simple linen cloth to cover the body down to their knees, which they can fashion

Fig. 9.1. Warriors inspect the fortress from outside. Photograph by Sergei Remizov, near Saranpaul, 2016. Courtesy of the photographer, CC-BY-ND.

according to their own taste. Yet the hierarchy of traditional attire is still preserved, since the chosen Mansi princess must wear a traditional Mansi dress and have the most beautiful braids. The "princess" must endure some pain, since she wears heavy braids beautified with metal rings and coins, amounting to two kilograms of extra weight. The quality of a girl's dress stands in direct relationship with her ability to work on herself and her skills, and simultaneously if she is doing well, organisers stress her links with the female side of her family, for example by saying "look, she is just like her grandmother!".

The introduction of such rules is meant to channel the attention of participants to "right" actions and objects. By setting the frames and inventing new rules, educators and older participants exercise power over younger ones. A rule prescribes that the girl who has the best hand-sewn dress and scarf takes the role of the "Mansi princess" for whose sake the battle takes place. The jury commission who makes the decision consists of female educators as well as "grandmothers" who are seen as authentic representatives of tradition. In contrast, during previous years, the role of the princess was given by chance: all girls had to draw lots. The transfer from random chance to a formal process of election signals a more educative thrust in the play and emphasises the importance of hand-made aesthetics. One young female educator and long-term participant of the camp laughed: "When we are in the city I can't force these girls to sew anything. They are always busy with something else. But here they do it by themselves". This observation suggests that the medium of play, especially when embedded in a particular place, speaks to young people and seems to resolve the problem of their lack of interest in ethnic tradition and language. In Saranpaul' or Khanty-Mansiisk young people may find "ethnic tradition" as worthy of being preserved, but still too "boring" to get engaged with.

But even if educators expect the young warriors to select their respective bride on the basis of her skills rather than her bodily appearance, in general boys do know in advance whom they would like to "marry" or they mutually arrange "marriage" with the girl they like. They memorise the dress or scarf of the girl before the ceremony. Girls also leave signs for boys, so they stay recognisable. One nineteen-year-old girl stated that she would prefer the role play without a scarf, so she stays recognisable for elite warriors and can be married to a chief. Remarks and strategies of players show that their views diverge from the camp leaders' educational thrust. Contradictions, inconsistency, and fluidity in attitudes not only between players and educators, but also within the groups make the role play and the revival project a continuous playful process of negotiation over power and meaning.

Girls have diverging opinions about their own role in the role-playing game and the reference framework beyond the play. Thus, sewing is not every girl's favourite activity. For some of them it is a question of personal "talent" and "endurance" rather than a task to be mastered by each and every woman, as it used to be in the past. Some of them mentioned that if they had a choice they would rather contribute to the game with other skills and talents they have. The degree of devotion to the educational objectives of the camp may impact on the benevolence from the side of leaders.

Other female participants pursue ethnic self-stylisation as their own leisure-time project. They take an initiative to talk to elders in their community outside the camp and are eager to learn how to sew a traditional dress, plait braids, and make other accessories. After the crafting process they hope to enjoy the possibility to wear their accessories during ethnic festivities in the district or other events such as future summer camps. However, the personal motivation of girls to

Fig. 9.2. A warrior chooses his bride. Photograph by Sergei Remizov, near Saranpaul, 2016. Courtesy of the photographer, CC-BY-ND.

get skilled in handicraft is usually rooted in their wish to take part in the role-playing game and in the internal competition among them to have the best outfit during the marriage ceremony. I was amazed how much creativity and sophistication they employed within a very short time to decorate empty sheets of fabric with old shreds, coloured threads and beads to attain an individual and outstanding look.

Girls' opinions on their own engagement in the role-playing game cover the whole range from wishing to be involved in fighting to deliberately respecting the "tradition" and performing their roles as wives the best they can. One girl named Nastia (aged 22 at the time of interviewing) stated: "For me the game is a connection with the world of our ancestors. Everything has been lost and now we try to resurrect that. I see how boys are fighting with so much enthusiasm and interest and I like it. And then I fantasise that the gods in the sky are happy that it is all preserved, it is alive and not forgotten". Most of the participating girls agree that they would like to have different, more exciting tasks, e.g. in the strategy-planning and decision-making process of the game. Some of them voice their wishes during common meetings, but also put to use their agency during the course of the role play, finding possibilities of action that are not yet codified in rules. However, they often find themselves restricted by fear of being excluded from playing for breaking the rules. Most girls keep their minds on plaiting friendship bracelets, telling each other stories, and supporting their husbands, while the warriors are thinking of strategies and searching for their enemies in the forest.

In the first year of the *Time of Singing Arrows*, girls were not even allowed to go to the fortress and did not play any role in the game at all. They beautified the camp and waited until boys came back from the battle. In the following years they were granted roles as wives and were eager to take part in the playing process. As of 2012, however, even the "Mansi princess" played a merely symbolic role and did not decide the course of the game. While in previous years girls used to scream, shout, and cry when their tribe faced an attack, now they restrain themselves from showing emotions and sit together silently in a circle, holding each other's hands. They channel the "energy" to their husbands to make them strong and courageous. Some girls report about an inner feeling of "strength" that emerges in them during such exercises. Their behaviour is a result of a comment made by a Mansi scholar on some girls' emotional outbursts during attacks. She reminded them that a Mansi woman used to be even-tempered, did not show her emotions, and cried only if a situation required it (for example, during a funeral ceremony).[5] This "traditionalist" view was indirectly challenged by a psychologist, who was also invited to the camp to assist adolescents and youth to foster their self-confidence. She counselled participants from a "western" psychology perspective, implying that it is healthier to express one's emotions instead of suppressing them. Both contrasting views on personhood find their implementation in discourses and practices of the role-playing game depending on the situation. Especially men are seen to be prone to unrestrained emotional and physical behaviour. As one young woman, 23-year-old Zhenia, stated:

> A man is a warrior anyway. It does not depend on their nationality. For a long time it is written in their genes. It is better if they get rid of their energy (*vypleskivat' energiiu*) here than in brawls in discos and cafés. It happens anyway. And men are fairer than women. The female [gender] is always about emotions. Look at psychology! And men can stand it if they have a bodily injury. Girls should have another role [than men].

---

5   Lapina (2008) provides similar accounts of female ethics among Khanty.

Her argument mirrors public discourses in Russia that embrace two contrasting views on men: on the one hand, their physical as well as mental superiority in relation to women, and on the other, men's susceptibility to aggressive behaviour, drinking, and violence (Kay 2006: 21ff.). While men need spaces to channel their excessive energies — as in the logic of the role-playing game — in order to be rational and reliable, women are naturally involved with emotions such as care and tenderness. This view dismisses the fact that girls are also now and then involved in quarrels and express aggressive behaviour. In everyday life in Saranpaul', girls and women face violence in a direct or indirect way and need to defend themselves. As one girl expressed it: "I have a third world war at home: my father is drunk". I often heard from young women about how they try to let out their aggression at home, in a bar, or a disco. I would like to quote a young female participant, twenty-year-old Ania, who stressed the importance of resurrecting the image of a "female warrior" too. We were locked in the fortress for the whole day and waited for attacks from the invading tribe. Ania passionately commented:

> I came here and wanted to play [...] And then on Mansi territory it is forbidden for girls to fight. OK, but [at least] I want to see the fight [...] there should be rules, but not that fixed. I don't see the sense [in it if] as soon there is an attack, we have to run into the hut. We cannot see anything, we can only listen [...] We came here and can only cook tea and soup. And I don't think that it is so interesting. We stay just like slaves. I want to see this fight. If I cannot participate, I would like to look at it. But we can't [...] I need to see the tactic, so that it helps me in the future. But I don't see anything [...] Women in our modern time are like victims. Daughter[s], wife[s], sister[s] are mainly like victims. But there are female warrior archetypes; they disappeared a long time ago. And now we have to try to resurrect that. Because indigenous people, Khanty and Mansi, they are also like victims. I think it would be very important.

Ania mentions a double vulnerability of indigenous women: as being subjects of Russian colonial power and a paternalistic state as well as patriarchal family structures. She is also looking for empowerment through "tradition", but with an alternative message. Similar to educators she also wants to instrumentalise the role-playing game for the purpose of self-cultivation and at the same time to retrieve her ancestral memory of a female warrior archetype.

Young men: "the spirit of the warrior"

Fantasies of male participants expand the notion of local ethnic belonging and reach out to game avatars and other media heroes they associate with. As Pasha, aged nineteen at the time of interviewing, puts it: "The strategies we use are from computer games and literature. We combine the old written sources and computer games, so that no-one knows what our next step is". Most adolescents and young men play computer games such as *Warcraft* or *Counter-Strike* at home (a public computer salon was opened in Saranpaul' in 2012). Young people emphasise that because of physical involvement in the battle they experience it as emotionally more intense than a computer game. For example, 22-year-old Tolik says: "In the computer game I don't have such a feeling. In the battle I felt myself as a real warrior. I had a sensation, I wanted to go and fight". However, young people also incorporate the rhetoric of elders into the reflection of their own experiences. Tolik goes on to say:

> During the camp the spirit of the warrior wakes up. Exactly through the dances, taking part in martial art workshops, you start to open your treasure chests and the ancestral memory wakes up. This memory is revealing itself during the battle when you run through the forest or direct the troops or fight with someone.

From my observation, the imaginative connection of warriors to their powerful, skilful ancestors stands often in sharp contrast to the loose links between (living) members of different generations and to the lack of knowledge of one's family history. So Tolik admitted that although he visits the camp every year, he has never been to his grandfather's old house located in a Mansi village not far from Saranpaul'.

Most male players are interested in making the role play fairer among themselves and are less concerned with addressing the girls' wishes and ideas. Nevertheless, they comment that the boredom of girls sometimes undermines the fighting spirit of warriors and disturbs the course of the game. The direct or indirect support of the strict dichotomy in gender roles echoes their views about the ideal of patriarchal family relations at home. "A woman should listen to her husband" is one frequent answer, but at the same time some are admitting that in daily life everything can be different.

Masculinity should not only be displayed at home but also on the street. Risk-taking behaviour and quarrels happen almost on a day-to-day basis, especially when alcohol is consumed in a disco or a bar. The term *patsan* is commonly applied as a respectful reference to an adolescent or a young man who is fair, "straight", can stand up for himself and the "weaker" sex. A *patsan* should not show fear to enter a fight, but also be eloquent in colloquial language. Expressing one's weaknesses means to be bullied by others, a fact that can spoil a boy's self-confidence and affect his performance in the army where bullying is part of hierarchical relationships (cf. Kay 2006: 48–49). As one young man mentioned, the role-playing game can provide an adolescent with skills to use his head first, and to think of a strategy when he is insulted or bullied rather than responding with physical force.

A contrasting view of a *patsan* was mentioned by another young warrior, Aleksandr (aged twenty at the time of interviewing), who explained to me that from his own observations young men today are not self-reliant, are afraid to take any initiative in love affairs, and cannot cope with broken relationships. From his point of view, a short-term role-playing game is an insignificant contribution to strengthen the willpower (*ukreplenie voli*) in young people, which should rather be trained throughout the whole year at school and other institutions. He sadly mentioned a friend who recently committed suicide. The deceased boy attended the camp in 2009 and was chosen as a tribe's chief in the role-playing game. Being back in the settlement he could not handle the problems that accumulated in his family, relationship, and job. According to Aleksandr, people might lose their "inner core" (*vnutrennii sterzhen'*) when "tradition" becomes just an attachment to the everyday life. According to his view, "tradition" and beliefs give a human a "core" in life. For him the game is less about "fighting", and more an "immersion into ancient times". Players should sense the atmosphere of that period, try to use their head when making decisions, and be less concerned about winning the game.

In fact, the emotional and physical investment of male players causes them even to lose their voices for a day or two at the end of the game. Denis, a 22-year-old tribe chief stated:

> It is really a lot of adrenaline, a surge of adrenaline. You can say [people are] fully engaged in the battle and they are tearing off each other's

braids. It means that skill and strength are the most important factors. It depends on your own level of development. It makes you think: if you are a good warrior, then you are a good warrior. If a man is somehow weak, then in the battle he will lose very fast.

Particular actions in the play frame may give players a feeling that they are surpassing their present selves. For example, the experience of dancing may change the self-perception of a young person. As one young warrior mentioned: "We danced and raised our spirit. I felt myself higher than a warrior somehow [...] Not as a warrior, but something higher". He did not have exact words for his experience and turned silent after mentioning it. Other warriors experience unexpected strength and are able to do things that go beyond their usual everyday abilities. One young man reported that he jumped over a two-meter high fortress wall in one jump in order to "save his life".

The "full engagement" in the game means that warriors not only have heroic feelings, but are also confronted with their own fears. Some adolescents tear down their own braids to leave the game, or are strongly frightened when they have to jump down into the fortress. Players who are particularly fearful are an object of discussion between educators and adult players in supervision meetings, who then think of strategies to involve them into the game. One young man told me in an interview: "There are people you have to work with a lot, so they overcome their fear". Again, the narrative of gendered "working on oneself" and on others is coming through in such value judgments of one's own and other people's performances. Those warriors who have shown extraordinary courage, agility, and cunning are publicly rewarded by educators as well as co-players at the end of the game.

Not all players use a meta-language to reflect upon the role-playing game rules, its goals, and educational thrust. That may differ according to their age and status in the game and in the camp. In interviews young players spoke passionately about their experiences, emotions, victories, and defeats in the role-playing game. Their comments support the view of play-theorists that "rhetoric and the play are never identical" (Sutton-Smith 1997: 77). For many of them the role play is self-referential and does not point to anything beyond the play itself. It is about fun, performance, friendships, and courting the opposite sex.

Conclusion

As this case study shows, play entails competing and contrasting messages. I argue that play with its ambiguous nature enables social actors to shift between the secular and sacred, the subjunctive and indicative, the real and imaginative. According to Sutton-Smith (1997) religion and play have something in common — a power of alterity. The role-playing game allows players to imagine themselves as someone else and yet to anchor themselves in their own local history and identity. The play offers an experimental way to reimagine the pre-colonial Mansi past and to make it more appealing for youth. Yet the playful engagement with the indigenous past in the camp should not be seen as fake, superficial, or "stylised". As the statement of the camp director indicates, it is a serious endeavour: "we don't play life here, we live here" (*my ne igraem v zhizn', my zdes' zhivem*). The imaginative past is played out in the present Mansi village, where spirits may be evoked and where the game has tangible effects on its participants.

The Soviet legacy and post-Soviet turn to essentialised identities and the desecularisation of culture provide a sounding board for social actors to shift between the secular and the sacred. Therewith female educators contested the Soviet view on pedagogy that a human can be shaped like a sculpture and claimed that nature plays an important role in the right upbringing of the young generation. Such characteristics as one's sex and ethnic background should be taken into account when encouraging young people to cultivate themselves. I suggest that the Soviet secular ideal of "working on oneself" and the semi-religious idea of "ancestral memory", even though they seem to contradict each other, are intertwined and at times complement each other. Engagement with objects and practices rendered as "traditional" serves both ends: it is integral to cultivating one's skills and moral attitudes on the one hand, and potentially evokes one's innate knowledge, belonging, and spirituality, on the other. Ideally, educators hoped that each participant of the camp would recognise themselves in terms of their ethnicity and would be interested to find out more about their ethnic roots after leaving the camp.

The generated world of the role-playing game and the camp in general are rendered to be more authentic than everyday life since they stimulate participants to discover their "real self". In the context of a marginal socio-economic situation, educators' rhetoric and practice is such that play is framed as a ritual that intends to transform the players — firstly young men and thereby indirectly also young women — to alter their sense of self and the meaning of their existence. Visual aesthetics serves a double function that is oriented inward and outward: on the one hand, to mediate particular values to young people, and on the other, to communicate social difference in the public space. It is meant to oppose negative aspects that are publicly associated with youth from a socially disadvantaged background in general and with Mansi in particular. The distinct mode of being in the summer camp amounts therefore to a temporary lifestyle within a micro-community of the camp, which may turn into a sense of lifestyle (in Chaney's terms) for those who participate repeatedly. Participants are meant to acquire a sense of life in their "real life" which would translate into particular sensibilities and certain practices.

Participants in their turn negotiate and perform values of what they consider Mansi tradition, re-fashion themselves, and accumulate particular forms of knowledge. As I argued elsewhere: "Youth emphasized various self-subjectivation practices and used a range of possibilities to articulate their ethical sensibilities, which selectively embraced values promoted in the camp and combined them with other practices and conceptions that surrounded them" (Schröder 2017: 182). The multiple framing allows girls and boys to manoeuvre between the interpretation of the role-playing game as "just play" or "tradition" according to the situation. While both sides were interested to raise their stakes for the opposite sex, girls felt that their aspiration to play a more prominent role in the game did not find resonance among educators. Similar to boys they also wished to have fun and to engage themselves in the playful side of the event. In her analysis of play, Lindquist challenges a conventional romantic view of play as intrinsically free. For her, play can serve the relations of domination and submission (Lindquist 2001: 18). The recognised Mansi identity inside the camp implied that girls needed to accept gender hierarchies and male leadership as "natural". Yet, they were also able to shift to the subjunctive mode and refer to gender hierarchies as "play".

For many participants, the role-playing stays self-referential as an intense experience within the liminal space of the camp. The camp life is contrasted to life in the settlement or the city as two different and not reconcilable realities. After the camp season is over it continues to live in their memories, on visual media, and the social network side VKontakte. They dream on about who will be their spouse in the next year's role play and a few get involved in the social organisation of the camp for the next summer vacation.

References

Bassin, Mark & Catriona Kelly (eds). 2012. *Soviet and Post-Soviet Identities*. Cambridge: Cambridge University Press, https://doi.org/10.1017/CBO9780511894732

Bateson, Gregory. 2000 [1972]. *Steps to an Ecology of Mind*. Chicago, IL: University of Chicago Press.

Barchunova, Tatiana & Natal'ia Beletskaia. 2009–2010. "Are play regiments really for play? Military practices in Novosibirsk: simulation of military actions in role-playing games for young people and militarized games for adults". *Anthropology & Archeology of Eurasia*, 48 (3): 9–30, https://doi.org/10.2753/aae1061-1959480301

Broz, Ludek. 2009. "Substance, conduct, and history: 'Altaianness' in the twenty-first century". *Sibirica*, 8 (2): 43–70, https://doi.org/10.3167/sib.2009.080202

Chaney, David. 1996. *Lifestyles*. London: Routledge, https://doi.org/10.4324/9780203137468

Donahoe, Brian & Joachim Otto Habeck (eds). 2011. *Reconstructing the House of Culture: community, self, and the makings of culture in Russia and beyond*. New York: Berghahn.

Droogers, André. 2012. *Play and Power in Religion: collected essays*. Berlin: De Gruyter.

Eward, Elizabeth & Michael O'Hanlon (eds). 2007. *Body Arts and Modernity*. Wantage: Sean Kingston.

Fedorova, Elena G. 1988. "Rebënok v traditsionnoi mansiiskoi sem'e" [The child in traditional Mansi family]. In: *Traditsionnoe vospitanie detei u narodov Sibiri*, ed. Igor' S. Kon & Chuner M. Taksami, pp. 80–95. Leningrad: Nauka.

—. 2000. "The role of women in Mansi society". In: *Hunters and Gatherers in the Modern World: conflict, resistance, and self-determination*, ed. Peter P. Schweitzer, Megan Biesele & Robert K. Hitchcock, pp. 391–98. New York: Berghahn.

Habeck, Joachim Otto. 2014. *Das Kulturhaus in Russland: postsozialistische Kulturarbeit zwischen Ideal und Verwahrlosung* [The House of Culture in Russia:

post-socialist culture work between ideal and degradation]. Bielefeld: transcript, https://doi.org/10.14361/transcript.9783839427125

—, Brian Donahoe & Siegfried Gruber. 2011. "Constellations of culture work in present-day Siberia". In: *Reconstructing the House of Culture: community, self, and the making of culture in Russia and beyond,* ed. Brian Donahoe & Joachim Otto Habeck, pp. 137–60. New York: Berghahn.

Halemba, Agnieszka E. 2006. *The Telengits of Southern Siberia: landscape, religion and knowledge in motion.* London: Routledge, https://doi.org/10.4324/9780203008102

Hobsbawm, Eric J. & Terence Ranger (eds). 1999 [1983]. *The Invention of Tradition.* Cambridge: Cambridge University Press, https://doi.org/10.1017/CBO9781107295636

Holland, Dorothy, William Lachicotte Jr, Debra Skinner & Carole Cain. 2001. *Identity and Agency in Cultural Worlds.* Cambridge, MA: Harvard University Press.

Kay, Rebecca. 2006. *Men in Contemporary Russian Society: the fallen heroes of post-Soviet change?* Aldershot: Ashgate, https://doi.org/10.4324/9781315249162

Khlinovskaya Rockhill, Elena. 2010. *Lost to the State: family discontinuity, social orphanhood and residential care in the Russian Far East.* New York: Berghahn.

King, Alexander. 2009. "Dancing in the house of Koryak culture". *Folklore: Electronic Journal of Folklore,* 41: 143–62, https://doi.org/10.7592/fejf2009.41.king

Kuebart, Friedrich. 1989. "The political socialization of school children". In *Soviet Youth Culture,* ed. Jim Riordan, pp. 103–22. Bloomington, IN: Indiana University Press, https://doi.org/10.1007/978-1-349-19932-7_5

Lapina, Maina A. 2008. *Etika i etiket khantov* [Ethics and etiquette of the Khanty]. Ekaterinburg: Basko.

Lindquist, Galina. 2001. "Elusive play and its relations to power". *Focaal: European Journal of Anthropology,* 37: 13–23.

Linnekin, Jocelyn. 1992. "On the theory and politics of cultural construction in the Pacific". *Oceania* 62 (4): 249–63, https://doi.org/10.1002/j.1834-4461.1992.tb00356.x

Luehrmann, Sonja. 2005. "Recycling cultural construction: desecularisation in post-Soviet Mari El". *Religion, State and Society,* 33 (1): 35–56, https://doi.org/10.1080/0963749042000330857

Popova, Svetlana A. 2003. *Obriady perekhoda v traditsionnoi kul'ture mansi* [Rites of passage in traditional Mansi culture]. Tomsk: Izdatel'stvo Tomskogo Universiteta.

Povoroznyuk, Olga, Joachim Otto Habeck & Virginie Vaté. 2010. "Introduction: on the definition, theory, and practice of gender shift in the North of Russia". *Anthropology of East Europe Review*, 28 (2): 1–37.

Schröder, Ina. 2017. "Shaping Youth: quest for moral education in an indigenous community in western Siberia". Doctoral thesis, Martin-Luther-Universität Halle-Wittenberg.

Sokolova, Zoia P. 2009. *Khanty i mansi: vzgliad iz XXI veka* [Khanty and Mansi: view from the twenty-first century]. Moscow: Nauka.

Ssorin-Chaikov, Nikolai. 2003. *The Social Life of the State in Subarctic Siberia*. Stanford, CA: Stanford University Press.

Sutton-Smith, Brian. 1997. *The Ambiguity of Play*. Cambridge, MA: Harvard University Press.

Ulturgasheva, Olga. 2012. *Narrating the Future in Siberia: childhood, adolescence and autobiography among the Eveny*. New York: Berghahn.

Wiget, Andrew & Ol'ga E. Balalaeva. 2011. *Khanty: people of the taiga — surviving the twentieth century*. Fairbanks, AK: University of Alaska Press.

Zakon. 2004. Zakon "O perechne trudnodostupnykh i otdalennykh mestnostei [...]" [On the list of hard-to-access and remote locations]. Law issued by the Khanty-Mansi Autonomous Okrug — Yugra on 31 December 2004 (with later amendments), http://pravo.gov.ru/proxy/ips/?doc_itself=&backlink=1&nd=187014894&page=1&rdk=11#I0

Zigon, Jarrett (ed.). 2011. *Multiple Moralities and Religions in Post-Soviet Russia*. New York: Berghahn.

10. A Taste for Play

Lifestyle and Live-Action Role-Playing in Siberia and the Russian Far East

Tatiana Barchunova and Joachim Otto Habeck

The goal of this chapter is to understand how participation in Live-Action Role-Playing (LARP) influences the lives and self-perceptions of those Siberians who are involved in this scene, and how the boundary between play and "real life" is being continually constructed and yet often disregarded at the same time. We start with a short overview of the present-day Siberian LARP scene; then we discuss taste, play, and game in relation to the concept of lifestyle; further, we examine the construction and transcendence of the borders that delineate "play" and "reality" as different modes of existence. Finally, we discuss the varying degrees of involvement that different players have in the game — from casual players to those for whom LARP is all-encompassing — which, in our opinion, is the key factor when it comes to understanding LARP as a distinct lifestyle.

Theoretically, we proceed from four ideas: first, the connection between *taste and lifestyle*, established by Pierre Bourdieu, and second, David Chaney's notions of *lifestyle and play* (both these ideas will be exposed in detail in the second section). Third, we draw on Mikhail Bakhtin's concept of *chronotope* to describe the designation of a certain space as a playground with its own rules and temporal setting. Fourth, we discuss Johan Huizinga's ideas on the *separation of play and real life*.

 https://doi.org/10.11647/OBP.0171.10

In conclusion, we will argue that role players transcend this boundary frequently, and for the most devoted role players, the differentiation between game and life is not applicable.

Empirically, we draw on interviews conducted in the framework of the CLLP project (presented in the Appendix) with a dozen interviewees in Novosibirsk (carried out by Tatiana Barchunova, henceforward abbreviated as TB) and six interviewees in Vladivostok (carried out by Natal'ia Beletskaia, and analysed for this chapter by Joachim Otto Habeck). The authors also make use of interviews and participant observation in other LARP settings.

Live-action role-playing (LARP) in Siberia today

The Siberian LARP scene emerged in the early 1990s and then grew rapidly, with a diversification into different genres. It covers the so-called historical re-enactment games, based on various periods of world history (including the reconstruction of global historical events or of certain periods in the history of indigenous peoples); fantasy games, based on books or film plots; freely invented scenarios, written by LARP leaders; strike-ball games, etc. The participants of these various playing activities often describe themselves as members of the "movement of role-playing games" (*dvizhenie rolevykh igr*). However, recently, the term "role-playing games" has come to be used to designate computer games too. In order to differentiate between computer and live-action games, the acronym LARP is now colloquially used for the latter. It refers to a variety of games beginning from large-scale field games with hundreds of participants and ending with pavilion games with only two or three people involved. LARP games are thus part of a wider ludic[1] scene which also includes computer games, "classic" table games, gambling, quiz sessions and other contests, geo-cashing, urban games at night time, car-based quests, cosplay, and many more.

The first role-playing game in Russia was held in Krasnoiarsk in 1990. It was arranged along the lines of J. R. R. Tolkien' s writings and was called *Hobbit games* (*Khobbitskie igrishcha*).[2] Since then, the movement has

---

1   The term "ludic" is used here as a shorthand for "related to play".
2   http://vk.com/club19866195 — "Letopis' Pervykh KhI [Khobbitskikh Igrishch] [Chronicle of the First Hobbit Games] (1990)" on the social networking site VKontakte.

spread over the whole country and diversified significantly (Barchunova & Beletskaia 2004). It is hard to tell how many people were involved in the original movement or any of its later diversified fractions. In the beginning, the LARP movement was publicly almost invisible; it was either ignored or maligned as some sort of deviance. Some priests of the Orthodox Church discussed "tolkienism" as a dangerous occult movement (Steniaev 1999) and mainstream journalists often categorised it as a "subculture" with all the pejorative connotations of the word, including the idea of diversion from and degradation of "proper" culture. However, since approximately the mid-2000s, a small number of publications have analysed various aspects of the LARP scene in Russia (for an overview, see Pisarevskaia 2011: 24–31; see also Kopytin 2016; Vorobyeva 2015).

Nowadays, every big city or town in the Russian Federation seems to have its own LARP club(s), informal association(s) of players, and/ or regular LARP events. Besides spontaneous and well-planned annual games of all sorts, there exist various regular and irregular conventions and festivals of role players being held in Bratsk, Cheliabinsk, Ekaterinburg, Kazan', Magnitogorsk, Moscow, Novgorod, Novosibirsk, St Petersburg, Samara, Tomsk, and other places. These are gatherings of different scale with tens or hundreds of participants from Russia and neighbouring countries. In this chapter, we will refer to the participants as "larpers" (as the English equivalent of the emic term *roleviki*, literally "role persons"). Our usage of larpers includes participants of both fantasy role-playing games and historical re-enactment games. The reason for this indiscriminate usage is that the most prominent event of the ludic scene in Novosibirsk (and arguably, Siberia in general) is the so-called "military-historical role-playing game 'Makarena'" (*Voenno-istoricheskaia rolevaia igra "Makarena"*), which is a mixed form of role-playing and historical re-enactment, as illustrated in subsequent sections.

At the first stage of the LARP movement, the so-called "curtain larpers" (*zanovesochniki*) had to use any pieces of leather, metal, lace, fabric (including used curtains) at hand under the conditions of the shortage of consumer goods in the 1990s. As of now, some participants produce rather sophisticated costumes and equipment for the games, they buy expensive natural materials (leather, linen, lace, beads) in special shops and on the internet. The logistics of the games have also become more complex. Some larpers use their own cars to travel to the game sites, sometimes they rent buses and cars for the equipment. The organisation of LARP conventions and festivals is also more elaborate now. The accommodation standards and demands tend to be higher.

The concept of lifestyle and its relevance to taste, play, and game

Taste is one of the key elements in the acquisition and expression of specific lifestyles. In his book *Distinction*, Bourdieu argued:

> Taste, the propensity and capacity to appropriate (materially or symbolically) a given class of classified, classifying objects or practices, is the generative formula of life-style, a unitary set of distinctive preferences which express the same expressive intention in the specific logic of each of the symbolic sub-spaces, furniture, clothing, language or body hexis (1984: 173).

In other words, personal predilections that shape the ambience of one's home or determine the choice of apparel should be understood as part of the "same expressive intention", and such expressive intention also comes to the fore in the domain of play and other leisure activities. Individuals have a propensity to cluster around shared expressive intentions: it is through such communities of taste that lifestyles become manifest as inter-personal, i.e. social phenomena. We will show in this chapter that this statement is valid for those members of the LARP community who pursue role-playing with a certain frequency and intensity.

According to Chaney, lifestyle "is a style, a manner, a way of using certain goods, places and times that is characteristic of a group but is not the totality of their social experience" (1996: 5). This interpretation is relevant to the subject of our research for several reasons. First of all, it addresses the appropriation of space and time and the usage of goods available. LARP in all its different forms, especially in the version of historical re-enactment or modelling of the future, deals with a special form of appropriation of time and space (more about that below), and it always entails the construction and application of paraphernalia (game accessories, or to use the emic term — *anturazh*, from the French word *entourage*).

Let us begin with the latter aspect, i.e. the material side of the games. The concept of lifestyle in Chaney's interpretation underlines the importance of patterns of consumption as reflexive projects (1996: 14–24, 112–13). The acquisition or do-it-yourself production of material objects are to be understood as meaningful acts, and it is in this way that consumption also entails production of meanings as well as it presupposes a certain attitude to the value of production in general. Within LARP this dialectic of consumption and production also takes place. There are common trends in mass consumption of goods among both mainstream[3] and marginal groups, including participants of ludic practices: for example, since the early 2000s, both mainstream and larpers' patterns of consumption decreasingly feature self-made things. Consumption is getting increasingly commercialised, differentiated, and sophisticated. This tendency is a subject of a public discussion in which individuals express their views on consumption and position themselves ethically around this issue. The value of what is self-made (or home-grown) as opposed to what is ready-made is a frequent theme of discussion and self-stylisation, and in the LARP scene this issue has gained particular topicality, as shall become clear further below.

Discussing the problem of identity (self) and consumption, Chaney draws on game as a metaphor and connects it with the idea of unpredictability:

> [...] if the meanings of things we are using or employing are unpredictable, then at least part of what they, the objects, will be taken to mean is dependent upon who is using them and how they are being used. And in the same way who we are — as active players in the *games* of consumption — is constructed and displayed through how we employ the resources of the *game* (1996: 113, emphasis added).

Contrary to the common sense understanding of consumption as a routine practice of consuming pre-established and pre-given items, Chaney thus stresses its creative aspects: it is both consumption and cultural production. In his chapter on lifestyle sites and strategies, he

---

3   The term "mainstream" is used here for tastes and preferences widely accepted as normal, not necessarily in need of explanation, and in this sense not necessarily reflexive.

portrays lifestyles as creative projects, as "forms of *enactment* in which actors make judgements in delineating an environment" (Chaney 1996: 92, emphasis added).

Second, in his analysis of the lifestyle concept Chaney stresses some other aspects of this notion which are related to games and playing. These are: "theatrical sociality", "dramaturgy of modern life", "playful forms" of civilised conduct, and modern life as a spectacle. A special section of Chaney's book on lifestyles deals with various concepts of lifestyle as symbolic exchange. One of the forms of symbolic exchange which is an important constituent of lifestyle is fashion. Here he refers to the account by Jean Baudrillard, who discusses fashion as "theatrical sociality" (Baudrillard 1993: 94, quoted by Chaney 1996: 54). The term is meant to express the idea that the display of fashion and other elements of outer appearance follows its own logic and purpose: display has the goal to attract the attention of others, and it is in this sense that sociability attains "theatrical" character. Though role-playing does not presuppose an audience (spectators) as such, it obviously belongs to a theatrical form of sociality, as we will argue in the conclusion.

Furthermore, in discussing the research of the origins of "civilized behavior" by Norbert Elias (1978: 79), Chaney mentions the importance of "playful forms" of human conduct (1996: 115). For Chaney, one of the essential elements of lifestyle is displaying difference, which he categorises through the concept of surfaces: "The *play* of surfaces creates distinctions that are matters of framing rather than qualitative difference. In the *dramaturgy* of appearance all actions are forms of performance" (1996: 123, emphasis added). The significance of surfaces, in its turn, is associated with the general trait of the unstable, fluid reality of modern "societies of spectacle" (ibid: 93). Not only here, but also in several other contexts does Chaney apply notions of game, play, and spectacle to his analysis of lifestyle and mass culture. For instance, when he analyses the approach to social practices by Michel de Certeau, he mentions that de Certeau suggests three types of practices through which "actors in everyday life manipulate established forms of knowledge and discourse in order to appropriate the 'stuff' of mass society for idiosyncratic perspectives" (Chaney 1996: 74). Those are "games, accounts, and tales and legends" (ibid.).

The above conceptualisations of lifestyle in terms of ludic elements — dramaturgy, spectacle, enactment, and game — seem to be following the trend of approaching social reality in terms of performance and enactment, which can clearly be seen in recent social theory, empirical research, and all sorts of playful simulations used in psychotherapy, business, and teaching.

The universal application of ludic metaphors to the analysis of social reality makes the analysis of games and playing *per se* a special challenge, as can be seen already in Huizinga's influential book *Homo Ludens* (1949), in which he exposes the history of culture as the history of playing. For Huizinga, human civilisation is rooted in playing: every sphere of life is imbued with ludic elements. However — and this deserves special attention — he argues that game and play are separated from "real life" in space and time (Huizinga 1949: Chapter 1). This act of universalising of the ludic element, on the one hand, and the act of separating it from the "real life" experience, on the other, seems to be a contradiction that calls for closer examination (Getsy 2011: xii; Hankiss 2001: 222; Norbeck 1974: 2), to be achieved through research of particular forms of games and play. To formulate this game/life paradox in other words: if playing is indeed separated from the "real world", then how can one argue that every sphere of life is imbued with ludic elements? In this paper we are going to address this paradox empirically through the analysis of LARP activities and participants' degrees of involvement.

LARP as practice: separation and mixture of game and reality

LARP is a practice that has several key variables: the intensity and duration of preliminary organisation of the game, the space appropriated, duration of the game (or enactment as such), the number of participants, the quantity and quality of financial and other resources involved, intensity, and means of communication before, during, and after the game. Additionally, games differ considerably in their aesthetic design, the level of ludic conventions and symbolism, institutional support, and organisation.

The paradigm case of LARP is a big field game which can be characterised through its core and periphery. The core of the game is the enactment of the game scenario by the majority of participants, which happens at a certain location over a certain period of time, usually a long weekend but occasionally up to more than one week. The conventional term for this site is the Russian word *poligon* (the same as *polygon* in English), and used by the military to refer to shooting ranges. Many (though by far not all) LARP sites are in fact located on territories of abandoned army grounds.

The space of the *poligon* is symbolically appropriated through the ascription of ludic temporality. In other words, by delineating the space and relocating it in time, the place is taken out of the surrounding reality and undergoes historical stylisation. Thus, time and place in this case are merged together and constitute a time-place conglomerate which can be referred to by Bakhtin's term *chronotope*.[4]

The delineation of the site, the declaration of a particular chronotope, is an obvious act of separating the game from the "real world" in Huizinga's sense. Moreover, there are certain stages, some of them carefully ritualised, that mark the passage from the real world into the chronotope of the game (cf. Pisarevskaia 2011: 148–51; Copier 2005: 9). The journey to the *poligon*, the change of dress, and the opening parade are the most important of these, as will be discussed below. Similarly, several events mark the passage from the game back into the real world. The organisers have to arrange and maintain these "gates" and they do so very consciously. The participants are usually fully aware of such passages and experience them with heightened attention. For novices in particular, the experience of entering the field is a very emotional one. This passage definitely has strong resemblance with what has been described as the transformative potential of rituals (Turner 1969; see also Carlson 2004: 16–17). In some of the opening rituals, organisers purposefully push novices into a state of *communitas*, disconnecting them from the outer world and integrating them mentally into the chronotope.

Having said that, there are many aspects in the preparation of the game, the discussion after the game, and also critical moments that may occur during the game which deny the idea of a strict separation. This

---

4   Bakhtin applies this concept to interpret various forms of interpretation of connection between time and space in different narratives (Bakhtin 1981; for a recent exegesis see Bemong & Borghart 2010). A similar concept of time-space is used by John Urry (2007: 15, 29, 118–24).

is not only a problem of border maintenance or a question of where to draw the line between the core of the chronotope and the periphery, but it is more generally about the unintended or intentional intermingling of game and "real life", about the transposition of objects, language, and ethical judgements from one world into another (cf. Tychsen et al. 2006: 268). The analysis below is centred on a big field game, "Makarena", and exemplifies this subversion of the classical distinction between game and actual life as separate modes of existence.

Fig. 10.1. A scene from the live-action role play "Black Prince" (*Chërnyi Prints*) in 2018 as part of the annual "Makarena" events. Source: https://vk.com/club27365038?z=album-27365038_253779390

Organisers and participants

A field game is a creative project; it constitutes a mode of cultural production. The project is usually organised by a group of masters headed by a leader, or "main master" (*glavnyi master*). The game masters select a game site, write the game scenario, and thereby establish the ludic reality which is called "the world" (*mir*). The scenario may be either completely invented or based on a historical event, an episode borrowed from a fictional book, or a plot of a movie. The scenario should draw on commonly shared cultural resources (for instance, deal with famous historical figures like Joan of Arc, Julius Caesar, King

Arthur, important historical events, or familiar fictional characters) and still be original enough to attract potential players. However, even if the scenario is based on historical facts or a fictional story, it is not designed to follow all details or historical data. The outcome of the game is open: there can be anachronisms or historically unconfirmed participants or events. In the case of the historical re-enactment scene of Novosibirsk, it is never strictly adherent to history. As Andrei Mel'nikov, one of the most prominent leaders of the Novosibirsk role-playing movement, says: "Well, in general, history is one thing and a game is something totally different. Here, everything can be, sort of, turned in a completely different way. Most important here is not to go beyond the frame of historical events".

The ludic world is constituted by roles, rules, and a plot. The plot determines some principal tasks to be fulfilled by people in different roles. Roles can be distributed by masters and/or the leader. But there can be individual participants who decide about their roles themselves. On a par with individual participants there are teams which have their own leaders. Inclusion of individuals — and even more so, whole teams — is usually subject to negotiation. For example, the online site (group) of Makarena 2013, the world of which is England in the early eleventh century, contained an announcement: "Applications from small teams of Scottish mercenaries will be considered separately".[5] The site also has links to documents that lay out the historical context and the protagonists, the "rules of fighting, rules of fortification, siege, of healers and methods of healing, economy and capture, and also the land of the dead".[6]

The Makarena forum currently counts more than 3,000 subscribers and the announcement of the 2018 game attracted approximately 3,500 clicks, though by far not all of the visitors of the online site actively participate in the games or online discussions. The actual number of participants in a game can vary from several tens to several hundred. The age of participants grows with the age of the movement itself — there are more elderly participants now than ten years ago, and it is no longer unusual to see people in their late thirties and forties.

---

5   http://vk.com/wall-27365038?own=1 — message posted to the group *Voenno-istoricheskaia rolevaia igra "Makarena"* on 24 May 2012 on VKontakte.

6   Ibid., message posted on 3 November 2012.

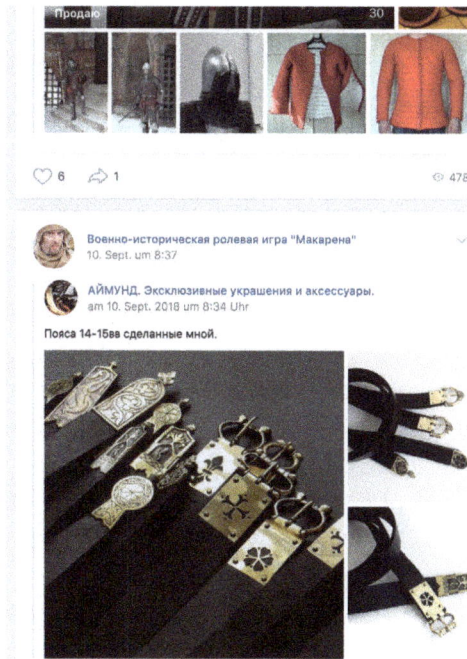

Fig. 10.2. Online forum for the "Makarena" on VKontakte. Screenshot as of 10 September 2018. The forum contains many posts about clothes, gear, weapons, etc. offered for exchange, purchase, or free of charge. Source: https://vk.com/club27365038

The majority of games are based on all kinds of militarian[7] actions against a symbolic enemy. However, there are moments of negotiations between alien parties, and periods of armistice. The civil life with its everyday economy is indispensable in the game, though up to now it has been secondary. Women can participate in the militarian activities through cross-dressing, but more often they are engaged in religious activities, medical care, and management of the ludic household. Game leaders tended to think that such ancillary roles are most suitable for women. Some of them came to acknowledge the need for paying more attention to the non-militarian aspects of the ludic world. The ludic life of women has become more diverse since the introduction of historical dances from about 2007. One of the first games when they were introduced was

---

7   The concept "militarian" was introduced by Tatiana Barchunova to designate various forms of symbolic representation of martial element in everyday life (Barchunova & Beletskaia 2009–2010).

Burgundian Wars (the Makarena event organised in 2007). Debates about ludic roles of women happen not only in Novosibirsk, but also, as Ina Schröder points out in Chapter 9 of this volume, in other regions and role-play settings.

While the masters and leaders set the rules of the game, they also participate and perform in it. Vadim Zevlever (nickname: Makar), the major master and name patron of the Makarena games, comments on this: "I also want to play. Why should I sit all dressed in camouflage on a chaise-longue drinking Cognac? That's not my business. Unlike football, a role-playing game allows the trainer also to play, at least a little bit." Sometimes, however, a master may decide to let the chronotope crack on purpose for a moment. Later we will return to the question of "being within" the chronotope and simultaneously "being beyond it".

Preparation of the game

The preparation of a big field game can take several months. The preparation covers advertisement of the project (as exemplified above), registration of participants, physical training of the teams, exercises in dancing, fencing, and other skills, sewing costumes, making armaments, providing artefacts for construction or reconstruction of everyday economy, and assembling other items of equipment. According to one of the game leaders, the best exercises to teach the skills of role-playing are verbal games: "Imagine that you are X, doing Y in situation Z". These exercises have some similarity with exercises in professional drama schools. They mark the initial stage of the participants immersing into the ludic world and identifying with their roles. The *anturazh* (additional equipment, accessories) is sometimes highly sophisticated and much time is invested in its creation. For instance, for the big field game *War of the Roses* (Makarena 2006) the girls who played students at a mediaeval university had designed a library collection. They printed out mediaeval philosophical treatises using Gothic fonts. The covers were decorated by strasses. The paper they used was tinted by tea so that the books would look authentically aged.

The final stage of preparation involves engineering and construction work at the game site itself. Field games are normally being held outside the urban space, in a forest or on abandoned military terrains.

Wood is available on the spot, but all the other building material needs to be transported to the game site, which usually requires cars or vans. Volunteers build symbolic civilian and militarian constructions which are used during the game. For example, for the same game a model of a temple was constructed, with vitrines made of transparent plastic films.

The format of the advertisement and organisation of games has substantially changed with widespread access to the internet since the 2000s. Initially, games were advertised at LARP conventions, through booklets printed by LARP community members, public bulletin boards (for instance, there was such a board at Novosibirsk State University), and informally, through mouth-to-mouth communication. Currently, LARP conventions are also used to present new projects and upcoming events. Small booklets are still printed and distributed but the printout has shrunk to several tens. The major means of sharing information is the internet. In the late 1990s there appeared the website rpg.nsk.ru for advertising games, assembling the LARP archive, and maintaining communication. Over the last years advertisements and communication are mostly facilitated through social networks such as VKontakte (vk.com). Every big game has its own group or site on the internet.

The process of preparation undermines the strict division between game and "real life" to a great extent. In the intervals between big field games their participants meet for training sessions; they arrange tournaments, festivals, and conventions in preparation of future games. In the framework of these interim sessions the game project participants wear ludic costumes, call each other by their ludic names, and learn about the rules and traditions of the ludic world. Therefore, according to Mel'nikov, the entry into the game actually begins at the stage of its preparation when participants learn to deal with each other as ludic characters.

Game entry

How does the transfer to the virtual world take place? How is the ludic identity acquired? Part of it, as we have seen, is already built up in the preparatory stage, but the journey from one's home or workplace to the game site is usually perceived as the moment when one "leaves behind" one's everyday life and gets mentally attuned to the ludic world.

Especially when team members travel together, they are in high spirits, jointly looking forward to the things to come, enjoying the tension of the unpredictable, exchanging stories (*baiki*) of earlier events, making final stitches on their garments, etc., as is revealed by the interviews with Vladivostok larpers. Denis B. (Lans), one of the most prominent larpers of Vladivostok (interviewed by Beletskaia), stated that "A journey with the club to some place is of course very useful for the club because it unites the team [...] The further you travel, the stronger will be the test [of integration], accordingly". A similar characterisation of the journey as a rite of passage is presented by Dina Pisarevskaia in her study on larpers in the European part of Russia: "the behavioural reactions of the neophytes are memorised, which later can have an influence on their reputation in the community" (2011: 150).

Travel to the game site may take several hours or even days. According to one of our interviewees, Aleksandra Anikina, packing and moving to the site is not very different from hiking and tourist camping. The most striking difference from tourism is that rank-and-file participants should bring their own accessories and ludic costumes with them, put them on upon arrival, and settle down at the camp. The act of changing dress is, for many people, the most decisive point in the passage from one reality to the other, and hence it is also an emotionally intensive moment. The organisers have also to deliver various ludic equipment (flags, bells, carriages, etc.) for modelling the life in the fictional world. Some participants begin to immerse into the fictional atmosphere before the game, at the stage of traveling to *poligon*, or even earlier, at the stage of reading the relevant materials long before the game. There are emic terms for the process of identification with the fictional character, all of which entail some literal meaning of "loading" (*zagruz, vgruz, pogruzhenie*). It is used to designate both the instructions of the game master and the self-identification with the fictional character.

Even though the start of the game is more or less fixed, not all participants enter the game at the same time. Therefore, while some of them are already *in* the game, the others are still preparing or tuning themselves to the action in what can be called the sub-ludic space (see below). In order to summon all the participants and to introduce them to each other, the game begins with a parade. At the parade, the teams and individual participants are already dressed up in the costumes of the ludic world, and this is the moment when they stop using their non-ludic names. The parade usually includes a presentation by the major leader, short presentations by the teams, and the official opening speech act. This is the moment when the delineation of the chronotope (the ludic world against "real life") is maintained at its strongest, and by many also experienced at its strongest. However, even here there is a link between the real and the ludic world, as participants take pictures of groups and individuals before the parade and sometimes after it. After the parade everybody briefly returns to his or her camp, and after this return the game events *per se* begin. If somebody appears in non-ludic clothes after the parade, the participants may joke: "Look, there is a naked chap over there!"

Chronotopic core: the feel of reality in the ludic world

The concept of the ludic chronotope helps us to describe how the borders between game and "real life" are constructed and maintained, but it has already become clear that this strict separation gets blurred in multiple ways. This brings up the question of game reality, of how this mode of existence is experienced. One of the Novosibirsk interviewees, Aleksandra Anikina, makes a strong statement on the ontological status of the ludic world: "A game is a reality of the notions of the participants about what is going on. Therefore, when loads of people in a particular location think that they are on the territory of Ancient Gaul [laughs], this is becoming real to a certain extent". The success of the game, according to her, depends on the intensity of emotional and imaginative reality construction. If the level of this intensity is high enough, if the ludic reality becomes "dense", if the ludic interaction is vivid, then everyone is happy with the game.

For many participants, the virtual world of the game reinforces their perception of reality in a mystical way. Anikina related a story that happened during one of the Makarena games and that in her narrative sounded like a miracle. In a game about Gallic wars she was playing a role of a Helvetian priestess. She recounted that all the Helvetians were destroyed and then said: "But on top of all of us being destroyed, it began to rain. I thought: 'It's started to rain — that's all we need!'" In order to make the rain stop she went to the shrine and performed a series of rituals. And then she observed that the sky began to clear exactly over the Helvetians' settlement. She was amazed to see how sharp the border between the blue sky and the thick clouds was, and to see that then finally all the clouds disappeared. It is obvious that she did not perceive the disappearance of the clouds and her magic as a mere coincidence; in her interpretation it sounded as ironic faith. For her, the virtual, the ludic, and the magic had the force to impact the natural events in the "real world". This is a particularly telling case of the contamination of the virtual with the real which we have encountered frequently.

Denis B. (Lans), the Vladivostok larper whom we introduced in the previous subsection, gave another impressive example of his emotional experience in which game and reality became blurred:

> On the issue of immersion in the image, in the role: at this game something happened to me which has never happened to me again. At a certain point, the game has become — well, not as if reality [...] but the emotions which I began to feel through the game became real. [...] Once there was a situation when [...] I went to the far edge of the *poligon* and then returned. While I was away our camp was attacked. And all people of our tribe [...] were either killed or taken as prisoners. I was the only survivor [...] and our enemies noticed me and also injured me. And I am lying near their wall quietly and I am dying under a warm sun (*pomiraiu na solnyshke*). And there arises, from inside, somewhere, the anguish, which is so real that you can reach it with your hands and touch. I [then] was saved by a girl I had no idea who she is. I was hosted by a different tribe, by a different team. I was dressed and fed. And this feeling that you are the only survivor, and the feeling of the presence of people who saved you, helped you, that there is someone to lean on, it was so real.

This episode illustrates that Lans — although being himself one of the organisers of the game, responsible for controlling the chronotopic entry and exit gates — is "lost" in the reality of the game. Similarly, Anikina's experience is an indication of how the game affects the outer sphere and makes the "real world" part of the ludic world. It is exactly this density of the mixture of the ludic and the real that is cherished by the larpers. To sum up this subsection, these two examples illustrate *one* of the different ways in which the ludic and the real get blurred. In the next subsection we will present the reverse case: the density of the mixture can be so overwhelming that the chronotope must be temporarily annihilated — though not necessarily completely.

Sub-ludic space and temporal discarding of the chronotope

Even though the chronotopic core of the game fits the classical definition of a game by Huizinga — it is set apart from "real life" in space and time — there are some typical situations during the game when the border between the ludic and the real must be transcended for practical reasons, in order to keep the game going.[8] Andrei Mel'nikov has called this the *sub-ludic space* (*podygrovoe prostranstvo*). This may be a tent or a room that is reserved for consultations of team leaders. One of the sub-ludic spaces is the campfire where the food is cooked and where team members come together during the evening or night. During these evenings it is not necessary for larpers to keep playing; they can interact as "real" persons. Mel'nikov perceives this sub-ludic space as the space for game management by the team leaders who have to control the sustenance of their camp life and the emotional state of their team members.

Also, there may be some emergency situations when players quit the game world and deal with each other in "reality". This happens, for instance, when a ludic conflict turns into a situation of real aggression. In this case, according to Vadim Zevlever, the master has to break into the conflict by means of irony or comedy:

> It happens that suddenly [...] as it is called, the boys went berserk (*perekrylo parnei*). With swords in their hands, just about to threaten each other's life. [In that case] one has to joke, you know, on a distracting topic, one has to say "Suddenly in the dragon's pocket a mobile phone is ringing". Everybody [in amazement]: "What mobile phone?" — "Nokia. A red one". The dragon says: "Hold on! Hello? I can't talk right now, I am in a fight" [...] "What do you mean: which fight?" "With the crusaders [of course], what a question! As soon as I am done, I will phone you back". And everybody sits [and thinks] "wow" and I say: "All right, smoking break! Everybody go for a smoke".

Game exit

While the opening parade is a "compulsory" ritual, the closing parade is usually an optional procedure. Thus, the end of the game

---

8   Schröder states in Chapter 9 of this volume that "in the role-playing game actors are constantly moving between the subjunctive and indicative frames". We interpret "subjunctive" as equivalent of the ludic mode and indicative for that what needs to be denoted as off-play (the "sub-ludic space").

is less ritualised and less sharp a moment in time. At the end of the game while some people already quit the game, the others still identify with their roles, wear their ludic outfit, and keep playing. The disassembling of the buildings and the clearing of the site may take several hours or even days; it is carried out by a smaller group of people who do not have to rush back to the city. People travel home in smaller groups or even individually; they are usually much more tired and less talkative than they were when travelling to the game site. Participants experience the departure from the ludic world very differentially and often individually rather than collectively. Group photos, hugs, and handshakes at a bus stop or railway station mark one of the latest stages of passage back into everyday life. Such photos often show groups of mixed clothing, with some people still wearing ludic attire and others dressed in their "civil" clothes.

As an ultimate stage of releasing oneself from the ludic identity, upon arrival at home, participants clean their clothes and boots and store them away (though not everything, and not everybody does; see below). What follows is a period of relaxation: people take a bath, quietly reflect on what has happened, meet their loved ones and give first reports, and generally try to get back into "real life". For some of our interviewees, this can happen within hours. For others, the emotional ludic status can last much longer, especially when the role of the player was ambiguous or problematic. Then, the help of the master may be needed. One of the game leaders we interviewed mentioned a girl who had a dramatic role and he kept communicating with her through email long after the game.

Usually a couple of days after the end of the game, the online forum gets increasingly frequented again. This is the time when photographs and personal assessments are exchanged. It comes with what some may see as a significant liminal rite: the game analysis (*razbor poletov*, literally the "assessment of the flights"). The commitment that individual forum members spend on these discussions is indicative of their general identification with the scene; in other words, participants take their ludic reality more or less serious throughout their "real life". All these phenomena support the idea that the border between the ludic and the real is not fixed. However, we also know of larpers that *never* stop being involved in play, and of those who incorporate their ludic personage into their "civil" identity.

The issue of participants versus spectators

According to our interviewees and other sources, LARP events generally do not presuppose any spectators to be present during the event. However, there is an essential element of LARP games which implies the existence of an audience, and therefore transforms LARP events into performances: the visual documentation by means of photo and video representations of every game. The visual materials created at all stages of any game and especially during the game event are diverse and abundant. At the very beginning of the role-playing movement, the first visual documents were black-and-white photographs which were kept in albums of almost every role player. Then, video materials were added to the personal archives. And now, with the access to digital cameras, every game is documented by hundreds of digitised pictures and video clips.

These various visual forms are multifunctional. First, they are representations of games which serve both to record past events and advertise upcoming events of the same type. Second, they are the form of a collective memory which facilitates the formation of collective identity (Chaney 1996: 31). And finally, visuality constitutes the performative element of LARP. The game becomes a spectacle for the viewers, many of whom participated in the same game. Visual documentation thus facilitates the mental return into the chronotope and reflects what happened collectively.

Since most of the visual materials circulate online, the permanent access of the visual materials to the spectators also undermines the spatial and temporal borders between the game and the real world. The spectators comment on the visual materials online and thus provide feedback for the performers. The difference between this feedback and theatrical feedback is that in the case of LARP it is a delayed and continued communication. The vast spectrum of visual representations of games allows us to consider LARP a theatrical form of sociality — one in which the actors are among their own spectators and critics.

All the experiences which undermine the border between the game and the real world produce the feeling that the game never ends. Says the leader of Makarena: "I hate the final parade. In 1996 at the very first Makarena, when half of the game had passed, a girl came up to me and asked: 'Tell me, Makar, when does the game come to the end?' And I responded: 'it never does'".

LARP and lifestyle: casual, regular, and total larpers

As we have seen above, a game as a practice covers preparation for the game, entry into the game (which involves travelling to the game site), non-ludic events at the site, the chronotopic core of the game (the enactment part or the game *per se*), exit from the game, game analysis shortly after the game, and communication of visual materials. We would like to identify three groups of larpers, based on the level of participation at these stages of the game: casual larpers, regular larpers, and total larpers.

Casual larpers are not involved in the organisation of the game, their appearance in the role play is usually restricted to basic functional roles — for example, that of an adept, a recruit, etc. — and the experience of the game usually does not exert a sustained influence on the way they see themselves and want to be seen by others.[9] We may thus assume that casual participation in LARP does reflect certain predilections and sensibilities, but it does not exert a significant impact on the lifestyle of a person in the sense of shaping that person's habits or their outer appearance. Casual larpers perceive games as single experiments that may be continued but also stopped.

According to Vadim Zevlever, the majority of participants are not capable of feeling their role, they just try to do what is prescribed by the game scenario. By implying that certain people simply have no talent for identification with the role, Zevlever ignores the very likely possibility that some participants do not find satisfaction in the game and therefore quit the scene after a short time. They may turn to other role-playing games or other types of play or sport. The interviews also show that the change of professional status, the beginning or end of university studies, and similar biographical turning points may force a role player to stop participating, which also explains the volatility of membership in many clubs.

---

9   As one of TB's informants, a student from Krasnoiarsk, described her experience playing an elf in a fantasy game: "You get some ears stitched on and receive a spear, and off you go" (*Ushi prishili, kop'ë dali i idi*). By that, she meant that she was a casual player, not having made any preparations before the game.

Regular larpers participate in field games and other LARP events. A regular larper can become a member of the master group and be involved in the organisation of a game. However, his or her LARP participation does not develop into a life-long project. Regular larpers communicate with each other outside the game chronotope, and in this communication they can use idiomatic expressions originating in various games. In their everyday life they may wear certain clothes or accessories which display their LARP experience as signs of shared experience to anyone who recognises them. But most aspects and activities of their life are not affected by the impact of their LARP experience, or to return to Chaney's definition of lifestyle mentioned above, their LARP experience "is not the totality of their social experience" (1996: 5). Moreover, the person does not see the LARP engagement as something that deserves or requires to be publicised, to be shared with people outside the LARP community. Several of our interviewees said they did not tell their relatives or colleagues at work that they were participating in role-playing games for many years. Nonetheless, the person's participation in the LARP community has such a degree of importance that a significant part of leisure time is spent with other larpers, even outside the context of the actual games.

An interesting example of this was related by Natasha Permiakova. As a role player she identifies herself with the ludic Celtic clan *Kallanmor*, founded on the occasion of the 1998 Makarena, though currently she does not play because she has a small child:

> In the same year [1999] in our company Kallanmor there happened the first wedding. And I went to participate in this wedding and we all came together in Omsk. And it was quite a performance. They got married at the Central Marriage Registration Office of Omsk. They had their Celtic costumes on, made of tartan, according to the traditional authentic Scotch wedding design. [...] This wedding was, of course, very heartfelt, because it was the first one. And also because we all came together with a very special cordial feeling.

This story of two larpers who decided to celebrate their marriage within the ludic community and mark their belonging to the ludic community by appropriate ritual clothes illustrates how ludic identities attain relevance in "real life", yet without fully occupying it. It is yet another example of how larpers wilfully transcend the boundary between the game and "reality".

Fig. 10.3. Natasha Permiakova during a LARP event near St Petersburg, August 2001. Photo: Tatiana Barchunova's interviewee (with permission),

The ludic/real border is especially ambiguous in the case of the so-called clan games (*klanovushki*). These games, according to Mel'nikov, are non-stop. People stay involved in the game even when they are at work: "When someone goes to work or to school, his foes may, in game mode, kill him or carry out any other game-related action on him. They are not inhibited by any objection, 'I am at work', or 'I am busy'. Once you have decided to take part, you must take part".

Aleksandra Anikina during a certain period of her life was teaching at a school. At one of the games she played a similar role: she acted as a bachelor responsible for the enrolment of students to her university. By coincidence, one of her real students came to the field game and had to deal with her as a teacher. He was not well prepared for the camping aspect of the game and had not brought a tent or a sleeping bag. She took patronage of him both as a real and as a virtual teacher: "Well. I gave him my mat and my sleeping bag […] That's it. Because I began to feel responsibility right away [laughs]. The situation was… how to say that? […] identical, homological to the situation in life in that I was teaching and he was my student […] That's it."

What is remarkable about the second group of larpers is their high mobility, which is both geographical and virtual, i.e. imagined

Fig. 10.4. Aleksandra Anikina hitch-hiking from the outskirts of Novosibirsk towards Tomsk, summer 2007. Photo: Tatiana Barchunova's interviewee (with permission), CC-BY-ND.

(cf. Urry 2007: 9). In addition to travelling to LARP events in regions distant from home, they show a general propensity to travel. Two young women among TB's interviewees should be mentioned in this case. Anikina travelled through Russia, Europe, and the Asian part of Russia by many possible means: on foot, hitch-hiking, by bicycle, by train, by bus, by aeroplane. She made one trip to Europe together with the above-mentioned student of hers. Permiakova travelled to many cities and towns of the Russian Federation, to most former Soviet Union countries, to Europe, Japan, and Thailand. Their geographical mobility was facilitated by their personal inventiveness and creativity in terms of logistics (Zuev 2008). They used all possible organisational venues for travel and accommodation: standard tourist services, informal services, couch-surfing networks, and networks of friends and other role players. The prearranged accommodation and travel did not always work out: both women had moments when they were completely broke and miserable.

The virtual mobility of regular larpers can be called chronotopic mobility. By this we mean the ability and desire to move back and forth between different worlds, which may exist as "mere" fiction or as an imaginary connected to a certain "real" place, such as a historical site.

In other words, the "spatial imaginary" (cf. Chapter 5 in this volume) of regular larpers and their travel biographies come to include sites of importance experienced or narrated in the ludic world. Chronotopically mobile people are sensitive to stories and cosmologies of the past, and their geographical travels are often imbued with history. Thus, Anikina travelled to the Altai Mountains to see the Ukok plateau, which has become widely known for a major archaeological discovery (Broz 2009; Halemba 2008). She is also interested to see places related to Celtic history. Chronotopic mobility also includes the ability to get immersed in ludic reconstruction of the past, and participate in futurological games. An interesting case of chronotopic mobility was related by Natal'ia Vinichenko: she participated in a game where she had to live under extreme "prehistoric" conditions in order to test her survival abilities.

Chronotopic mobility does not necessarily imply intensive geographical mobility. Chronotopically mobile people might not have enough economical and network resources for long-distance travels in physical space. The major instrument of chronotopic mobility in this case is the power of imagination reinforced by ludic communication. A low degree of physical mobility and a lack of material resources do not necessarily reduce the intensiveness of play, and are often compensated for through the ingenious application of those resources which are at hand. We believe that chronotopical mobility — the ability and desire to travel between different worlds — is a highly important ingredient of the life experience of regular larpers, and connected with it is the readiness to transpose different elements — objects, words and concepts, moral values — from one reality to another (as is exemplified by the Celtic wedding in Omsk described above).

This readiness is even more true for the third category, the *total larpers*. Most of them are the leaders and organisers of games. They oftentimes "structure their whole life" (to use the words of one of TB's interviewees, Andrei Mel'nikov) so as to participate in LARP. They are involved in all stages of LARP events. They are attached to a particular style of clothes, so that their ludic attire is never really stored away in the wardrobe or chest. In addition, some of them tend to use terms or even a specific linguistic style that derive from their interest in historical re-enactment.

Among TB's interviewees, almost all the total larpers are in some way professional historians in their "real life". For them, the modelling of historical events through playing is a cognitive resource. The acquisition of military technologies of the past through their reconstruction and practicing, according to Vadim Zevlever, is a sensory experience essential for any historian:

> A true historian is willing not only to read but also to touch and feel [...] A person who sits in a study and describes the deeds of the detachment of parachute troops and who has never bailed out himself, is ridiculous [...] Thus, now, thanks to my own experience I know what the gallop attack of bayonets is. I see it quite differently. Before I practiced it myself, I have not known, for instance, how a horse would move... How it moves, how it behaves when the cannons thunder around. One should sit on it and feel it.

Total larpers tend to have jobs that enable them to invest significant time into the organisation of games and participation in other LARP events. They are either freelancers, or they find jobs that allow them to accommodate their LARP experience with paid employment. The organisation of a big field game with several hundred participants takes, according to Zevlever, several months. Even the organisation of a small-scale game of one or two days demands more than a month. Three Novosibirsk interviewees who belong to the category of total larpers are professional pedagogues who have positions of extra-curriculum teachers at special clubs for children of a particular city district. Their lifestyle is definitely constituted by LARP and can be characterised as historical romanticism, often with a particular stress on military history. The majority of games they arrange or participate in are about historical reconstruction of different historical events. Lans, the leading figure of the Vladivostok role-playing movement, works as a system administrator. He says: "My work satisfies me in terms of self-realisation. [...] I can keep the balance that I have been always looking for: between the spare time [...] and salary". This interviewee also has a deep interest in history, but more in the ethical than martial aspects of it, and he recounts how the excessive focus on fights and weapons in earlier role-playing games in Vladivostok gradually led to an impasse that could only be overcome by redesigning the games in a more encompassing way.[10]

---

10   Above we have mentioned that some game leaders now increasingly think beyond militarian action and try to integrate other aspects more strongly into the game scenarios.

What is characteristic for Lans and other total larpers is their intention and capacity not only to travel between different worlds, but to make these worlds accessible to other people. In other words, they do not just live in a "dream world" — they rather provide the basis for other people's dreams to come true. Transposition of symbols, narratives, and normative orders is for them more than just a periodical or regular experience; rather, it is a mechanism whereby to communicate systematically their worldview to others. Often this goes hand in hand with the desire to make the "real world" a better place. Simultaneously, a new reality is constructed — one that follows and emulates certain models and conventions and yet exists in its own right.[11] We identify these larpers as "total larpers" because the value that they attribute to the chronotopical existence is so strong that this form of existence itself turns into a sensibility — into a moral purpose, to be shared with others.

The nexus of chronotopical mobility, romanticism, inventiveness, and a certain educatory mission comes to the fore in many leaders' self-descriptions, and we introduce two of them in more detail here. Both are from Novosibirsk. Andrei Mel'nikov, a pedagogue in an extra-curricular school, is very explicit in expressing his style of travelling, which for him is primarily associated with hiking and overcoming hardship. He perceives hiking as a chronotopic experience since traveling makes him closer to his ancestors who had to overcome difficulties that modern people do not face. They had to light fire, they did not have warm running water. He and his associates make most of their ludic clothes themselves. In opposition to the general tendency from self-made to purchased accessories mentioned earlier, they perceive the production of clothes as a vital and authentic activity since its final product is not a "decorative", disposable ludic costume but a functional outfit that has to protect the body from natural and human vicissitudes.

When Mel'nikov was asked by TB if he could describe his lifestyle he said that he would liken himself to early Mediaeval man (*chelovek*) and his values, especially his respect for nature. Mel'nikov sees his

---

11   From this point of view their experience is close to the experience of Indianists, described and interpreted by Petra Tjitske Kalshoven who in her turn refers to Michael Taussig's ideas. She argues that "by embodying an imagined model steeped in mimetic capital" one can go "beyond representation" and produce something being "its own thing, where something new is at stake" (Kalshoven 2012: 225).

role model as a Viking, though not literally transferred to modern life. He is a partisan of a healthy way of life, without smoking or extensive alcohol drinking. He wants to create an environment based on rules and respect for freedom of others. The major problem he faces in arranging games is other participants' laziness and the lack of responsibility. He argues that the sense of responsibility in young men and women is undermined by playing computer games. The victories in computer games produce feelings of pseudo-achievements which, in his words, are pure phantoms. He stresses the importance of manual skills and physical fitness for personal development.[12]

Another total larper among TB's interviewees is Vadim Zevlever (nicknamed Makar). His notion of high cognitive value of embodiment of historical experience is similar to that of Mel'nikov. But unlike Mel'nikov he presents himself as a cosmopolitan, a citizen of Planet Earth, who has basic knowledge of several European languages and identifies himself as a descendant of Portuguese, Spanish, Dutch, German, Polish, Belarusian, Ukrainian, Russian, and Jewish ancestors.

Like Mel'nikov, Zevlever is interested in material culture and skills, and he too is a partisan of physical exercises. He sewed his ludic costumes himself. In his interview he mentioned that his apartment looks like a workshop filled with raw materials, game accessories, and toy soldiers. He is the head of the Napoleonica club in Novosibirsk. Like Mel'nikov, he teaches in the system of extra-curricular education. One of his courses is historical fencing. Zevlever graduated from the department of history of the Pedagogical University in Novosibirsk. He writes about the Napoleonic Wars and for him historical reconstruction in games is a field of experimental history. The "Makarena" games we have been discussing above were named in honour of Zevlever's nickname, Makar. However, the Makarena games are not only about the Napoleonic Wars, they also employ other historical motifs: Zevlever and his associates have already arranged 24 games about different periods of European and early Russian history. For example, *The Black Prince* (*Chërnyi Prints*), took place near Novosibirsk in May 2018.[13]

---

12   Compare the note about "healthy way of life" (*zdorovyi obraz zhizni*) in Chapter 11.
13   http://vk.com/club27365038 — the Makarena group on VKontakte.

Fig. 10.5. Vadim Zevlever (Makar). Cropped version of a photo published on 20 July 2019 in the forum for the "Makarena" on VKontakte on the occasion of the forum having reached 3,000 members. Source: https:// vk.com/club27365038.

According to Zevlever, the annual Makarena is an important event in terms of LARP fashion in the region: "It looks as if, in general, I set the fashion. For after the Makarena all summer the folks participate in other games in the costumes they have made for my game". Role models for him are soldiers of the past. A true soldier according to him has to perceive death as something which is inevitable and which one has to face with pride and dignity:

> If a woman from Sparta lost her husband in a battle, she got happy, it was her day of celebration, since he met his death face-to-face. That's it. And we know lots of similar cases in the history of the human society. For instance, with Scandinavians who lived to die beautifully. As a matter of fact, if the hour of your death has come, die beautifully![14]

And he seems to be serious about it, both in terms of ludic and real death. Of all examples of moral judgements and stylisation among larpers,

---

14   The notion of death in role-playing games would deserve a detailed account on its own. Though the death of the personage in a LARP game is a virtual event, we have often heard in the interviews that it is emotionally uprooting and demands special psychological support. In fact, the game world has an institution which is responsible for the psychological rehabilitation — the so-called "place of the dead" (*mertviatnik*).

this is probably the most expressive statement. With this example of an ultimately deadly ethical and aesthetic personal project, we turn to our conclusion.

Conclusion

Writing about playing is a challenge. Besides different games as an organised form of playing, we are involved in numerous ostentatiously performative activities. We cheat, fantasise, play tricks on our neighbours, come up with surprises, blackmail, risk unusual social roles and outfit. All of us have a taste for play, as has been mentioned by such writers as Baudrillard, de Certeau, Chaney, and Elias. However universal the act of playing is for human beings, some players invest special effort into games and receive especially deep satisfaction from it. Total larpers exemplify this special commitment. For total larpers, the taste for play is the generative principle of their lifestyle.[15] They invest lots of imagination, time, and resources into arranging various games and participating in them. Inasmuch as they are willing to share this passion with others, they come to be the protagonists not only of a particular game, but also of a community of taste and a distinct lifestyle with the "same expressive intention" (Bourdieu 1984: 173) in their ludic-and-real existence. Their experience allows us not only to understand how specific forms of leisure and consumption have developed, but also to grasp the nature of play and its relation to the real.

Returning to the concept of theatrical sociality, which we have borrowed from the writings of Chaney and Baudrillard: at the core of this term is the idea that the display of clothes and other elements of outer appearance has some self-referential aspect: it is a purpose unto itself. Nonetheless, such display may bear a subversive element (Chaney 1996: 54, with reference to Baudrillard 1993: 94), and has the potential to create irony. The larpers that we interviewed use clothes and other accessories with clear reference to some historical or fictional setting;

---

15 It is clear that for total larpers the game is (to use the words of Bakhtin about carnival) "life itself", but "exposed in a special ludic way" (*oformlennaia osobym igrovym obrazom*) (Bakhtin 1986: 297). However, for total larpers games and real life are not two separate worlds as they were in the mediaeval carnival culture. Rather, games and real life constitute one single world, one single lifestyle.

in that sense the notion of self-referentiality may seem not applicable for role plays. However, what is strongly manifest is the notion of performance and theatrical forms of communication: participants take on certain roles that are to be enacted over several hours or days, and they immerse themselves in a play that reflects both the sensibilities of an earlier period or a fictional world *and* their own sensibilities around morality and emotional experience, transposed from the context of real life into the role play. Participants in role-playing games make use of the opportunity to try out themselves in a theatrical setting — a play in which actors and spectators are identical.

Common sense suggests that games are different from the real world. The rules and conventions of a game are different from those norms that regulate our operations in the real world. It is limited in space and time. We know when the game begins and when it ends. Game accessories are kept in special containers, to be taken out, worn, and displayed on certain leisure-related occasions only. This common sense is perfectly consistent with the conventional approach to games based on Huizinga's *Homo Ludens*. However, the empirical research of LARP events seems to undermine this approach.

Let's imagine the chronotopic core of the game when several hundred young men and women come together in a spring forest. It is early May, relatively warm during the day, freezing at night. They are all wearing special clothes, styled according to the historical period they enact. They feel themselves English aristocrats involved in dynastic wars, or Romans fighting against barbaric tribes. They are being aroused by the spring winds, sunsets and sunrises, contingencies of battles, intrigues of the courts, the romance of music near the fireplace, and the heroic deeds they have to accomplish. It is the ludic world, separated from the real one, the latter consisting of urban routines full of traffic jams, daily chores, service centres, IT departments, school, and college rooms with their artificial light and sober interior.

However, if we look at the game as a practice, the boundary between the real and the ludic is undermined in multiple forms. In this chapter, we have discussed four main ways in which the border is put into question. First, the border is not a fixed moment in time, because people prepare more or less intensively, arrive and depart at different times, etc. The five-day game core event is preceded by a long period of preparation and training and followed by an extended time of evaluation and reflection by both participants and non-participants of the games. Second, the border disappears as the reality of the ludic world merges with that of the other world. As we have seen, the virtual magic of the game comes to be perceived as a "real" means to influence the forces of nature. Emotions, though emergent from within the ludic context, can grow as strong as to be taken for "real" experience. Third, participants temporarily leave the ludic space and enter the sub-ludic one. The management of logistics by game masters and the tackling of emergency situations such as real aggression or sickness, require an intermediate zone which has been succinctly called the sub-ludic space by one of our interviewees. This sub-ludic space as well as the "land of the dead" where dead characters have to stay before re-entering the game as different personalities, does not subvert the ludic conventions; rather, it makes them work. Finally, there are individuals whose ludic identity gradually merges with their "civil" identity (through transposition of items, language, and moral and aesthetic judgements).

The notion of game as a practice unfolding through several stages is also heuristic in answering the general question of this chapter: what is the impact of participation in games on a person's lifestyle? We have identified three categories of participants: casual larpers, regular larpers, and total larpers. Casual larpers have a taste for play, but are not involved in its preparation. Regular larpers' taste for play is revealed in the repertoires of roles they play, commitment to serial games and teams, and their involvement in the preparation of the games. They are familiar with all game sites and belong to the relevant social networks. Total larpers are not only leaders and organisers of the games at all stages, but they come to connect their activities with moral principles that apply to life in general, regardless of conventional differentiations between the ludic and the real. They are pedagogues in the most general sense of the word. From this point of view, they are similar to the leaders of the ethnic identity games described in Chapter 9. They have teaching expertise, they are supposed to be role-models for their students and proponents of a healthy and decent lifestyle. They are convinced that participation in role-playing games offers important moral lessons for life and provides for creative ways of consumption and self-experience. Their taste for play is their passion, and they want to share this passion with others.

References

Bakhtin, Mikhail. 1981. "Forms of time and of the chronotope in the novel", trans. Caryl Emerson & Michael Holquist. In: *The Dialogic Imagination: four essays by M. M. Bakhtin*, ed. Michael Holquist. Austin, TX: University of Texas Press, pp. 48–254.

—. 1986. *Literaturno-kriticheskie stat'i* [Critique of literature articles], ed. G. Bocharov & V. V. Kozhinov. Moscow: Khudozhestvennaia literatura.

Barchunova, Tatiana & Natal'ia Beletskaia. 2004. "Without fear and reproach: the role-playing games community as a challenge to mainstream culture". *Sibirica*, 4 (1): 116–29, https://doi.org/10.1080/13617360500070947

—. 2009–2010. "Are play regiments really for play? Military practices in Novosibirsk: simulation of military actions in role-playing games for young people and militarized games for adults". *Anthropology & Archeology of Eurasia*, 48 (3): 9–30, https://doi.org/10.2753/aae1061-1959480301

Baudrillard, Jean. 1993. *Symbolic Exchange and Death*, trans. Iain Hamilton Grant. London: SAGE, https://doi.org/10.4135/9781526401496

Bemong, Nele & Pieter Borghart. 2010. "Bakhtin's theory of the literary chronotope: reflections, applications, perspectives". In: *Bakhtin's Theory of the Literary Chronotope: reflections, applications, perspectives*, ed. Nele Bemong, Pieter Borghart, Michel de Dobbeleer; Kristoffel Demoen, Keun de Temmerman & Bart Keunen. Gent: Academia Press, pp. 3–16, http://www.oapen.org/xtf/download?type=document&collection=oapen&doc id=377572; https://doi.org/10.26530/oapen_377572

Bourdieu, Pierre. 1984 [1979]. *Distinction: a social critique of the judgement of taste*, trans. Richard Nice. London: Routledge & Kegan Paul.

Broz, Ludek. 2009. "Substance, conduct, and history: 'Altaian-ness' in the twenty-first century". *Sibirica*, 8 (2): 43–70, https://doi.org/10.3167/sib.2009.080202

Carlson, Marvin. 2004. *Performance: a critical introduction*. 2nd edition. New York: Routledge.

Chaney, David. 1996. *Lifestyles*. London: Routledge, https://doi.org/10.4324/9780203137468

Copier, Marinka. 2005. "Connecting worlds: fantasy role-playing games, ritual acts and the magic circle". *Proceedings of the DiGRA 2005 Conference — Changing Views: worlds of play*. No place: DiGRA, http://www.digra.org/dl/display_html?chid=http://www.digra.org/dl/db/06278.50594.pdf

Elias, Norbert. 1978. *The Civilizing Process*, vol. 1. Oxford: Blackwell.

Getsy, David. 2011. "Introduction". In: *From Diversion to Subversion: games, play, and twentieth century art*, ed. David J. Getsy. University Park, PA: Pennsylvania University Press, pp. i–xvii.

Halemba, Agnieszka. 2008. "'What does it feel like when your religion moves under your feet?' Religion, earthquakes and national unity in the Republic of Altai, Russian Federation". *Zeitschrift für Ethnologie*, 133 (2): 283–99.

Hankiss, Elemér. 2001. *Fears and Symbols: an introduction to the study of Western civilization*. Budapest: Central European University Press.

Huizinga, Johan. 1949. *Homo Ludens: a study of the play-element in culture*. Abingdon: Routledge.

Kalshoven, Petra Tjitske. 2012. *Crafting "the Indian": knowledge, desire, and play in Indianist reenactment*. New York: Berghahn.

Kopytin, Sergei M. 2016. "Youth subculture of RPG community: on the problem of methodological description". *Journal of the Siberian Federal University, Humanities and Social Sciences*, 6 (9): 1480–89, https://doi.org/10.17516/1997-1370-2016-9-6-1480-1489

Norbeck, Edward. 1974. "The anthropological study of human play". *Rice Institute Pamphlet — Rice university studies*, 60 (3), https://scholarship.rice.edu/handle/1911/63156

Pisarevskaia, Dina Borisovna. 2011. *Subkul'tura rolevykh igr v sovremennom obshchestve* [The subculture of role plays in contemporary society]. Moscow: Rossiiskaia Akademiia Nauk, Institut etnologii i antropologii im. N. N. Miklukho-Maklaia.

Steniaev, Oleg. 1999. "Pis'mo Tsentra reabilitatsii zhertv netraditsionnykh religii N°47/23 ot 15 avgusta 1999 direktoru Pravoslavnogo obshchestva 'Panagiia' M. Yu. Medvedevu po povodu dvizheniia tolkienistov" [Letter of the Centre for Rehabilitation of Victims of Non-Traditional Religions no. 47/23, dated 15 August 1999, to the director of the 'Panagiia' Society, M. Yu. Medvedev, on the issue of the Tolkienist movement]. Religioznaia bezopasnost' Rossii, http://www.stolica.narod.ru/occult/tolkien/tol1.html

Turner, Victor 1969. *The Ritual Process: structure and anti-structure*. Chicago, IL: Aldine, https://doi.org/10.4324/9781315134666

Tychsen, Anders, Michael Hitchens, Thea Brolund & Manolya Kavakli. 2006. "Live action role-playing games: control, communication, storytelling, and MMORPG similarities". *Games and Culture*, 1 (3): 252–75, https://doi.org/10.1177/1555412006290445

Urry, John. 2007. *Mobilities*. Cambridge: Polity Press, https://doi.org/10.4324/9781315595733

Vorobyeva, Olga V. 2015. "Constructing of group identity during live-action role-playing games". *Anthropology & Archeology*, 54 (1): 68–80, https://doi.org/10.1080/10611959.2015.1132094

Zuev, Dennis. 2008. "The practice of free-traveling: young people coping with access in post-Soviet Russia". *Young*, 16 (1): 5–26, https://doi.org/10.1177/110330880701600102

11. Conclusions

Joachim Otto Habeck

The authors of the preceding chapters hope to have contributed to the theoretical exploration of the concept of lifestyle, drawing on David Chaney (1996), Pierre Bourdieu (1984), and other social scientists' works. Beyond that theoretical contribution, it is hoped that this volume has reached the goal of documenting the rich diversity of everyday-life experiences in communities small and large across Siberia and the Far North of Russia. Each individual life project and biography should be encountered with sincerity, even if occasionally interviewer and interviewee had very different approaches to the meaning of certain norms and values, questions of social inclusion, and the future trajectories of society in Russia. Beyond the two biggest cities of the country — Moscow and St Petersburg — the authors have sought to capture hopes and concerns connected with personal fulfilment and social well-being in less central, in some cases very peripheral communities of Russia. This is a relevant pursuit in its own right, considering the prevailing image of Siberia as remote and generally backward.

Open boundaries, transnational exchanges, and the potential of communication via the internet have facilitated a degree of proximity between "home" and "research community" that many of us research-team members could not foresee at the time when we started ethnographic work in the respective community (usually in the 1990s). Notwithstanding this new proximity and openness, many of us also see a growing tendency of estrangement between Russia and western

 https://doi.org/10.11647/OBP.0171.11

European countries when it comes to mass media and public discourse. "Talking past each other" is one of the ramifications of internet-based social networks, and the undebatable existence of a language barrier aggravates old and new stereotypes.

In the sections to follow, I will first sketch out some trends that have come to exert pervasive influence on Russian society in recent years, then address the central research questions that the project has explored. I then return to the concept of lifestyle and discuss it in the context of the findings of this research project. Finally, I look into the meanings of modernity in the Siberian context, since lifestyle is often considered to be a phenomenon typical for high-modern and post-modern societies.

Beyond 2011: an update on social and cultural shifts in Russia

The chapters of this volume are all based on ethnographic research that took place around the year 2011. The research attempted to capture the diversity of lifestyles in Russia and simultaneously to examine factors that circumscribe and pose limits to individual aspirations and activities. The contributing researchers conducted fieldwork among a broad range of communities and social groups, each of them arguably constituting some reality of their own, notwithstanding the diverse types of connectedness of these communities and notwithstanding the different roles that individuals take on in their everyday life.

This volume may be read as a documentation of the breadth of social realities and ambitions in Siberia and northern Russia twenty years after the end of the Soviet Union. Eight years have passed since the time of the fieldwork; but nonetheless, the authors are positive that their observations and conclusions continue to have relevance and validity in the present time. Simultaneously, the members of the research team perceive gradual and wide-reaching changes in the communities in which they conducted research, and in Russian society at large over the last years. These changes have taken place not only in the domain of infrastructure (e.g. the completion of the road between East Siberia and the Russian Far East in late 2010) and telecommunication (e.g. the advent of GSM in about 2015 in remote rural settlements). Recent years have also seen a noticeable shift in public discourse and — to return to Chaney's notion — sensibilities, as has also been observed by other social scientists, to be discussed in this section.

Generally, we can speak of a conservative turn in Russia.[1] This conservatism has been dubbed "blurry" inasmuch as it allows for a wide range of political stances and tropes of memory (Bernsand & Törnquist-Plewa 2019: 4, with reference to Laruelle). It emanates from the centre of power, finding support — sometimes superficial, at other times very intensive — on the part of local politicians and among the inhabitants, including the urban and rural communities where we conducted research. This does not mean that the range of possible forms and practices of self-expression has shrunk altogether; rather, the range has come to incorporate explicitly patriotic, religious, spiritual, and strongly traditional conceptions of self and social interaction. Many liberal convictions and lifestyles have become subjected to criticism that emerges from a disenchantment with pro-western and "democratic" trends of the 1990s and a nostalgic longing for a Soviet past when life was supposedly more "in order". To be sure, such developments did not proceed in a steady, gradual, undisputed manner. Important discursive shifts occurred with the political events in Crimea and the eastern part of Ukraine in 2014, with the ensuing sanctions and financial difficulties.

Disenchantment with the "liberal" 1990s

There is a widely shared and persuasive feeling among large parts of Russian society that the 1990s were a decade of disorder (*bespredel*). The policies of privatisation, market liberalisation, and pertinent reforms intended a very clear break with the collectivist ideology of the Soviet past. These policies derived from and simultaneously promoted a bundle of sensibilities around individual initiative, experimenting with new

---

1   Discussing this view with several colleagues from within Russia and beyond, I received divergent responses. Some of the contributors to this volume hold that conservative attitudes are not a new but rather persistent phenomenon, articulated by the juxtaposition of Russian values against those of the west. Similarly, Alexander Agadjanian (2017: 42) argues that the Russian Orthodox Church "actually served as one of the channels transmitting continuity with the Soviet past, thereby assuming some substantial elements of the late Soviet, predominantly conservative ethos". Other commentators imply that Russia's current policies must be seen in the context of western countries' geopolitical advances and active alienation of Russia (e.g. Chris Hann in his controversy with Alessandro Testa, see Hann 2015: 90).

cultural forms and means of self-expression, not only but importantly through consumer choices. For the inhabitants of the biggest cities, it was arguably easier to develop new personal and familial strategies in terms of livelihood; the window of new opportunities was simply larger than in the more provincial parts of the country, where the economic restructuring often led to an almost complete devastation of the formerly state-owned or collective enterprises. At present, differences in life standards, livelihoods, and political attitudes continue to be determined by place of residence and centrality/remoteness (Zubarevich 2013).

The reforms of the 1990s were explicitly connected with democracy and liberal society modelled on North American and western European societies, but in the course of the 1990s it became clear that the "reforms" did not prevent, but rather nurtured illicit (in many cases, clearly criminal) methods of accumulating wealth and non-transparent practices of decision-making. Therefore, it is understandable that "democracy" and "liberalism" attained pejorative connotations in the political opinion of many inhabitants, who rather demanded a "strong hand" (*sil'naia ruka*) to rule the country. In the almost two decades since Vladimir Putin's accession to power in 2000, the political design of a "strong hand" came to be real, which explains his popularity to a large extent. Regardless of how one evaluates the political success and moral basis of the government under Putin, many observers (within and outside Russia) agree that the country has regained its former geopolitical importance. Despite the very palpable economic ups and downs over the last twenty years, there is almost unanimous agreement among the populace that the economic and social conditions in Russia are now more stable than in the 1990s.

The disenchantment with the pro-western and "democratic" trends of the 1990s is accompanied with a nostalgic longing for a Soviet past (Bernsand & Törnquist-Plewa 2019). Such nostalgia is rarely connected with a desire to return *tout court* to the Soviet ways; it rather constitutes a selective reading of memories to be kept — to be kept, on the one hand, because they define moments of "good life" and happiness in personal biographies (as described in Chapter 6 of this volume); on the other hand, they also recall the absurd difficulties of everyday life in past decades, conjuring up a sense of bygone sociality and documenting the practical creativity of the narrator(s) in "getting by". But nostalgia is not just personal; it is also created and celebrated in public, at state level. The resurrection of the grandeur of the Soviet Union and earlier periods of Russian history surely carries an integrative function — a point of convergence that most citizens can identify with. It also serves to rehabilitate the nation's "sense of self" and establish political legitimacy through emphasis on historical continuity instead of rupture.

Putin's political agenda has been characterised as generally conservative, and Putin himself does not shy away from using this characterisation himself.[2] This is not to say that Putin's leadership has no critics; in fact, even within the inner circles of the leading party, divergent opinions and conflicts about the meaning of conservatism exist, as becomes clear from Katharina Bluhm's (2016, 2018) close reading of conservative manifestos and her analysis of political groupings. Bluhm argues that conservatism in Russia cannot be simply equated with "Putinism" (2016: 6). To be sure, the government actively (and top-down) tries to create and maintain "a 'loyal' civil society" (ibid: 8), but conservative values have strong currency also among other actors and institutions, notably the Russian Orthodox Church (see below). Despite ongoing altercations about the "right" conservative path, there is a collection of values on which most conservative thinkers would agree: these include "justice, patriotism, social solidarity, the will to strong leadership and self-discipline. Beyond that, the 'traditional values and ideas of the majority of the people' (for example, in what

---

2   The emphasis on traditional values is exemplified by Putin's presidential address to the Federal Assembly on 12 December 2013, which contained the following statement: "Today, in many countries, norms of morals and morality are under revision, national traditions and the differences between nations and cultures become blurred. Society is now asked to show healthy acceptance of everyone's right to free conscience, political views and private life, but — however strange this may seem — also to show obligatory acceptance of the equality of good and bad [as] notions of opposite sense. Such a destruction of traditional values 'from above' leads not only to negative consequences for the societies, but [is] fundamentally anti-democratic, inasmuch as its implementation into life derives from abstract, diverted ideas against the will of the people's majority, which does not accept the current turn and the envisaged revision. — And we know that there are more and more people in the world who support our position on the defence of traditional values that for thousands of years constituted the spiritual and moral basis of civilisation and of each people: the values of the traditional family, of genuine human life, which also includes religious life, life that is not only material but also spiritual, the values of humanism and diversity of the world" (Poslanie Prezidenta 2013).

concerns marriage and family) should be resolutely defended" (ibid: 25). Moreover, there is widespread agreement among the political elites and large parts of society that Russia's future depends on technological innovation, the strengthening of infrastructure and institutions, and the "connection between modernization and geopolitics" (ibid: 13). To regain strength, it is assumed, Russia must combine technological development with a return to its own spiritual and cultural riches.

Marlène Laruelle, long-time observer of the patriotic turn in Russia, sums up these feelings and explains how they provide the basis and motivation for the work of organisations that engage in the promotion of patriotic education:

> All the activists share the same negative views of the 1990s, the state's collapse, the market economy and the so-called Westernisation (*vesternizatsiya*) of Russian society. They exhibit values that can be considered conservative: respect for hierarchy, emphasis on order, paternalism, fraternity, concern for one's neighbour, respect for the elderly and social responsibility. Added to this is the idea that Russian society has become ill because it has forgotten its history (2015: 19).

Patriotism and patriotic education

While the organisations engaged in patriotic education cover only a section of youth activities, they exemplify very profoundly the ways in which conservative values and self-reliance are transmitted from the older to the younger generation. A process that was already well underway in the 2000s (Laruelle 2009; Le Huérou & Sieca-Kozlowski 2008; Oushakine 2009) has gathered further momentum in the last few years. Laruelle (2015) argues that the terms patriotic and patriotism have come to stand for an almost indefinite range of stances and political aims. She offers a typology of organisations, spanning the range from extracurricular clubs based at schools or municipal cultural institutions to clubs affiliated with the Orthodox Church, through to clubs under the supervision of former military staff. In addition, Laruelle also includes clubs engaged in historical re-enactment (2015: 14).

In the domain of historical re-enactment one can see considerable overlap in the personnel of these organisations and the people who organise live-action role-playing games ("larpers") portrayed in Chapter 10. Public appeals to patriotic education resonate well with some larpers' views on the pedagogic function of role-playing games. The theme of patriotic education also appears, albeit less directly, in the summer camps that aim to train (male) youth to find inner strength, as described in Chapter 9: the field game *Zarnitsa* with markedly military features has been taken out of its earlier context of Soviet patriotic education and customised to fit an indigenous educational mission. Whichever the context of youth camps in present-day Russia, there is nothing unusual in the prospect of children and youth arrayed in camouflage, which is owed to the outdoor character of activities and underlines a sense of comradeship.

Among the manifold facets of patriotic education that Laruelle points to is the interrelation of household income, place of residence, and leisure activities on offer for young people:

> A kind of correlation probably exists between patriotism and social stratification but it needs to be studied in greater depth and with sociological tools. The poorer a person is, the more one's leisure activities depend on public service offerings. [...] [P]atriotism also has a territorial marker. The larger the spectrum of leisure activities on offer in general, in Moscow and the main Russian cities, the smaller the recruitment pool for patriotic clubs and the less appeal they have to anyone outside their captive audience (those seeking free leisure activities); while in smaller towns and even more so in villages, the patriotic activities sponsored by the town hall, former military personnel or the local parish are often the only ones available, so they enjoy a form of monopoly by default (2015: 18).

In small towns and rural settlements, different types of leisure activities are indeed limited in choice; moreover, many parents are on too tight a budget to be able to use commercially provided leisure activities. Village clubs or municipal Houses of Culture continue to offer (more or less regularly and successfully) extracurricular and leisure activities mainly for children at school age at little or no cost. Although I agree with Laruelle on the necessity to examine spatial and income-related aspects of engagement in patriotic activities, I see a wider spectrum of activities in the public sphere of culture, comprising genres of music, dance, and creative arts that may correspond to patriotic values, but do not necessarily do so (Habeck 2014). I agree with Laruelle that there is a noticeable slant towards patriotism as a moral value to be imbued in young people's minds through school and extracurricular education; this is in line with the general trend of a conservative turn.

The Russian Orthodox Church

Numerous anthropological studies have looked at the strengthening influence of the Russian Orthodox Church after the end of the explicitly atheist Soviet state (e.g. Agadjanian 2017; Benovska-Sabkova et al. 2010; Köllner 2012; Luehrmann 2005; Tocheva 2017; Zigon 2011). One can also generally observe a growing popularity of other religious denominations with a long-standing presence in Russia (Islam, Judaism, Buddhism), of indigenous belief systems such as shamanism, and of religious groups that arrived to Russia rather recently and do not enjoy the legal status of "traditional religion" (e.g. Pentecostalists or Jehovah's Witnesses). Notwithstanding the diversity of denominations, the Russian Orthodox Church certainly holds the leading position. It is hard to ignore the immense number of church buildings in all parts of the country, some of them being restored as a result of the restitution of clerical property, others being built from scratch in towns and settlements at the extractive resource frontier. The position of the clergy is vested in personal, ideological and institutional "entanglements" (Köllner 2018) with local politicians, entrepreneurs, and the military at the national, regional, and local scale.

Despite some degree of diversity of interpretations within the Russian Orthodox Church, the predominant majority of the clergy shares the conviction that Russian society suffers from having lost its cultural values and its spirituality (*dukhovnost'*), and that only the restoration of the latter can help overcome existing social ills. In line with this thought, occasions abound for critiquing individualism, consumerism, and hedonism as "non-Russian" and a sign of degradation. While the general concern about *dukhovnost'* may seem timeless, the particular lessons drawn from it create novel responses: Kristina Stoeckl sees the Russian Orthodox Church as a "norm entrepreneur [...] calling attention to issues that hitherto have not been named" (2016: 133). The concern about social and personal wellbeing through spirituality should be considered as a sensibility in its own right, with newly developing or re-emerging aesthetics and norms of proper conduct, including patterns of consumption and mobility. For example, the practice of fasting has attained widespread popularity (Mitrofanova 2018), as has the practice of pilgrimage (Kormina 2010; Naletova 2010).

While the church as an institution understandably emphasises its continuity in Russian history, religious rites and everyday practices were largely disbanded or reframed in Soviet times, so that now many individuals perceive the need to acquaint themselves and their children with these old-new practices and the belief system on which they are based. Some authors have discussed this realignment under the term *votserkovlenie* ("enchurchment") (Benovska-Sabkova et al. 2010). The personal ambitions and aspirations that accompany the turn towards religiosity, the stream of communication with others about morality and appropriateness, the combination of a shared set of norms with practical exercise, and the repetitive character of the weekly and annual cycle of congregations add up to an expressive mode of identification, and is thus constitutive of a distinct lifestyle. Jarrett Zigon (2008) in particular discusses notions of morality in Russia in the context of practice.

Arguably more than others, adherents of the Russian Orthodox Church — or to do justice to the diversity of believers, more specifically the clergy — are very pronounced in their judgement when it comes to family, sexuality, reproduction, and the institution of marriage (Agadjanian 2017: 43–45). Inasmuch as this is supported by a general conservative turn in Russian politics and society, and the conflation of patriotic behaviour with a healthy nation, the opportunities for public expression of lifestyles diverting from these norms seem to diminish, as has been alluded to in recent publications (e.g. Luehrmann 2017; Mitrokhin 2013; Rakhimova-Sommers 2019; Stähle 2015).

Consumption and critique of consumerism

Not the least important element in the conservative discourse is the critique of consumerism implicitly understood as the blind pursuit of hollow (market-driven) promises and the zeal to gain satisfaction from the act of purchasing or consuming in its own right. In Russian public discourse, consumer culture is frequently portrayed as a phenomenon that has entered Russia from "the west". The term "lifestyle" (*stil' zhizni*) and along with it, the idea of stylisation (*stilizatsiia*), easily acquire the connotation of something spurious (exemplified in Chapter 9), devoid of authenticity and spirituality. Indeed, consumption is often considered to be the key marker of distinctive lifestyles not only in academic scholarship but also in mass media (the latter also pertains to Russia).

In some of the theoretical literature on lifestyle, the linkage between lifestyle and consumption is presented as straightforwardly direct: lifestyle can be analytically exposed through patterns of consumption (see the discussion of Michael Sobel's interpretation of lifestyle in Chapter 1) and consumption is a prime domain of social distinction. It is true that in contemporary Russia, there exists a range of lifestyles that derive their distinctive force largely from the display of fashion, cars (Broz & Habeck 2015), and other consumer goods, sometimes clearly bearing the signs of fetishisation of certain brands and commodities. More generally, the gradual spread of shopping malls in Russian (including Siberian) cities is just one indicator of the unfettered attractiveness of personal and household consumption (cf. Roberts 2016). Yet consumption did not appear suddenly with the turn from a socialist to a market economy: distinctive practices of consumption existed also in Soviet times, and in spite of the overall ideological emphasis on production, private consumption attained public legitimacy in the 1960s under Khrushchev (see Crowley & Reid 2010).

An example of current perceptions of taste and patterns of consumption is a recent study on clothing: Ol'ga Gurova (2014) uses interviews from St Petersburg and Novosibirsk to examine middle-class clothing preferences. She identifies gender, age, class affiliation, and place of residence as the main factors that shape the ways in which people select clothes, want to see themselves, and want to be seen by others. She argues that most male interviewees show a much higher awareness about dress and taste than in Soviet times and the 1990s. Older cohorts of interviewees continue to judge clothes in accordance with "classic" patterns, paying much attention to "cultivated" attire that suits the social occasion. Older people at times complain about the provocative manner of young people's attire, whereas most of the young interviewees emphasise that dress should express individuality and personality.

Gurova's study indicates a general tendency towards individualisation. The concern about finding one's personal style (*stil'*) comes to the fore in interviews with both young and middle-aged informants. Gurova considers middle-class consumers as the main target group of marketing, and middle-class youth as those who are most prone to experimenting with new styles. Among her interviewees, there is awareness about (and usually respect for) people with very low income who nonetheless invest much of their scarce resources in "proper" or tasteful attire. Middle-class perceptions of the upper class have changed to some extent: the image of *nouveaux riches* in raspberry-red jackets and golden necklets, which was typical for the 1990s, is giving way to a different type of appearance, oriented towards a well-groomed body and higher quality garments.

Gurova notes that people in Novosibirsk dress more brightly and simultaneously more "grey-ish" and less individually than in St Petersburg, which is characterised by its restrained and yet individual apparel. There seems to be a paradox — bright versus grey — which may be explained by seasonality (cold winters do not offer many opportunities for bright clothing) and additionally by some sort of "herd instinct" (*stadnyi instinkt*) of Novosibirsk urbanites, who are generally prone to follow the latest fad, as one of Gurova's interviewees said.[3] Gurova also pays attention to the spatial hierarchy of trends in taste and dress: Novosibirsk largely follows and emulates trends received from St Petersburg and Moscow — with some local variation, which may partly be explained by its proximity to China and Far-Eastern markets. According to my interviewees in Novosibirsk, inhabitants of smaller industrial cities, such as Kemerovo, are even less individualist in terms of apparel, less refined and more trivial in their taste. People in district centres take the regional capital's fashion as a yardstick, whereas villagers seek to incorporate the fashion that they observe in the district centre.

As such, these statements are not very surprising, but there are two points that deserve particular attention: first, despite the ethnic diversity of Siberia, very seldom do elements of regionally or ethnically

---

3   From my own observations, in the city centre of Novosibirsk it is indeed possible to dress in very ostentatious and "individualist" ways, but a few blocks further, towards the city's suburbs, such statements of individualism will be met by stern glances and occasionally by sneering comments. See Habeck & Schröder (2016) on spatial aspects of explicit xenophobia and homophobia in some parts of the urban fabric of Novosibirsk.

specific dress enter the flow of fashion. There have been artistic and academic projects to identify distinct Siberian brand symbols, playing with existing stereotypes about Siberia (Press 2012). Nonetheless, fashion designers and managers in this domain continue to look for inspiration from Moscow, St Petersburg, and western countries, in some cases ultimately deciding to relocate there.[4] It should be added, however, that in some of the ethnically defined territories of Russia — such as the Republic of Sakha (Yakutia) — visible expressions of personal sensibilities that evolve around ethnicity can be seen clearly in the domestic and the public sphere (see Chapter 7). Second, the argument about the spatial hierarchy of fashion loses some of its clout in specific situations and spaces; and interestingly, it is in very remote villages as well as in large cities that research team members met individuals who show stubborn indifference to fashion as much as to the comments of their neighbours (exemplified in Chapter 3). Attire may look odd as long as it is practical.

Gurova mentions anti-materialist attitudes among some of her interviewees, both amongst the senior and the junior cohort. The former are likely to comply with the request from Soviet days "not to get obsessed with things" (*ne zatsiklivat'sia na veshchakh*, 2014: 60), whereas the latter display anti-materialist attitudes with the aim to express critique towards capitalism and consumerism. There is ample congruence here with normative appeals around *dukhovnost'*, discussed in the previous section, and also with the phenomenon of voluntary simplicity that has developed as a sensibility in its own right in Russia (cf. Il'in 2015) as well as in other societies. In the course of our research project, we came across many examples — and have presented them in this volume — of lifestyles and subcultures that continue to value self-made objects, home-grown food, regional products, economic self-sufficiency, a livelihood close to nature and the skills that come with it, and traditional crafts and skills as part of a regional — in some cases, indigenous — identity. Returning to one of the general arguments, any attempt to analyse lifestyle through the proxy of consumption remains insufficient if the sensibilities that lay at the core of these lifestyles are not understood in detail.

---

4   Two of my interviewees for this project did.

Increase in mobility and international tourism

Mobility has the potential to make people more aware of the range of lifestyles that exist outside their immediate sphere of everyday life: it offers manifold opportunities to realise in which ways others (relatives, friends, acquaintances, and members of the general public) live under very diverse conditions and pursue very diverse forms of work and pastime activities. A particularly strong version of this argument has been made by Vladimir Popov with regard to international tourism as a trigger for tolerance and democracy:

> Russian tourists can be considered as the subjects trying actively to master new forms of transnational practice, identity and subjectivity after a long stay in actual closedness during the days of the Soviet era and the following economic crisis of the 1990s. Except for the transnational mobility, hardly any phenomenon in the cultural aspect has contributed to the weakening of the dominant codes of behaviour which have remained an inheritance from previous historical periods. Many forms of social and cultural life seen outside, especially in the advanced Western countries, have appeared extremely attractive and acted as ideals of what many would seek in their daily lives. It is felt that the experience, acquired in the practice of international mobility, has appeared as the important reason encouraging social changes in Russia towards a more open and democratic society (2012: 160–61).

While I agree with the statement that transnational mobility fosters a sense of openness and awareness of other modes of living, I am more sceptical about the tenet that the experience of having been abroad encourages a more democratic and tolerant society. Acquaintance with other people's living conditions and comparison with one's own mode of living does not necessarily mean that travellers accept other countries' social arrangements and other people's values as applicable in their own societal context.[5] In the oft-discussed comparison of "us" in Russia with people living elsewhere, I frequently encountered statements to the effect that Russia needs to pursue its own way. Having said that, from among the interviewees of our research project, many of the urban and

---

5   Dennis Zuev (personal communication) observed that Russian *Work-and-Travel* students visiting the United States for a mid-term period (up to four months) did not generally develop a stronger sense of tolerance or acceptance of alternative life-ways.

some of the rural inhabitants judge their stays abroad very positively, with some taking the decision to spend part of their life in a different country (in North America, Europe, Southeast Asia), quite frequently moving back and forth between their new home abroad and their home town in Russia in a sense that clearly shows the marks of a transnational existence.

Popov's assessment is based on statistical data from across Russia; it does not account for regional differences. While travelling to Mediterranean countries or Thailand came to be something of a mass phenomenon in the 2000s, it nonetheless remains the privilege of urban inhabitants; whereas those living in rural settlements continue to arrange their travels in dependence on relatives in Russian cities, combining a host of practical issues (shopping, provisions, healthcare, etc.) with the maintenance of familial networks. Exceptions of this rule are some rural communities in the vicinity of Russia's state boundary, e.g. with China or Finland, but in these cases, the aspect of pleasure in travel is usually less important than its economic aspect. Regional disparities of mobility are stark across the different parts of Russia, as has been recently shown by Bolotova, Karaseva & Vasilyeva (2017) — a point to which I will return below in line with the discussion of mobility patterns in the rural settlements of our research project.

Lifestyle, habits of travelling, and visual forms of self-presentation

The research project was designed with the purpose of studying two questions:

(a) What is the mutual relationship between changing technology and infrastructure on the one hand, and lifestyles, on the other, *as exposed by habits of travelling*?

(b) What is the mutual relationship between changing technology and infrastructure on the one hand, and lifestyles, on the other, *as exposed by changing visual forms of self-presentation*?

An examination of the above was achieved through the prism of three sub-questions: (i) How have technology and infrastructure changed over time?; (ii) How have habits of travelling changed over time?; and (iii) How have visual forms of self-expression changed over time?

How have technology and infrastructure changed over time?

Chapter 2 of this volume discusses changes in technology and infrastructure in detail, and only general trends shall be repeated here. In comparison to present times, travel in the last Soviet decade was harder and easier: it was harder inasmuch as there was a general shortage of tickets, and passengers had very little choice when it came to selecting their travel time and means of transport, let alone a full itinerary of travel. It was easier inasmuch as larger parts of society felt travels to be affordable, even if regulated through a complex balance of entitlements and limitations. The dendritic character of infrastructure (mirroring administrative hierarchies) was specific for the Soviet Union as a country with a centrally managed economy and a vast territory; in present-day Russia, this condition continues to exert its impact on the movements of people for all kinds of purposes, including touristic ones.

After a period of the state's inability to sustain infrastructure in the Far North and Far East of Russia during the 1990s, one can now witness a technological overhaul of the main arteries and also gradual expansion of infrastructure. These tasks figure high on the political agenda: they reflect the intention to "catch up" with other countries; they are partly influenced by geopolitical considerations; and — in the remoter parts of the country — continue to be guided by the development of resource extraction. Many settlements in the Far North and Far East owe their existence to resource extraction and/or the maintenance of railways and roads, and this phenomenon is likely to continue in future years.

Internet connection is now of essential importance in many spheres of life, and younger people experience the necessity to have access to the internet arguably more strongly than members of the older generation. The implementation of a reliable and high-speed internet connection in rural and remote areas of Russia proceeds at comparatively fast pace. Within only two decades, the mobile phone has become an indispensable part of everyday communication and personal logistics for nearly all inhabitants of the region. Mobiles and the internet have also laid the ground for an exponentially growing production and circulation of photographs, continuing the legacy of home photography of the last Soviet decades and expanding visual forms of self-presentation in terms of quantity and also diversity of content.

However, GSM and internet coverage are regionally disparate, as is the transportation network. The number of privately owned cars has increased rapidly, facilitating individually arranged travel and loosening the dependence on trains. Trains and public bus services now compete with commercial bus and *marshrutka* services. The latter offer a much higher degree of flexibility in planning one's movements, but this depends on personal income and is thus subject to social stratification.

How have habits of travelling of travel changed over time?

With regard to tourism in Soviet times (notably, the 1960s to 1980s), Brož and Habeck have highlighted the intricate interplay of tourism organised by institutions and so-called "wild", individually arranged tourism (Chapter 4). Purposes and destinations in the institutional segment of tourism were largely prescribed by ideological considerations. Leisure was not *per se* a reason to travel; instead, tourism required a "noble cause" such as the restoration of health and productivity, acquaintance with the history and socialist present of the country, or, in the case of trips outside the Soviet Union, the idea of a "friendship of nations" (*druzhba narodov*). Journeys abroad were strongly controlled by state and party organisations and considered a special privilege. Yet also within the Soviet Union, the allocation of travel vouchers and similar entitlements occurred in a rather arbitrary way, despite a belief in the equality of citizens. Individually arranged travels relied either on networks of relatives and friends, or on the use of largely informal services at the margins of the state-provided tourist infrastructure. Yet alternative lifestyles and modes of "getting around" also existed in Soviet times, as is illustrated by the informal network of person-to-person recommendations (*sistema*) among hippies who were willing and ready to offer their flat as a hang-out or transit lodging to like-minded people.

Characteristic for the 1990s and even more so for the 2000s is an increasing diversity of modes and motivations of tourism, facilitated by the shift towards more flexible and more individual arrangements of transport (Chapter 2). This diversity is also in line with a post-Soviet interest in exploring new types of leisure activities, often in response to commercially created desires and images of exotic destinations (Chapter 4). The consequences of the social stratification of tourism — and of mobility more generally — are manifold. In Novosibirsk and other Siberian cities, a mushrooming number of travel agencies started to cater for different desires and different household budgets from about 2000 onwards. In later years, part of this market segment has moved towards online sales. In addition, couch-surfing and other travel practices based on online social networks have contributed to the growth of a non-commercial (or at least, less commercial) touristic infrastructure, which is of great importance for young (more often than not, urban-based) travellers with a limited budget, creating the basis for a spontaneous and cosmopolitan attitude towards travelling.

The above remarks about changing habits of travelling are not meant to downplay the scope of *personal topographies* (cf. Chapter 5) of those inhabitants that we interviewed in remote rural settlements; rather it means to say that they differ from each other. Several of our rural interviewees combine extended stays in roadless forest or tundra areas with regular visits to the respective regional centre, which may be several hundreds of kilometres away from their place of residence. Towards the tundra or forest "end" of their personal ambit of action, they frequently find themselves outside the area covered by GSM or the internet, being left to their own navigational abilities (for many urbanites, a frightening prospect); whereas in the other direction, their travels usually follow pathways that continue to be prescribed by administrative hierarchies and dendritic infrastructure. Earlier, it was suggested that inhabitants of rural communities travel significantly less to foreign countries and that their holiday itineraries closely follow their networks of relatives and friends, usually with the purpose of accessing services and goods that they do not have at their place of residence. This suggestion is supported by the data that research team members collected in the three rural communities of Novoe Chaplino, Saranpaul', and Chavan'ga; yet what also comes to the fore are important differences in each community's configuration of mobility patterns.

The case of Novoe Chaplino (briefly portrayed in Chapter 6) corresponds quite closely with the blueprint of pathways constituted by institutions and kinship ties; however, part of this community's kinship networks went beyond the Soviet border and were severed for that reason. The historically existing connections with communities across the Bering Strait were revived during a short period in the 1990s but have largely been discontinued. Occasionally, a cruise ship came along to bring visitors from abroad to the village, creating insecurity among local inhabitants of "what to show", in other words, what to present as locally and culturally unique. The potential asset of Novoe Chaplino's location on the Bering Sea has not sparked the emergence of new pathways, so that personal topographies remain geared to the district and regional centre. Spatial imaginaries include Anadyr', Magadan, and also Moscow, St Petersburg and Black Sea resorts nine time zones away in much more vivid form than any place in neighbouring Alaska or neighbouring Kamchatka. Due to the extremely high costs of travelling, holiday trips are predominantly dependent on state benefits.[6]

Inhabitants of Saranpaul' (Chapter 9) speak of their place as an island, hard to reach and then hard to leave behind again. Arrangements of logistics and travel reflect the limited range of transportation and consumer goods in the village. Having said that, the summer camps for young people organised by indigenous pedagogues draw visitors from far afield, and there has been a regular exchange of youth between the summer camp and Germany. It is the secluded location and indigenous cultural heritage that make Saranpaul' a tourist destination, and both local and visiting youth experience the camp as an opportunity for self-cultivation and discovering one's talents.

Chavan'ga (Chapter 3) used to be a rural settlement economically based on agriculture and fishing, but is gradually turning into a weekend or summer-cottage settlement. Much depends on the concerted efforts of individuals to make a living in this village. The village may by now be abandoned, were it not for the fact that several individuals decided to stay or return at their own discretion, sometimes to the amazement of their relatives. More than in the other two rural settlements, one gets the impression that inhabitants pursue some individual life

---

6   Life projects can be discerned in the narratives of many photo-elicitation interviewees of Novoe Chaplino, but there were also interviewees who did not perceive any necessity to narrate their biography in any sense of a coherent "project".

projects which, when taken together and notwithstanding personal animosities, engender a sense of social cohesion and identity of the place.

In the discussion of changing patterns of mobility, I have gradually shifted the emphasis from tourism to other motivations for travelling, particularly the habit (by necessity) of inhabitants of remote communities to draw upon family members who now live in different locations. Out-migration of young people is a common phenomenon in rural communities, but it is not necessarily a one-way road. This also accounts, in the long run, for some of our indigenous interviewees' journeys in search of "roots", which may occur several generations after an ancestor's relocation (see Chapter 5). In both Soviet and post-Soviet times, people travel towards a distant (Siberian, Far Northern, or Far Eastern) "home", the initial reasons for which go back to the metropolitan-bound mobility of the indigenous intelligentsia. In recent years, travelling in search of "roots" has been increasingly associated with spiritual well-being.

For most of our "rural" interlocutors, it is not unusual to combine rural and urban places of residence in their biographies. Higher education and the search for a job require young people from rural communities to move to the district centre or "the city" (often the regional capital). Our research has shown that young people's decisions about moving (leaving, returning, commuting) are judged by others in very ambivalent ways. On the one hand, parents are aware that higher education and career necessitate their children to move away. On the other, there are hopes that young people will then come back to support and maintain the household and the rural community. Villagers may be sceptical about a young person's return from the city to the native village, especially if higher education has not been completed. Such cases may be viewed as personal failure, even though the person themselves may view it differently. Chapter 3 provides examples of individuals who have decided to go for voluntary simplicity, to forfeit a better salary of a job in town for the benefit of personal freedom and a less stressful working day in the village. These observations are indicative of a more general trend among young people to balance work-life requirements with individual ideas of self-fulfilment.

Bolotova, Karaseva, and Vasilyeva (2017) conducted anthropological field research among youth in three different regions of the Far North: Kirovsk (a town in Murmansk Oblast), Yagodnoe (a small town in the uplands of Magadan Oblast), and Syndassko (a rural settlement near the Arctic Ocean, in the north-eastern "corner" of the Krasnoiarsk Region). The juxtaposition of the three cases vividly underscores the stark disparities of Far Northern regions in terms of transportation and infrastructure, and it also illustrates the strong influence of these conditions on young people's patterns of mobility and their life decisions. As Bolotova reports, many youths and also some older residents of Kirovsk conduct regular trips to the regional capital, to other towns in the region, and also occasionally to Finland and Norway. An important reason to return to Kirovsk is the beauty of the surroundings and a range of outdoor activities, particularly skiing. A high degree of connectedness also comes to the fore in virtual communities:

> New technology contributes to the transformation of the perception of space: due to the high level of Internet accessibility in the Murmansk region, there are numerous groups on social networks that are popular on the regional level. For example, there are travel companion groups, regional virtual communities, and interest clubs that also organize regular off-line meetings, such as climbers, Hare Krishna followers, cyclists, role-playing gamers, anime fans, and many others (Bolotova, Karaseva & Vasilyeva 2017: 89).

Compare this with Vasilyeva's description of life in Syndassko, which to outsiders comes over as rather bleak:

> [Y]oung people's planning horizon is short, and the decisions about relocation and life change can be spontaneous. Therefore, young people's life strategies and related movements are often not caused by purposeful action but happen on a whim. At the same time, one's biography usually includes a lot of mobility, which can last for many years (Bolotova, Karaseva & Vasilyeva 2017: 113).

Here again we see an obvious connection between living conditions and the predictability of pursuing a life project. By extension we see that the conditions and limitations of lifestyle diversity — where lifestyle is seen as expressive and intentional practice evolving around certain sensibilities and ambitions of self-formation — depend on infrastructure and predictability of transport. In remote small communities, there is also a particularly palpable connection between the possible range of lifestyles and local strategies of procurement through land use, barter and exchange, public-sector jobs, pension payments, and other state-granted benefits. Connectedness is defined as being positioned in far-extending social networks of kinship and direct exchange, much more than through any virtual social network (Syndassko does have access to the internet, but it is reportedly very slow and highly expensive).

Yagodnoe, the third location of Bolotova, Karaseva, and Vasilyeva's study, occupies an intermediate position, and yet a precarious one in view of the mass out-migration from Magadan Oblast to the "mainland", i.e. the European part of Russia or more southerly parts of Siberia. As Karaseva reports, inhabitants judge the condition of the road to Magadan and the state's willingness to invest in road maintenance as an indicator of the town's future prospects; the road takes on the position of a lifeline. Movement in search of higher education and also weekend entertainment are so strongly oriented towards the regional capital, some 500 kilometres away, that the sense of place comes to include Yagodnoe, Magadan, and the road as a dispersed notion of "here". An internet connection exists and some inhabitants have experience with online shopping, but the logistics of delivery are complicated enough to induce residents of Yagodnoe to do their shopping in Magadan (Bolotova, Karaseva & Vasilyeva 2017: 98).

The findings of these three authors resonate with those of our research, in that they point out stark disparities in young people's mobility. They complement our interviews with people above the age of forty, i.e. those that remember conditions and practices of travelling in Soviet days compared to today. To sum up the post-socialist shifts: in comparison to Soviet times, personal topographies and spatial imaginaries (Chapter 5) attained a larger ambit and diversity in the first and especially the second post-Soviet decade — for many inhabitants of Siberia, but not for all. Depending on the household's location and economic situation, the withdrawal or continuation of state-subsidised transportation, and social ties outside their own place of residence, the interviewees that we met in the framework of our research project largely differ in their capacity to develop personal ambitions and life projects beyond the level of "making ends meet".

How have visual forms of self-presentation changed over time?

In the 1960s and 1970s, visualisation through photography put the work collective at centre stage and also paid reverence to the family as a social institution; whereas in the 2000s, new technological means of photographing and sharing photographs have been instrumental in the visualisation of leisure activities and everyday life, with the family remaining a focal point of reference in the lives of most of our interlocutors. What has also become apparent over recent years is a heightened or renewed concern with spiritual fulfilment and the expression of spiritual values through visual means.

As Jaroslava Panáková put it in Chapter 6, "happiness is part of an individual lifestyle project, its 'architect' and 'companion', and sometimes its ultimate goal. We seek to do what we think will make us happy, even if it does not necessarily end up this way". What has changed over the decades is the configuration of the self and the collective: work has shifted from being seen as something beneficial for the collective and the entire society to something that should be both socially and individually fulfilling (Chapter 3); it has shifted from visually framing one's own role as a self-within-the-collective towards self-within-the family, self-with-children, self-with-friends, or simply self in an immense range of activities and places (Chapter 6).

As a result of this shift, there is a growing willingness of individuals, alone or together with others, to picture and present themselves in a larger diversity of roles. The role of the committed worker, the role of the caring mother/father/relative, and the role of the cheerful traveller have already been present in the portfolio of visual forms of self-expression in earlier decades. These are now complemented by additional roles — free time permitting — of more leisurely and informal pursuits. This is a result of two processes: on the one hand, of the shift from the professional (and concomitantly, time-consuming and infrequent) art of photography towards the everyday, ubiquitous (and concomitantly, trivial) practice of photography. On the other hand, it is the result of a wider array of socially relevant moments that deserve to be depicted.

These findings are exemplified by two domains of self-expression that figured most strongly in Chapters 7–10 of this volume: ethnicity and role play. Ethnicity, as has been established by Eleanor Peers in Chapter 7, underwent a specific form of "moulding" in Soviet times, and the mould comprised a certain range of genres (attire in the first place; along with music, literature, theatre and opera, and cuisine) through which ethnic peculiarities were to be expressed within the framework of the brotherhood of peoples. These genres and expressive forms have well survived into post-socialist times. As Artem Rabogoshvili shows in Chapter 8, this does not prevent ethnic communities' members and activists from treating such expressions as sincere statements. Rather, they may take advantage from clues that are easily recognisable to others and as such create a "surface" for public consumption, notwithstanding their individual views on the source and significance of ethnic belonging as part of personal identity.

To put it differently, donning a Tatar costume is a statement in reverence to Tatar cultural traditions, but it is neither just role play, nor is it necessarily an outward sign of deeply felt Tatar identity. *Some* members of ethnic communities intentionally incorporate publicly recognisable expressions of ethnicity into the ambience of their home even though the artefacts may look artificial; *some* ethnic activists debate the "authenticity" of certain elements; and *some* others combine them in creative and ironic ways with different, and at first glance inappropriate, genres. If ethnicity is understood as a sensibility in its own right, then the manifold stances towards the use of dress and other visual symbols can be read as individual positions about style and veracity. It would be facile to underestimate the political power of statements about ethnic belonging: as the first scene of Chapter 7 illustrates, people in power, regardless of their own ethnic background, feel required to comply with the populace's expectations about regional loyalty.

A differentiation is made in Chapter 8 between *old-time residents,* i.e. ethnic groups that were already in Soviet times acknowledged as minorities by some or all of Russia's administrative units; and *newcomers,* i.e. groups that in the Soviet Union had their "own" republics or territories but are now usually considered as migrants from *Blizhnee zarubezh'e* ("Near Abroad"), mainly from Central Asia. For both groups, dress and other visual clues are important means to show their presence in a multicultural social fabric. Public festivities and national holidays carry much currency in this endeavour, and in that respect, newcomers have to invest considerable energy in following the patterns already established among the old-time residents. The degree of commitment varies among members of communities of both groups. Such differential degree of involvement can be taken as a criterion of immersion into a distinct lifestyle, similarly manifest in live-action role-playing (LARP) communities, even though the basis of LARP is usually not ancestral and much more intentional.

Role play involves a quite specific form of stylisation, which requires the self to be someone else and yet to be oneself. Inside the *chronotope* of live-action role-playing games, change of dress is mandatory, and a huge amount of attention is paid to the aesthetics of garments and accessories. The apparel is not only prescribed by the scenario but also the subject of personal style and taste. These costumes, the dramatic moments of the action, and the strong emotions of the actors are all recorded using photographs and films. The photo-elicitation interviews with larpers and our visits to their online forums provide abundant visual clues to self-as-other-and-yet-self, starting with black-and-white photographs from the late 1980s and ending with fully-fledged photo albums to be shared widely and publicly through the social network VKontakte. This has also helped larpers to see themselves not as lone oddballs, but as followers or participants of a large community, albeit with different degrees of commitment. As Tatiana Barchunova and Joachim Otto Habeck show in Chapter 10, there are different degrees of personal involvement in the "world" of the game, and the most devoted larpers draw no clear boundary between play and reality. As Barchunova found out, many larpers see "real life" as one variation of other worlds. By transferring items of dress or accessories into "real life", they visually demonstrate their readiness to make playful self-stylisation an element of their everyday life.

As Ina Schröder shows in Chapter 9, ethnicity and role play come together in summer camps organised with the purpose of teaching young people to rediscover traditional cultural values. In the camp that Schröder studies near Saranpaul', video footage is broadcast daily to campers in a quasi-news format so that participants can judge their own and other's performance and discuss what went well or not so well. This results in a dense daily cycle of action, visualisation, and evaluation. Like the games described in Chapter 10, there is also an annual cycle of preparation, enactment, evaluation, and exchange of memories. The games differ, however, in the extent of irony versus pedagogical ambition: the summer camp near Saranpaul' is earnestly didactic in its role play.

To conclude this section, let me add a general observation. More often than in earlier decades, visual forms of self-expression contain a smile. The smile may be interpreted variously: as a sign of hedonistic self-indulgence; as an ironic twinkle that signals a subversion of social norms and expectations; or as the warm glow of mutual care and sympathy. All of these interpretations contribute to the exploration of lifestyles: they may be read as expressions of a consumer-culture attitude to fulfilling material desires and the satisfaction of bodily senses; as the temporary joy of diving into subcultural diversions from "grey" everyday life and serious behaviour; or as the more perennial happiness of being together with loved ones. Let readers be reminded that photographs usually depict only happy moments, and that the stories that surround them have many different shades. By the same token, self-expression through visual means almost always carries a message about personal ambitions and intentions, about trying to be good to oneself and others, and about trying to be good at something.

Reassessing the concept of lifestyle

In the introduction to this volume, I argued that lifestyle can be seen as a particular *mode* of identification: it is expressive, routinised, and stylised. It is expressive inasmuch as the practices and choices are meant to convey a message about one's self to others (and frequently, they are deliberately deployed for that purpose); it is routinised through repeated action (with some procedures taking on such a habitual character that they no longer depend on active reflection); and it is stylised in that it combines collective ideas and fashions with a certain degree of personal variation and play with conventions. (The latter point could also be described as individual positionings towards and around sensibilities.) Lifestyle is a particular mode of identification among other modes of a less expressive kind, i.e. modes of identification which are not articulated in the public or have to be completely hidden (which does not imply that these modes are less serious or less intensive an experience for the individual).

One of the conclusions to be drawn from the research presented in this book is the interconnection of lifestyle, repeated action, and reflexivity. When embarking on this project, research team members pondered on the question whether (and if so, in what ways) lifestyle requires any form of reflection on the part of the individual. We agree with the suggestion that repeated action leads to habitualisation — and that it perpetuates and reproduces structures of social interaction. We also follow Bourdieu in claiming that tastes and predilections are strongly influenced by existing conventions, institutions, and social positions — to such an extent that individual "choices" are not a matter of choice but rather non-reflexive enactments of class-dependent patterns of taste. However, on behalf of the research team, I argue that this is not sufficient to chart the explanatory potential of the concept of lifestyle.

Under the constraints of time, energy, and social and economic resources which every human being experiences, some type of action always occurs at the expense of another type, and thus some choice of activity reduces the potential for other choices. On this basis, it is possible to discern different degrees of involvement in certain activities. The more intensive the involvement in an activity, the higher the significance in the life of the individual. The cases presented in several chapters illustrate different degrees of involvement — in some cases, obsession — with certain activities, and the most devoted practitioners can be most clearly identified with a distinctive lifestyle. With the gradual enskillment of practices related to the personally significant activity, individuals develop habitual (and largely non-reflected) patterns of actions, i.e. routines, and also patterns of self-expression. The intensity of involvement and the personal significance of the activity, however, become objects of self-reflection.

Moreover, individuals pursue personally significant activities not in isolation, but usually in communication, co-presence, and/or interaction with others. In the framework of such exchanges, enskillment comes to be a topic of communication. The process of training, the acquisition of a specific vocabulary, and also the comparison of one's own competencies with those of others all bring about self-inspection, dialogue about things worthy to be achieved, collectively shared ambitions, and also individual aspirations ("reaching the next level", so to speak). In the process of learning and practicing together, in the constant flow of concerns and ideals, individuals develop their own way of doing things "right". They develop their own style and their own responses to what they have come to acknowledge as a shared sensibility, to return again to Chaney's concept, and this by necessity has an expressive aspect to it, including visual clues that in composition result in "surfaces".

This can be observed with regard to outdoor adventurers and activists interested in maintaining the cultural memory of a small place (Chapter 3), activists of ethno-cultural organisations (Chapter 8), indigenous pedagogues (Chapter 9) as well as among regular larpers (Chapter 10). It can also be observed among those who pursue a spiritually rewarding life, be it in search of the healing power of nature and the spiritual forces residing therein (Chapter 4) or under the auspices of the Russian Orthodox Church. Likewise, the quest for a renewed engagement with indigenous traditions (Chapter 7 and Chapter 9) entails an expressive and reflexive element of self-formation and a personal response to issues of modernity, cultivation, and social and individual progress.

Lifestyle and modernity in post-Soviet Russia

On a more general level, the research team also pursued the question of whether a focus on lifestyle in Siberia helps to generate an anthropological contribution to scholarly debates about *modernity*. Some authors have argued that lifestyle is a feature of modern, high-modern, or post-modern societies (see Chapter 1). Does the concept have any explanatory value in a non-western setting such as "provincial" Russia? Do notions of modernity and progress carry any relevance in the historical and contemporary context of Siberia?

Much has been written by anthropologists and historians about the Soviet modernisation project (e.g. Kotkin 1995; Volkov 2000; for Siberia and the Far North: Slezkine 1994). The Soviet government and the Communist Party actively pursued the goal to spur progress not only in technological terms, but also to create a "new person", a "Soviet person" (*sovetskii chelovek*, Smirnov 1973) and thus to induce shifts in people's convictions, ambitions, self-perception, and behaviour. Such social engineering has held sway over large parts of the country's population, and it should not be forgotten that explicitly deviating views or open resistance were not tolerated.

The effects of modernisation were notably strong in rural and indigenous communities: the "old" way of life was to disappear — a mandate that was accompanied by dramatic and at times violent disruptions in all spheres of life. At the same time, the Soviet modernisation project opened up new trajectories of personal fulfilment and aspirations, notably through formal education, a diversified range of occupations and careers, and also through a country-wide flow of cultural production, creating a shared Soviet cultural space. Indigenous forms of cultural expression were permitted to persist — but only in a sanctioned form — to be utilised for public displays of diversity in the framework of a "modern" Soviet conviviality. (As we have seen, this type of display of indigenous culture also has reverberations in present-day Russia).

In the light of the quest for modernity and progress, which had pervasive power in all parts of the country, there was a wide variety of individual and collective responses to the idea of how to be "modern" in different domains of life. These responses depended not only on changing political priorities, but also on the individual's involvement in different social networks. Moreover, Yurchak (2006) has convincingly shown how the very institutions and mechanisms which served to create an ideologically legitimate frame for activities simultaneously created spaces for unofficial, informal, and partly illicit activities at the margins (such as the boisterous parties at the fringe of socialist manifestations that everyone was expected to attend).

The heightened significance of visuality constitutes an important part of modernity — and of lifestyle (Chaney 1996: 101). This trope is most clearly addressed in Chapters 6 and 7 of the volume. Panáková shows in Chapter 6 (with reference to Sontag 2005) that visual media is a key phenomenon of the "modern": images come to determine demands, mingling with and replacing the immediacy of first-hand experience. Similarly, Peers argues in Chapter 7 (with reference to Chaney 1996) "that the anonymity of [...] urban space, the development of cultures of consumption, along with mass advertising and fashion, and the fracturing of pre-modern hierarchies have led to a new emphasis on visualisation in the formation and negotiation of social structuration and identity" (p. 262). Later in the chapter, she expands on this point and identifies as one of the characteristics of the "essentially modernist nature of the Soviet project" the power of the Party and the government to create "normative conceptions of aesthetic experience" and "legitimate patterns of sensibility" (p. 275). This, I would add, generated new ways for individuals to perceive their own role in society, and the lifestyles available to them.

If one accepts the power of images and imaginaries to be a central feature of modernity, then the Soviet Union was embracing modernity from its very beginning, considering the intensity of visual messages emanating from the centres of power and mirrored by local performances of progress in the peripheries. In addition to these official displays of well-being, the development of home photography — i.e. mass production of cameras for private use — since the mid-1960s was instrumental in capturing vernacular interpretations of what "good life" looks like (Chapter 6), and these personal interpretations themselves largely drew on the aesthetics ideologically promoted by Soviet design and media (Chapter 7).

Aesthetics and the whole array of societal changes were promoted pervasively across the country,[7] yet the promotion and implementation proceeded at different speeds; moreover, they were negotiated regionally and locally in divergent ways. Some of the authors have referred to Nikolai Ssorin-Chaikov's book *The Social Life of the State in Sub-Arctic Siberia* (2003), which captures vividly the "advent" of the state in Central Siberia, its local applications, and the unfinished character of this process, always with the prospect of a better future yet to arrive. Regional variations of Sovietisation come to the fore in Chapter 7: Yakut/Sakha interpretations of progress and the "good life" gave the project of modernisation a specific slant. In other areas of Siberia, too, staged performances of "progress" underwent regional variation, though usually they largely complied with the frame of a general Soviet "mould" of cultural expression. Nonetheless, such performances occasionally entailed subtle undertones, to be interpreted as critique by spectators who could read between the lines. To add one

---

7   The distinctive style of Soviet architecture, design, artworks, and cultural performance is often associated with the avant-garde of the 1920s (Mally 2003); however, it is possible to discern typically Soviet forms of artistic and aesthetic expression also in subsequent decades (Papernyi 2007).

more observation, even in places where the appurtenances of modernity (and technical progress) arrived with significant delay and were continually limited in stock, inhabitants creatively combined — through *bricolage* — the items they had at hand, often in pursuit of individual ideas about "how to be modern".

Modernity was also defined through mobility and the extension of infrastructure and (state-controlled) accessibility of all parts of the country; in other words, the Soviet state made immense investments in order to reduce remoteness. What disappeared in the process of modernisation were earlier indigenous patterns of mobility, itineraries, means of transport, and the skills needed to handle them; these were replaced by a new form of mobility, reaching as far as Moscow, Leningrad and the Black Sea, requiring new skills but also widening indigenous individual's social networks throughout the Soviet Union. Such new modes of mobility were regarded as a metaphor of the country's progress. As Panáková puts it, these changes resulted in "an initiation into another understanding of what one should be, wants to be, or can afford to be through displacement" (Chapter 6 (p. 226)).

The first post-Soviet decade, the 1990s, saw large-scale experimenting with new ways of being at the societal and personal levels; this shift was strongly oriented towards consumer goods, social practices, and lifestyles from outside the country, often from "the west".[8] Such experiments often included self-expression and the display of wealth through shiny and glittery forms of attire (among these, the raspberry-coloured jackets mentioned earlier in this chapter). Curiosity about distant destinations was first impeded by generally low financial resources, but in the early 2000s, travelling abroad became achievable for considerable numbers of Russians. At about the same time, digital photography and communication via the internet provided the basis for a hitherto unexperienced and dazzling flow and diversity of images, apparently marking Russia's entry into a post-modern condition, whereby the grand political narratives lose their pervasive power, the quest for happiness is relegated to the individual, and the "necessity to choose" one's own way (Giddens 1991) becomes mandatory.

---

8   The collected volume *Consuming Russia* edited by Barker (1999) puts consumption at centre stage but extends far beyond consumption in the narrow sense, depicting a large array of shifts in popular culture and aesthetics in the first decade of post-Soviet society.

Notwithstanding, the 2000s and the 2010s do not fully comply with such a conceptualisation of the post-modern condition. In contemporary Russia, the *multitude* of moral norms and convictions is rarely given credit as a value in its own right; state institutions, the Orthodox Church and other "norm entrepreneurs" (Stoeckl 2016, see above) apprehend it with scepticism. Norms and convictions thus undergo a process of consolidation. The conservative turn, however, does not negate a simultaneous quest for modernisation. The ingredients of the new type of modernity combine technological and infrastructural development with an inward-looking reassessment of the past and the search for moral values and sources of inspiration from within Russian history. The search for spiritual revival and the refusal of consumerism and individualism have already been portrayed as sensibilities in their own right, and they resonate with current critiques of consumerism elsewhere in the world. One more factor influencing current conditions and limitations of lifestyle plurality in Russia is the fact that the experimenting with goods and ideas "from outside" now takes place in a calmer manner, possibly resulting from a certain degree of saturation. This shift is very much in line with the pervasive emphasis on patriotic forms of behaviour and morality.

Towards the end of the conclusion, let us come to the question of whether lifestyle can be applied in the context of *indigenous* Siberia — more precisely, in the context of a region with many ethnic groups whose members continue to pursue hunting and herding as "traditional" forms of resource use and derive a sense of identity from them. By now it should have become clear that such application is not only possible, but also has explanatory value in the analysis of social change in socialist and post-socialist societies. This is not to say that pre-revolutionary, "traditional" indigenous societies were exempt from expressions of lifestyle (a tenet that was discussed in Chapter 1). While it may appear that in "traditional" society, the rigidity of social institutions limited the room for manoeuvre of individual actors,[9] it is nonetheless clear that livelihoods in the tundra, taiga, or steppe also

---

9   Sántha and Safonova (2010) have made an explicit statement about the egalitarian, non-hierarchical character of Evenki society, where authority is not determined by inherited status but by individual competency and success in pursuing tasks necessary for the well-being of the community, up to the point of Evenki interlocutors ridiculing any form of social hierarchy.

depended on individual talents and skills developed through training and in communication with others. It also relied on individual ideas about how to do things right, with concomitant variation in aesthetic predilections. The retrospective application of lifestyle to "traditional" indigenous societies of Siberia (say, two or three centuries ago) would need to be based on safer empirical ground, but at least the possibility should not be ruled out. The conventional historiographic differentiation between the pre-revolutionary and the Soviet period of indigenous peoples' history went hand in hand with a differentiation between a dark past and a bright future; it left little descriptive space for shades in between.

Finally, the pedagogical mission of indigenous teachers and activists to revive traditional skills and indigenous spiritual values, along with the decision of indigenous families to make a living by hunting, fishing, or herding, can again be read as personal positionings towards sensibilities — statements about specific moral values that one should strive for. Neo-traditionalism (Pika 1999) may thus contribute to the formation of a distinct lifestyle in its own right, especially so when traditional attire comes to be used for the creation of a "surface" to be acknowledged by the wider public.

This research project has sought to elicit hopes and sensibilities of indigenous as well as other inhabitants of Siberia. The purpose was to show the contemporary breadth of ambitions, some of them being particularly Siberian, but in no way disconnected from other places. Our interviewees and friends often share with us (the members of the research team and contributors to this volume) their latest photos, taken in reindeer herders' camps, tourist camps in the Altai mountains, at school or the workplace, at home with their families, during their travels to their grandparents' home, or to Paris, London, or New York. We hope to continue to share our exchanges and friendship with them in future years.

References

Agadjanian, Alexander. 2017. "Tradition, morality and community: elaborating Orthodox identity in Putin's Russia". *Religion, State & Society*, 45 (1): 39–60, https://doi.org/10.1080/09637494.2016.1272893

Barker, Adele (ed.). 1999. *Consuming Russia: popular culture, sex, and society since Gorbachev*. Durham, NC: Duke University Press, https://doi.org/10.1215/9780822396413

Benovska-Sabkova, Milena, Tobias Köllner, Tünde Komáromi, Agata Ładykowska, Detelina Tocheva & Jarrett Zigon. 2010. "'Spreading grace' in post-Soviet Russia". *Anthropology Today*, 26 (1): 16–21, https://doi.org/10.1111/j.1467-8322.2010.00711.x

Bernsand, Niklas & Barbara Törnquist-Plewa. 2019. "Introduction: cultural and political imaginaries in Putin's Russia". In: *Cultural and Political Imaginaries in Putin's Russia*, ed. Niklas Bernsand & Barbara Törnquist-Plewa, pp. 1–9. Leiden: Brill, https://doi.org/10.1163/9789004366671

Bluhm, Katharina. 2018. "Russia's conservative counter-movement: genesis, actors, and core concepts". In: *New Conservatives in Russia and East Central Europe*, ed. Katharina Bluhm & Mihai Varga, pp. 25–53. London: Routledge, https://doi.org/10.4324/9781351020305

Bolotova, Alla, Anastasia Karaseva & Valeria Vasilyeva. 2017. "Mobility and sense of place among youth in the Russian Arctic". *Sibirica: Interdisciplinary Journal of Siberian Studies*, 16 (3): 77–123, https://doi.org/10.3167/sib.2017.160305

Bourdieu, Pierre. 1984 [1979]. *Distinction: a social critique of the judgement of taste*, trans. Richard Nice. London: Routledge.

Broz, Ludek & Joachim Otto Habeck. 2015. "Siberian automobility boom: from the joy of destination to the joy of driving there". *Mobilities*, 10 (4): 552–70, https://doi.org/10.1080/17450101.2015.1059029

Chaney, David. 1996. *Lifestyles*. London: Routledge, https://doi.org/10.4324/9780203137468

Crowley, David & Susan E. Reid. 2010. "Introduction: pleasures in socialism?" In: *Pleasures in Socialism: leisure and luxury in the Eastern Bloc*, ed. David Crowley & Susan E. Reid, pp. 3–51. Evanston, IL: Northwestern University Press, https://doi.org/10.2307/j.ctv43vtgm.4

Gurova, Ol'ga Yur'evna. 2014. "'U vas tak yarko odevaetsia narod!': sotsial'nye razlichiia v potreblenii odezhdy v Sankt-Peterburge i Novosibirske" ["People dress so brightly here!": social distinctions through clothing in St Petersburg and Novosibirsk]. *Etnograficheskoe obozrenie*, 3: 52–70.

Il'in, Vladimir I. 2015. "Daushifting [sic] kak voskhodiashchaia sotsial'naia mobil'nost'" [Downshifting as upward social mobility]. *SocioTime/Sotsial'noe vremia*, 1: 78–90.

Habeck, Joachim Otto. 2014. *Das Kulturhaus in Russland: postsozialistische Kulturarbeit zwischen Ideal und Verwahrlosung* [The House of Culture in Russia: post-socialist culture work between ideal and degradation]. Bielefeld: transcript, https://doi.org/10.14361/transcript.9783839427125

— & Philipp Schröder. 2016. "From Siberia with love or angst in the city? On the idea of merging research projects in Novosibirsk and co-teaching in Hamburg and Berlin". *Ethnoscripts: Zeitschrift für aktuelle ethnologische Studien*, 18 (1): 5–24, https://journals.sub.uni-hamburg.de/ethnoscripts/article/view/1010/937

Hann, Chris. 2015. "Declining Europe: a reply to Alessandro Testa". *Anthropology of East Europe Review*, 33 (2): 89–93.

Köllner, Tobias. 2012. *Practising Without Belonging? Entrepreneurship, morality, and religion in contemporary Russia*. Zürich: LIT.

—. 2018. "Religious conservatism in post-Soviet Russia and its relation to politics: empirical findings from ethnographic fieldwork". In: *New Conservatives in Russia and East Central Europe*, ed. Katharina Bluhm & Mihai Varga, pp. 245–59. London: Routledge, https://doi.org/10.4324/9781351020305-12

Kormina, Jeanne. 2010. "Avtobusniki: Russian Orthodox pilgrims' longing for authenticity". In: *Eastern Christians in Anthropological Perspective*, ed. Chris Hann & Hermann Goltz, pp. 267–86. Berkeley, CA: University of California Press, https://doi.org/10.1525/california/9780520260559.003.0012

Kotkin, Stephen. 1995. *Magnetic Mountain: Stalinism as a civilization*. Berkeley, CA: University of California Press.

Laruelle, Marlène. 2009. *In the Name of the Nation: nationalism and politics in contemporary Russia*. New York: Palgrave Macmillan, https://doi.org/10.1057/9780230101234

—. 2015. "Patriotic youth clubs in Russia: professional niches, cultural capital and narratives of social engagement". *Europe-Asia Studies*, 67 (1): 8–27.

Le Huérou, Anne & Elisabeth Sieca-Kozlowski (eds). 2008. *Culture militaire et patriotisme dans la Russie d'aujourd'hui* [Military cult and patriotism in present-day Russia]. Paris: Karthala.

Luehrmann, Sonja. 2005. "Recycling cultural construction: desecularisation in postsoviet Mari El". *Religion, State & Society*, 33 (1): 35–56, https://doi.org/10.1080/0963749042000330857

—. 2017. "'God values intentions': abortion, expiation, and moments of sincerity in Russian Orthodox pilgrimage". *HAU: Journal of Ethnographic Theory*, 7 (1): 163–84, https://doi.org/10.14318/hau7.1.015

Mally, Lynn. 2003. "Exporting Soviet culture: the case of Agitprop theatre". *Slavic Review*, 62 (2): 324–42, https://doi.org/10.2307/3185580

Mitrofanova, Anastasia. 2018. "Orthodox fasting in a postsecular society: the case of contemporary Russia". *Religions*, 9 (9): 267–88, https://doi.org/10.3390/rel9090267

Mitrokhin, Nikolay. 2013. "Gottes Wort und Priesters Tat: die Orthodoxe Kirche und die Homosexualität" [God's word and priest's deeds: the Orthodox Church and homosexuality]. *Osteuropa*, 63 (10): 71–85.

Naletova, Inna. 2010. "Pilgrimages as Kenotic communities beyond the walls of the church". In: *Eastern Christians in Anthropological Perspective*, ed. Chris Hann & Hermann Goltz, pp. 240–66. Berkeley, CA: University of California Press, https://doi.org/10.1525/california/9780520260559.003.0011

Oushakine, Serguei. 2009. *The Patriotism of Despair: nation, war, and loss in Russia.* Ithaca, NY: Cornell University Press, https://doi.org/10.7591/9780801459108

Papernyi, Vladimir. 2007. *Kul'tura Dva* [Culture Two], 2nd edition. Moscow: Novoe literaturnoe obozrenie.

Pika, Aleksandr (ed.). 1999. *Neotraditionalism in the Russian North: indigenous peoples and the legacy of Perestroika*, ed. in English by Bruce Grant, with a new afterword by Boris Prokhorov. Edmonton: Canadian Circumpolar Institute; Seattle: University of Washington Press. (Originally published in Russian in 1994 under the title *Neotraditsionalizm na Rossiiskom Severe*.)

Popov, Vladimir. 2012. "The culture of new mobility in Russia: networks and flows formation". *Mobilities*, 7 (1): 151–69, https://doi.org/10.1080/17450101.2012.631816

Poslanie Prezidenta. 2013. "Poslanie Prezidenta Federal'nomu Sobraniiu: Vladimir Putin oglasil yezhegodnoe Poslanie Prezidenta Rossiiskoi Federatsii Federal'nomu Sobraniiu" [Presidential Address to the Federal Assembly: Vladimir Putin read out the annual address of the President of the Russian Federation to the Federal Assembly], http://kremlin.ru/events/president/news/19825

Press, Sergei. 2012. "Festival' 'Sibirskie brendy', Novosibirsk, fevral' 2012" ["Siberian Brands" Festival, Novosibirsk, February 2012]. *DP (Delovoi Peterburg)*, 1 February 2012. https://www.dp.ru/a/2012/01/26/Festival_SIBIRSKIE_BREN

Rakhimova-Sommers, Elena. 2019. "'Your stork might disappear forever!': Russian public awareness advertising and incentivizing motherhood". In: *Cultural and Political Imaginaries in Putin's Russia*, ed. Niklas Bernsand & Barbara Törnquist-Plewa, pp. 177–91. Leiden: Brill, https://doi.org/10.1163/9789004366671

Roberts, Graham H. 2016. *Consumer Culture, Branding and Identity in the New Russia: from five-year plan to 4x4.* New York: Routledge. https://doi.org/10.4324/9781315858302

Safonova, Tatiana & István Sántha. 2010. "Gender distinctions in an egalitarian society: the case of Evenki people of the Baikal region". *Anthropology of East Europe Review*, 28 (2): 120–39.

Slezkine, Yuri. 1994. *Arctic Mirrors: Russia and the small peoples of the North.* Ithaca, NY: Cornell University Press.

Smirnov, Georgii L. 1973. *Sovetskii Chelovek: formirovanie sotisalisticheskogo tipa lichnosti* [The Soviet Person: formation of the socialist type of personhood]. Moscow: Politizdat.

Sontag, Susan. 2005 [1977]. *On Photography*. New York: Rosetta.

Ssorin-Chaikov, Nikolai. 2003. *The Social Life of the State in Subarctic Siberia*. Stanford, CA: Stanford University Press.

Stähle, Hanna. 2015. "Between homophobia and gay lobby: the Russian Orthodox Church and its relationship to homosexuality in online discussions". *Digital Icons: studies in Russian, Eurasian and central European new media*, 14: 49–71.

Stoeckl, Kristina. 2016. "The Russian Orthodox Church as moral norm entrepreneur". *Religion, State and Society*, 44 (2): 132–51, https://doi.org/10.10 80/09637494.2016.1194010

Tocheva, Detelina. 2017. *Intimate Divisions: street-level orthodoxy in post-Soviet Russia*. Münster: LIT.

Volkov, Vadim. 2000. "The concept of *kul'turnost'*: notes on the Stalinist civilizing process". In: *Stalinism: new directions*, ed. Sheila Fitzpatrick, pp. 210-230. London: Routledge.

Yurchak, Alexei. 2006. *Everything Was Forever, Until it Was No More: the last Soviet generation*. Princeton, NJ: Princeton University Press, https://doi. org/10.1515/9781400849109

Zigon, Jarrett. 2008. *Morality: an anthropological perspective*. Oxford: Berg.

— (ed.). 2011. *Multiple Moralities and Religions in Post-Soviet Russia*. New York: Berghahn.

Zubarevich, Natalia. 2013. "Four Russias: human potential and social differentiation of Russian regions and cities". In: *Russia 2025*, ed. Maria Lipman & Nikolay Petrov, pp. 67–85. London: Palgrave Macmillan.

Appendix

On Research Design and Methods

Joachim Otto Habeck and Jaroslava Panáková

Anthropology of Siberia has a long and venerable history. Regional studies and ethnographies have made many compelling contributions in several fields of general anthropology, yet there are also neglected topics and blind spots. In the light of the revival (*vozrozhdenie*) of ethnic identity and indigenous culture in the late 1980s and early 1990s, many Russian and western anthropologists alike were first and foremost interested in studying ethnicity (and the different ways in which ethnic identity is expressed and negotiated through traditional forms of land use, religion, language, and political representation). In the last two decades, anthropological debates around Siberia have been moving beyond the concepts of ethnicity and identity, placing them into wider debates of social practice and societal change. This also implied a modified understanding of the research "object", which was no longer limited to indigenous groups alone, but gradually came to include research among other ethnic groups living in Siberia, in urban settings, non-traditional spheres of production (e.g. extractive industries), and leisure-oriented and also occasionally virtual social networks (for an overview of the field, see Vitebsky & Alekseyev 2015).

The Siberian Studies Centre (2003–2014) of the Max Planck Institute for Social Anthropology hosted several groups of researchers during its existence, and the authors of this volume were all affiliated with the Siberian Studies Centre from 2008 onwards. Supporting and promoting the shifts in the research agenda of anthropology of Siberia, we sought to go beyond an exclusive focus on ethnic identity and traditional forms of land use. Hence our decision to take a closer look at how the inhabitants of Siberian cities and villages see themselves, seek to "realise" themselves, and define what is most dear and important to them. In other words: what are the activities and identities that people choose, and try to master?

A concept that has the potential to facilitate such research is *lifestyle*, because it connects habitualisation with self-reflexivity, norms and values with embodied practice, ambitions with resources, and identity with display (see Chapter 1 for a theoretical grounding of the concept). At the Siberian Studies Centre, we employed this concept as the theoretical core of a research project. "Conditions and Limitations of Lifestyle Plurality in Siberia" was chosen as the title for this study, which commenced in 2008 (cf. Habeck 2008) and officially ended in 2013.

The team met on a regular basis and also conducted workshops in Halle and elsewhere in September 2008, May 2010, October 2010, February 2011, November 2011, May 2012, and November 2012. The composition of the team changed to some extent: apart from those who conducted field research (see Table 12.1), additional members of the team were Kirill Istomin, Stephan Dudeck, Elena Liarskaya, and Vladislava Vladimirova. They too provided substantial input, e.g. in the first phase of the programme, when a preliminary definition of lifestyle was formulated: *Lifestyle is what one does in order to be what one thinks one should be.* This early definition aimed to combine practice, intentionality, a certain degree of reflection, behaviour influenced by social norms, and aspirations to reach a certain idea without necessarily reaching it. Lifestyle, in other words, is a combined expression of what one should be, wants to be, and can afford (or manage) to be. We soon came to realise that this definition of ours had some resemblance to that provided by David Chaney (1996: 37), as discussed in Chapter 1: "Lifestyles are reflexive projects: we (and relevant others) can see (however dimly) who we want to be seen to be through how we use the resources of who we are".

Discussions at this early stage of the programme centred around the conceptual separation of choice (usually considered to have less-lasting consequences) versus decision (with long-term consequences likely to ensue). Further, we debated if lifestyle should include the element of intentionality, if and how our interlocutors' *ex-post-facto* rationalisation of their previous actions should be taken in account, and whether or not to use lifestyle as an emic concept. There was unanimous agreement that the team should use lifestyle as an etic concept, and as *explanandum* rather than *explanans*; in other words, the aim was not to use the concept as a category by which to explain differences within society at large, but rather as a concept that itself needs to be explored. We agreed later that the term should be investigated particularly in connection to changes in technology (telecommunication and transportation).

By early 2010, the team had decided to approach the study of lifestyle from two different vantage points, or focus themes: first, the changing habits of travel; and second, visual forms of self-presentation. While these two focus themes make the study of lifestyle and technological change more concrete, they are nonetheless broad enough to cover a vast range of interviewees' biographical experiences; they also allow individual researchers to adapt the research questions to the particular economic and infrastructural conditions in their respective field sites.

Our two focus themes could be framed by the questions: (a) What is the mutual relation between changing technology and infrastructure on the one hand, and lifestyles, on the other, *as exposed by habits of travelling*?; and (b) What is the mutual relation between changing technology and infrastructure on the one hand, and lifestyles, on the other, *as exposed by changing visual forms of self-presentation*?

An examination of these two questions then requires the study of a set of more basic questions:

- How have technology and infrastructure (in the region) changed over time?

- How have habits of travel changed over time?

- How have visual forms of self-presentation changed over time?

- How are these changes related to each other?

Our first focus theme, devoted to investigating changing habits of travelling over the last forty years, was triggered by several important developments in our area of study. First, as a result of the collapse of aviation in the 1990s, many inhabitants of rural Siberia found themselves "trapped", so to speak, because, quite suddenly, they could not travel at all. Second, we were interested in the gradual "revival" of aviation in several, but not all, areas. Third, many but (again) not all parts of

Siberia gradually became more accessible for overland transportation, and generally in Russia the number of cars per capita has been growing over the last three decades (Chapter 2 provides details).

Finally, we wanted to look into changing practices of holiday-making, to be studied through our interlocutors' holiday biographies. In Soviet times, tourism was officially organised in groups. Individual tourism was considered as "wild" tourism (*dikii turizm*, see Chapters 4 and 5). Thirty years later, there is a wider range of destinations, events, and activities. Already in the 1990s and 2000s, Russia saw a pronounced upsurge of tourism — of holiday travels to and within Siberia, but also from Siberia to China and the Mediterranean Sea. Simultaneously, there are new forms of inequality and stratification. Who can afford to travel where, if at all? What makes people decide to go to a certain destination? Tourism and holiday-making have come to constitute a major field of social distinction.

However, our research was not restricted to tourism alone. We were also concerned with traders, long-distance commuters, settler populations and their links to the so-called mainland, and individuals who combine life in the tundra or forest with life in the village or city. Changing habits of travelling point to changing degrees and meanings of mobility for the individual. Therefore, we planned to examine what significance these journeys or spaces have in our respondents' lives, how they interpret them, and to what extent they interpret them as elements in coherent stories of themselves. There are many reasons for occasional travelling, for example visits to relatives, participation in festivals, contests, role-playing games, tournaments, concerts, etc. Participation in such activities or events can provide a key to studying lifestyles in practice. Usually, people are eager to document their presence at such sites and occasions.

Our second focus theme — visual forms of self-presentation — started from the question of how individuals and collectives stylise and document their presence at major events and destinations. Individuals highlight particular aspects of their activities and social networks, and often they do so through visual means. They keep record of memorable events by taking photographs for their album, or for sharing online. Groups — whether united by ethnicity, work, or other attributes — express a corporate identity through the display of key symbols, using old and new media technologies. The internet, in particular, offers a large virtual space for people with limited physical spaces for such representation. We intended to relate the ways that people "want to be seen" to the predilections and conventions that their lifestyles manifest. As part of this theme, we explore the concept of "self" as expressed by visual means, through photo elicitation interviews (see Chapter 6).

In spring 2010, we had agreed on a collection of eleven texts (Bourdieu 1993, 2000; Chaney 1996; Giddens 1991; Goffman 1990; Harper 2002; Löfgren 1999; Omel'chenko 2003; Urry 2002; Weber 1946) as key readings in English and Russian, enabling a shared understanding of key concepts. Further, we designed the following guidelines for semi-structured interviews for the exploration of both focus themes (see the guidelines for interviews at http://hdl.handle.net/20.500.12434/5fbdd7ae).

1. With regard to the first theme — travel biographies — the interview guideline started with questions about "home", the semantic difference between *poezdka* and *puteshestvie* (both Russian words can be translated as "travel") and the request to recall a very memorable journey. Next, the focus was set on different decades, starting from the ten years before the time of the interview (the 2000s), then moving to the distant past (for most interviewees, the 1970s) and then the decades in between. For each decade, researchers asked about holiday trips, business trips, visits to relatives, and cases of relocation. Interviewees were then encouraged to recall one particular journey for each decade, expanding on its purpose and destination, remarkable moments, the preparation of the journey, and its organisational and financial aspects. The journey was then to be discussed in the more general context of conditions and limitations of personal mobility in the respective decade. Finally, the interviewee was asked about plans for future travels and a final, particularly curious episode.

2. With regard to the second theme — visual forms of self-presentation — each researcher was to conduct photo elicitation interviews, asking informants to select six photographs that would best describe them "as a person" (*kak lichnost'*) usually several days before the actual photo elicitation interview. Of importance were the interviewee's comments as to the

circumstances of selecting photographs and his or her way
of arranging the photographs during the interview itself (as
described in Chapter 6). Beside the photo elicitation interviews
and the collections of the photos that the informants selected in
the elicitation process, researchers also a) gathered other home
photographs, photo albums, and digital photo collections; b)
documented the social life of home photographs, i.e. the ways
in which photographs are treated, archived, and/or displayed
at home or circulated among people; c) occasionally made their
own photo documentation of events or situations where visual
forms of self-presentation come to the fore, such as celebrations
of the Day of the Fisherman, the Day of the Reindeer Herder,
Yhyakh and other indigenous peoples' festivities, local festivals,
sport events, etc.). This part of the research was done in each
region; its range and depth depended on the field site, the
individual researcher's capacities, and local informants'
exposure to home photography.

3. Researchers compiled short CVs for each interviewee,
   capturing their place of residence in different years or decades,
   their education and professional biography, marital status and
   family members, ownership of individual means of transport,
   and language skills (Russian, English, native language, etc.).
   Data on interview settings and situations (place, duration,
   possible disturbances, etc.) were also compiled.

4. In addition to jointly working out the interview guidelines and
   the instructions of photo elicitation, we also agreed to collect
   basic information on transportation, telecommunication, and
   the technical basis of (home) photography in the communities
   under study. Compiling such information for the late 1980s,
   late 1990s, and 2011–2012 (partially also for pre-1980 years)
   in a simple way from published sources, online reports,
   interviewees' memories, and our own knowledge, we sought
   to obtain an overview of technological innovation and change,
   which in turn was in line with the research questions.

For the project, we conducted fieldwork in ten different locations
across Siberia and the Far North of Russia. Research team members
went to field sites where they had already worked in earlier years.

Among these ten field sites are six big cities with several hundred thousand inhabitants — Novosibirsk, Krasnoiarsk, Irkutsk, Ulan-Ude, Vladivostok, and Yakutsk; the seventh site is Chemal, a village in the Altai Republic, with c. 4,000 residents and a significant influx of tourists during the summer months. The other three locations are remote villages across the Far North of the country: Novoe Chaplino at the coastline of Chukotka; Saranpaul' near the eastern foothills of the Ural Mountains; and Chavan'ga, located in the European part of northern Russia. Brief portraits of the field sites are given in Chapter 2 of this book.

Researchers used snowball sampling and occasionally convenience sampling for identifying interviewees. Snowball sampling commenced from the contacts that the researcher had established during previous stays at their field site, gradually reaching out to these interviewees' acquaintances, neighbours, etc. Convenience sampling also included cases of individuals (chance acquaintances in the local grocery store, for example) who were spontaneously ready for an interview. In small communities, it is sometimes hard to differentiate between a proper snowball sample and a convenience sample, because neighbours know each other well; and this in connection with social expectations and obligations may lead to a situation where a researcher is expected to visit or *not* to visit certain households. A particular case was that of Joachim Otto Habeck's interviews with students at the College of Cultural Work in Novosibirsk. It was at the discretion of the head teacher to choose students for photo elicitation and travel biography interviews.

Generally, in the larger settlements, researchers decided to get in contact with members of a group with a certain commonality (not necessarily a common lifestyle, but at least some shared *sensibilities* as defined by Chaney 1996: 8–10). The notion of a shared lifestyle is quite clearly applicable to *some* of these groups, as in the case of Tatiana Barchunova's and Natalia Beletskaia's interviewees, many of whom showed a strong commitment to live-action role-playing. Eleanor Peers, Luděk Brož, and Joseph Long conducted interviews mainly (but not exclusively) with individuals who identify with one of the Siberian indigenous peoples,[1] i.e. Sakha, Altaian, and Buriat respectively. Artem

---

1   "Indigenous peoples" here does not exclusively mean "numerically small indigenous peoples". The latter term stands for ethnic groups with less than 50,000 members. Altaians, Buriat, Sakha, and some other groups are numerically larger. The background and consequences of the differentiation between "numerically small" and other ethnic groups is discussed in Donahoe et al. (2008).

Rabogoshvili focused his research on representatives of diverse ethnic minorities in urban settings. Masha Shaw (*née* Maria Nakhshina) and Jaroslava Panáková worked in very small communities, where several weeks of fieldwork bring forth a large range of acquaintances. Ina Schröder conducted fieldwork in a similar setting, yet she directed particular attention to pedagogues and students (participants in youth camps). Dennis Zuev's range of interlocutors was defined by communication via the website CouchSurfing — an open-ended community which, we argue, carries clear signs of lifestyle commonality in view of shared practices, tastes, and patterns of communication. Habeck worked with two groups: (female) students at the College of Cultural Work in Novosibirsk and (male) residents of a relatively small, reputedly "working-class" neighbourhood within the same city.

Consequently, our overall sample is neither uniform nor coherent. The regional disparities, diverse access to the community under study, and the large scope of the field sites result in uneven distribution. Overall, however, the bias involves two features only: the sex and age of the informants. Of the 110 interviewees, the percentage of women is above sixty (altogether, we conducted interviews with 68 female and 42 male individuals). As to age cohorts, there is a strong bias towards people in their twenties (46 per cent aged between 21 and 30). Having said that, what comes to the fore is a large range of "cases" as regards place of residence (from highly urban to pronouncedly rural and/or remote); and level of formal education, profession, and employment status.

The structured approach of applying the same guidelines and procedures across different settings and field sites make individual interviews comparable and capture important moments in our interlocutors' biographies. In combination with historical analysis and ethnographically grounded research, this also allows for a deeper understanding of the social (educational, professional, and leisure-related) institutions that have shaped collective experiences and sensibilities in Soviet and post-Soviet times. Simultaneously, they provide the ground for discussing the strong regional disparities that characterise different parts of Siberia and the Far North, notably when it comes to individual patterns of mobility (cf. Bolotova, Karaseva & Vasilyeva 2017).

Table 12.1. Field sites of researchers and periods of fieldwork carried out under the programme "Conditions and Limitations of Lifestyle Plurality in Siberia". Sorted by location of field site (generally but not strictly from north to south). Note: data on population are based on the All-Russian Census of October 2010; the data serve to indicate the type of settlement (from small rural settlement to large city and through to metropole). (Table 2.1 in Chapter 2 provides data on population for 1 October 2010 and 1 January 2018).

Name of site	Administrative unit	Population as of 1 Oct 2010	Researcher's name	Period(s) of field research
Chavan'ga	Murmansk Oblast	Seasonal: c. 170 Permanent: c. 87	Masha Shaw	Different seasons of 2011–2012
Novoe Chaplino	Chukotka Autonomous Okrug	419	Jaroslava Panáková	July 2010 and Apr-May 2011
Saranpaul'	Khanty-Mansi Autonomous Okrug – Yugra	2,575	Ina Schröder	Different seasons of 2011–2013
Yakutsk	Sakha Republic (Yakutia)	269,691	Eleanor Peers	Dec 2010 and Jan-Apr 2011
Krasnoiarsk	Krasnoiarsk Region	973,826	Dennis Zuev	Mar-Apr 2011
Novosibirsk	Novosibirsk Oblast	1,473,754	J. Otto Habeck, Tatiana Barchunova	Apr-June 2011 June-July 2011 Mar-Apr 2012
Chemal	Altai Republic	3,973	Luděk Brož	June-Sep 2010
Irkutsk	Irkutsk Oblast	587,891	Artem Rabogoshvili, Joseph Long, Dennis Zuev	Apr-Dec 2011 June-Dec 2011 Mar-Apr 2011
Ulan-Ude	Republic of Buryatia	404,426	Joseph Long, Artem Rabogoshvili	Apr-Dec 2011 Oct-Nov 2011
Vladivostok	Primor'e Region	592,034	Natal'ia Beletskaia, Dennis Zuev	Aug 2011 July-Aug 2011

Lifestyle in Siberia and the Russian North

Table 12.2. Numbers of interviews conducted during fieldwork by members of the research programme "Conditions and Limitations of Lifestyle Plurality in Siberia". Note: interviews varied in length between fifteen minutes and 120 minutes.

	Photo Elicitation Interview (in tandem with travel biography) (both types of interviews were conducted with the same interlocutor)	Travel Biography Interview (in tandem with photo elicitation)	Additional Photo Elicitation Interviews Only this type of interview was conducted	Additional Travel Biography Interviews Only this type of interview was conducted
Tatiana Barchunova	5	5	1	2
Natal'ia Beletskaia	5	5	0	1
Luděk Brož	2	2	1	0
Joachim Otto Habeck	6	6	5	0
Joseph Long	4	4	1	4
Jaroslava Panáková	1	1	7	7
Eleanor Peers	2	2	4	5
Artem Rabogoshvili	5	5	0	0
Ina Schröder	8	8	3	0
Masha Shaw	5	5	1	4
Dennis Zuev	8	8	5	8

As can be seen from this table, research team members utilised the two focus-theme approaches to varying extent, yet all of them conducted both types of interviews. In sum, 79 photo elicitation interviews and 82 travel biography interviews were conducted with a total number of 110 individuals. The number of photo elicitation interviews analysed by Panáková in Chapter 6 is seventy. The difference is due to the fact that nine photo elicitation interviews were transcribed and shared with delay, so that they could not be included in Panáková's analysis.

Of key importance for the research project was a workshop in February 2011 in Berdsk near Novosibirsk, where researchers had the opportunity to present the project to colleagues at Novosibirsk State University and receive their feedback. The venue was chosen in view of several team members' ongoing fieldwork in different parts of Siberia. The workshop also had the purpose of discussing interim reports from all field sites. The conclusion of field research was marked by a further workshop in autumn 2011. By May 2012, we were developing our first ideas for structuring the publication, and in November 2012 the first drafts of chapters for this volume were discussed in the framework of an internal review process.

Data analysis has been a lengthy and uneven process. Of the different categories of data, the photographs collected through the photo elicitation interviews have been closely analysed by Panáková. In Chapter 6, she portrays in detail the method of the photo elicitation interviews, the procedure, and the overall corpus of photographs that the research team collected. Having analysed the set of 484 photographs, Panáková draws a synthesis in terms of content (i.e. message and arrangement) as well as material (technical) properties of the photographs, aiming to explain how technological change in tandem with changing social conventions have modified the range of "legitimate" forms and motifs of depiction and self-presentation.

With regard to travel biographies, Long analysed interviews conducted by himself and other research team members (Chapter 5) and establishes the concept of *spatial imaginaries* (i.e. collectively shared ideas about destinations, expectations, modes, and purposes of travel) and *personal topographies* (i.e. individual profiles of physical and also virtual mobility). As a next step, the latter might be combined with a quantitative analysis of interviewees' range of mobility and frequency of travel, in accordance with space-time path diagrams (Kwan 2000, Shoval et al. 2015; Vrotsou, Ellegård & Cooper 2007) and other methods developed in the domain of "time geography". Without any doubt, mobility patterns, reasons of travel, and collective and individual modes of travel have changed significantly, owing not only to changes in transport and infrastructure but also to personal predilections and socially constituted ideas about holiday-making and tourism.

Of the 79 plus 82 interviews conducted for this project, more than ninety per cent were audio recorded and the majority of these transcribed. All field research data have been systematised. Field research data, pertinent metadata, the fieldwork "toolkit" with interview guidelines and other instruments, the minutes of the workshops, a range of relevant theoretical and regional literature, and the presentations that team members held at different occasions are all stored in a way that permits an easy overview. In addition to individual team members, the Max Planck Institute for Social Anthropology has received a documented copy of the data set for the sole purpose of long-term data securement. Having said that, despite the exercise in spring and autumn 2011 of working out a common strategy for coding (along with the preparation of transcripts for qualitative data analysis) the actual step of coding could not be achieved in the remaining time of the programme's duration. What has not been done, therefore, is collective qualitative data analysis by means of pertinent software.

Habeck as coordinator of the project has drawn conclusions on the main research questions as formulated above, also with a view to summarising the findings on the project's secondary key concepts (modernity, mobility, photography, aesthetics, display of ethnic belonging, play, creativity, and self). These insights are given in Chapter 11. Moreover, each researcher has carefully gone through the data she or he collected, and identified commonalities and differences in the biographies and plans of their interviewees. Several of the chapters of this volume build upon this mode of analysis, closely and carefully portraying specific sites of shared practice and shared ambitions (Chapters 3, 7, 8, and 9). Three chapters were co-authored: Zuev and Habeck portray changes in transport and telecommunication from the late 1980s to the present, offering a point of departure for examination of how technological innovation and changes in lifestyles are interrelated

(Chapter 2). Brož and Habeck use their field research observations to discuss changing habits of travelling for leisure and to approach the ubiquitous situation of encounter between tourist and local cultural entrepreneurs (Chapter 4). Barchunova and Habeck look into the internal logics of live-action role play and discuss how players draw or dismiss the boundary between play and "real life" (Chapter 10).

To conclude with some general remarks about the research process, comparative endeavours of ethnographic fieldwork are not without challenges, even if research instruments (guidelines, forms for metadata, etc.) are prepared before field research. Over several decades, there has been a general tendency in social and cultural anthropology to conduct ethnographic research on an individual basis and then try to conduct comparison *ex post facto*. This project was conceptualised with the intention to prepare a comparative basis before the actual start of ethnographic fieldwork. It should be admitted that this was a time-consuming process, and it is fair to list the shortcomings of this project: firstly, the study is influenced by the selection of informants in favour of women and people in their twenties. Secondly, data analysis has been done individually (not collectively), partially after the end of the granted project.

Nonetheless, the chapters of this volume present numerous topical and intriguing insights gained during fieldwork, reflecting many hours of intensive discussion on methodology and theory resulting in a common understanding of the key concepts. Moreover, the comparison of travel biography data in Chapter 5 and of photo elicitation data in Chapter 6 illustrates that comparative analysis of data can be achieved in qualitative and quantitative ways. There has been some delay in the preparation of the collected volume, for reasons partly beyond the control of the editor and other team members. Notwithstanding, the research project "Conditions and Limitations of Lifestyle Plurality" offers more than just a snapshot of social and cultural dynamics in Siberia and the Russian North around the year 2011. As contributors to the volume, we hope that our findings make it easier for outsiders to embrace and appreciate livelihoods and life projects in smaller and larger places in Russia, by means of both ethnographic detail and a synthesis of historic shifts from the 1980s to the 2010s.

In addition, we hope to have shown how the concept of lifestyle has been helpful in the examination of modernity, mobility, photography, aesthetics, displays of ethnicity, play, creativity, and self as promising topics in future anthropological research on Siberia, and potentially beyond.

References

Bolotova, Alla, Anastasia Karaseva & Valeria Vasilyeva. 2017. "Mobility and sense of place among youth in the Russian Arctic". *Sibirica: Interdisciplinary Journal of Siberian Studies*, 16 (3): 77–123, https://doi.org/10.3167/sib.2017.160305

Bourdieu, Pierre [P'er Burd'e]. 1993. "Sotsial'noe prostranstvo i simvolicheskaia vlast'" [Social space and symbolic power], trans. V. I. Ivanova. *Thesis: teoriia i istoriia ekonomicheskikh i sotsial'nykh institutov i sistem*, 1 (2): 137–50.

—. 2000 [1986]. "The biographical illusion", trans. Yves Winkin & Wendy Leeds-Hurwitz. In: *Identity: a reader*, ed. Paul du Gay, Jessica Evans & Peter Redman, pp. 299–305. London: SAGE.

Bourdieu, Pierre, with Luc Boltanski, Robert Castel, Jean-Claude Chamboredon & Dominique Schnapper. 1990 [1965]. *Photography: a middle-brow art*, trans. Shaun Whiteside. Cambridge: Polity Press.

Chaney, David. 1996. *Lifestyles*. London: Routledge, https://doi.org/10.4324/9780203137468

Donahoe, Brian, Joachim Otto Habeck, Agnieszka Halemba & István Sántha. 2008. "Size and place in the construction of indigeneity in the Russian Federation". *Current Anthropology*, 49 (6): 993–1020, https://doi.org/10.1086/593014

Giddens, Anthony. 1991. "The trajectory of self". In: Anthony Giddens, *Modernity and Self-identity: self and society in the late modern age*, pp. 70–108. Stanford, CA: Stanford University Press.

Goffman, Erwin. 1990 [1956]. *The Presentation of Self in Everyday Life*. London: Penguin.

Habeck, Joachim Otto. 2008. "Conditions and limitations of lifestyle plurality in Siberia: a research programme". *Max Planck Institute for Social Anthropology Working Paper Series*, 104, http://www.eth.mpg.de/pubs/wps/pdf/mpi-eth-working-paper-0104

Harper, Douglas. 2002. "Talking about pictures: a case for photo elicitation". *Visual Studies*, 17 (1): 13–26, https://doi.org/10.1080/14725860220137345

Kwan, Mei-Po. 2000. "Interactive geovisualization of activity-travel patterns using three-dimensional geographical information systems: a methodological exploration with a large data set". *Transportation Research Part C: Emerging Technologies*, 8 (1–6): 185–203, https://doi.org/10.1016/s0968-090x(00)00017-6

Löfgren, Orvar. 1999. "Looking for tourists". In: Orvar Löfgren, *On Holiday: a history of vacationing*, pp. 260–82. Berkeley, CA: University of California Press, https://doi.org/10.1525/california/9780520217676.003.0009

Omel'chenko, Elena Leonidovna. 2003. "Kul'turnye praktiki i stili zhizni rossiiskoi molodezhi v kontse XX veka" [Cultural practices and lifestyles of Russian youth at the end of the twentieth century]. *Rubezh: al'manakh sotsial'nykh issledovanii*, 18: 145–66, http://www.ecsocman.edu.ru/rubezh/msg/141484.html

Shoval, Noam, Bob McKercher, Amit Birenboim & Erica Ng. 2015. "The application of a sequence alignment method to the creation of typologies of tourist activity in time and space". *Environment and Planning B: Planning and Design*, 42 (1): 76–94, https://doi.org/10.1068/b38065

Urry, John. 2002. "Mobility and proximity". *Sociology*, 36 (2): 255–74, https://doi.org/10.1177/0038038502036002002

Vitebsky, Piers & Anatoly Alekseyev. 2015. "Siberia". *Annual Review of Anthropology*, 44: 439–55, https://doi.org/10.1146/annurev-anthro-092412-155546

Vrotsou, Katerina, Kajsa Ellegård & Matthew Cooper. 2007. "Everyday life discoveries: mining and visualizing activity patterns in social science diary data". In: *IEEE International Conference on Information Visualisation 2007*, ed. Ebad Banissi et al., pp. 130–38. Los Alamitos, CA: IEEE, https://doi.org/10.1109/iv.2007.48

Weber, Max. 1946 [1922]. "Class, status, party". In: *From Max Weber: essays in sociology*, trans. & ed. Hans H. Gerth & C. Wright Mills, pp. 180–95. New York: Oxford University Press, https://doi.org/10.4324/9780203759240

List of Illustrations

Chapter 2

Chapter 3

Chapter 4

Chapter 5

Chapter 6

Chapter 7

Chapter 8

Chapter 9

Index

Buryatia 37, 53, 58, 74, 136, 176, 179,
181, 188, 205, 217, 295–296, 319,
441, 443

capitalism 5, 17, 140, 148, 206,
257–259, 262, 265, 268–269, 284,
410

Caucasus 64

Chaney, David 5, 11, 14–16, 19,
22, 27, 46, 92, 106, 132, 142, 196,
206, 257–259, 262–264, 267–269,
275–277, 283, 290, 298, 306, 324,
327, 332–333, 337–339, 361, 365,
368–370, 383, 385, 393, 399, 401,
425–426, 436, 439, 441

Lifestyles 14, 24, 35, 92, 191, 263

Cheliabinsk 234, 367

childhood 107, 118, 134, 145, 182, 231,
235, 246

Chita 175

Chukchi Autonomous Region 42, 45,
48, 56–57, 77, 79, 193, 202, 205, 207,
210–211, 217, 230–231, 236, 243,
441, 443

Novoe Chaplino 47–48, 50–51,
56–57, 89, 191, 206, 214, 230, 236,
415–416, 441, 443

Provideniia 57

Church, the. *See* religion

class

middle-class 9–10, 24, 44, 141, 206,
209, 326, 408–409

upper-class 141, 409

working-class 140–141, 442

climate change 70

collectivism 2–3, 27, 83, 132,
171, 216–217, 276, 281, 306,
382–383, 401, 425, 445, 447.
See also individualism; *See
also* memory: collective memory

collective identity 12, 21, 383

collectivist ideology 401

communitas 42, 322, 325, 372

community 3, 7, 10, 20, 35–37, 41, 44,
46, 49, 54, 56–57, 63, 69–70, 80, 85,
88, 92–93, 112, 120, 132, 154–155,
161–162, 170, 179, 181, 192, 194,
196, 216, 219, 246, 258–259, 262–
263, 265–267, 269–270, 272–273,
276–277, 280–282, 284–285,
288–290, 296–297, 299–300,
303–305, 313–315, 317–321,
323–324, 326–327, 333, 337, 346,
349, 353, 361, 368, 377–378, 385,
393, 399–401, 412, 415–419,
421–422, 426, 429, 440–442

community formation 258, 262,
280, 282, 290

svoi 3, 281–282, 289–290

consumerism 28, 45, 207, 406–407,
410, 429

Cossacks 51

creativity 2–3, 54, 106, 125–126, 188,
354, 387, 402, 446, 448

dance 41, 144, 260, 269–270, 285–288,
315, 322, 338, 343, 347, 357, 375,
405

ballet 285–286

circle dance 260

folk dance 286, 288

"The Twist" 144

death 63, 235, 245, 281, 344, 349, 392

funeral 236, 355

homicide 146, 192

suicide 192–193, 334, 336, 349, 358

de Certeau, Michel 208, 370, 393

democracy 19, 288, 401–403, 411

Dittrich, Rita 24, 26

Domaranskaia, Anna 23

drink

alcohol 57, 334–336, 358, 391

vodka 109, 261

wine 261

kumys 259, 261

tea 110–111

Droogers, André 343

economy

economic crisis 20, 57, 411

economic growth 20, 51

market economy 19, 150, 404, 408

This book need not end here...

At Open Book Publishers, we are changing the nature of the traditional academic book. The title you have just read will not be left on a library shelf, but will be accessed online by hundreds of readers each month across the globe. OBP publishes only the best academic work: each title passes through a rigorous peer-review process. We make all our books free to read online so that students, researchers and members of the public who can't afford a printed edition will have access to the same ideas.

This book and additional content is available at:
https://doi.org/10.11647/OBP.0171

Customise

Personalise your copy of this book or design new books using OBP and third-party material. Take chapters or whole books from our published list and make a special edition, a new anthology or an illuminating coursepack. Each customised edition will be produced as a paperback and a downloadable PDF. Find out more at:

https://www.openbookpublishers.com/section/59/1

Donate

If you enjoyed this book, and believe that research like this should be available to all readers, regardless of their income, please become a member of OBP and support our work with a monthly pledge — it only takes a couple of clicks! We do not operate for profit so your donation will contribute directly to the creation of new Open Access publications like this one.

https://www.openbookpublishers.com/supportus

Like Open Book Publishers

Follow @OpenBookPublish

Read more at the Open Book Publishers BLOG

You may also be interested in:

Life Histories of Etnos Theory in Russia and Beyond

Edited by David G. Anderson, Dmitry V. Arzyutov and Sergei S. Alymov

https://doi.org/10.11647/OBP.0150

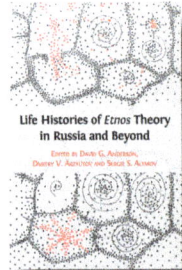

Mobilities, Boundaries, and Travelling Ideas: Rethinking Translocality Beyond Central Asia and the Caucasus

Edited by Manja Stephan-Emmrich and Philipp Schröder

https://doi.org/10.11647/OBP.0114

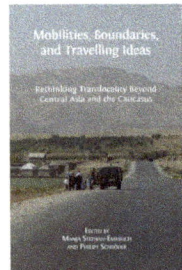

Frontier Encounters: Knowledge and Practice at the Russian, Chinese and Mongolian Border

Edited by Franck Billé, Grégory Delaplace and Caroline Humphrey

https://doi.org/10.11647/OBP.0026

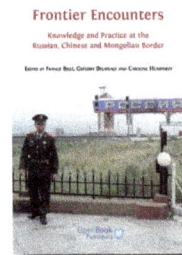